# STRUCTURAL PRINCIPLES IN EU EXTERNAL RELATIONS LAW

The law and practice of EU external relations is governed not only by general objectives (Articles 3(5) and 21 TEU and Article 205 TFEU) and values (Article 2 TEU) but also by a set of principles found in the Treaties and developed by the Court of Justice, which structure the system, functioning and exercise of EU external competences. This book identifies a set of 'structural principles' as a legal norm-category governing EU external relations; it explores the scope, content and function of those principles that may be categorised as structural. With an ambitious scope, and a stellar line-up of experts in the field, the collection offers a truly innovative perspective on the role of law in EU external relations.

# Structural Principles in EU External Relations Law

Edited by
Marise Cremona

·HART·
PUBLISHING
OXFORD AND PORTLAND, OREGON
2018

Hart Publishing
An imprint of Bloomsbury Publishing Plc

Hart Publishing Ltd
Kemp House
Chawley Park
Cumnor Hill
Oxford OX2 9PH
UK

Bloomsbury Publishing Plc
50 Bedford Square
London
WC1B 3DP
UK

www.hartpub.co.uk
www.bloomsbury.com

Published in North America (US and Canada) by
Hart Publishing
c/o International Specialized Book Services
920 NE 58th Avenue, Suite 300
Portland, OR 97213-3786
USA

www.isbs.com

HART PUBLISHING, the Hart/Stag logo, BLOOMSBURY and the
Diana logo are trademarks of Bloomsbury Publishing Plc

First published 2018

British Library Cataloguing-in-Publication Data
A catalogue record for this book is available from the British Library.

ISBN:  HB:  978-1-78225-997-8
       ePDF:  978-1-78225-995-4
       ePub:  978-1-78225-996-1

Library of Congress Cataloging-in-Publication Data

Names: Cremona, Marise, editor.

Title: Structural principles in EU external relations law / Edited by Marise Cremona.

Other titles: Structural principles in European Union external relations law

Description: Portland, Oregon : Hart Publishing, 2018.  |  Includes bibliographical references and index.

Identifiers: LCCN 2017048789 (print)  |  LCCN 2017051411 (ebook)  |
ISBN 9781782259961 (Epub)  |  ISBN 9781782259978 (hardcover : alk. paper)

Subjects: LCSH: European Union countries—Foreign relations—Law and legislation.

Classification: LCC KJE5105 (ebook)  |  LCC KJE5105 .S77 2018 (print)  |  DDC 342.24/0412—dc23

LC record available at https://lccn.loc.gov/2017048789

Typeset by Compuscript Ltd, Shannon
Printed and bound in Great Britain by CPI Group (UK) Ltd, Croydon CR0 4YY

To find out more about our authors and books visit www.hartpublishing.co.uk. Here you will find extracts,
author information, details of forthcoming events and the option to sign up for our newsletters.

# CONTENTS

**Part III: Systemic Principles**

# LIST OF CONTRIBUTORS

**Loïc Azoulai** is Professor at Sciences Po Law School, Paris; he holds an Excellence Chair with a project on 'Forms of Life and Legal Integration in Europe (FOLIE)'.

**Edoardo Chiti** is Professor of Administrative Law at the Università degli studi della Tuscia.

**Marise Cremona** is Professor Emeritus at the European University Institute, Florence.

**Geert de Baere** is a Judge at the General Court of the EU and Associate Professor of EU Law and International Law at the University of Leuven.

**Mireia Estrada Cañamares** is an Associate at Cuatrecasas law firm, Madrid.

**Inge Govaere** is Professor of European Law, Jean Monnet Chair in EU Legal Studies and Director of the Ghent European Law Institute (GELI) at Ghent University, as well as Director of the European Legal Studies Department at the College of Europe, Bruges.

**Christophe Hillion** is Research Professor at the Norwegian Institute of International Affairs (NUPI), Professor of European Law at the Universities of Leiden and Gothenburg, and researcher at the Swedish Institute for European Policy Studies (SIEPS) in Stockholm.

**Joris Larik** is Assistant Professor of Comparative, EU and International Law at the University of Leiden and a Senior Researcher at the Hague Institute for Global Justice.

**Päivi Leino** is Professor of International and EU Law, UEF Law School and Academy of Finland Research Fellow.

**Jed Odermatt** is a Postdoctoral Researcher, University of Copenhagen, Centre of Excellence for International Courts (iCourts).

**Anne Thies** is Associate Professor in the School of Law, University of Reading.

**Ilaria Vianello** is Senior Research Fellow, Max Planck Foundation for International Peace and the Rule of Law, Heidelberg.

# LIST OF ABBREVIATIONS

| | |
|---|---|
| ACTA | Anti-Counterfeiting Trade Agreement |
| AFSJ | Area of Freedom, Security and Justice |
| AG | Advocate General |
| ASEAN | Association of Southeast Asian Nations |
| CCP | Common Commercial Policy |
| CFSP | Common Foreign and Security Policy |
| CJEU | Court of Justice of the European Union |
| CLS | Council Legal Service |
| CSDP | Common Security and Defence Policy |
| EAEC | European Atomic Energy Community |
| ECHR | European Convention on Human Rights |
| ECJ | European Court of Justice |
| ECSC | European Coal and Steel Community |
| ECtHR | European Court of Human Rights |
| EEA | European Economic Area |
| EEAS | European External Action Service |
| EFTA | European Free Trade Association |
| EIDHR | European Instrument for Democracy and Human Rights Worldwide |
| EMU | economic and monetary union |
| ENP | European Neighbourhood Policy |
| EPC | European Political Cooperation |
| ESM | European Stability Mechanism |
| ESMA | European Securities and Markets Authority |
| EU | European Union |
| FAC | Foreign Affairs Council |
| FAO | Food and Agriculture Organization |
| GATT | General Agreement on Tariffs and Trade |
| GC | General Court |
| GSP | Generalised Scheme of Preferences |
| HR | High Representative of the Union for Foreign Affairs and Security Policy |
| IA | Impact Assessment |
| IcSP | Instrument contributing to Security and Peace |
| ILO | International Labour Organization |
| IMO | International Maritime Organization |
| ITLOS | International Tribunal for the Law of the Sea |

| | |
|---|---|
| JHA | Justice and Home Affairs |
| MDG | Millennium Development Goals |
| MFA | macro-financial assistance |
| NGO | non-governmental organisation |
| SAP | Stabilisation and Association Process |
| SEA | Single European Act 1987 |
| TEC | EC Treaty |
| TEU | Treaty on European Union |
| TFEU | Treaty on the Functioning of the European Union |
| TSCG | Treaty on Stability, Coordination and Governance |
| TTIP | Transatlantic Trade and Investment Partnership |
| UN | United Nations |
| UNASUR | Union of South American Nations |
| WTO | World Trade Organization |

# Part I

# The Concept of Structural Principles

# 1

# Structural Principles and their Role in EU External Relations Law

MARISE CREMONA

## I. Introduction

Our starting point is an observation, based on earlier work on the Court of Justice of the European Union and European Union (EU) external relations objectives.[1] This is that in the external policy field, the Court has not been a driving force behind the EU's policy agenda in the same way that it has shaped the concept of Union citizenship or the way in which its interpretation of the substantive treaty provisions on discrimination, competition policy or free movement have been geared to the creation of the single market. This might be the result of a reluctance to engage with external political choices, but our purpose in this book is not to look for what might motivate the Court. It is rather to explore what role law plays in EU external action and whether, to what extent, law may operate differently in the external from the internal context.

The nature of the Treaty provisions on EU external action, with a set of open-ended policy objectives and fewer policy-directed legal obligations on the Member States, has left much to the agenda-setting of the political institutions. This seems natural: surely it is in the nature of foreign relations to be politics-driven and for law to play a minor role? But in fact law *does* play an important role in EU external relations. The Court has had no hesitation in establishing principles and far-reaching rules governing the scope and nature of Union external competence, institutional questions concerning the exercise of that competence, and the consequent obligations on the Member States, both of compliance and cooperation. For example: its insistence that legal basis is a matter of constitutional significance and subject to judicial control;[2] its insistence on the importance of judicial

---

[1] M Cremona, 'A Reticent Court? Policy Objectives and the Court of Justice' in A Thies and M Cremona (eds), *The European Court of Justice and External Relations Law: Constitutional Challenges* (Oxford, Hart Publishing, 2014) 15.
[2] For example, Opinion 2/00, EU:C:2001:664; Case C-91/05 *Commission v Council*, Judgment, EU:C:2008:288; Case C-263/14 *European Parliament v Council*, Judgment, EU:C:2016:435.

review and the priority of EU primary law;[3] its development of the doctrines of exclusivity and pre-emption, thereby curtailing the Member States' treaty-making powers;[4] its development of the duty of cooperation, now based on Article 4(3) of the Treaty on European Union (TEU), requiring the Member States to exercise their own powers in ways which are compatible with Union law,[5] which do not hinder the Union's exercise of its competence,[6] and which do not jeopardise the 'unity of international representation' of the Union.[7]

What explains the contrast between these cases and the Court's reticence when it comes to the EU's external policy agenda, and how can we characterise the role that law plays in EU external relations?

The Treaties set broadly-defined policy objectives, or orientations, for EU external action but they do not establish an end-point to which they seek to move the Union. Insofar as there are purposive or set goals (e.g. reduction of poverty, liberalization of trade, sustainable development) these are not objectives which are realizable by the EU alone; it must work towards them in partnership with third countries. And these goals are not prioritised over other EU objectives, such as the pursuance of the EU's interests. We do not find in the Treaties defined policy choices governing external action such as the openness of EU markets or even non-discrimination.[8] Rather, the Union is given a task: to develop relations and build partnerships with third countries and international, regional or global organisations; it is given a number of policy fields in which to operate, a range of instruments, and a set of orienting, open-ended and non-prioritised objectives (international peace and security, sustainable development …).

Against this background, the direction and goals of EU external policy must be set by the institutions themselves. As Article 22 TEU provides, '[o]n the basis of the principles and objectives set out in Article 21, the European Council shall define the strategic interests and objectives of the Union'. The Court is very rarely driven to find that the Union's external powers have been misused;[9] it emphasises

---

[3] For example, Joined Cases C-402/05P and C-415/05P *Yassin Abdullah Kadi and Al Barakaat International Foundation v Council and Commission,* Judgment, EU:C:2008:461; Joined Cases C-584/10P, C-593/10P and C-595/10P *European Commission, United Kingdom and Council v Yassin Abdullah Kadi,* Judgment, EU:C:2013:518.

[4] For example, Case 22/70 *Commission v Council,* Judgment, EU:C:1971:32; Case C-45/07 *Commission v Greece,* Judgment, EU:C:2009:81; Opinion 1/03, EU:C:2006:81.

[5] Case C-476/98 *Commission v Germany,* Judgment, EU:C:2002:631.

[6] Case C-266/03 *Commission v Luxembourg,* Judgment, EU:C:2005:341; Case C-433/03 *Commission v Germany,* Judgment, EU:C:2005:462; Case C-205/06 *Commission v Austria,* Judgment, EU:C:2009:118; Case C-249/06 *Commission v Sweden,* Judgment, EU:C:2009:119; Case C-118/07 *Commission v Finland,* Judgment, EU:C:2009:715.

[7] Case C-246/07 *Commission v Sweden,* Judgment, EU:C:2010:203.

[8] Gareth Davies describes the EU's internal policy competences as essentially purposive as opposed to sector-specific, the former being defined in terms of the power to take measures to achieve a specific goal, the latter being defined in terms of a particular field: G Davies, 'Democracy and Legitimacy in the Shadow of Purposive Competence' (2015) 21 *European Law Journal* 2.

[9] There have been only two cases where the Court has found that the EC had no external competence. In Opinion 2/94, EU:C:1996:140, the Court based itself on its view that accession to the ECHR would have 'fundamental institutional implications for the Community and for the Member

the need for the institutions to retain their discretion, their room for manoeuvre. It is non-interventionist, tending to take those choices at face value (basing itself on statements in legal instruments and policy documents); it does not question them, nor seek to define or shape them.[10] Instead, it has taken on another role: it ensures that the institutions act within their powers, and that the Member States do not obstruct the formation and implementation of Union policy. It is in fact engaged in establishing and protecting an institutional space within which policy may be formed, in which the different actors understand and work within their respective roles.[11] The principles which have been drawn from the Treaties and elaborated by the Court to establish this institutional space I call 'structural principles'. They include the duty of sincere (and close) cooperation, the principles of conferral and institutional balance, mutual solidarity, subsidiarity, and the principle of autonomy. By identifying and developing these principles, which by their nature are flexible and capable of evolution, the Court of Justice exercises a formidable role in the governance of EU external action despite its hands-off approach to substantive policy choice.

This chapter seeks to explore further the nature and inter-relationships of these structural principles as legal norms, as a basis for the following chapters which examine each of the key structural principles in turn. It proceeds in three stages. First, it offers an explanation for the importance of structural principles in the EU's external relations by exploring the nature of EU external relations powers. Secondly, it begins an enquiry into the nature of structural principles: what does it mean to say that they are *principles*, that they are *structural*, and that they operate within *external relations*? Thirdly, it offers a tentative typology of structural principles and some ideas on the ways in which they may complement and operate in tension with each other.

## II. Absence of a *Telos* in EU External Policy

The original Treaty of Rome contained only two express external powers: the Common Commercial Policy (CCP) and Association Agreements. These original

---

States' and would exceed the Community's conferred powers. In Joined Cases C-317/04 and C-318/04 *European Parliament v Council*, Judgment, EU:C:2006:346, the Court took the view that internal powers could not be used as a basis for external action where the purposes of that action were expressly excluded by the internal legislation.

[10] Legal basis is a good example; while insisting that choice of legal basis should be based on objective factors amenable to judicial review, in practice the Court will normally derive the aim of a measure (important in the determination of legal basis) from the statements included in the Preamble which have of course been drafted with the desired legal basis in mind.

[11] *cf* R Post, 'Constructing the European Polity: *ERTA* and the *Open Skies* Judgments' in L Azoulai and M Poiares Maduro (eds), *The Past and Future of EU Law: The Classics of EU Law Revisited on the 50th Anniversary of the Rome Treaty* (Oxford, Hart Publishing, 2010) 234.

provisions set no specific end-goals; they gave the Community a field of activity in which to exercise its competence but without specifying the purposes of this action. The Common Commercial Policy, it is true, did mandate the establishment of a policy based on 'uniform principles' but here it is the uniformity that is important, the alignment of the different Member States' trade policies, not the content of the common rules.[12] Association Agreements were simply described as 'involving reciprocal rights and obligations, common action and special procedures'. And indeed we can see that these original external powers have been used for a wide variety of purposes, from establishing the World Trade Organization (WTO) to development-oriented selective trade preferences; from pre-accession to integration without accession; from preferential status for former colonies to free trade agreements with strategic trading partners. The EU's more recent express external powers, such as development cooperation or the Common Foreign and Security Policy (CFSP), share this open-ended character; they are competences to engage in a particular policy field.

In contrast, many (not all) of the EU's internal powers were, and are, designed to achieve specific objectives (the removal of obstacles to freedom of movement, achieving a common or internal market, undistorted competition, non-discrimination). And there is an overall purpose, recently expressed well by the Court in Opinion 2/13 as the *implementation of a process of integration*:

> The pursuit of the EU's objectives, as set out in Article 3 TEU, is entrusted to a series of fundamental provisions, such as those providing for the free movement of goods, services, capital and persons, citizenship of the Union, the area of freedom, security and justice, and competition policy. Those provisions, which are part of the framework of a system that is specific to the EU, are structured in such a way as to contribute—each within its specific field and with its own particular characteristics—to the implementation of the process of integration that is the raison d'être of the EU itself.[13]

The open-ended character of the Union's external competences is confirmed and even emphasised by the Lisbon Treaty, which creates a general list of external objectives in Article 21 TEU, without linking them to specific external powers. These objectives use words (verbs) which serve to orient policy rather than setting goals: safeguarding values; consolidating and supporting democracy and the rule of law; strengthening international security; fostering sustainable development; encouraging economic integration; the progressive abolition of trade restrictions; helping to develop international measures to preserve and improve the quality of the environment; promoting an international system based on stronger multilateral cooperation and good global governance. The fact that these objectives are general and not tied to specific external policies emphasises the ability of the

---

[12] M Cremona, 'The External Dimension of the Single Market: Building (on) the Foundations' in C Barnard and J Scott (eds), *The Law of the Single European Market: Unpacking the Premises* (Oxford, Hart Publishing, 2002) 351.
[13] Opinion 2/13, EU:C:2014:2454, para 172.

policy-makers to engage in their own prioritising and balancing between these objectives which may pull in different directions. It is difficult to see them being used to claim that a particular external act is invalid or that a power is being misused. To be clear: I do not seek to minimise the importance of these external objectives and their normative dimension; rather the contrary. I wish rather to draw attention to the fact that they do not serve to create or delimit competence. As expressed by Larik, 'they provide a sense of purpose as to the exercise of [the EU's] powers through the structures of the constitutionalized legal order'.[14]

What of policy fields which do not expressly mention external action but where this is deemed necessary to achieve the Treaties' policy objectives? This latter category of implied external powers introduced by the *ERTA* case-law and now 'codified' into Article 216(1) of the Treaty on the Functioning of the European Union (TFEU) is indeed tied to objectives, but these are *internal* objectives (i.e. the objectives of the internal power on which the implied external power is based). As recently expressed by the Court:

> [W]henever EU law creates for those institutions powers within its internal system for the purpose of attaining a specific objective, the EU has authority to undertake international commitments necessary for the attainment of that objective even in the absence of an express provision to that effect.[15]

Article 216(1) TFEU expresses the same principle. The link to internal objectives may limit the scope of the external powers to which they are linked; in Opinion 1/94 on the WTO, for example, the Court held that:

> [T]he sole objective of [the Treaty chapters on establishment and services] is to secure the right of establishment and freedom to provide services for nationals of Member States ... attainment of freedom of establishment and freedom to provide services for nationals of the Member States is not inextricably linked to the treatment to be afforded in the Community to nationals of non-member countries or in non-member countries to nationals of Member States of the Community.[16]

Thus, external action was not essential to achieve the Treaty's objectives in the field of establishment and services. The Court deliberately rejects an argument made by the Commission at the time that the Treaty power to act internally in the field of services automatically created an external power over trade in services.[17]

---

[14] J Larik, 'From Speciality to the Constitutional Sense of Purpose: On the Changing Role of the Objectives of the European Union' (2014) 63 *International and Comparative Law Quarterly* 935, 962.

[15] Opinion 1/13, EU:C:2014:2303, para 67, citing also Opinion 1/03 (n 4) para 114.

[16] Opinion 1/94, EU:C:1994:384, paras 81 and 86.

[17] ibid paras 74–75: 'The Commission argues, first, that there is no area or specific provision in GATS in respect of which the Community does not have corresponding powers to adopt measures at internal level. According to the Commission, those powers are set out in the chapters on the right of establishment, freedom to provide services and transport. Exclusive external competence flows from those internal powers. That argument must be rejected'. Note that in this Opinion the Court does not always differentiate clearly between the existence of implied external competence and its exclusive character; this is an important point but is not germane to the argument made here. See further P Eeckhout, *EU External Relations Law*, 2nd edn (Oxford, Oxford University Press, 2011) 87–95.

A couple of examples from recent cases on implied powers illustrate the link between implied external powers and internal objectives. In *United Kingdom v Council*,[18] the Court held that Article 48 TFEU was the appropriate legal basis for a Council decision establishing the Union position on the amendment of a European Economic Area (EEA) annex so as to incorporate revised EU legislation on social security coordination. This internal legal basis was preferred to other more 'external' options[19] because the Court held that the purpose of the EEA agreement was essentially to apply internal market law to the European Free Trade Association (EFTA) parties:

> The contested decision is thus precisely one of the measures by which the law governing the EU internal market is to be extended as far as possible to the EEA, with the result that nationals of the EEA States concerned benefit from the free movement of persons under the same social conditions as EU citizens.[20]

The power to adopt an act with external effects is based upon an internal power because its aim is characterised in terms of the application of internal free movement. In Opinion 1/13, the Court discusses the EU's competence in relation to the 1980 Hague Convention on the civil aspects of international child abduction; in finding that the EU has an exclusive external competence based on the existence of Regulation 2201/2003, the Court emphasised the close relationship between the Convention and the EU Regulation, and the risk, were Member States to take different positions on the accession of third countries to the Convention, of undermining the uniform and consistent application of the Regulation within the EU, especially the rules relating to cooperation between Member State authorities. It is the internal system of cooperation which drives the need for an exclusive external EU competence. Some more recently created internal powers from which external powers might be implied are themselves defined in an open-ended way. For example, the Treaty provisions on the common immigration policy have more in common with the common commercial policy (an emphasis on uniformity at external borders and the management of migration; little by way of substantive policy content) than with the Treaty provisions on internal freedom of movement.

Thus, the argument so far is that external powers do not characteristically establish a foreign policy end-goal but rather a field of action in which the EU can operate, and the Court has not created a role for the law (and itself) in determining the use made of those powers. Let me substantiate this in relation to the four key external relations policy competences: trade; association agreements; Common Foreign and Security Policy; and development cooperation.

---

[18] Case C-431/11 *United Kingdom v Council*, Judgment, EU:C:2013:589.
[19] The United Kingdom had argued for the use of Art 79(2) TFEU which refers to the rights of third-country nationals residing in Member States; AG Kokott had also canvassed the option of Art 217 TFEU on Association Agreements.
[20] *United Kingdom v Council* (n 18) para 58. See also paras 50–51.

The original Treaty of Rome focused on the need for a uniform trade policy rather than on its policy content. The recent post-Lisbon case-law on the scope of the CCP confirms the Court's traditional approach: a measure will fall within the CCP if it 'relates specifically to international trade in that it is essentially intended to promote, facilitate or govern trade and has direct and immediate effects on trade'.[21] An effect on trade is important, but those effects may include regulation and restriction of trade as well as liberalisation: the Common Commercial Policy is not likely to see a 'tobacco advertising' moment. Trade liberalisation is an objective of the EU's CCP (Article 206 TFEU) but this is subject to institutional policy choices. As expressed by the Court in a case where achieving uniform rules had been preferred over liberalisation, the 'objective of contributing to the progressive abolition of restrictions on international trade cannot compel the institutions to liberalise imports from non-member countries where to do so would be contrary to the interests of the Community'.[22] For the Court to find that the EEC was bound by the General Agreement on Tariffs and Trade (GATT) was a striking way of importing external policy content into the EU, but the lack of direct effect meant that even GATT norms were (and are) not directly enforceable against EU policy choice through EU courts; the institutions decide how to give effect to GATT/WTO.

And as long as a measure affects trade (positively or negatively), it might be designed to achieve any number of different further policy objectives: development; environmental protection; security of supply of strategic materials; granting or withholding political approval; or promotion of human rights. Trade policy has (of course) always been instrumentalised. For example, in 1982 it was agreed for the first time to use trade powers as the legal basis for a Community instrument imposing economic sanctions (by reducing quotas) against the Soviet Union, following European Political Cooperation (EPC) discussion and in the absence of a UN Security Council Resolution.[23] The political reason (events in Poland) is not mentioned explicitly in the Regulation, the Preamble merely stating that 'the interests of the Community require that imports from the USSR be reduced'. Later the same year, a Regulation imposing sanctions against Argentina over the Falkland Islands referred in its Preamble to the EPC discussions and this became standard practice. So the politics has always been there. The Lisbon Treaty is open about this: the Common Commercial Policy is to be 'conducted in the context of the principles and objectives of the Union's external action'.

In the case of Association Agreements, we see the Court accepting the very wide range of purposes to which they have been put, and insisting that their interpretation must be guided by those purposes. Thus, in its interpretation of

---

[21] Case C-137/12 *Commission v Council*, Judgment, EU:C:2013:675, para 57, citing also C-414/11 *Daiichi Sankyo and Sanofi-Aventis Deutschland*, Judgment, EU:C:2013:520, para 51.

[22] Case C-150/94 *United Kingdom v Council*, Judgment, EU:C:1998:547, para 67, interpreting a predecessor to Art 206 TFEU (Art 110 EC).

[23] Regulation 596/82/EEC [1982] OJ L72/15.

the Europe Agreements with the countries of central and eastern Europe that were to become Member States, the Court recognised their aim of progressive integration of the associated country into the Community and, despite the fact that the agreements contained no general objective of free movement of workers, offered this as a reason for extending its case-law on non-discrimination in conditions of employment to nationals of the associated country legally working in the EU.[24] As we have already seen, the degree of integration envisaged in the EEA has led the Court to espouse an internal legal basis for the adoption of a decision to adapt the EEA *acquis*.[25] This degree of integration was also the basis for a strong statement in *Ospelt* on the need for uniformity of interpretation.[26] In contrast, when interpreting the provisions on services in the Association Agreement with Turkey, the Court has contrasted the 'purely economic aims' of that Agreement with those of the EU Treaties in refusing to apply its case-law on recipients of services.[27] These are clear examples of the Court's willingness to accept the specific degree of integration apparently intended by the parties to these different Association Agreements, despite the fact that they are concluded under the same legal basis. The Court has never tried to extract from the Treaties an 'ideal-type' of Association to which it would seek to mould the agreements it is asked to interpret.

In defining the scope of the EU's development cooperation competence, the Court has been guided by policy documents such as the European Consensus on development,[28] as well as secondary legislation. Although the Treaty states that the reduction of poverty is the 'primary objective' of the EU's development cooperation policy,[29] the general external objectives of Article 21(2) TEU are also to be taken into account,[30] and the Court has contextualised the poverty objective by drawing on references in the European Consensus to sustainable development and the pursuit of the Millennium Development Goals.[31] Even a readmission clause in an international agreement was held to 'contribute to the pursuit of the objectives of development cooperation' on the ground that it formed part of an Article headed 'Cooperation in Migration and Development', and migration is included in the European Consensus.[32] As Broberg and Holdgaard comment, 'the real benchmark for determining the scope of the Union's development cooperation policy competence appears to be derived not from Articles 208 TFEU and 209 TFEU but from the European Consensus and the Development Cooperation instrument'.[33]

---

[24] See, eg Case C-162/00 *Pokrzeptowicz-Meyer*, Judgment, EU:C:2002:57.

[25] *United Kingdom v Council* (n 18).

[26] Case C-452/01 *Ospelt*, Judgment, EU:C:2003:493, para 29.

[27] Case C-221/11 *Demirkan*, Judgment, EU:C:2013:583, para 53.

[28] Joint Statement by the Council and the Representatives of the Governments of the Member States meeting within the Council, the European Parliament and the Commission on European Union Development Policy: 'The European Consensus' [2006] OJ C46/1.

[29] Art 208(1) TFEU.

[30] Case C-377/12 *Commission v Council*, Judgment, EU:C:2014:1903, para 37.

[31] ibid para 42.

[32] ibid paras 52 and 55.

[33] M Broberg and R Holdgaard, *EU External Action in the Field of Development Cooperation Policy: The Impact of the Lisbon Treaty*, SIEPS Working Paper 2014/6 (2014) 46.

Perhaps even more striking, since it involves the CFSP, in addressing a challenge by the European Parliament to the choice of procedure for concluding an agreement with Mauritius on the transfer and trial of suspected pirates, the Court simply went along with the Parliament's acceptance that a CFSP legal basis was appropriate in substantive terms.[34] Despite the boundary between the CFSP and other external powers, which while not such a gulf as prior to the Lisbon Treaty, is still significant,[35] the Court argued the case on purely procedural grounds and, unlike the Advocate General, did not address at all the institutions' choice of substantive legal basis. Of course, it is true that neither party sought to contest that substantive legal basis, but since the Court was to hold that the procedural legal basis should follow the substantive legal basis, this would have given it a ground on which to critique the choice of substantive legal basis if it had chosen to do so.[36]

This section has pointed to a characteristic of EU external competence as defined in the Treaties, that is, its absence of concrete end-goals. Whereas, in its internal policies, the Union is generally instructed to construct *something* (an internal market, an area of freedom, security and justice, a system of undistorted competition),[37] in its external policy, the Union is called upon to construct *itself*, to build its actorness and agency. As a result the law (and the Court) does not interfere with the institutions' choice of specific policy objectives or with the use of external competences for varied purposes. When, on the other hand, we turn to the issues which define the institutional structure of EU external policy-making, we see law being used, through structural principles, to construct the Union as an autonomous international actor.

# III. Concept of Structural Principles

The position I have described, of a Union which is granted certain broad policy fields in which to exercise its external capacity, with little by way of clear guidance in the constituent Treaties as to the ends for which those powers have been given, may seem to have much in common with a sovereign state as an international actor. However, the Union, as we know, has international legal capacity but is an

---

[34] Case C-658/11 *European Parliament v Council*, Judgment, EU:C:2014:2025, paras 44–45.

[35] Art 40 TEU.

[36] Advocate General Bot agreed that a CFSP legal basis was appropriate and sufficient. In a similar subsequent case the Court was specifically asked to address the choice of a CFSP legal basis and accepted that the agreement fell 'predominantly within the scope of the CFSP' because it was designed to facilitate and serve the objectives of an EU naval mission: Case C-263/14 *European Parliament v Council*, Judgment, EU:C:2016:435, para 55.

[37] Where the Union is mandated to create a policy (e.g. employment, environment, energy) it is generally made clear what that policy should entail: responsive labour markets, a high level of employment, preserving protecting and improving the quality of the environment, security of energy supply.

organisation of attributed powers; it does not have the autonomous competence of a state that flows from its recognised sovereign statehood. The fact that the EU is a rule-based (international) actor, the fact that it operates through law, that its powers are derived from law, is strongly evident. When we examine the external relations of the EU we find that law is central to the development of the EU as an international actor—possibly even influencing the type of international actor that the EU is.[38] Given the Court's unwillingness to interfere with the institutions' policy agenda-setting, how is it doing this? My argument is that the Court, through an interlocking set of structural principles, is establishing a framework expressed in (or implied from) the Treaties, protecting an institutional space within which policy may be formed, in which the different actors understand and work within their respective roles. These structural principles are both found in the Treaties and developed by the Court of Justice; they structure the system, functioning and exercise of EU external competences and are designed to promote a smooth artic-ulation of the EU's system of external relations and its effective presentation of an international identity. They regulate the relationships between the different actors in the complex EU system, which includes not only the EU institutions themselves but also the Member States and (indirectly) individuals and third countries, so as to enable the creation of an EU actorness. Structural principles are therefore not concerned with the *substantive content* of policy, but rather with *process* and the *relationships* between the actors in those processes, and their normative content reflects this.

## A. What Does It Mean to Say that These are *Principles*?

These principles are legal norms; they have a legal function and breach of them may result in the illegality of the resulting measure.[39] But a principle is a differ-ent type of norm from a rule. A rule is designed to operate in and to govern a

---

[38] *cf* the literature on the EU as a normative actor, including I Manners, 'Normative Power Europe: A Contradiction in Terms?' (2002) 40 *Journal of Common Market Studies* 235; H Sjursen, 'The EU as a "Normative" Power: How Can This Be?' (2006) 13 *Journal of European Public Policy* 235; I Manners, 'The Normative Ethics of the European Union' (2008) 84 *International Affairs* 45. Although outside the scope of this chapter, the law also plays an important part in shaping the content of EU external policy. The EU characteristically uses law as an instrument and objective of its foreign policy, and sees itself as a promoter of a *rule-based international order* (European Security Strategy, adopted by the European Council in December 2003, 9–10). The EU shapes its external relationships through legal instruments and the promotion of a rule-based approach to international relations is threaded through its Treaty-based external objectives. With varying degrees of success, it increasingly seeks to play a part in the development of international law, through the United Nations and in multilateral negotiations: F Hoffmeister, 'The Contribution of EU Practice to International Law' in M Cremona (ed), *Develop-ments in EU External Relations Law* (Oxford, Oxford University Press, 2008) 37. It can be argued that this fundamental characteristic of the EU as an external actor is a function of its own law-based nature.

[39] Their legal effects may be direct or indirect; for example, it can be argued that the principle of coherence operates through other principles such as conferral and sincere cooperation: see further section IV below.

specific set of circumstances. A principle has a more fundamental character; we may say that rules flow from, and should be consistent with, underlying principles. As Tridimas has said, a general principle expresses a core value.[40] It is perhaps in this sense that the Treaties refer in Article 21(1) TEU to 'the principles which have inspired [the Union's] own creation, development and enlargement', these being essentially the values expressed in Article 2 TEU, on which the Union is founded. A principle is somehow fundamental, justifying and underpinning the specificity and detail of rules, both procedural and substantive.

How do principles interact with rules? How do the principles we are examining here, such as the duty of sincere cooperation or the principle of transparency, operate in relation to (say) the rules applicable to the negotiation and conclusion of treaties? Clearly, principles may be translated into specific rules (e.g. an inter-institutional agreement[41]) in which case they will inform and guide the interpretation of those rules. Thus, in the *Transfer of Suspected Pirates* case, the Court held that '[t]hat rule [i.e. the duty imposed in Article 218(10) TFEU on the Council and Commission to keep the Parliament informed throughout the process of negotiation of an agreement] is an expression of the democratic principles on which the European Union is founded'.[42] But the fundamental nature of principles, their generality as opposed to the specificity of rules, means that principles will inform and guide the interpretation of rules even where those rules have not been adopted to give them specific expression.[43] Thus, for example, in the *CITES* case the Court based its ruling on the principles of legal certainty and conferral, dismissing somewhat cursorily the parties' 'terminological arguments' and concluding that 'in principle, any measure producing binding effects is subject to the obligation to state reasons'.[44] Since general principles rank with primary law, they may constitute grounds for reviewing the legality of legal acts or rules adopted by the institutions. In several recent cases, the institutional parties have based claims of illegality on breaches of the principles of institutional balance, conferral or the duty of sincere cooperation. To take a single example, in the *ITLOS* case, the Council alleged (unsuccessfully on this occasion) that the Commission, by making a formal submission on behalf of the EU to the International Tribunal for the Law of Sea (ITLOS) without the prior approval of the Council, had infringed the principles of conferral of powers, institutional balance and sincere cooperation, all found in Article 13(2) TEU.[45]

---

[40] T Tridimas, *The General Principles of EU Law*, 2nd edn (Oxford, Oxford University Press, 2007) 1.

[41] See, eg, Case C-25/94 *Commission v Council*, Judgment, EU:C:1996:114, para 49: '[S]ection 2.3 of the Arrangement between the Council and the Commission represents [the] fulfilment of that duty of cooperation between the Community and its Member States within the FAO'.

[42] *European Parliament v Council* (n 34) para 81.

[43] The interaction between principles and rules has long occupied legal scholars; for a discussion of the well-known Hart-Dworkin debate, see, eg, J Mackie, 'The Third Theory of Law' (1977) 7 *Philosophy and Public Affairs* 3; S Shapiro, 'The Hart-Dworkin Debate: A Short Guide for the Perplexed' in A Ripstein (ed), *Ronald Dworkin* (Cambridge, Cambridge University Press, 2007) 22.

[44] Case C-370/07 *Commission v Council* (*CITES*), Judgment, EU:C:2009:590, para 42.

[45] Case C-73/14 *Council v Commission* (*ITLOS*), Judgment, EU:C:2015:663.

Principles point to a particular direction of argument or line of reasoning. One result of this character of principles is that they may be held in tension with one another without being seen as contradictory or conflicting. Principles may legitimately pull in different directions. This might raise a question as to whether some principles are more fundamental than others, and should thus be given greater weight. Should we seek to establish a hierarchy of structural principles? At this stage it seems to me that the nature of principles is not to be hierarchic; they accommodate each other and a principle may be given more weight in one case than another. That does not perhaps preclude the possibility of determining that the Court appears to privilege certain principles over others.

Let us take an example from a recent judgment, which is a strong example since one of the principles is conferral, which if any might have a claim to be considered especially fundamental. In *Germany v Council*, Germany contested the use of Article 218(9) TFEU for the adoption of a Council decision determining the position to be adopted by the Member States in the context of an international agreement to which the EU is not a party.[46] Article 218(9) covers Council decisions 'establishing the positions to be adopted on the Union's behalf in a body set up by an agreement, when that body is called upon to adopt acts having legal effects'. Germany's argument was that it would be contrary to the principle of conferral to apply this provision in the case of an agreement concluded by the Member States and not the EU.[47] The Court rejected this argument. It did not (of course) deny the principle of conferral, it simply found that it was not contravened in this case, by giving an interpretation of Article 218(9) that (while textual) was fundamentally influenced by the principle of effectiveness. Its argument (following a line of earlier cases) was that in cases where the EU is not a party to an agreement which nevertheless falls within EU competence, the EU may exercise that competence through its Member States acting jointly on its behalf and in its interest.[48] And in the Court's view, there was nothing in the wording of Article 218(9) which prevented it being used to address a decision to the Member States in such a case, where they are to adopt a position 'on the Union's behalf'.

Since principles are not designed to give a once-and-for-all answer to a concrete question (which does not prevent them from being decisive in a particular case), they are open to adjustment and re-interpretation over time and in changing circumstances. In 1971, in the *ERTA* case,[49] for example, the Court conceived the conferral of external powers as a transfer from the Member States to the Community, and consequently treated external competence as naturally excluding the

---

[46] Case C-399/12 *Germany v Council (OIV)*, Judgment, EU:C:2014:2258.
[47] ibid para 33.
[48] ibid para 52. See further M Cremona, 'Member States as Trustees of the Union Interest: Participating in International Agreements on Behalf of the European Union' in A Arnull, C Barnard, M Dougan and E Spaventa (eds), *A Constitutional Order of States: Essays in European Law in Honour of Alan Dashwood* (Oxford, Hart Publishing, 2011) 435.
[49] *Commission v Council* (n 4).

Member States (either the Member States or the Community could act, but not both). Rather quickly that view started changing: conferral of powers on the Union does not necessarily disempower the Member States, and we see an emphasis on the need to manage the combined action of Union and Member States through (among others) the principles of 'unity in the international representation of the Union and its Member States',[50] and of sincere cooperation.[51] This example illustrates the dominant role of the Court of Justice in identifying and interpreting principles; their flexibility allows them to develop from small beginnings to powerful tools in the hands of the Court and to take on somewhat unpredictable forms on occasion.[52]

## B. What Does It Mean to Say that These Principles are *Structural*?

Structural principles can be seen as a type of general principle. Some of the principles that I have identified as structural are usually included in lists of general principles: effectiveness, transparency, and proportionality and equality (which are ingredients of the rule of law). Others, however, are not, including conferral, sincere cooperation, autonomy and institutional balance. I am not convinced that we gain much from attempting to ascertain whether there is a canon of general principles and that a structural principle somehow gains greater weight by having (also) been categorised as a general principle, or whether all structural principles are to be regarded as general principles.

It might also be argued (and Tridimas does argue) that the value of a classification of general principles is limited. So does it increase our understanding of EU external relations law to identify these principles as 'structural'? I argue that it does, in that it helps us to make sense of the phenomenon identified in the first section of this chapter and the very particular role played by legal norms *as structural principles* in shaping the decision- and policy-making processes of EU external relations: the contribution to policy-making of each different actor (Member States as well as the institutions) and the balance and constructive relationships between them; their accountability to individuals and third countries affected by their decisions and the transparency that underpins that accountability. This role is important precisely because the substantive content of that policy is left so undefined by EU Treaty law.

These principles are structural in the sense of defining and being inherent to the deep structure of the EU. As principles operating to structure EU external

---

[50] *Commission v Sweden* (n 7) para 104.

[51] C Hillion, 'Mixity and Coherence in EU External Relations: The Significance of the Duty of Cooperation' in C Hillion and P Koutrakos (eds), *Mixed Agreements Revisited: The EU and Its Member States in the World* (Oxford, Hart Publishing, 2010) 87.

[52] See, eg, mutual trust, elevated into a principle of 'fundamental importance' in Opinion 2/13 (n 13) para 191.

policy-making they have a specific function. This is both internal and external in effect. Internal in the sense of structuring internal processes (how decisions are made). External in the sense that the legal particularities of the EU as an international actor,[53] e.g. joint participation of EU and Member States in mixed agreements, or the status of international law within the EU legal system, find their source in these principles.

These principles are structural in the sense of being concerned with the process of policy-making rather than its content. In this sense they can be distinguished from the objective-oriented principles of EU external relations policy which we find in Article 21(1) TEU and which reflect the Union's foundational values as expressed in Article 2 TEU, providing a basis for the Union's relations with third countries and international organisations, and playing an important part, along with the objectives set out in Article 21(2) TEU, in guiding the direction of its external policy. The focus on process rather than policy choice in the role that law plays in governing EU external relations, while it can be seen as protecting the institutions' policy space, may also have the effect of de-politicising genuine disputes. Conflicts are framed, so as to engage the Court, in terms of structural process-related principles rather than policy content and this reduces the scope for open and engaged policy contestation.

## C. What Does It Mean to Say that These are Structural Principles of *External Relations* Law?

There are two dimensions to this question, which are inter-related. The first is simple to state (though not to answer). All the principles discussed here also operate in the context of internal action. Do they operate differently when the action is external and if so how? We might argue that all principles, by their nature as principles, operate in their particular context and the external context is simply a manifestation of that inherent contextual operation of principles. So there is nothing special about structural principles operating in external relations, although the sectoral context will have an impact.

But there is another dimension. What if the 'structure' takes a different shape in the case of internal and external action? Structural principles in the internal context may be concerned primarily with the structure that it is the Union's mission to build: that is, its construction of an Area of Freedom, Security and Justice (AFSJ), of an internal market, of an economic and monetary union (EMU) (Article 3 TEU). Thus, the unity of the market may be an important structural principle for the EU. So also might be the internal space within which freedom of movement may take place, or the mutual trust between courts and between Member State

---

[53] M Licková, 'European Exceptionalism in International Law' (2008) 19 *European Journal of International Law* 463.

authorities which is at the heart of the AFSJ, the internal market, and indeed (in theory) of the EMU.

In the external context, in contrast, insofar as the EU has a mission to construct, it is to construct the EU itself as an effective external actor. Thus, for example, unity becomes a question of the unity of the international representation of the Union and its Member States.[54] It is given the task to build partnerships and relations with third countries in order to pursue together certain broad objectives. Thus, structural principles should provide a solid foundation for the construction of the EU as an international actor, a treaty-maker, a participant in international negotiations. They are concerned with the articulation of power of the EU's constituent parts (including the Member States, who play an important part in building the EU's international presence). They are concerned with the ability of the EU both to establish a distinct identity as a global actor and to project the policies it has developed, and with its need to operate within a system of international law: hence the need for systemic as well as relational principles, principles that define the operation of the system as a whole as opposed to the relations between its constituent parts. It is this dimension which turns these principles from being simply institutional to being structural. In the next section, we turn to look at these different types of structural principles and their functions.

## IV. A Tentative Typology of Structural Principles

In clarifying what it means to talk of structural principles in EU external relations, it could be helpful to identify two types of function and thus two types of structural principle: relational and systemic.

*Relational* principles govern the relationships between actors or legal subjects (not norms); the structure here refers to the framework within which the actors in the EU's system of external relations can play their roles, deciding and implementing policy. In its recent Opinion 2/13 on the proposed accession of the EU to the European Convention on Human Rights (ECHR), the Court of Justice referred to the 'specific characteristics' of the EU and EU law, which include 'those relating to the constitutional structure of the EU, which is seen in the principle of conferral of powers referred to in Articles 4(1) TEU and 5(1) and (2) TEU, and in the institutional framework established in Articles 13 TEU to 19 TEU'. These 'essential characteristics' of EU law 'have given rise to a structured network of principles, rules and mutually interdependent legal relations linking the EU and its Member States, and its Member States with each other'.[55] For the Court these principles are the core of the 'constitutional structure' which is specific to the EU and which

---

[54] *Commission v* Sweden (n 7) para 104.
[55] Opinion 2/13 (n 13) paras 165–67.

is based on common values and mutual trust.[56] The common values provide the normative content of the relational principles and are a source of the mutual trust which is a basis for the principles of (for example) sincere cooperation and mutual solidarity, transparency, institutional balance and conferral of powers.

*Systemic* principles are concerned with the operation of the system as a whole, with building the EU's identity as a coherent, effective and autonomous actor in the world. They make it clear that structural principles are not simply concerned to define the static relations between actors, but are designed to guide their conduct, to ensure that the actors do in fact act, and that their action is directed at constructing an EU capable of fulfilling the external mandate it is given in Articles 3(5) and 21 TEU.

In the following paragraphs I outline these two types of principle, the aim at this stage being illustrative rather than analytic.

## A. Relational Principles

In the EU system we can identify four relational axes and each of these is governed by one or more structural principles.

### (i) Member State–Member State

Being a member of the EU entails obligations to fellow Member States as well as to the EU as such and this operates in external policy as well as internally. In fact, it is perhaps more explicitly stated in the Treaties in the foreign policy context. The principle of *mutual solidarity* is mentioned three times in Article 24 TEU which introduces the CFSP, twice as 'mutual political solidarity'. It is described as the basis of the EU's own policy (the CFSP), and it is also linked to the Member States' duty of loyalty to the EU as an effective and cohesive force in international relations (Article 24(3) TEU). Further than this are the 'solidarity clauses' which provide for Member States to assist each other in case of external threats or natural disasters: the obligation of aid and assistance in cases of armed aggression under Article 42(7) TEU (with suitable references to Article 51 of the UN Charter, to NATO and to the 'specific character of the security and defence policy of certain Member States'); and the obligation to act jointly to assist a Member State which is the victim of a terrorist attack or natural or man-made disaster under Article 222 TFEU. In less dramatic contexts, we can see evidence of the principle of mutual solidarity in Article 34(2) TEU, which provides that Member States represented in international organisations or international conferences where not all the Member States participate must keep the other Member States and the High Representative informed of any matter of common interest.

---

[56] ibid para 168.

We can argue that on the basis of the principle of mutual solidarity, the Member States owe obligations to each other as well as to the EU when operating collectively with the EU (e.g. in the context of a mixed agreement) or when operating collectively where the EU cannot participate (e.g. within the United Nations (UN)). Participating as an EU Member State should entail *inter se* obligations as well as obligations towards the EU. As the Court put it in Opinion 2/13:

> [T]he Member States have, by reason of their membership of the EU, accepted that relations between them as regards the matters covered by the transfer of powers from the Member States to the EU are governed by EU law to the exclusion, if EU law so requires, of any other law.[57]

If so, what would these obligations consist of? Information and consultation, presumably, genuine efforts to find common positions, and perhaps also to accommodate and support a fellow Member State's specific needs and concerns. Although there is no obligation to abstain from *inter se* dispute settlement, the Member States' obligations towards the EU may require disputes to be resolved within the EU framework.[58]

Thus, mutual solidarity between Member States is both a precondition for the development of the Union's foreign policy and one of the outcomes or expressions of that policy. Opinion 2/13 also demonstrates that the need to protect the high levels of mutual trust between Member States may constrain the EU in the external obligations it contracts, demanding a degree of separation, or autonomy from general international law, in Member States' *inter se* relations.

## (ii) Member State–Institutions

The principle of *conferral* is important in determining the basis for EU powers and in deciding whether they are exclusive or not. To take a recent restatement of this principle:

> [S]ince the EU has only conferred powers, any competence, especially where it is exclusive, must have its basis in conclusions drawn from a comprehensive and detailed analysis of the relationship between the envisaged international agreement and the EU law in force.[59]

Given that 'competences not conferred on the Union in the Treaties remain with the Member States',[60] conferral is the principle that delimits the boundary between EU and Member State competence. And the principle of conferral requires that

---

[57] ibid para 193.
[58] Case C-459/03 *Commission v Ireland*, Judgment, EU:C:2006:345; *cf* also Opinion 2/13 (n 13) paras 207–13.
[59] Opinion 1/13 (n 15) para 74; see also Opinion 1/03 (n 4) para 124, and Case C-114/12 *Commission v Council*, Judgment, EU:C:2014:2151, para 74.
[60] Article 4(1) TEU.

the boundaries do not become blurred, even in the interests of unity in international representation. Thus, it should be clear whether a decision is adopted by the Council or by the Representatives of the Member States.

In the recent *Air Transport Agreement* case,[61] the Commission challenged the legality of a decision on the signing and provisional application of an international air transport agreement, adopted jointly by both the Council and the Representatives of the Member States (a so-called 'hybrid' decision). The Council argued that the hybrid decision was an expression of the duty of sincere cooperation. Since it was common ground that the agreement should be mixed (concluded by both the Union and the Member States), the Council argued:

> it is incumbent upon the Member States and the European Union to cooperate closely with regard to mixed agreements and to adopt a common approach in order to ensure unified representation of the European Union in international relations. The adoption of a joint decision is the expression of the cooperation thereby imposed.[62]

In an earlier case also involving a hybrid decision Advocate General (AG) Sharpston had accepted that cooperation is an 'essential condition' for the exercise of shared competence and that 'a joint decision is an expression of perhaps the closest form of cooperation'; nevertheless she argued both that 'procedural rules cannot be set aside in the name of the principle of sincere cooperation',[63] and that the principle of sincere cooperation 'can be relied upon only by an institution acting within the limits of its competences'.[64] In *Air Transport Agreement*, the Court agreed:

> [T]hat principle [the duty of cooperation] cannot justify the Council setting itself free from compliance with the procedural rules and voting arrangements laid down in Article 218 TFEU.[65]

The procedures laid down in Article 218 were compromised as the Member States participated in the adoption of an act which under Article 218(5) should have been adopted by the Council alone, and the position of the Council was compromised by participation in a decision of the Member States.[66] AG Mengozzi in fact took the view that the principle of sincere cooperation requires that the Member States should not interfere with the autonomy of the institutions. In his view, the merger of the Union and the intergovernmental decision into one indivisible whole could 'constitute a dangerous precedent of contamination of the autonomous decision-making process of the EU institutions that is liable, therefore, to cause damage to the autonomy of the EU as a specific legal system'.[67]

---

[61] Case C-28/12 *Commission v Council*, Judgment, EU:C:2015:282.
[62] ibid para 28.
[63] Case C-114/12 *Commission v Council*, Opinion of AG Sharpston, EU:C:2014:224, para 195.
[64] ibid para 175. On that occasion the Court did not decide the issue, since it took the view that competence was in any case exclusive.
[65] *Commission v Council* (n 61) para 55.
[66] ibid para 50.
[67] Case C-28/12 *Commission v Council*, Opinion of AG Mengozzi, EU:C:2015:43, para 80.

The principles of conferral and sincere cooperation are, as this case illustrates, closely connected. The duty to cooperate does not alter the allocation of powers between the EU and the Member States. Although the duty of cooperation 'is of general application and does not depend either on whether the Community competence concerned is exclusive or on any right of the Member States to enter into obligations towards non-member countries',[68] what is required by the duty of cooperation will vary depending on whether competence is exclusive or shared. In cases of exclusive competence, the Member States may act *only* through joint or collective action.[69] In cases of shared competence the duty of cooperation is more flexible; it can involve an obligation not to obstruct the EU if an international initiative such as the negotiation of an agreement is underway; it can involve an obligation to act jointly with the EU institutions in particular circumstances (e.g. decision-making within mixed agreements or international organisations):

> When [a mixed] agreement is negotiated and concluded, each of those parties [the Union and the Member States] must act within the framework of the competences which it has while respecting the competences of any other contracting party.[70]

This proposition can come under strain: *Commission v Sweden* demonstrates a strong reading of the duty of cooperation in the case of a mixed agreement, and while it can be defended it comes perilously close to a denial of Member State competence to act at all.[71]

Despite the centrality of the principle of conferral, there have been very few cases where it has been found that the EU has no competence at all.[72] So we could argue that this principle is not in practice so important as a power-limiting principle, but more because it makes clear the role of law (and therefore the courts) in structuring EU external power; it is a principle which establishes the need for a legal structure to EU power.

While conferral establishes the need for the EU (and each institution) to act within the limits of its powers, the principle of *subsidiarity* governs the decision to exercise that power. The operation of subsidiarity in the external context is not altogether clear. Subsidiarity in the sense of Article 5(3) TEU refers to the choice between EU or Member State action against a background of shared competence. In external relations this choice between Member State or Union action does of course exist, but is complicated in a number of ways. External action is characterised by the fact that the EU and Member States often operate side by side, concluding agreements together. Some important external competences are complementary rather than pre-emptive in effect. In the case of so-called parallel

---

[68] *Commission v Sweden* (n 7) para 71.
[69] Case C-45/07 *Commission v Greece*, Judgment, EU:C:2009:81.
[70] *Commission v Council* (n 61) para 47.
[71] *Commission v Sweden* (n 7). A Delgado Casteleiro and J Larik, 'The Duty to Remain Silent: Limitless Loyalty in EU External Relations' (2011) 36 *EL Rev* 524.
[72] See n 9 above.

competences such as development cooperation and humanitarian aid, it is explicitly stated that the exercise of Union competence shall not result in the Member States being prevented from exercising theirs.[73] This is the case also for the exercise of competence under the Common Foreign and Security Policy. The principles governing these complementary competences are coherence and cooperation.[74] We could even see the use of mixed agreements, in particular where not strictly required by the absence of Union competence over part of the agreement, as an expression of subsidiarity. The Union acts, but not to the exclusion of the Member States. In such cases, the constraints on the Member States arise not from the operation of subsidiarity and its effect on the decision to exercise competence, but rather from the principle of sincere cooperation and its effect on the ongoing exercise of competence by the Member States.

Subsidiarity is also complicated by the interaction between the internal powers and implied external powers. The exercise of an internal competence, itself subject to the principle of subsidiarity, may lead to a situation of exclusive external competence on the basis of Article 3(2) TFEU, and thus the exclusion of subsidiarity at the external level.[75] We may say, then, that in the context of external policy-making, the choice between Member State or Union action inherent in the concept of subsidiarity is not a clear-cut either/or decision, and when the choice for Union action does preclude action by the Member States this will generally be the result of a (subsidiarity-based) choice to adopt internal legislation at Union level. This leads us to question what role subsidiarity should play in relation to external action. The choice between external action by the Union and external action by the Member States does not imply a choice between different levels of action—national or Union level—since both would act internationally. If we are to maintain the idea of choosing an appropriate level of action (acting as closely as possible to the citizen) which underlies the conception of subsidiarity,[76] then we may consider applying subsidiarity to the choice between acting at EU level (internally) and acting globally (externally).[77] In this sense, implied external powers could be seen as an expression of the principle of subsidiarity based on the decision to use the EU's competence to act at the most appropriate level to achieve its objectives.

---

[73] Article 4(4) TFEU.

[74] See Art 208 TFEU for development cooperation, Art 210 TFEU for humanitarian aid, and Arts 24(3) and 26(3) TEU for the CFSP.

[75] See, eg, *Commission v Council* (n 59). It is, of course, not always the case that the adoption of internal legislation will lead to exclusive external competence on the basis of Art 3(2) TFEU; an examination of both the legislation and the international agreement will be required.

[76] According to the Preamble to the TEU, decisions are to be taken 'as closely as possible to the citizen in accordance with the principle of subsidiarity'.

[77] B de Witte and A Thies, 'Why Choose Europe? The Place of the European Union in the Architecture of International Legal Cooperation' in B Van Vooren, S Blockmans and J Wouters (eds), *The EU's Role in Global Governance: The Legal Dimension* (Oxford, Oxford University Press, 2013) 23.

## (iii) Inter-institutional Relations

The principles of conferral and sincere cooperation are closely linked also in the inter-institutional context. Article 13(2) TEU makes this clear:

> Each institution shall act within the limits of the powers conferred on it in the Treaties, and in conformity with the procedures, conditions and objectives set out in them. The institutions shall practice mutual sincere cooperation.

In the institutional context, conferral of powers is associated with institutional balance, recognising the different functions of each institution and the importance of the way those powers interact and affect each other. We see this in the choice of legal basis, and especially where there is a possibility of incompatible legal bases.[78] And the institutions have roles and prerogatives that they may seek to defend: the Commission's duty (and right?) to ensure the Union's external representation as provided in Article 17(1) TEU, and in particular its prerogatives as negotiator;[79] the Council's right to conclude international agreements;[80] the European Parliament's position as co-legislator, its right to give or withhold consent to the majority of international agreements, or simply its right to be consulted or to be informed. In determining the Parliament's prerogatives, the Court has referred to democracy as a Union value: for example, in the *GSP* case the obligation to consult the Parliament (as it then was) was said by the Court to be based on the principle of institutional balance and on the 'fundamental democratic principle' of consultation of people through their representatives.[81] In the *Transfer of Suspected Pirates* case, the right of the Parliament to be informed even in the case of a CFSP agreement was held to be an essential procedural requirement, breach of which resulted in the annulment of the Council's act:

> [T]he Parliament's involvement in the decision-making process is the reflection, at EU level, of the fundamental democratic principle that the people should participate in the exercise of power through the intermediary of a representative assembly.[82]

The other institutions may not be able to claim such an exalted basis for their prerogatives but this does not mean that the institutional balance is always tipped in favour of Parliamentary involvement.[83]

The Lisbon Treaty introduced for the first time an explicit reference to *the duty of sincere cooperation* applied to the institutions, although the Court had already

---

[78] Case C-130/10 *European Parliament v Council*, Judgment, EU:C:2012:472.

[79] In Case C-114/12, the Commission argued that 'By acting as it did, the Council blurred the personality of the European Union and its presence and standing in international relations'. Opinion of AG Sharpston (n 63) para 191. See also Case C-425/13 *Commission v Council*, Judgment, EU:C:2015:483, in which it was held that although the Council was entitled to establish a consultative committee in an international negotiation, it had infringed the Commission's prerogative as negotiator by giving the committee the power to determine negotiating positions.

[80] Case C-660/13 *Council v Commission*, Judgment, EU:C:2016:616.

[81] Case C-65/93 *European Parliament v Council*, Judgment, EU:C:1995:91.

[82] *European Parliament v Council* (n 34) para 81.

[83] *European Parliament v Council* (n 78) para 82.

interpreted the general duty of cooperation as also applying to them.[84] Sincere cooperation is increasingly referred to by the institutions in litigation,[85] and the Court is starting to give some substance to the principle, as it has in dealing with Member State–EU relations. For example, the Court has held that 'the principle of sincere cooperation requires the Commission to consult the Council before-hand if it intends to express positions on behalf of the European Union before an international court'.[86] Whereas institutional balance applies to the allocation of institutional roles in the Treaties, sincere cooperation operates on the institutions when acting *within* their respective spheres of competence.[87] So while the European External Action Service may be seen as an institutionalised opportunity for (though not the 'fulfilment' of) the duty of cooperation between the Council, the Commission and the Member States,[88] Article 40 TEU, which requires the preservation of and respect for the distinct 'procedures and the extent of the powers of the institutions' under CFSP and non-CFSP competences, can be seen as an expression of the principle of institutional balance. As we have already seen, sincere cooperation cannot be used to justify a departure from the allocation of competences to the different institutions. The 2010 inter-institutional agreement between the Commission and the European Parliament, including its provisions on the negotiation of international agreements, is clearly intended to provide a framework for 'sincere cooperation', as well as the effective and transparent exercise of the institutions' respective powers.[89] The Council has taken the view that the agreement nevertheless threatens the institutional balance established in the Treaties, although the possibility of legal action threatened in 2010 has not materialised.[90]

Mutual sincere cooperation expresses the idea that each institution should respect and allow full expression to the powers of the other institutions: '[E]ach

---

[84] See, eg, *European Parliament v* Council (n 81).

[85] See, eg, *Commission v Council* (n 61); *Commission v Council* (n 79); *Council v Commission* (n 45); Case C-48/14 *European Parliament v Council*, Judgment, EU:C:2015:91.

[86] *Council v Commission* (n 45) para 86.

[87] ibid para 84: 'Under Article 13(2) TEU, the European Union's institutions are to practice mutual sincere cooperation. That sincere cooperation, however, is exercised within the limits of the powers conferred by the Treaties on each institution. The obligation resulting from Article 13(2) TEU is there-fore not such as to change those powers'.

[88] Council Decision 2010/427/EU of 26 July 2010 establishing the organisation and functioning of the European External Action Service [2010] OJ L201/30.

[89] Framework Agreement on relations between the European Parliament and the European Commission [2010] OJ L304/47. According to the Preamble, 'this Framework Agreement does not affect the powers and prerogatives of Parliament, the Commission or any other institution or organ of the Union but seeks to ensure that those powers and prerogatives are exercised as effectively and transparently as possible'.

[90] 'The Council notes that several provisions of the Framework Agreement have the effect of modi-fying the institutional balance set out in the Treaties in force, according the European Parliament pre-rogatives that are not provided for in the Treaties and limiting the autonomy of the Commission and its President. The Council is particularly concerned by the provisions on international agreements, infringement proceedings against Member States and transmission of classified information to the European Parliament.' Council Statement on relations between the European Parliament and the Com-mission, 21 October 2010, Council doc 15172/10.

of the institutions must exercise its powers with due regard for the powers of the other institutions'.[91] This is not just a question of respecting institutional balance and the other institutions' prerogatives, although it does encompass this. It also means that the institutions in their mutual relations should seek to maximise the degree to which each can fulfil its functions in the EU system. Each institution has an autonomy, which is represented by its particular role, but that autonomy should not be exercised at the expense of the autonomy of the other institutions. Here, perhaps, we can see the meaning of mutuality and the sense in which mutual cooperation is needed to preserve, or achieve, institutional balance.

This aspect of mutual sincere cooperation requires an understanding, not only of the formal legal powers of each institution but also the purpose of those powers: what function it serves, and the role it plays in a particular process or specific procedural context. In the process of treaty-making, for example, we need to understand the part played by the Council, the Commission and the European Parliament, as well as that of the Court of Justice. As expressed by the Court itself, the mutual sincere cooperation required by Article 13(2) TEU 'is of particular importance for EU action at international level, as such action triggers a closely circumscribed process of concerted action and consultation between the EU institutions'.[92] From this perspective, mutual sincere cooperation may contribute to the interpretation of the scope of the institutions' powers, as well as to how they are exercised.

The principle of *transparency* expresses the need for communication and information-sharing between institutions. It is implemented, *inter alia*, via inter-institutional agreements and in this context transparency serves the aims of institutional balance (for example, enabling the Parliament to play its role by initiating debate and passing resolutions on policy choices) and the systemic principles of effectiveness and coherence, facilitating effective policy-making and enabling the institutions to ensure that the EU's external face is unified and coherent. This invites the question: to what extent is transparency a principle in its own right, and to what extent is it a means of ensuring that other principles are respected? It is perhaps in the fourth axis of relations, between the EU and individuals and third countries, that the principle of transparency takes on a more autonomous and normative role.

### (iv) EU Institutions–Individuals/Third Countries/International Organisations

The structuring of the EU as an international actor implies the need to structure its relationships with those 'outside' itself, individuals affected by its actions, as well of course as the third countries and international, regional and global organisations

---

[91] *Commission v Council* (n 79) para 69.
[92] ibid para 64.

with which the Union is mandated to 'develop relations and build partnerships' (Article 21(1) TEU). The fact that we may claim that these relations are governed by principles of EU law, and not simply the constraints of international law, illustrates the extent to which the EU as an international actor is legally bounded. And while it is the EU itself which establishes these principles, it nevertheless conducts those relations within the legal environment of international law. Put another way, the autonomy of the European Union necessary to establish its identity as an actor does not imply that the EU is closed to international law and legal relationships (that EU law and international law 'pass by each other like ships in the night' to use the metaphor of AG Maduro in *Kadi I*[93]). The principle of autonomy and its relationship to the task of contributing to the 'strict observance and development of international law' which is at the heart of EU external action (Article 3(5) TEU) operates as a systemic principle, a principle which helps to define the actorness of the EU. But there is also a need to address the principles which govern the EU's conduct towards individuals and its international partners in a relational sense. Here, we will turn to two principles in particular: the rule of law (itself a compendium) and transparency.

The conception of a Union based on the *rule of law*, of the rule of law as a founding value of the EU (Article 2 TEU) which it is to uphold and promote in the wider world (Article 3(5) TEU), and one of the principles which 'inspired its own creation, development and enlargement, and which it seeks to advance in the wider world' (Article 21(1) TEU) implies certain obligations on the Union in its dealings with individuals affected by its actions[94] and perhaps also towards third countries. I am not here referring to the substantive content of policy (the EU as a promoter of the rule of law in third countries, or the EU's ability to discriminate in terms of substantive policy between countries or individuals through trade preferences or visa requirements[95]). The claim is rather that the framework of external action needs to abide by certain procedural standards. Some outlines of this principle have been developed through the case-law on restrictive measures, including the obligation to state reasons, and rights of judicial review. The *Schrems* case is rather special, since the Data Protection Directive explicitly requires that the Commission in adopting a 'safe harbour' or adequacy decision must be satisfied that the level of protection of fundamental rights in a third country is at least equivalent to that in the EU, but it raises the question of the more general applicability of Charter rights of effective judicial protection and good administration to external action.[96] In the recent judgment in *H*, the Court of Justice accepted jurisdiction

---

[93] *Yassin Abdullah Kadi and Al Barakaat International Foundation v Council and Commission* (n 3) para 22.

[94] ibid.

[95] Of course, the EU may commit itself to the principle of non-discrimination through political choice through its membership of an international organisation (such as the WTO), its international treaty commitments or the adoption of autonomous measures.

[96] Case C-362/14 *Schrems v Data Protection Commissioner*, Judgment, EU:C:2015:650.

(despite the limits imposed by Article 24(1) TEU and Article 275 TFEU) to review a decision adopted by a CFSP head of mission on the grounds that it concerned staff management. Its judgment, reversing that of the General Court, refers to the Union being founded on the 'values of equality and the rule of law', effective judicial review being 'inherent in the existence' of the rule of law. The principle of the rule of law is here used to help to define the scope of the Treaty rule excluding the Court's jurisdiction over provisions relating to the CFSP and acts based on those provisions.

The principle of *transparency* in this context is concerned in particular with public access to documents, and the tendency of the EU institutions as well as governments towards secrecy in matters of international relations. There are perhaps two angles of transparency to consider: towards the EU public, and towards the outside world. A more traditional approach has argued that the need to restrict access of third countries to information justifies restricting information also to the EU public.[97] However, the Court has not interpreted the international relations exception in the Access to Documents Regulation as simply excluding all questions of external relations from transparency requirements.[98] It requires justification in each case that the EU's interests will be damaged. And there are signs that the general expectations are changing: witness the decision (finally) to release the Transatlantic Trade and Investment Partnership (TTIP) negotiating mandate. This is at least in part due to a realisation that if the EU is to achieve the aims it has set itself in its external relations it needs to convince not only its external partners but also its own institutions (in particular the European Parliament) and its own public.[99]

## B. Systemic Principles

The structural principles that we may call *systemic* characterise the type of international actor the EU is, and the norms it produces in its external policy-making. They are concerned with the operation of the system as a whole as opposed to the interaction between its individual components, with building the EU's identity as a coherent, effective and autonomous actor in the world. Autonomy is reflective of the EU's need to project its international identity as distinct from its Member States, and also of the Court's insistence that the EU represents a system autonomous from international as well as national law. The institutional policy-making space which is built and protected by the structural principles is open to international

---

[97] Regulation 1049/2001 regarding public access to European Parliament, Council and Commission documents [2001] OJ L145/43, art 4.

[98] Case C-350/12P *Council v Sophie in't Veld*, Judgment, EU:C:2014:2039; Case T-301/10 *Sophie in't Veld v Commission*, Judgment, EU:T:2013:135.

[99] The cases of the SWIFT and ACTA agreements provide ample evidence of this, as does the current debate over TTIP.

law,[100] but the relation is mediated through rules of EU law, established in the Treaty and developed and applied by the Court of Justice. Coherence and effectiveness are assessed with reference to the Union's objectives, as defined in the Treaties and operationalised by the political actors.

How do these systemic principles interact with relational principles? In the discussion of relational principles we have referred several times to these systemic principles and it is clear that they work closely together. They may be complementary. On the one hand, the relational principles are designed to further the systemic principles: the Member States, for example, in an expression of the principles of loyalty and solidarity, are to refrain from any action 'likely to impair [the Union's] *effectiveness* as a *cohesive* force in international relations' (Article 24(3) TEU). On the other hand, the systemic nature of coherence, effectiveness and autonomy implies that these principles serve to guide and shape the other structural principles and their implementation. Thus, the principle of effectiveness, based on the conception of the EU as an actor with international legal capacity, is behind the interpretation given to the principle of conferral in *ERTA* so as to allow for the emergence of implied external powers. The principle of autonomy underpins the Court's approach to the rule of law in *Kadi* and to mutual trust in Opinion 2/13. The principle of coherence has been used by the Court to guide its interpretation of the principle of institutional balance reflected in the relationship between substantive and procedural legal basis in Article 218 TFEU.[101] There may also be tensions between them, for example, between coherence and the principle of conferral; or between effectiveness and the principle of transparency; as well as tensions between the two systemic principles of coherence and effectiveness, in the sense of consistency versus *real-politik*, and between relational principles such as conferral and sincere cooperation.[102]

# V. Conclusion

This chapter has introduced the concept of structural principles in EU external relations law by putting forward a preliminary assessment of their rationale, their nature and their function. It starts from an observation about the character of external relations competences: the task of the Union, guided by its values, is to

---

[100] To take a couple of examples: the Court's recognition that the EU is bound by customary international law, and its use of the canons of interpretation of international law in its interpretation of the EU's international treaty commitments. For a critique of the Court's approach to international treaty law, see J Odermatt, 'The Use of International Treaty Law by the Court of Justice of the European Union' (2015) 17 *Cambridge Yearbook of European Legal Studies* 121.

[101] *European Parliament v Council* (n 34) paras 52–60.

[102] On the latter, see *Commission v Sweden* (n 7), and the Opinion of AG Sharpston in *Commission v Council* (n 63).

'develop relations and build partnerships' with third countries and international organisations, and to work for a high degree of cooperation in order to further its objectives (Article 21 TEU). The Treaty does not establish end-goals for the Union's external policy, its objectives being orientational and general rather than functional. This is not to downplay their importance, but rather to understand the nature of their role. Policy goals certainly exist, but they are created as a result of policy-making by the Union's institutional framework, giving concrete shape to the Union's objectives in specific situations or on particular issues.

The chapter then argues that this characteristic of EU external competence shapes the role of law in external relations. Its focus is not on shaping the uses to which that competence is put, but rather on shaping or constructing an institutional space within which policy can be made. The legal structure thus created is protective of the policy autonomy of the Union, of the powers of the different actors in the system, and has developed principles which govern their relations.

These principles I have termed structural, since they help to define the structure of the EU as an international actor, both internally and externally. As principles they operate alongside rules, they may find their expression in detailed rules (e.g. rules of procedure) and they may help to interpret or apply rules in specific cases. They may complement but may also be in tension with each other. As structural principles they are concerned with process rather than the content of policy, and this has an impact on the context in which policy contestation can take place and the role that law and the courts can play in this process. The chapter identifies two types of structural principles, relational and systemic. Relational principles operate on the different relational axes between Member States, institutions and individuals or third countries. They concern the existence and exercise of competence, solidarity and cooperation, transparency both between the EU institutions and towards the public, and observance of the rule of law. Systemic principles are concerned with the solidity of the structure: the building of the EU as a coherent and effective and autonomous actor. The following chapters will address each of these principles individually; our hope is that this attempt to look at EU external relations through the lens of structural principles will help us to understand better the role that law plays in this construction project.

# 2

# Structural Principles in EU Law: Internal and External

LOÏC AZOULAI

## I. Reference to Structure in EU Law

This chapter will be an attempt to situate structural principles in external relations law within the broader context of the evolution of EU law. It purports to explore the role such principles play in EU external relations law with respect to the role they have in the internal field. The hypothesis is that for all that they share (which essentially is an existential tension between the independence of Member States and their coexistence within a common framework for action), EU internal law and EU external relations law take, at least originally, a different approach to the question of structural principles. This becomes clear if we consider the distinct contexts in which these principles emerge. The very nature of what we call 'structural principles' changes from one context to the other.

The original and central project of Community law was both internal and structural in nature. It was to build a new economic and social order based on pre-existing domestic orders. From the outset, the European project went beyond the mere transformation of domestic orders. It engaged in an order-building enterprise. For the first generation of Community lawyers this primarily meant building the 'Common Market' through bureaucratic and judicial means and by relying on the functional objectives enshrined in the EC Treaties. For the EU lawyers, the meaning of the challenge has changed: it is to build a constitutional order based on founding EU values in a manner which is more respectful of the constitutional diversity found within the Union. As it extends and affects ever larger areas of national law and deeper sets of socioeconomic sectors, it becomes apparent that EU law cannot rely solely on its own resources and content itself with purely market integration goals. It must now be seen within a wider constitutional and pluralist context, dealing with external references and non-market rationales while keeping in mind its market-building project. It is now fashionable in EU law circles to treat the original functionalist and supranationalist projects as *passé*, in favour of what is thought of as the more complex picture involving a multiplicity of actors, jurisdictions and constitutional orders. This latter project is commonly known as 'constitutional pluralism'.[1] These changing ways of constructing Europe (and their myriad variations) differ in the way they conceptualise legal and political integration. They share, however, the basic assumption that EU law just like EC law does not make sense independent of an 'overarching frame of reference' underpinning the ensemble of EU legal provisions. Pescatore calls it 'an idea of order',[2] von Bogdandy a 'grand structural plan',[3] Maduro 'the European legal system' as a whole.[4]

In an interview given rather late in his life, Pescatore summarised the legal method prevailing in the Union: 'Riphagen taught me the importance of what are called structural principles in law. Before one can talk of the substance of legal norms, one must see what the structure into which these norms are integrated is'.[5] In his view, EU norms are integrated into a unique structure that may not be compared to a classical international organisation. The novelty of the EC/EU system derives from its 'new principles of representativity': a series of doctrines that justify an unconditional transfer of loyalty to a new centre of power, the EU institutional system, and a clear allocation of tasks and responsibilities between the European institutions setting the objectives and the Member States implementing them.[6] But there is more than a reference to a specific organisation and institutional framework in this. The legitimation of the European Union requires more than a unique institutional system; it needs a new form of legal knowledge and legal practice. Pescatore relies on 'structural principles' as a method to interpret and to make EU legal norms. On this view, EU law must rest not only on a set of norms but also on a set of principles. These principles are used to introduce new and concrete forms of action, but at the same time they are capable of providing a solid and coherent basis for the whole construction. These principles are both sources of EU law and principles of interpretation of EU legal sources, yet at the same time meta-principles which help to define the overall nature of the EU legal order.[7] This is exactly how concepts such as primacy, non-discrimination on

---

[1] For an account of the doctrinal dimension of this approach see K Jaklic, *Constitutional Pluralism in the EU* (Oxford, Oxford University Press, 2014).

[2] P Pescatore, *The Law of Integration: Emergence of a New Phenomenon in International Relations, Based on the Experience of the European Communities* (Leiden, Sijthoof, 1974).

[3] A von Bogdandy, 'Founding Principles of EU Law: A Theoretical and Doctrinal Sketch' (2010) 16 *European Law Journal* 95.

[4] M Poiares Maduro, 'Three Claims of Constititional Pluralism' in M Avbelj and J Komarek (eds), *Constitutional Pluralism in the European Union and Beyond* (Oxford, Hart Publishing, 2012) 67.

[5] The transcript of this interview dated 2013 is to be found at www.cvce.eu/histoire-orale/.

[6] Pescatore, *The Law of Integration* (n 2). For an early illustration of this idea of structure in the case-law of the Court see Case 76/70 *Wünsche & Co.*, Judgment, EU:C:1971:51, para 10. See also Opinion 1/76, EU:C:1977:63, para 12.

[7] See, on the examples of direct effect and primacy, B de Witte, 'Direct Effect, Supremacy and the Nature of the Legal Order' in P Craig and G de Búrca (eds), *The Evolution of EU Law* (Oxford, Oxford University Press, 1999) 177.

grounds of nationality or *effet utile* currently work in EU law. Their multifaceted and confusing role qualifies them as 'structural principles of EU law'.

The most ambitious intellectual and practical accomplishment in the field of EU law has always been to establish the set of structural principles on which the whole construction of EU law is based. Both the Court of Justice of the European Union and legal scholarship have been busy with this task.[8] Structural principles are seen as forms of rationalisation of a highly valuable but essentially instable project. To make EU law subject to structural principles is to make it and the EU more resilient. This is essential so that EU law may stand as a solid barrier between the fragile supranational structure and what is perceived to be the constant risks of political disintegration, legal fragmentation and social disaffection. Thus, the formulation of structural principles aims to embed political, economic and social relations and forces that structure the process of integration into the legal form and into certain patterns of thought favourable to integration. On this view, the political and the factual are pushed out of the domain of EU affairs and consigned to the local or national forum. In the history of the European construction, this conceptual endeavour was supported by a form of political and social mobilisation that allowed for the creation of a common culture of integration within a group of influential individuals belonging to different institutional contexts.[9]

Transposed to the external relations field, this endeavour immediately encounters a serious difficulty: the difficulty of coping with the many different actors both within and outside the Union participating in and struggling for visibility on the international plane. The range of international actors, both state and non-state actors, and the expansion of international law-making make this project particularly difficult to achieve.[10] It is in the field of external relations that the tension between existence and coexistence between Member States is at its most acute. Moreover, in this field, there is no easy means to control the third parties involved.[11] The concern herein is constructing the EU itself as a credible and effective actor rather than constructing any substantive order.[12] The 'external project' is to affirm the presence and visibility of the EU on the 'polyphonic' and low regulated international scene.[13] External relations law engages with the outside

---

[8] See, for instance, T Tridimas, *The General Principles of EU Law*, 3rd edn (Oxford, Oxford University Press, 2006).

[9] See on this point the work of a 'new' sociologists and historians of integration: A Vauchez, *Brokering Europe: Euro-Lawyers and the Making of a Transnational Polity* (Cambridge, Cambridge University Press, 2015); M Egan, 'Towards a New History in European Law: New Wine in Old Bottles?' (2013) 28 *American University International Law Review* 1223.

[10] *cf* D Thym, 'Foreign Affairs' in A von Bogdandy and J Bast (eds), *Principles of European Constitutional Law*, 2nd edn (Verlag CH Beck, Hart Publishing, 2009) 315.

[11] *cf* L Azoulai, 'The Acquis of the European Union and International Organisations' (2005) 11 *European Law Journal* 196.

[12] See Marise Cremona, Chapter 1.

[13] See Joris Larik, Chapter 7. The 'polyphonic nature of the Union's external action' was first outlined by C Hillion, 'Mixity and Coherence in EU External Relations: The Significance of the "Duty of Cooperation"' in C Hillion and P Koutrakos (eds), *Mixed Agreements Revisited: The EU and Its Member States in the World* (Oxford, Hart Publishing, 2010) 87.

world and the domain of power relationships. Politics (the elaboration of a proper settled position in a contested environment) is, in a way, central to this project. The conceptual origins of the EU external relations law field are to be found in the *AETR* case in which the Court established the Community as a political actor, as a new form of power.[14] It is all about the independence of action of the Community in its external relations. This is not to say that law is not central to the project—it is: law is not only a technical instrument to conclude international agreements; it is the main instrument for structuring the Union's power.[15] Therefore the problem of structure as it appears in this context is not a problem of the normative foundation of a new substantive order. It is a problem of ensuring the consistency and the credibility of the EU as a political actor in the international arena. It is about structuring collective action in a multilayered environment. The Court hinted at this in its famous *Defrenne* judgment of 1976 on social policy and equal treatment when it made a fine distinction between the two distinct uses of the concept of 'principles' in relation to the first part of the Treaty and to Article 113 of the EC Treaty on commercial policy. The former use of the concept of 'principles' concerns, the Court stated, 'the very foundations of the Community' whereas the latter concerns 'the coherence of its external relations'.[16]

Taking this distinction seriously for analytical purposes, I would like first to explore further these two conceptual universes and to make clear how structural principles operate in both fields. In section II, the role structural principles play in the internal field is analysed. Section III briefly examines the way structural principles eventually emerged in the external relation field. Then, in section IV, I propose to look at the way in which, in practice, each field accommodates what the other field takes as its main concern: how EU internal law deals with political realities, and how EU external relations law deals with substantive values and constitutional principles. Rather than two separate fields of law, these are two different legal dynamics communicating with each other and contaminating each other. This may lead us to rethink both fields from the perspective of the other.

# II. Structural Principles: Internal

EU law has an uneasy relationship to something which may be called 'the society of Member States', the relationship between Member States, which it imagines as rather combative and uncertain terrain. The 'law of integration' aims at

---

[14] Case 22/70 *Commission v Council (AETR)*, Judgment, EU:C:1971:32.
[15] *cf* L Azoulai, 'The Many Visions of Europe: Insights from the Reasoning of the European Court of Justice in External Relations Law' in M Cremona and A Thies (eds), *The European Court of Justice and External Relations Law: Constitutional Challenges* (Oxford, Hart Publishing, 2014) 165.
[16] Case 43/75 *Defrenne v Sabena*, Judgment, EU:C:1976:56, para 29.

'establishing a special type of relationship between States'.[17] EU law is based on a rejection of the old diplomatic system based solely on relationships of power. It intends to create a distinction between law and power. Relationships based on power alone are to be transcended in favour of the establishment of a 'common framework'.[18] This is done through a series of legal doctrines, such as the obligation to take action within the EU institutional system, the obligation not to undermine the EU institutional framework while acting outside the framework, or the prohibition to rely on mechanisms of reciprocity.[19] But the goal of EU law does not stop here: it is not purely institutional. The goal is to erect a plane or viewpoint above the fray of inter-state relations from which the situation of states and individuals is to be assessed. This is the point of view of the Treaties' objectives, say for instance the establishment of the internal market. EU law is not the law of intersubjective relations. It is the law of an objective legality instrumental to the creation of a substantive order to which institutional players and private parties are uniformly bound. This is why it would be misleading to speak of 'EU *internal relations* law' as mirroring 'EU *external relations* law'. In building this 'transcendental' order, EU law seeks to remain agnostic about political preferences and social conflicts, ideological differences and value choices.

However, it should be clear that this construction is deeply problematic. On the one hand, EU law presents itself as the law of a new overarching socioeconomic order but it does not possess the corresponding means, instruments and scope of action to displace domestic socioeconomic and legal orders. Further, it is not able to affect all social and legal relationships concerned with the establishment of an encompassing European order. It entirely depends on Member States structures, rules and institutions. On the other hand, EU law claims to be agnostic in terms of values and principles of justice but it directly impinges on welfare state structures and it extends to areas where conflicts of values often arise. EU law faces a series of contradictions inherent in the integration process. In this context, the reference to structural principles emerges as one of the techniques developed by EU law and its principal organ of interpretation, the Court of Justice, to both justify and overcome these contradictions. The idea is to provide a 'structure' or an identity of its own to a system factually and functionally dependent on external resources and references. The development of structural principles is used for differentiating EU and national law. It is presented by EU law itself as a disjuncture between principles and policies. The former is the proper realm of EU law while the latter refer to domestic conflictual rationalities.

This is reflected in the very peculiar way in which these principles are identified and implemented by the Court. These principles may be classified as 'general

---

[17] Pescatore, *The Law of Integration* (n 2) Preface.

[18] See Case 232/78 *Commission v France*, Judgment, EU:C:1979:215, para 7 (preferably in the French version, the working and drafting language of the Court).

[19] See Editorial Comments, 'Union Membership in Times of Crisis' (2014) 51 *CML Rev* 1.

principles', 'fundamental principles' or they may even not be expressly termed 'principles'.[20] They are concerned with the position of the individual under EU law, the nature of the EU legal order as well as the relations between institutions. What is distinctive about these principles is not their label nor their specific content but their mode of operation. To name just a few, these are the principles of non-discrimination, free movement, primacy, *effet utile*, judicial review, institutional balance and loyal cooperation. These principles operate as ways of structuring EU law, separating it from what is seen as the highly political, mundane and fragmented domestic legal practice. As a result, they have an impact on the representation of the defining features of the EU legal order and more broadly on the nature of the European Union.

First of all, some principles work as means of detaching or separating EU law from the reality 'on the ground' in which EU law operates. For instance, the primacy of EU law as a structural principle is mainly about this. As the Court made clear in *Winner Wetten*, 'rules of national law, even of a constitutional order, cannot be allowed to undermine the unity and effectiveness of Union law'.[21] Constitutional arrangements have no direct bearing on the development of EU principle-based law. As a result, the incorporation of EU law into domestic legal systems responds to its own logic and modalities; it should be free from the constraints set out by national constitutional orders. Even further, it aims to modify the distribution of places between the Union and its Member States, making the latter parts of the former conceived of as a whole. The reliance on the principle of non-discrimination on grounds of age in *Mangold* may be seen as a similar example of this separation of EU law and political reality, by making EU law indifferent to the particular social environment in which national policies are developed.[22] This mode of operation is even more striking in cases of *renvoi* when EU law itself refers to national law as precondition for its application. Many EU law provisions refer to national law in order to provide a definition or specific conditions. In interpreting such provisions, the Court often resorts to the 'principles underlying EU law' as a way to limit or even to remove the reference to national law, giving an autonomous meaning to the terms and conditions inserted in EU law provisions.[23] Taken a step further, this reference to 'structural principles' may well be used to circumvent the constitutional constraints provided by the Treaties. As the argument goes, the reference to underlying principles would provide the

---

[20] For an account of this terminological variation in the case-law of the Court, see Case C-101/08 *Audiolux*, Opinion of Advocate General (AG) Trstenjak, EU:C:2009:410, para 67. B de Witte rightly points out the fact that primacy is originally rarely referred to as a 'principle': see 'Institutional Principles in the Judicial Development of the EU Legal Order' in F Snyder (ed), *The Europeanisation of Law: The Legal Effects of European Integration* (Oxford, Hart Publishing, 2000) 89.

[21] Case C-409/06 *Winner Wetten*, Judgment, EU:C:2010:503, para 61.

[22] Case C-144/04 *Mangold*, Judgment, EU:C:2005:709.

[23] See, eg, Case C-363/05 *JP Morgan*, Judgment, EU:C:2007:391, para 22.

constitutional foundations of the EU such that the revision procedure provided by Article 48 TEU could not be allowed to alter.[24]

Secondly, structural principles act as agents of 'totalisation' of EU law. They ensure that EU law has maximum coverage and operates with overarching conceptions across the sectoral fields of EU law and sometimes also beyond the strict boundaries of EU law. This represents of form of 'perfectionism' typical in EU law.[25] For instance, rules considered as 'fundamental principles' such as the rule of non-discrimination on grounds of nationality extend to non-EU treaties such as the Euratom Treaty.[26] More intriguingly, the reference to fundamental principles may be used to extend the scope of application *ratione materiae* or *ratione personae* of a piece of EU legislation. The case-law on non-discrimination on grounds of age is an excellent illustration of this technique. In *Mangold* and *Küciükdeveci*, the Court developed the strange figure of a principle not 'laid down' in a Directive but to which the Directive 'gives specific expression'.[27] As a result of this operation, EU legislation extends to matters and private relationships not initially covered by it. This structural development stands in sharp contrast with the recent and now famous *Dano* case on access to social benefits by non-economically active EU citizens. In this case, the principle of non-discrimination is said to be given specific expression in EU legislation but to the effect that EU provisions must be strictly interpreted.[28] What we have here is a *'clausebound'* interpretation as opposed to the constructivist and teleological approach to interpretation usually relied on by the Court of Justice.[29]

Finally, structural principles operate as holistic modes of expression. They are used as a way to make all actors realise that they are part of the same global system. The principle of sincere cooperation has its origins in this context. In *Commission v France* in 1969, the Court made clear that even when acting within their sphere of 'reserved powers' (the field of monetary policy at the time), Member States are obliged to 'cooperate in a spirit of loyalty' and abide by the most fundamental rules of the Treaties, namely the internal market and competition rules. This is justified by 'the solidarity which is at the basis of ... the whole of the Community system in accordance with the commitment provided for in Article 5 of the Treaty (now Article 4(3) TEU)'.[30] Member States must have due regard to the Union system as a whole. In some other cases, this reference to the whole works not as a constraint but as a source of empowerment. The case-law

---

[24] *cf* von Bogdandy, 'Founding Principles of EU Law' (n 3).

[25] J Bomhoff, 'Perfectionism in European Law' (2013) 14 *Cambridge Yearbook of European Legal Studies* 75.

[26] Case C-115/08 *ČEZ*, Judgment, EU:C:2009:660, para 88.

[27] *Mangold* (n 22); Case C-555/07 *Küciükdeveci*, Judgment, EU:C:2010:21.

[28] Case C-333/13 *Dano*, Judgment, EU:C:2014:2358.

[29] G Itzcovich, 'The Interpretation of Community Law by the European Court of Justice' (2009) 10 *German Law Journal* 537.

[30] Joined Cases 6/69 and 11/69 *Commission v France*, Judgment, EU:C:1969:68, para 16.

on primacy is illustrative of this. In its seminal judgments in *Costa v Enel* and *Simmenthal*, the Court refers to the 'foundations of the Community'.[31] The conflict is presented not as a conflict between a national measure and a specific Community provision but as conflict between a national measure and notion of the Community as a whole: the reference point is 'the legal basis of the Community itself'.[32] This operation is to empower the national courts by making them realise that they are part of a new whole. This should allow them to emancipate themselves from previous constitutional affiliations. Hence, the link the Court regularly makes between primacy and sincere cooperation.[33] Through this reference, national courts and other domestic actors are brought into a new legal and conceptual order which floats above 'political disorder'.

However, in some cases, this may not be enough. Political disorder may break the structure of the EU legal order. There are two typical sets of cases. The first concerns disputes between Member States. In such cases, Member States are inclined to rely on EU law as an instrument of distrust. *Hungary v Slovakia* is such a case.[34] This case concerned Slovakia's refusal to allow the entry of the Hungarian President, who sought to participate in a commemoration organised by the Hungarian community living in Slovakia, to the territory of Slovakia. In that case, the Court stated that because the situation was governed by international law, in particular the law governing diplomatic relations, EU law was not applicable. It is clear that the Court was reluctant to engage in what it perceived as a highly sensitive political question. In this case, the Court stepped backward by considering that the general relationship between the Member States is not covered by the structural principles of EU law. In his opinion, Advocate General Bot timidly argued that the commitment of Member States to maintain good-neighbourly relations is 'consubstantial with their decision to join the Union', and may therefore be covered by EU law and in particular the principle of loyal cooperation. Indeed, it may be assumed that any serious conflict between Member States, even more so with questions relating to the protection of minorities and mutual respect, is likely to disturb the proper functioning of the Union. This suggestion was not taken up by the Court.

The second set of cases concerns instances of cooperation between Member States outside the institutional framework of the EU. The *Pringle* case, concerning the validity of the Treaty establishing a European Stability Mechanism (ESM), is a case in point.[35] It has been rightly noted that the practice of a number of Member States in acting outside the EU legal framework and making use of the EU institutions for this purpose is not a new one and, indeed, has been accepted by the Court

---

[31] Case 106/77 *Simmenthal*, Judgment, EU:C:1978:49, para 18.

[32] Case 6/64 *Costa v ENEL*, Judgment, EU:C:1964:66.

[33] See, eg, Case C-213/89 *Factortame*, Judgment, EU:C:1990:257, para 19: '[T]he duty to apply EU law and to set aside conflicting rules of national law has been presented by the ECJ as an application of the principles of cooperation laid down in Article 5 of the EEC Treaty'.

[34] Case C-364/10 *Hungary v Slovakia*, Judgment, EU:C:2012:630.

[35] Case C-370/12 *Pringle*, Judgment, EU:C:2012:756.

in two previous judgments.[36] There is, however, one essential difference between the context of these judgments and the *Pringle* case. The mechanism at issue on this case has as its objective to 'safeguard of the euro area as a whole' which itself is considered to be central to the furtherance of the integration project or, as the Court put it, as part of 'the general interest of the Union'. As a result of this judgment, in a domain essential to the attainment of the Union's objectives, Member States are allowed to act outside the EU framework and enjoy a large degree of autonomy. True, the validity of the mechanism is made subject to a 'duty to comply with European Union law'. However, this refers to strict conditionality substantiated by the measures of budgetary discipline adopted by the Union and not to the structural principles governing the Union (such as primacy, institutional balance, fundamental rights).[37] What is particularly striking is the ease with which the Court accepts the use of the EU institutions in a context which is profoundly adverse to the development of the legal and institutional culture of the EU. Moreover, this decision stands in sharp contrast with the external relations case-law on the setting up of mechanisms borrowing elements from the EU framework, where the Court was keen to protect the EU institutional structure.[38] In other words, the Court has failed to defend the conceptual and normative assumptions underpinning the EU legal order.[39] The lesson to be drawn from this is that, in both cases, confronted with matters of a deeply political nature, the Court retreated from the structural principles of EU law.

## III. Structural Principles: External

External relations law was developed on a different conceptual and normative basis. It is not about a form of 'perfect and inalterable order' floating above politics, but rather as a means to exist in the realm of international political realities. This is evidenced by the fact that the Court accepts that the system may be *affected* by international law and transnational realities. This notion of 'affect' is a recurring concept in external relations case-law. As from 1977, the Court acknowledges that by responding to 'the problems resulting from requirements inherent in the external relations of the Community', the autonomy of the Community may be affected.[40] In recent Opinions, the Court has made clear that 'an international

---

[36] Joined Cases C-181/91 and C-248/91 *Parliament v Council* and *Parliament v Commission*, Judgment, EU:C:1993:271; Case C-316/91 *Parliament v Council*, Judgment, EU:C:1994:76.

[37] Following a different path, the German Federal Constitutional Court has made the constitutionality of the European Stability Mechanism (ESM) Treaty subject to the respect of the constitutional objective of prices stability (joined cases 2BvR 1390/12, 2 BvR 1421/12, 2 BvR 1438/12, 2 BvR 1439/12, 2 BvR 1440/12, 2 BvE 6/12, paras 203–6).

[38] Opinion 1/91, EU:C:1991:490, paras 34–35; Opinion 1/76 (n 6) paras 10–12.

[39] See M Dawson and F de Witte, 'Constitutional Balance in the EU after the Euro-Crisis' (2013) 76 *MLR* 817.

[40] Opinion 1/76 (n 6) para 12.

agreement entered into by the Union ... may affect the powers of the Union institutions, without, however, being regarded as incompatible with the Treaty'.[41] The main issue in this area is to what extent may the power of the Union be externally affected without compromising its independence of action and altering its internal structure. The Court accepts that, in the general capacity conferred on the Union in the external sphere, there is not only a capacity to act but also an ability to be affected. What is decisive is that this 'does not alter the essential character of the powers conferred on the Union institutions'.[42]

External relations law is less structural in spirit than institutional. To be sure, 'the autonomy of the EU legal order' and the 'internal constitution of the Union' are core concepts in this field too, but viewed through the eyes of an external relations lawyer, these concepts do not amount to any kind of independent legal order endowed with its own basis of validity. Instead, they refer to an institutional space, to a machinery based on a set of institutional relations between the Union and the Member States, between the Union institutions themselves, and among the Member States. The essence of the system lies in its relational dimension. In the case-law of the Court, the Union is dignified as an institutional project carrying out common interests that are concurrently or alternatively defended by the Union institutions and by the Member States bound together.

To summarise, the problem of EU internal law is that of establishing a structural order *above* the Member States. The problem of EU external relations law is to establish loyal and efficient relationships *between* the main European institutional players involved. The Court's original way of setting up these relations was to substitute as far as possible Community action for the unilateral or joint action of the Member States. This is the result of the *AETR* doctrine.[43] Whereas the internal lawyer aspires to objective order, the external relations lawyer aspires to build institutional relations. However, once posed this way, it is clear that our understanding should be nuanced. The difference is one of emphasis, not of nature. Yet, as a starting point, this helps explain why the internal lawyer seems comfortable with structural principles and uncomfortable with power, while the external relations lawyer coming to grips with power relationships is wary of the involvement of substantive structural principles. As a matter of fact, substantive structural principles are not conducive to political flexibility. The Court has repeatedly made clear that the exercise of political discretion in international negotiations is to be protected.[44] It insists that there is a need to preserve freedom of action for

---

[41] Opinion 1/92, EU:C:1992:189, paras 32 and 41; Opinion 1/00, EU:C:2002:231, para 20.

[42] Opinion 1/00 (n 41) para 20. This is a variation on the expression found in Opinion 1/76 (n 6) para 12, mentioning 'the alteration of essential elements of the Community structure as regards both the prerogatives of the institutions and the position of the Member States *vis-à-vis* one another'.

[43] *cf* Azoulai 'The Many Visions of Europe' (n 15).

[44] On this see M Cremona, 'A Reticent Court? Policy Objectives and the Court of Justice' in M Cremona and A Thies (eds), *The European Court of Justice and External Relations Law: Constitutional Challenges* (Oxford, Hart Publishing, 2014) 15, 24–25.

the Union in the future.[45] In *FIAMM*, the Advocate General made it clear that the Union institutions should be left a 'margin of political freedom' in the context of the WTO,[46] recognising the institutions' 'political prerogatives'. This results in denying the recognition of the direct effect of the WTO agreements and in refusing the principle of liability of the Union in the absence of fault. Structural principles and constitutional guarantees as classically understood in the internal realm are not compelling in the external field.[47]

In this field, the need for the emergence of particular types of structural principles arose in two specific contexts. One way was through the admission that, despite the fact that they enjoy exclusive external competence, Union institutions may be unable to act in a particular situation. In such situations, a form of regulation of Member States' action was needed. This regulation came in the form of allowing Member States to act but also binding them to act in the interest and on behalf of the Union and in accordance with the duty of cooperation.[48] The need for structural principles arose more pressingly out of the realisation that the approach adopted in the *AETR* case establishing the absolute precedence of the Union's institutional framework in the conduct of external action within the ambit of EU law was no longer tenable. The Court has progressively admitted the participation of Member States along with Union institutions in the conduct of external action. This has led to a frequent use of mixed agreements.[49] Moreover, the development of the sphere of Member States' joint action outside the EU institutional framework cannot be ignored any longer.[50] Finally, the rise of the democratic ideology and the ever greater exposure of the Union's activities to the public have forced the Union to organise this cooperation transparently.[51] The emergence of structural principles may be seen as a response to these various factors.[52] It is based on the pluralisation of EU external action and the subsequent default position of shared responsibilities between the Union institutions and the Member States authorities. This explains the prevalence in this field of procedural or 'relational' principles.[53] The focus now is on the need to organise the 'close

[45] Opinion 1/03, EU:C:2006:81, para 126; Opinion 2/91, EU:C:1993:106, para 25.

[46] Joined Cases C-120/06P and C-121/06P *FIAMM*, Judgment, EU:C:2008:476, para 35.

[47] See, eg, Case 52/81 *Faust v Commission*, Judgment, EU:C:1982:369, para 9, cited by Cremona, 'A Reticent Court?' (n 44) 24.

[48] *AETR* (n 14) paras 77, 90. See M Cremona, 'Member States as Trustees of the Union Interest: Participating in International Agreements on Behalf of the European Union' in A Arnull, C Barnard, M Dougan and E Spaventa (eds), *A Constitutional Order of States? Essays in EU Law in Honour of Alan Dashwood* (Oxford, Hart Publishing, 2011) 435.

[49] See CWA Timmermans, 'The Court of Justice and Mixed Agreements' in A Rosas, E Levits and Y Bot (eds), *The Court of Justice and the Construction of Europe: Analyses and Perspectives on Sixty Years of Case-Law* (The Hague, Asser Press, 2013) 659.

[50] See Case C-114/12 *Commission v Council (Protection of Neighbouring Rights)*, Judgment, EU:C:2014:2151.

[51] Case C-280/11P *Council v Access Info Europe*, Judgment, EU:C:2013:671; Case C-658/11 *Parliament v Council*, Judgment, EU:C:2014:2025.

[52] See on the duty of loyalty, C Hillion, 'Cohérence et action extérieure de l'Union européenne' in E Neframi (ed), *Objectifs et compétences dans l'Union eiropéenne* (Brussels, Bruylant, 2013) 315.

[53] See Marise Cremona, Chapter 1.

association' of the main institutional players involved within the Union through procedures of cooperation, obligations of loyalty and solidarity.

This may also help explain the special feature of these structural principles. These are mainly concerned with rules of conduct and attitudes. The *PFOS* case is certainly the best illustration of this feature.[54] In this case, EU law amounts to a real discipline to adopt a 'common attitude'.[55] Indeed, the Court ruled that in an area of shared competence, absent a formal decision of the Council to act externally, the Member States are still bound by the 'concerted common strategy within the Council'.[56] This strategy proving an intention not to act for the time-being is a sufficient basis to consider that a common framework was in place. As such, it triggers an obligation of abstention on the part of the Member States. In this context, even though the legal nature of the common position was not totally clear, an individual course of action was seen as a deliberate act of 'dissociation' from the common discipline and deemed to be a breach of former Article 10 EC (Article 4(3) of the Treaty on the Functioning of the European Union (TFEU)). Beyond prompting a process of 'socialisation',[57] the Court enacts a form of institutional ethics: each Member State is bound to adopt a certain attitude of loyalty towards the partners and the Union institutions.

# IV. Reversal of Structural Styles

If we look at each field from the opposite perspective, we find that cross-fertilisation and contamination may happen. EU internal law may in some instances be willing to accommodate political sensitivities whereas EU external relations law may sometimes be open to substantive structural principles, also called 'constitutional principles'. I will be brief on the first perspective. It seems that EU lawyers and legal actors have long underestimated the extent to which national political structures and sensibilities (whether constitutional identities or local cultures and values) influence Member States' engagement with the EU legal order. We might observe in the recent case-law of the Court of Justice the development of arguments and techniques based on social choices, political preferences and the essential functions of the Member States. The Court is becoming more sensitive to national and local sensibilities. This is evident in the growing reference to the national identities as set out in Article 4(2) TEU.[58]

---

[54] Case C-246/07 *Commission v Sweden (PFOS)*, Judgment, EU:C:2010:203.
[55] The notion is to be found in Case C-205/06 *Commission v Austria*, Judgment, EU:C:2009:118, para 44.
[56] *PFOS* (n 54) para 91.
[57] See the reference to 'processes of socialization' in Joris Larik, Chapter 7.
[58] See further L Azoulai, 'The ECJ and the Duty to Respect Sensitive National Interests' in M Dawson, B de Witte and E Muir (eds), *Judicial Activism at the European Court of Justice* (Cheltenham, Edward Elgar, 2013) 167.

On the other side, the involvement of a structural 'internal-style' mode of reasoning in the external field may be observed in two interesting cases. The first one is the *TNT* case.[59] It is a case of *renvoi* of EU law to international law. The Brussels Regulation on Jurisdiction and the Recognition and Enforcement in Civil and Commercial Matters (44/2001) provides that it 'shall not affect' international conventions to which Member States are parties. However, as the result of the Court's interpretation, it turns out that one of these conventions, the Convention on the Contract for the International Carriage of Goods by Road, 'cannot compromise' the principles which underlie the Brussels Regulation, in particular the free movement of judgments and mutual trust in the administration of justice in the Union. In other words, we have here a clear transposition of the internal mode of reasoning: a reference to international law is turned into a mere reception of a foreign concept and transformed into a EU law source consistent with the broad normative foundations of EU law. The Court refuses to let EU law be affected by international law. It turns its back on the will of the EU legislature and on its own case-law which recognises the necessity to take account of international law which is binding on all the Member States.[60] How are we to explain such a move in the external field? One plausible interpretation is that this decision is concerned, in fact, with a genuine constitutional principle: the principle of mutual trust between Member States within the Union. The Court defends what in *NS* the Court called the *raison d'être* of the European Union, namely the trust that Member States place in each other.[61] That the value of mutual trust is deemed to prevail over any other reference, including the respect for fundamental rights and constitutional identities, seems to be demonstrated in the *Melloni* case and in Opinion 2/13.[62]

The second interesting case is a more famous one. In *Kadi*, the Court famously stated that all Union measures, including measures transposing UN Security Council measures providing for sanctions, must be compatible with EU fundamental rights.[63] By no means may EU measures challenge 'the principles that form part of the very foundations of the [EU] legal order'. In fact, 'the obligations imposed by an international agreement cannot have the effect of prejudicing the constitutional principles' of the Treaties.[64] In this case, the Court introduced

---

[59] Case C-533/08 *TNT*, Judgment, EU:C:2010:243.

[60] See on this reading, M Cremona, *The Internal Market and Private International Law Regimes: A Comment on Case C-533/08 TNT Express Nederland BV v AXA Versicherung AG*, EUI Working Papers LAW 2014/08 (2014). For an example of the Court's openness to international law in the harmonisation context, see Case C-377/98 *Netherlands v Parliament and Council*, Judgment, EU:C:2001:523, para 58.

[61] Joined Cases C-411/10 and C-493/10 *NS*, Judgment, EU:C:2011:865, para 83. See the reference to 'the principle of mutual trust' at para 55 of this ruling (see also *TNT* (n 59)).

[62] See Case C-399/11 *Melloni,* Judgment, EU:C:2013:107, para 63; Opinion 2/13, EU:C:2014:2454, para 168.

[63] Joined Cases C-402/05P and C-415/05P *Yassin Abdullah Kadi and Al Barakaat International Foundation v Council and Commission*, Judgment, EU:C:2008:461.

[64] ibid paras 285, 304.

into the external field the reference to the structural principles as understood in the internal realm with the reference to judicial review and fundamental rights as 'constitutional guarantees'.[65] But, interestingly, it did so by relying on an argument which was initially framed in the context of the external case-law: namely, that it is all derived from the need to respect the 'allocation of powers' enshrined in the Treaties. What is to be protected is the Union's specific order of competences.[66] This is a clear reference to 'the autonomy of the EU legal order' as classically defined in the external field.[67] What the Court says in this case is that this structural feature of EU external relations law includes a heavily value-laden dimension, a substantive justice dimension. In other words, it makes explicit the link between the relational paradigm prevalent in external relation law with the constitutional paradigm applied in the internal realm.

To account for this shift, it must be said that this decision was issued in the specific context of international sanctions targeting individuals. We are here at the edge of the external field, since this is about measures adopted by the Union internally in compliance with obligations imposed by the law of the United Nations. More importantly, this regime of sanctions goes to the heart of what the Union claims to be about: the protection of the individual, of the person. The decision may be seen as a reaction to a challenge concerning the underlying core normativity of the Union's project and of its legal system. If this is so, the decision should not be over-interpreted as a challenge to the primacy of Security Council law and sanctions in international law, neither as a challenge to the status and value of international law in EU law, nor as a discontinuation of the doctrine of political freedom in international action.

# V. Conclusion

This change in perspective may be pushed further and prompt a rethinking of EU law, both internal and external, as a regime combining constitutional and relational structural elements. Rethinking EU internal law as a regime for dealing with the 'relational space' that has developed between the Member States and their peoples, alongside the EU institutional framework, is a project which has only just begun. We may call it 'a regime of mutual membership'.[68] It requires a shift in perspective which blends EU law and politics or diplomacy instead of opposing them.[69] The construction of this regime may learn a lot from external relations

---

[65] ibid para 316.
[66] ibid para 282.
[67] See Opinion 1/91 (n 38) para 35.
[68] See Editorial Comments, 'Union Membership in Times of Crisis' (n 19).
[69] Pointing in this direction see L van Middelaar, *The Passage to Europe* (New Haven, CT, Yale University Press, 2013).

law and its insistence on political freedom, flexibility and extended obligations of loyal cooperation. Central to this regime would be new forms of solidarity and horizontal transfer of loyalty among state constituent entities. This is not to break away from the idea of a structural EU legal order but to revitalise it.[70]

What results from rethinking EU external relations law as a 'constitutional' project? Such an exercise would require going beyond the basic idea of Europe that drove the project of self-affirmation of the Union's identity in the international arena. It would require identifying the core doctrines necessary for establishing a kind of substantive structural order beyond the boundaries of the law of the Union. This, of course, cannot be based on the pure projection of the Union interest and a formal principle of unity of representation. EU external relations law must be seen within a wider constitutional and pluralist context, dealing with external references and competing actors while keeping in mind the broad value-based project pursued by the Union.[71] It would need to engage in normative considerations with regard to the set of EU fundamental principles applicable in international law. Conversely, the Court should be capable of demonstrating some awareness of the 'constitutional identity' of international law regimes. This may well be the only way to continue making sense of the experience of integration as an external project now that the possibility of referring to a structural unity based on the absolute precedence of the Union's institutional framework and interests is no longer available.

[70] See further L Azoulai, 'Appartenir à l'Union européenne. Liens institutionnels et liens de confiance dans les relations entre Etats membres' in *Liber Amicorum en l'honneur de Vlad Constantinesco* (Brussels, Bruylant, 2015) 11.

[71] More broadly on global plural constitutionalism, see D Halberstam, 'Local, Global and Plural Constitutionalism: Europe Meets the World' in G de Búrca and JHH Weiler (eds), *The Worlds of European Constitutionalism* (Cambridge, Cambridge University Press, 2012) 186.

# 3

# Enforcement of and Compliance with Structural Principles

EDOARDO CHITI

## I. Introduction

Enforcement and compliance are complex processes, which are difficult to analyse in all their components (typically, rule-making, administrative and judicial components, interacting one with the others) and to conceptualise in a convincing way. They also represent a rather unexplored field of research. There is, of course, a rich legal and political science literature on enforcement of and compliance with European Union (EU) law,[1] but it rarely refers to the enforcement of and compliance with principles and it rather deals with transposition of Directives and compliance with preliminary rulings and Court of Justice of the European Union (CJEU) judgments. This chapter takes seriously the difficulties of an inquiry on enforcement and compliance with structural principles. Its purpose is to explore this field of research by proposing some tentative ideas, organised around some basic questions: what are the processes through which structural principles governing EU external action are enforced and complied with? What are their functional and normative rationales? How can one explain their development? And how could they be refined? The aim of this chapter is therefore a very preliminary one: that is, to describe the enforcement processes, to point to their distinctive features, to identify the

---

[1] See, eg, the essays collected in M Cremona (ed), *Compliance and the Enforcement of EU Law* (Oxford, Oxford University Press, 2013); S Andersen, *The Enforcement of EU Law: The Role of the European Commission* (Oxford, Oxford University Press, 2012); J Pelkmans and A de Britto, *Enforcement in the EU Single Market* (Brussels, Centre for European Policy Studies, 2012); D Beach, 'Why Governments Comply: An Integrative Compliance Model that Bridges the Gap between Instrumental and Normative Models of Compliance' (2005) 12 *Journal of European Public Policy* 113; J Tallberg, 'Paths to Compliance: Enforcement, Management, and the European Union' (2002) 56 *International Organization* 609; GG Falkner, O Treib, M Hartlapp and S Leiber, *Complying with Europe: EU Harmonization and Soft Law in the Member States* (Cambridge, Cambridge University Press, 2005).

issues they raise. The limits of an inquiry of this kind are self-evident: the chapter is more interested in recognising the development and consolidation of the mechanisms through which structural principles are enforced than in contributing to the general theoretical reflection of enforcement and compliance in the EU; moreover, it proposes a general overview of the enforcement processes of structural principles, leaving aside many details of these processes and not paying the due attention to law in action. Despite these shortcomings, we expect the inquiry to provide a number of indications on which further reflection on compliance with structural principles could usefully rely.

The chapter is structured as follows. It opens with a clarification of a number of points which frame the inquiry (section II). It then analyses the features of the enforcement processes which have emerged and been consolidated over the years (section III). In this section, it is argued that a fundamental bifurcation exists between, on the one hand, the cases in which the structural principles govern relationships between EU subjects and, on the other hand, the cases in which the structural principles govern relationships between the EU and subjects external to the EU (third countries, international organisations, etc). Two different processes of enforcement correspond to these two groups of relations. The remainder of the chapter is devoted to three questions about the enforcement processes which have been identified. First, do the two types of enforcement processes incorporate different functional and normative rationales (section IV)? Secondly, why do the structure and rationale of the enforcement processes change depending on the type of relationships involved by structural principles (section V)? Thirdly, how should a process of adjustment and reform of the existing enforcement processes be constructed (section VI)?

## II. Four Claims

Before going through the analysis of the processes through which structural principles are enforced, it is convenient to clarify that the inquiry carried out in this chapter rests on four claims.

To begin with, the terms 'enforcement' and 'compliance' are here used to denote, respectively, a process and an outcome. 'Enforcement' refers to the whole of ongoing negotiations, political and legal processes, and institutional change that are involved in the execution of EU structural principles and are functionally orientated to give them full effectiveness. This is, admittedly, a broad understanding of enforcement. Differently from much of the literature on enforcement,[2] we do

---

[2] See, eg, Tallberg, 'Paths to Compliance' (n 1); Andersen, *The Enforcement of EU Law* (n 1); and K Raustiala and A-M Slaughter, 'International Law and Compliance' in W Carlsnaes, T Risse, and B Simmons (eds), *Handbook of International Relations* (Sage, 2002) 538.

not give enforcement a specific coercive meaning, but we rather assume that it covers 'all activities designed to ensure appropriate compliance with legal norms'.[3] 'Compliance' refers to the result of obedience which is sought through the enforcement process. Process and outcome, in any case, are inevitably intertwined, as obedience is an outcome which is gradually constructed within the process itself. Moreover, the process of enforcement is not clearly separated from the process of emergence of a principle. It is not possible to say, for example, that the formation of a principle is a matter of interpretation and its enforcement a matter of application. Enforcement largely implies interpretation and contributes to the development of the principle at stake.

Secondly, enforcement and compliance represent a crucial dimension of the process of establishment and consolidation of structural principles in EU external relations. Structural principles are not only orientated to sustain specific lines of reasoning. In order to perform their structuring function, they should also be able to provide answers in specific cases and to constrain the action of the various actors involved in the relationships they are meant to govern. They therefore need to rely upon mechanisms of judicial enforcement, through which they may operate as grounds for reviewing the legality of legal acts adopted by all actors at stake. They also need to be operationalised through specific regulatory frameworks. More generally, enforcement is necessary to demonstrate the actual relevance of structural principles, to realise the expected benefits for all actors involved, to determine the effective capability of structural principles to shape and stabilise the institutional framework within which EU external policy is formed and implemented.

Thirdly, enforcement is certainly shaped by a variety of elements, such as the policy field at stake, the available legal instruments and the orienting objectives. Indeed, the various structural principles that have been discussed in the various chapters are enforced through a highly ramified system. A myriad of enforcement processes coexist, each involving specific actors, exploiting its own instruments, and based on peculiar strategies. And the attempt to identify some overall patterns brings with itself a danger of over-simplification, if not of reductionism. Yet, the processes of enforcement and compliance ultimately depend on the types of relationships which are governed by the various structural principles. As most structural principles aim at structuring an institutional space by governing a number of relationships, the enforcement processes make sense, both in descriptive and in normative terms, insofar as they are oriented to ensure the smooth functioning of such relations. This does not mean that the enforcement processes are not conditioned by other elements, such as the policy field in which the individual principle operate and the legal instruments that the relevant EU institutions and bodies may use in that field. It means, however, that the enforcement

---

[3] C Harlow and R Rawlings, *Process and Procedure in EU Administration* (Oxford, Hart Publishing, 2014) 172.

processes are primarily linked to the relations which are governed by the structural principles. It is in this light that enforcement and compliance should be analysed and assessed.

Finally, the relationships governed by structural principles involve a great variety of actors and legal subjects. This chapter proposes to further articulate the framework provided by Marise Cremona in Chapter 1 and it identifies eight main relational axes: (i) EU Member State–EU Member State; (ii) EU Member State–EU institutions; (iii) EU institution–EU institution; (iv) EU institutions–EU natural or legal persons; (v) EU–third countries; (vi) EU–third countries' natural or legal persons; (vii) EU–international organisations; (viii) EU–global regulatory systems. It is in the light of these eight lines that the processes of enforcement and compliance are to be discussed. While the first seven types of relations are self-explanatory, the last one requires a quick clarification. Global regulatory systems are here meant as the vast array of new types of administrations beyond the state which have emerged and proliferated in the last decade and which cannot be conceptualised as formal international organisations, being less formalised and institutionalised, but equally or even more able to exercise an influence on states, individuals and collective entities such as corporations and NGOs. This is the case, for example, of formal and informal intergovernmental regulatory networks and coordination arrangements (eg the Basel Committee and the International Organization of Securities Commissions), administrations by hybrid intergovernmental-private arrangements (eg the Codex Alimentarius Commission), and administrations by private institutions with regulatory functions (eg the International Standardization Organization.[4] Admittedly, the importance of the relational axes involving, respectively, the EU and international organisations and the EU and global regulatory systems should not be over-estimated. They are only potentially relevant, as it is not possible to identify, at the current stage of development, any structural principle really governing the relationship between the EU and an international organisation or a global regulatory system. This does not mean, however, that structural principles governing those relationships might not emerge in the future: this could be the case, for example, of a principle of loyal cooperation between the EU and international organisations and global systems.

---

[4] On the various types of global regulatory systems see especially B Kingsbury, N Krisch and RB Stewart, 'The Emergence of Global Administrative Law' (2005) 68 *Law and Contemporary Problems* 15, 20; S Cassese, *The Global Polity: Global Dimensions of Democracy and the Rule of Law* (Seville, Global Law Press, 2012) 22; and S Battini, 'The Proliferation of Global Regulatory Regimes' in S Cassese (ed), *The Research Handbook on Global Administrative Law Handbook* (Cheltenham, Edward Elgar Publishing, 2016).

# III. A Bird's-Eye View on the Enforcement Processes Consolidated so Far: A Basic Divide

Structural principles are not self-enforcing. They are operationalised, it has already been observed, through a multiplicity of enforcement processes. Such processes vary one from the other as regards the actors involved, the instruments which are used and the underlying strategies. The great number of variations in the enforcement processes depend on variables such as the policy field in which the relevant principle operates, the public and private interests at stake, the legal instruments that are available in a certain context. At the same time, enforcement processes primarily depend on the type of relationship which is governed by each structural principle.

When focusing on the relationships involved, one may identify a basic divide between two different situations: on the one hand, the cases in which the structural principles govern relationships between EU subjects; on the other, the cases in which the structural principles govern relationships between EU subjects and subjects external to the EU (third countries, international organisations, etc). The processes of enforcement which have emerged and consolidated over the years reflect this divide. Two different processes of enforcement correspond to the two groups of relations. When structural principles govern relationships between EU subjects, they are operationalised through enforcement processes which rely not only on monitoring and sanctions, but also on proceduralisation. When they govern relationships between the EU and subjects external to the EU, instead, their enforcement processes take a different form. In this case, enforcement rarely relies on proceduralisation. Moreover, the very limited exploitation of proceduralisation is only partly compensated by recourse to instruments based upon monitoring and sanctions, as administrative control is underdeveloped and judicial review presents a number of shortcomings. When they take place, though, administrative control and judicial review seem capable of promoting the elaboration of procedural techniques of enforcement.

## A. Operationalization of Structural Principles Governing Relationships Between EU Subjects: Enforcement Through Proceduralisation

The first group of enforcement processes refers to structural principles governing relationships between EU subjects or actors. The following relational axes are therefore relevant: (i) EU Member State–EU Member State; (ii) EU Member State–EU institutions; (iii) EU inter-institutional; (iv) EU institutions–EU natural or legal persons. One might assume that structural principles involving these relational axes essentially rely on judicial enforcement, as it is indeed suggested by most of the chapters of this book. Yet, when they govern relationships between EU subjects, structural principles are usually operationalised through a more complex enforcement chain, based not only on monitoring and sanctions, but also on a set of administrative mechanisms aimed at making compliance possible, that is, at putting the conditions for an effective enforcement of the principle by the relevant EU actors.

Three aspects are important in these enforcement processes. First, they are usually regulated by EU law only, rather than being subject to a combination of EU law sources and international law sources interacting between themselves. Of course, the relevant EU law provisions may have been adopted in order to implement international law at the regional level. The enforcement process, though, is directly regulated by EU law only. EU law, moreover, is here to be understood as the whole of the relevant rules, not only of legislative nature, developed by EU institutions and bodies. Secondly, a structural principle is usually operationalised through EU rules and practices which lay down what we may call 'concretising figures': for example, access to information is a concretising figure of the principle of transparency. In their turn, such concretising figures need to be operationalised through procedures which are laid down by EU rules (the rules envisaging the concretising figure or further rules). The procedure is then implemented by political institutions or by EU administrations. It may imply different types of actions, ranging from the exercise of high political discretion to the simple and mechanical application of rules. Thirdly, the process of enforcement also relies on monitoring and sanctions, both of administrative and judicial nature. Administrative control is mainly directed to scrutinise Member States' conduct, while judicial control operates as a mechanism to review the actions of EU and national institutions. As enforcement mechanisms, both administrative control and judicial review may be used to directly enforce a structural principle, although judicial control is made subject to some limitations in specific policy domains, such as the Common Foreign and Security Policy (CFSP) and the Common Security and Defence Policy (CSDP). More often, however, administrative control and judicial review ensure the enforcement of the rules laying down a concretising figure or its implementing arrangements.

Several examples may illustrate this phenomenon. As for structural principles governing the relationships between two or more EU Member States, one may refer to the principle of mutual solidarity. On the basis of the structural principle of mutual solidarity, the Member States owe three main sets of reciprocal obligations: the obligation of aid and assistance in cases of armed aggression under Article 42(7) of the Treaty on European Union (TEU); the obligation to act jointly to assist a Member State which is the victim of a terrorist attack or natural or man-made disaster under Article 222 of the Treaty on the Functioning of the European Union (TFEU); the obligation of information and consultation of Member States not represented in international organisations or international conferences under Article 34(2) TEU. These obligations, often referred to as 'solidarity clauses', may be considered as concretising figures of the principle of solidarity. In their turn, they need to be operationalised through specific implementing arrangements. This functional chain, from the structural principle to the concretising figure and implementing arrangements, is explicitly recognised by Article 222 TFEU, which both provides for the solidarity clause and calls on the Council to define the 'arrangements for the implementation by the Union of the solidarity clause by a decision adopted on the basis of a joint proposal by the Commission and the High Representative of the Union for Foreign Affairs and Security Policy'. In this case, the implementing arrangements are essentially procedural and involve EU political actors. Council Decision 2014/415/EU, laying down the arrangements for the implementation by the EU of the solidarity clause,[5] provides for a procedure involving mainly national governments and the Council and characterised by a high degree of political discretion. The procedure is opened by an 'invocation' of the solidarity clause by the political authorities of the affected Member State to the Presidency of the Council. It goes on to the arrangement of a 'Union response' by the Council, acting also on the basis of proposals put forward by the Commission and the High Representative of the Union for Foreign Affairs and Security Policy. It ends when the Member State which invoked the solidarity clause indicates that there is no longer a need for the invocation to remain active. The structure of the procedure clearly reflects the political sensitivity of the relationships between Member States in this field of EU action and is in line with the requirement of Article 222(2) TFEU, according to which Member States are to coordinate between themselves in the Council in order to comply with their own solidarity obligations.

A second example is that of subsidiarity, which is a structural principle governing not a horizontal relationship between Member States, but a vertical relationship between EU Member States and EU institutions. The relevance of subsidiarity for EU external relations is a contested issue, which is discussed in a later chapter of this book.[6] While the principle of subsidiarity applies to the external aspects of the EU policies implemented through EU legislation in the same way as it applies to other legal acts,[7] its application to international agreements and to certain policy fields, such as the CFSP, is far less obvious. What is here relevant, however, is that the principle of subsidiarity, insofar as it is applicable to the external action of the EU, is operationalised through a test which is in its turn implemented by a procedure. Both the test and the procedure are envisaged by EU law sources (respectively, Article 5 TEU and the Protocol on the Application of the Principles of Subsidiarity and Proportionality). The enforcement process is therefore structurally similar to that of the solidarity principle. One should not overlook, though, the specificities of the subsidiarity implementing procedure. Like the solidarity procedure, the procedure envisaged by the Protocol involves the EU political institutions and certainly implies political discretion. Yet, it brings about a specific

---

[5] Council Decision 2014/415/EU [2004] OJ L220/3.
[6] See Geert de Baere, Chapter 5.
[7] See Case C-411/06 *Commission v European Parliament and Council*, Judgment, EU:C:2009:518.

balance between the intergovernmental, multinational and supranational voices, building on the tradition of the Community method and including national parliaments in the decision-making process. Moreover, the exercise of political discretion is structured as an argumentative process, oriented to the discussion of the various reasons justifying or denying the coherence of a proposed EU measure with subsidiarity.[8]

A further example, illustrating the enforcement of structural principles governing a relationship between EU political institutions, is that of inter-institutional sincere cooperation. This principle is envisaged by Article 13(2) TEU, together with the principle of institutional balance, and is operationalised through several concretising figures, each of which rely upon a procedure involving EU political institutions or administrative bodies and imply a wider or more narrow political discretion. One concretising figure is the obligation of inter-institutional cooperation envisaged by the Arrangement concluded in 1991 by the Council and the Commission and regarding preparation for the Food and Agriculture Organization (FAO) meetings, statements and voting. The obligation of inter-institutional cooperation involves the Commission and the Council and is implemented through a voting procedure in the cases in which an agenda item deals with matters containing elements both of national and of EU competence. A CJEU judgment illustrates the relevance of judicial control in this enforcement process. Called by the Commission to assess a decision taken by the Fisheries Council and giving the Member States the right to vote in the FAO for the adoption of a specific agreement, the Court of Justice held that the Arrangement is a binding commitment towards the Commission and the Council and 'represents fulfilment of the duty of cooperation between the Community and its Member States within the FAO'. The decision of the Fisheries Council was therefore annulled as an unlawful breach of the Arrangement.[9] A second concretising figure is that envisaged by Rules 23 to 29 of the Framework Agreement on relations between the European Parliament and the European Commission.[10] Those Rules of the Framework Agreement establish an obligation of inter-institutional cooperation in the negotiation and conclusion of international agreements. Cooperation takes place through a detailed procedure, regulated by Annex III and implying a limited degree of discretion by the Commission, which is required to provide information to Parliament at all stages of the process and to take Parliament's views as far as possible into account.

Finally, one may refer to transparency as an example of structural principles governing a relationship between EU institutions and EU natural or legal persons

---

[8] For a recent account of the functioning of the procedure, providing 'facts and figures', see European Parliament, *State of Play on Reasoned Opinions and Contributions Submitted by National Parliaments under Protocol No 2 of the Lisbon Treaty* (Brussels, Directorate-General for the Presidency, Directorate for Relations with National Parliaments, Legislative Dialogue Unit, 9 April 2014).

[9] See Case C-25/94 *Commission v Council*, Judgment, EU:C:1996:114.

[10] Framework Agreement on relations between the European Parliament and the European Commission [2010] OJ L304/47.

(EU citizens and residents). Transparency is now envisaged by Article 11 TEU, calling on EU institutions to maintain 'an open, transparent and regular dialogue with representative associations and civil society', and by Article 15(3) TFEU, requiring the EU institutions and administrative bodies to 'conduct their work as openly as possible'. Access to information is an obvious concretising figure. It is disciplined by an EU law source, Regulation (EC) 1049/2001 of the European Parliament and of the Council, regulating public access to European Parliament, Council and Commission documents by EU citizens and residents.[11] The extent to which such Regulation applies to EU bodies carrying out external actions is a contested issue, although a broad interpretation of the scope of application of the Regulation seems justified by the circumstance that a legal basis for public access to documents is now provided by Article 15(3) TFEU and the Commission has proposed that Regulation 1049/2001 be amended to make it clear that it applies also to the European External Action Service (EEAS).[12] What is here relevant, in any case, is that Regulation 1049/2001, insofar as it is applicable to documents held by EU institutions and bodies and concerning the external action of the EU, envisages a detailed administrative procedure, involving the institution or body holding the document. Such procedure implies a very limited degree of discretion and may be followed by a complaint to the Ombudsman and or by court proceedings against the relevant institution or body. The quite rich litigation before the CJEU on the application of Regulation 1049/2001 shows the relevance of judicial control over the correct application of the procedure through which access to documents is implemented.[13]

All these examples show that structural principles governing relationships between EU subjects are usually operationalised through enforcement processes which rely less on monitoring and sanctions than on proceduralisation. Judicial control is certainly relevant, but it is only one component of the enforcement process. A structural principle is usually operationalised through EU rules and practices which lay down concretising figures that in their turn operate through procedures implemented by EU political institutions or administrative bodies, subject to the CJEU's judicial control. It goes without saying that this general framework could be detailed in many ways. Two aspects deserve to be noted here. First, there is nothing peculiar in what has been presented as the general pattern of enforcement of structural principles governing relationships between EU subjects. This pattern does not differ from that of the enforcement processes of structural principles which apply internally. The former has the same basic structure as the latter. Secondly, neither the concretising figures not their implementing procedures are neutral. Quite to the contrary, they shape the structural principle at

---

[11] Regulation (EC) 1049/2001 of the European Parliament and of the Council [2001] OJ L145/43.

[12] COM(2011)137. See also Council Decision 2010/427/EU [2010] OJ L201/30, whose Art 11 provides that the EEAS is to apply Regulation 1049/2001; and Decision 2011/C 243/08 of the High Representative [2011] OJ C243/16, laying down the relevant implementing rules.

[13] See Päivi Leino, Chapter 8.

stake and stress some of its possible meanings or dimensions. For example, the solidarity clause envisaged by Article 222 TFEU and its implementing procedure characterise mutual solidarity as a principle highly respectful of the political will of national governments, starting with that of the Member State in danger. The subsidiarity test and procedure shape subsidiarity as a principle aimed at ensuring that a specific deliberative process takes place within the EU decision-making proceedings. And the various obligations implementing the principle of inter-institutional sincere cooperation privilege the joint exercise of external functions over other possible objectives of the principle, such as, for example, the protection of each institution's sphere of competences.

## B. Operationalisation of Structural Principles Governing Relationships Between EU and Non-EU Subjects: Enforcement Through Limited Judicial Review

Structural principles governing relationships between EU and non-EU subjects are quite limited in number. Relations between EU and non-EU subjects are crucial in the domain of EU external relations and take place through a plurality of axes, which have already been recalled: (i) EU–third countries; (ii) EU–third countries' natural or legal persons; (iii) EU–international organisations; (iv) EU–global regulatory systems. In spite of the high relevance of these relations, however, structural principles mainly govern (in their current state of development) interactions taking place within the EU legal order. Only a few structural principles among those which have already emerged and consolidated actually involve relationships between the EU and third actors. The most prominent example is that of the rule of law, which applies not only to the relations between the EU subjects, but also to the relations between EU and non-EU actors. Other structural principles are possibly in the making: this is the case, for example, of loyal cooperation between EU political institutions and administrative bodies, on the one hand, and international organisations and global regulatory systems, on the other, which is indirectly recognised as a principle by an increasing number of EU legislations, global measures and EU and international judicial decisions. For the time being, however, the rule of law is the main example of a structural principle governing relationships between EU and non-EU actors.

Admittedly, one might expect that the enforcement process of the rule of law does not vary according to the type of relations involved. When it applies to relations between EU and non-EU subjects, the rule of law is likely to be operationalised through mechanisms subject to a combination of EU and non-EU sources, rather than to EU sources only. Such complication of the legal framework, though, should not modify the structure of the enforcement process, which should still rely on rules laying down a number of concretising figures and a set of implementing procedures. Moreover, one might expect that a particular relevance is granted to the administrative component of the enforcement process, given that the development of the administrative rule of law in the relationships between the EU and third actors is one of the most suitable ways to stabilise and structure such relationships.

Legal reality, though, proves to be quite different. First, when it applies to relation between EU and non-EU subjects, the rule of law is not at all operationalised through arrangements requiring an administrative action. The EU establishes a huge variety of relationships with third countries, citizens and legal persons of third countries, international organisations and global regulatory systems. Such relationships are regulated by a combination of EU and non-EU measures, such as international treaties and soft law measures. But this legal framework can hardly be reconstructed (through an *ex post* exercise) as a framework operationalising the rule of law through the establishment of a number of concretising figures to be implemented by EU and non-EU actors. Secondly, the very limited exploitation of proceduralisation is only partly compensated by techniques of enforcement based upon administrative control and judicial review. Both administrative control and judicial review are emerging as two relevant channels of enforcement of the rule of law in the EU–third parties' relationships. But this development is, for the time being, quite rudimentary and limited. Thirdly, administrative control and judicial review may sometimes lead to the elaboration of techniques of enforcement based on proceduralisation.

This overall dynamic may be illustrated through a number of examples.

Ilaria Vianello in Chapter 9 points to several developments showing the tendency not to operationalise the rule of law in the relations between EU and non-EU actors through rules laying down a number of concretising figures and the relative implementing procedures.[14] As Vianello makes clear, both the Stabilisation and Association Process (SAP) and the European Neighbourhood Policy (ENP) imply the adoption of a great number of administrative measures, such as progress reports, action plans, and delegated and implementing acts. Far from being routine measures, they have a significant impact on the countries to which they are addressed as well as on third countries' citizens. At its current stage of development, however, the regulatory framework implementing the SAP and the ENP cannot be reconstructed as a framework oriented to operationalise the rule of law in relations between the EU and third countries and their citizens and legal persons. This is, as Vianello suggests, a genuine shortcoming, given that the standards and values developed in liberal Western democracies and encapsulated in the Lisbon Treaty require the development of rules and practices capable of making EU administrative action subject to the rule of law.

Vianello's chapter also provides interesting examples illustrating the limited role currently played by administrative and judicial control in the enforcement process. One example is the decision of the European Ombudsman on a complaint concerning the Commission's alleged failure to use its powers to suspend the

---

[14] See Ilaria Vianello, Chapter 9.

EU–Vietnam cooperation agreement in the face of serious violations of human rights by the Republic of Vietnam.[15] In that Decision, the Ombudsman observed that the EU legislator seemingly intended to confer a large degree of discretion on the Commission for the interpretation and application of the human rights clause. This does not mean that the power can be exercised out of any limit and control: 'Very broad discretionary powers may exist, but they are always subject to legal limits'.[16] The Ombudsman, though, relied on a rather narrow understanding of those limits, which were identified 'in the general principles that the Commission has imposed on itself in the operation of human rights clauses'.[17] Moreover, the Ombudsman proved quite complacent about the Commission's discretion, accepting without any genuine discussion its argument that the suspension of the agreement would have deprived the EU of the possibility of using EU-funded cooperation programmes to support the reform process in the country and that it was therefore preferable to make use of measures different from the suspension of the Agreement, in accordance with the self-imposed guidelines.

The *Kadi* saga, instead, may be taken as an example to illustrate how the judicial enforcement of the rule of law in the relations between EU and non-EU subjects may ultimately trigger a process of development of a regulatory framework or at least administrative practices implementing the rule of law. In *Kadi I*, the CJEU pointed to the need to balance Kadi's fundamental rights, as protected by the EU, with the interest of international cooperation.[18] This induced the United Nations (UN) Security Council to introduce a first set of administrative guarantees and to establish a general de-listing procedure, which individuals may activate through a national government. Analogously, several changes were introduced in the EU regime, although it remained disputed whether the new legal framework was sufficient to afford effective protection to the individuals and organisations listed at UN level.[19] In *Kadi II*, the CJEU held that preventive measures should be based on grounds fully reviewable by a court,[20] thus imposing a strict burden of proof on the UN Security Council and the Commission.[21]

The example of the rule of law shows that structural principles governing relationships between EU and non-EU subjects are operationalised through

[15] Decision of the European Ombudsman on Complaint 933/2004/JMA against the European Commission, 28 June 2005, available at www.ombudsman.europa.eu/cases/decision.faces/en/2153/html.bookmark#hl0.

[16] ibid para 1.6.

[17] ibid.

[18] See Joined Cases C-402/05P and C-415/05P *Yassin Abdullah Kadi and Al Barakaat International Foundation v Council and Commission*, Judgment, EU:C:2008:461.

[19] E Spaventa, 'Counter-terrorism and Fundamental Rights: Judicial Challenges and Legislative Changes after the Rulings in *Kadi* and *PMOI*' in A Antoniadis, R Schütze and E Spaventa (eds), *The European Union and Global Emergencies* (Oxford, Hart Publishing, 2011) 105, 114.

[20] See Joined Cases C-584/10P, C-593/10P and C-595/10P, *Commission and others v Yassin Abdullah Kadi*, Judgment, EU:C:2013:518.

[21] M Savino, 'What if Global Administrative Law is a Normative Project?' (2015) 13 *International Journal of Constitutional Law* 492.

enforcement processes which are slightly different from those implementing principles concerning relations between EU actors. The latter rely on procedur-alisation, complemented by administrative and judicial control. The former are characterised by a more nuanced dynamic. They are not organised around a fully accomplished set of enforcement techniques. Concretising figures are under-developed, and administrative control and judicial review, which are emerging as the main relevant channels of enforcement, present several shortcomings. Judicial review, however, is potentially capable of leading to the elaboration of techniques of enforcement based upon proceduralisation. Two aspects of this type of enforcement processes should be pointed out. First, they differ from the enforcement processes of structural principles which apply to fields of EU inter-nal action. This does not happen, as we have observed, when structural principles for EU external action govern relationships between EU actors. The implication is that the processes of enforcement do not change on the basis of the internal or external character of EU action. They change in relation to the actors involved in the relationship that the principle intends to structure. Secondly, the circum-stance that concretising figures and implementing procedures are largely under-developed implies that the meanings and dimensions of structural principles gov-erning relationships between EU and non-EU actors have not yet been precisely defined. The clarification of the meanings that the rule of law may assume as a principle applying to relations between EU and non-EU actors is still an ongoing and open process, which several forces might be willing to shape in the near future.

## IV. Rationales

In the previous paragraphs, it has been argued that structural principles governing EU external action are operationalised through two different processes. When they structure relationships between EU subjects, they are usually enforced through EU rules and practices laying down concretising figures that in their turn operate through implementing arrangements. We have characterised this type of processes as enforcement through proceduralisation. This points to the circumstance that most of the implementing arrangements establish procedures which structure the action of the EU actors involved in the relevant relationship. Proceduralisa-tion is then complemented by administrative control and judicial review, which also represent a crucial dimension of the enforcement process. The main function of administrative control is to scrutinise Member States' conduct, while judicial review usually operates as a control over compliance with the implementing pro-cedural arrangements by EU and national institutions and bodies. When struc-tural principles govern relationships between EU and non-EU subjects, instead, they are enforced through processes that rarely exploit procedural techniques. The enforcement processes of this group of structural principles are mainly based on administrative control and judicial review, although even this type of enforcement is far from being fully accomplished. Judicial enforcement, however, is potentially capable of promoting the elaboration of procedural techniques of enforcement, which might emerge in the near future.

The identification of two different types of enforcement processes, differing one from the other as regards their basic structure, suggests not to over-emphasise the relevance of judicial review. Judicial review is often at the heart of the analyses on the enforcement of structural principles. But it is only one of the various possible components of enforcement processes, which may rely also on proceduralisation and administrative monitoring. In those cases, courts come later, to sanction a violation by an EU actor of an implementing arrangement, and operate complementarily to administrative control. As for the role played by rules in enforcement processes, they certainly represent a fundamental mechanism for the operationalisation of most structural principles. They lay down the concretising figures and implementing arrangements through which structural principles become concretely relevant and actually capable of stabilising the institutional framework within which EU external policy is formed and implemented. At the same time, this is only one of the various ways in which the relationship between structural principles and rules operate. Such relationship does not only imply that rules may be used to operationalise structural principles. It also implies that principles 'inform and guide the interpretation of rules even where those rules have not been adopted to give them specific expression', as recalled by Marise Cremona.[22]

The empirical recognition of a basic divide between two types of enforcement processes also raises a number of questions, the first of which is whether the two enforcement processes encapsulate different strategies and normative preferences. Reflecting on the effective application of EU law, Harlow and Rawlings have recently observed that enforcement 'raises important issues of administrative policy and process, or discretion, procedural design and trade-off'.[23] There is much to agree with in this statement. It reminds us that enforcement should not be treated as a neutral and somehow mechanical process. It should rather be considered as a complex process encapsulating specific strategies and based on normative preferences. The enforcement processes of structural principles are not an exception. Which are, then, their functional and normative rationales?

As for enforcement of structural principles of the first group, governing relationships between EU subjects, one may immediately point to the combination of cooperative and coercive elements on which it is based. On the one hand, the enforcement process makes recourse to implementing procedures oriented to achieve compliance through negotiation and problem-solving. Negotiation and problem-solving are shaped and constructed in ways which vary from case to case. For example, the implementing arrangements of the solidarity clause envisaged by Article 222 TFEU tend to protect the political will of the government of

---

[22] See Marise Cremona, Chapter 1.
[23] Harlow and Rawlings, *Process and Procedure in EU Administration* (n 3) 170.

the Member State in danger, while the arrangements implementing the various obligations of inter-institutional cooperation promote the joint action of the EU institutions and bodies involved. In spite of the obvious peculiarities of each solution, however, the implementing procedures may be seen as proactive instruments to ensure that the objectives sought by the relevant structural principles are achieved. By structuring the action of the various actors involved in the relationship that the principle intends to govern, they are oriented to sustain ongoing dialogue between the actors, prevent problems arising, and ultimately promote compliance with the structural principle they serve. On the other hand, the enforcement process relies on the traditional tools of administrative and judicial control and sanction. These are *ex post*, reactive instruments, based upon coercion. They may be used as mechanism for the direct enforcement of the relevant structural principle. More often, however, they operate as instruments to enforce the concretising figures or implementing arrangements envisaged by EU law.

The result is a double-edged enforcement strategy, functionally oriented not only to face infringements and to solve compliance problems, but also to prevent such problems and to promote appropriate compliance with structural principles. This suggests that coercion and problem-solving are not necessarily alternative strategies, as it is often argued in the literature on compliance in the context of international and supranational legal regimes.[24] The distinction made in that literature between strategies of 'enforcement', based upon coercion, and 'strategies of management', relying on capacity-building, is obviously relevant as an analytical tool, but it is inappropriate where it is used to characterise the two strategies as incompatible alternatives. The way in which the processes of enforcement of structural principles are designed shows that the two strategies may be combined and are actually exploited together in the EU context.

The dual strategy which has been identified, moreover, does not simply respond to functional needs. It is also instrumental to normative goals. Indeed, the combination of cooperation and coercion promotes a stabilisation of the relevant relationships which implies the development of some form of solidarity between all actors involved. The establishment of cooperative instruments, of course, do not exclude that actors may be moved by self-interest and act according their own preferences. Yet, these instruments commit all actors involved, being Member States or EU institutions and bodies, to understand their respective roles in relation to the other actors involved, to solve possible value conflicts between them, and to avoid action based on short-term interest calculations. This does not mean, of course, that the current implementing arrangements are always well designed. What we are saying is rather that the strategy underlying the enforcement processes is potentially capable of sustaining the value of solidarity within the relationships between EU actors regulated by structural principles.

---

[24] An overview of the theoretical approaches to the issue of compliance in the EU context is provided by L Conant, 'Compliance and What EU Member States Make of It' in M Cremona (ed), *Compliance and the Enforcement of EU Law* (Oxford, Oxford University Press, 2013) 1.

The same cannot be said of the enforcement of structural principles governing relationships between EU and non-EU subjects. In this case, it is difficult to identify a clear enforcement strategy. Admittedly, the enforcement process is not oriented to problem-solving, cooperation, negotiation and rule interpretation. Procedural techniques are under-developed, although they might emerge in the future. For the time being, the enforcement process essentially relies on administrative and judicial control. This might reflect a low degree of commitment by the actors involved in this group of structural principles. The political science and international relations literature on compliance has traditionally argued that coercion methodologies of enforcement respond to the need to increase non-compliance costs in a context in which the relevant actors have an interest in deliberate non-compliance, while cooperation methodologies may be developed when actors have a high commitment to compliance. In this perspective, an enforcement process essentially based on administrative and judicial control could be understood as a process recognising the limited degree of reciprocal trust between EU and non-EU subjects and contrasting the possibility of deliberate non-compliance by increasing non-compliance costs. This point, however, would not adequately consider that even administrative and judicial control is far from being fully developed. The lack of cooperative techniques of enforcement is not really compensated by enforcement tools based on coercion, as administrative and judicial control on the compliance with this group of structural principles is subject to many limitations. If a clear enforcement strategy is missing, it is unsurprising that the enforcement process is not instrumental to any recognisable normative goal. The enforcement process does not operate as a source of legitimacy of the institutional space in which the relations between EU and non-EU actors take place. Unlike the enforcement process of the first group of structural principles, it does not promote a stabilisation of the relevant relationships based on the development of solidarity between EU and non-EU actors, due to the lack of cooperative tools. But it does not even organise the relationships between EU and non-EU actors according to a pluralist conception. Such conception would not imply any search for convergence on shared values and would defend the specific options and preferences of each actor. Yet, it would nevertheless require a relational understanding by each actor of its own role and position and an internalisation of its obligation to avoid self-interested behaviours. In this case, instead, the actors involved in the relationship have no real incentive to develop relational understandings of their own roles and are subject to very limited legal and political costs in case of non-compliance with structural principles.

# V. Explanations

The differences between the two groups of enforcement processes might be explained in several ways. One might suggest, for example, that the current asymmetry simply reflects the different degrees of development of structural principles which the two groups of enforcement processes operationalise. As the growth and articulation of relations between EU and non-EU actors is a relatively new institutional phenomenon, their juridification through structural principles may be said to have just begun. In this perspective, structural principles governing relationships between EU and non-EU actors are likely to be further developed in the near future and a gradual emergence of a pattern for their enforcement based on proceduralisation and judicial review is expected to take place. In a different vein, one might point to the fundamental differences between the legal contexts in which the relationships governed by structural principles operate. Relationships between EU subjects take place within the EU order, which has historically developed as a legal space oriented towards compliance with EU law. Relationships between EU and non-EU subjects, instead, are carried out in a legal context which is partly inside and partly outside the EU legal order. This structural difference might be said to prevent the gradual alignment of the enforcement processes aimed at operationalising the structural principles governing the two groups of relationships.

The position of this chapter, though, is that neither of these two possible explanations is really satisfying: one overlooks the relevance of the differences between the two legal contexts, the other over-emphasises it. While it is certainly true that the differences between the two legal contexts condition and influence the structure and rationale of the enforcement processes, the divide between enforcement processes which has been identified in the previous sections does not depend only on this factor, but it also reflects the self-restraint of the CJEU and a political orientation of the EU institutions.

The enforcement of structural principles governing relationships between EU subjects exploits the EU compliance mechanisms worked out over a 60-year long historical process. The mechanisms for the enforcement of EU law have evolved along three different and complementary lines. First comes the administrative control carried out through the infringement procedure as well as through the proceedings envisaged by several special regimes, such as competition and state aids.[25] Secondly, EU norms can be enforced through a system of judicial remedies which allows both the legislative and administrative measures of the EU and the acts of Member States to be reviewed for their conformity, respectively, with the Treaties and with EU law. Such system is the result of the use made by litigants, domestic courts and the CJEU of the remedies envisaged in the 1957 EC Treaty. The use made by the CJEU and national courts of the preliminary rulings procedure, in particular, has strengthened the capability of the system of judicial remedies of promoting compliance with EU law. It has also remarkably

---

[25] A Ibañez, *The Administrative Supervision and Enforcement of EC Law: Powers, Procedures and Limits* (Oxford, Hart Publishing, 1999); S Grohs, 'Article 258/260 TFEU Infringement Procedures: The Commission Perspective in Environmental Cases' in M Cremona (ed), *Compliance and the Enforcement of EU Law* (Oxford, Oxford University Press, 2013) 57.

differentiated the EU legal order from international law. As Weiler famously
put it, 'the Community legal order as it emerged from the Foundational Period
appeared in its operation much closer to a working constitutional order'.[26] Thirdly,
the EU has developed since the late 1980s means of enforcement different from
those based on administrative and judicial control. The compliance of private
actors and EU and national public bodies with EU law has been not only controlled
'externally' through administrative instruments such as the infringement proceedings or by litigants before a court. It has increasingly been driven and structured
within a European administrative system. Such a European administrative system obviously aims at carrying out the various public functions exercised by the
EU, from the management of the internal market to social regulation, and to the
emerging core of welfare and security activities. It also operates, however, as a set
of governance instruments aimed at enhancing compliance by the addressees of
EU policies through the facilitation and institutionalisation of negotiation, cooperation and mutual learning among the national public powers and private actors
to which EU law and policies are addressed. Compliance is therefore 'internalised'
in the European administrative system, which works, among other things, also as
a machine for a gradual development of obedience by private actors and EU and
national public powers.[27] This multilayered system, operating through coercive
administrative and judicial tools and compliance-promoting administrative tools,
has provided a robust infrastructure for the enforcement of EU norms. It comes as
no surprise, therefore, that structural principles governing relationships between
EU subjects are enforced through enforcement processes which combine proceduralisation, administrative control over domestic measures and judicial review
of EU and Member States' acts. This simply reflects the structure and rationale of
the enforcement system of EU law within the EU legal order. While administrative
control and judicial review ensure the judicial enforcement of this group of structural principles, as well as of their concretising figures, proceduralisation aims at
promoting compliance by structuring negotiation, cooperation and dialogue.

The different structure and rationale of enforcement processes of the second
group of principles, those governing relationships between EU and non-EU subjects, is due to a combination of legal and political factors. To begin with, the
enforcement of this group of structural principles cannot rely on administrative
or judicial control over domestic measures. As an instrument to ensure domestic
compliance with EU law, the EU system of administrative control and judicial
review operates in relation to Member States only. While Member States' measures are subject to administrative control and judicial review for their conformity
with EU law, including structural principles, neither the infringement proceedings nor preliminary rulings may be used to review the legality of acts adopted by

---

[26] JHH Weiler, 'The Transformation of Europe' (1991) 100 *Yale Law Journal* 2403, 2422.
[27] This point is developed by E Chiti, 'The Governance of Compliance' in M Cremona (ed),
*Compliance and the Enforcement of EU Law* (Oxford, Oxford University Press, 2013) 31, 36–42.

third countries. Structural principles may therefore constitute grounds for reviewing the legality of acts adopted by third countries, but no real enforcement is possible through the available judicial remedies. The EU system of judicial remedies, instead, allows the review of the measures of the EU itself for their conformity with structural principles. The efficacy of the available mechanisms, however, is far from clear. Indeed, the CJEU's jurisdiction is limited in certain fields of external relations, such as CFSP. The *locus standi* of third country individuals is a contentious and unsettled issue. A great number of highly relevant EU measures tend to escape, due to their non-binding nature, judicial review. Some of these shortcomings reflect the intergovernmental character of certain policy fields, others derive from the circumstance that the EU system of judicial remedies has been constructed over the years as a system functional to develop within the EU legal order the habit of obedience which is typical of constitutional orders.[28] The CJEU, in any case, could make a non-restrictive use of its powers and try to overcome some of the current shortcomings. For the time being, however, this seems to be a simple possibility, provided that the CJEU has shown a clear reluctance to enhance the effectiveness of judicial review in external relations.[29] On a different level, one could expect the enforcement processes to rely on a number of compliance-promoting administrative tools. Instruments of this kind might compensate the limits of judicial review over national and EU conducts. Yet, structural principles governing relationships between EU and non-EU subjects are hardly enforced through concretising figures and implementing arrangements. So far, the relevant EU political institutions have taken a rather defensive approach and proved disinclined to develop this type of enforcement mechanisms, probably with a view to protect their room for manoeuvre in the exercise of their external relations tasks.

## VI. Perspectives: Enforcement of Structural Principles as a Project of Institutional Design

This chapter has reconstructed the ways in which structural principles are enforced, pointed to the rationales inherent to the two main groups of enforcement processes which have been identified, and discussed the reasons explaining their development and features. This is, admittedly, only a first step in a large and deep field of research. It should be followed by a comprehensive empirical investigation, carried out with reference to individual structural principles, as well as by a reflection on the implications of the repertoire of regimes through which

---

[28] Weiler, 'The Transformation of Europe' (n 26) 2421–22.
[29] For an illustration of this attitude of the CJEU in relation to the structural principle of the rule of law in the SAP and ENP, see Ilaria Vianello, Chapter 9.

structural principles are operationalised on the theoretical reflection on enforcement and compliance in the EU order.

While leaving these issues to further research, we have here to observe that the inquiry conducted so far suggests some possible lines of development of the enforcement processes of structural principles. Once we unpack empirically the enforcement of structural principles and we notice that structural principles may be operationalised in different ways, reflecting specific rationales and incorporating normative preferences, we can better understand the nature of enforcement as a project of institutional design. Because the function of enforcement is here meant to cover all activities designed to ensure appropriate compliance with legal norms, as stated at the beginning of this chapter, one should not simply register the development of a number of processes of enforcement of structural principles, but should also point to the possibility to shape such processes in such a way as to allow the achievement of the objectives of structural principles. The challenge faced by all actors involved is to design enforcement regimes that deploy multiple modalities of enforcement for the achievement of the objectives sought by structural principles.

In this perspective, enforcement should ultimately be understood as a process which is to be designed in such a way as to serve the overall rationale of structural principles. As Marise Cremona has observed in Chapter 1, structural principles 'structure the system, functioning and exercise of EU external competences and are designed to ensure the smooth articulation of the EU's system of external relations'.[30] They regulate the relationships between the different actors operating in the field in EU external relations (EU institutions, Member States, individuals, third countries, etc) with the view of establishing an institutional space within which policy may be formed and the different actors, including the CJEU, clarify and respect their respective roles. The fundamental function of structural principles is therefore to stabilise the relationships between the actors involved instrumentally to the smooth functioning of the institutional routes through which EU external policy is elaborated. Enforcement processes of structural principles can be considered successful only if they are orientated to sustain this overall function of structural principles. Analogously, enforcement processes should promote the normative objectives of structural principles. Cremona has appropriately stated that structural principles are not concerned with the substantive content of policy, but rather with process and the relationships between the actors in those processes.[31] This does not mean, however, that structural principles do not incorporate any normative claim. On the contrary, they may operate as sources of legitimacy of the institutional space, partly internal and partly external to the EU legal order, in which the relationships between the various actors involved in the process of elaboration and implementation of the EU external policy take place.

[30] See Marise Cremona, Chapter 1.
[31] ibid.

For example, structural principles may be considered to operate as a factor of legitimacy when they promote solidarity between all actors involved.

The developments which have been reconstructed in this chapter suggest that the enforcement processes emerged and consolidated so far are not always orientated to the achievement of the functional and normative purposes of structural principles. The enforcement processes of structural principles governing relationships between EU and non-EU actors are under-developed. The rationale of this group of enforcement processes may have a realistic foundation insofar as it assumes that EU and non-EU actors may have a low commitment to compliance with structural principles and may deliberately take non-compliance actions. This rationale, however, is not appropriately developed, as the system of judicial enforcement of this type of structural principles presents several shortcomings. Moreover, it is a rationale which certainly does not promote that cooperation between actors without which structural principles are realistically unable to operate. As for the enforcement processes of structural principles governing relationships between EU actors, they are more sophisticated and coherent with the fundamental function of the principles that they serve. Their efficacy, though, should be tested through case studies and empirical analyses, having in mind that proceduralisation brings with it the risk of an excessive formalisation of administrative processes. This is not the place to launch an attempt to refine the existing enforcement processes in such a way as to design enforcement regimes really instrumental to the functional and normative objectives of structural principles. We can notice, though, that this is an inescapable issue for further research on structural principles. The development of structural principles requires a redefinition of enforcement processes as a project of institutional design, in which all actors involved, including the European legal scholarship, should be engaged.

# Part II

# Relational Principles

# 4

## To Give or To Grab: The Principle of Full, Crippled and Split Conferral of Powers Post-Lisbon

INGE GOVAERE

## I. Introduction

The principle of conferral of powers occupies a prominent place in the Lisbon Treaty. Not only is it stated as a fundamental and horizontal principle in the common provisions of the Treaty on the European Union (Article 5 TEU).[1] For the first time utmost care has been given to lay down, in a Treaty text, also the modalities and the consequences of the application of this principle.[2] As such, a catalogue of competence is introduced in Articles 2 to 6 of the Treaty on the Functioning of the European Union (TFEU) which lists the 'categories and areas of union competence' (Title I TFEU) whilst spelling out the nature of the competences conferred to the Union in those fields, for instance, exclusive, shared or complementary. Moreover, it is recurrently and firmly stated that powers which are not conferred to the Union by the Treaties are to remain with the Member States (including Articles 4(1) and 5(2) TEU). Especially those new additions in the Treaties are revealing of the currently prevailing political context whereby the Member States seek to get a renewed grasp on the formulation, interpretation and application of the Treaty principle of conferral. This can hardly be considered

---

[1] Article 5 TEU (Lisbon) stipulates as follows: '1. The limits of Union competences are governed by the principle of conferral. The use of Union competences is governed by the principles of subsidiarity and proportionality. 2. Under the principle of conferral, the Union shall act only within the limits of the competences conferred upon it by the Member States in the Treaties to attain the objectives set out therein. Competences not conferred upon the Union in the Treaties remain with the Member States'. Note that the text of the Lisbon Treaty is much more substantial than the prior formulation in the Nice Treaty and at that time inserted only in the EC Treaty pillar: Art 5 TEC (Nice): 'The Community shall act within the limits of the powers conferred upon it by this Treaty and of the objectives assigned to it therein'.

[2] On discussions and attempt pre-Lisbon, see, eg, G De Búrca, 'Limiting EU Powers' (2005) 1 *European Constitutional Law Review* 92.

in isolation from the development of case law of the Court of Justice of the European Union (CJEU), which deftly asserts exclusive jurisdiction to interpret this key structural principle of EU law.

The importance of the principle of conferral to determine the structure, functioning and exercise of European Union (EU) law can hardly be over-estimated. From a sequential perspective, the principle of conferral is necessarily the very first of all the structural principles to be applied. It may be difficult if not impossible to establish a full sequential order of the various structural principles underlying EU law, but all the other EU law principles are triggered only once this initial hurdle has successfully been cleared by the EU.

For a good understanding of the principle of conferral in all its complexity, it is opportune to clearly distinguish the following two functions.

The principle of conferral is first and foremost the core principle that determines the delimitation of competence between the Member States and the EU.[3] At the same time it impacts directly on the relations between the EU and/or its Member States with third countries and other international organisations as it underpins the limitations that may be placed on the legal personality of the Union.[4]

The application of the principle of conferral also determines whether or not a subject matter comes within the ambit of the autonomous EU legal order, which is characterised by the exclusive jurisdiction of the CJEU,[5] primacy and direct effect. As such, it is the only one of all the Treaty principles that serves to determine not only whether and to what extent the EU has any competence but, additionally, whether and to what extent the CJEU may exercise exclusive jurisdiction.

The outcome of the application of the principle of conferral may nonetheless be very different in terms of the EU autonomous legal order as compared to EU competence. The Lisbon Treaty formally abolishes the pillar structure and introduces one legal personality for the whole EU, but this is not always and necessarily fully matched in substance. In many if not most cases there will be a 'plain' or 'full' conferral with a perfect match in terms of EU competence and CJEU exclusive jurisdiction. However, the area of Common Foreign and Security Policy (CFSP) is still to a large extent kept outside the jurisdiction of the CJEU, as well as democratic control by the European Parliament.[6] This may lead to what one could call a *crippled* conferral, meaning that competence is conferred on the EU without the corresponding conferral to the autonomous EU legal order. Both judicial and democratic control are then left at the level solely of the Member States. Another complicating factor is that the integration of the former third pillar matters of

---

[3] Marise Cremona points to the following two dimensions for allocation of competence: the relationship between the EU–Member States and the relationship between internal and external powers, see M Cremona, 'EU External Relations: Unity and Conferral of Powers' in L Azoulai (ed), *The Question of Competence in the European Union* (Oxford, Oxford University Press, 2014) 65.

[4] Article 47 TEU reads: 'The Union shall have legal personality'.

[5] Article 19 TEU in conjunction with Art 344 TFEU.

[6] Article 24 TEU.

Justice and Home Affairs (JHA) into the autonomous EU legal system has entailed the importation of the corresponding opt-outs for certain Member States.[7] This implies that both EU competence and CJEU exclusive jurisdiction may be conferred on the Union by some Member States but not by others, thus leading to a situation of *split* conferral. It is not inconceivable that the possibility to adopt CFSP measures under the constructive abstention mechanism,[8] whereby a Member State allows the other Member States to go ahead without being bound by the measure itself, could in practice even give rise to claims of a *crippled split* conferral.

Especially since the Lisbon Treaty, it is therefore no longer sufficient to determine *whether* competence is conferred to the Union by the Treaties in any given case. The renewed line of questioning after the Lisbon Treaty is first of all *who* may determine whether competence has been transferred to the Union. The first section will therefore address the issue of whether conferral of competence is 'to give or to grab'. In other words, is this now placed firmly in the hands of the Member States as masters of the Treaties, through the insertion of the catalogue of competence? Or may the CJEU still continue to claim exclusive jurisdiction to settle EU competence issues, including the extent of its own jurisdiction?

The second section will tackle the other and perhaps even more important new development to be discerned in the case law. In a post-Lisbon setting, the outspoken or underlying question has increasingly become the determination of the *modalities* of the conferral of competence to the Union, be it in a plain, crippled or split form. As such, it is not only important to know whether the EU has been attributed competence but also on what legal basis this was, or should have been, done. A crucial question thus is to know whether it is the legal basis that determines the plain, crippled or split form of conferral, both in theory and practice, or whether the prospect of a crippled or split EU action in any way influences the finding of the proper legal basis.

By way of caveat, it should be underlined that the Lisbon Treaty reforms have sparked a renewed impetus of cases questioning the external competence of the Union in all its complexities. In spite of the sequential importance of the principle of conferral, it is in practice not always easy to 'isolate' this principle from other arguments, such as the application of the principle of institutional balance and/or the duty of sincere cooperation as laid down in Article 13(2) TEU and Article 4(3) TEU.[9] Conversely, it is not because the principle of conferral is invoked

---

[7] Protocol No 21, opt-out of the United Kingdom and Ireland; Protocol No 22, special opt-out for Denmark.

[8] Article 31 TEU.

[9] For a recent example, see Case C-73/14 *Council v Commission (IRLOS)*, Judgment EU:C:2015:663. For an analysis of prior cases relating to the duty of sincere cooperation, see, eg, M Klamert, *The Principle of Loyalty in EU Law* (Oxford, Oxford University Press, 2014); E Neframi, 'The Duty of Loyalty: Rethinking Its Scope Through Its Application in the Field of EU External Relations' (2010) 47 *CML Rev* 323; A Casteleiro and J Larik, 'The Duty to Remain Silent: Limitless Loyalty in EU External Relations?' (2011) 36 *EL Rev* 524.

in any given case that it is also really in dispute. For instance, in the *OIV* case, Germany expressly invoked the principle of conferral albeit it did not really dispute the competence of the EU in the matter. Germany rather seemed to oppose the implications for the Member States, as well as to question to modalities of exercise of EU competence in international fora.[10]

## II. Quest for Control of the Principle of Conferral

### A. Full Conferral of Competence: Proper Legal Basis

The Member States' endeavour to gain control over the principle of conferral as a reaction to prior case law of the CJEU can be discerned throughout the Lisbon Treaty. Contrary to what may be expected, this is not always and necessarily to restrict the transfer of competence to the Union. This is perfectly illustrated by the reaction in the Lisbon Treaty to prior case law of the CJEU concluding as to the absence of competence for the Union to adhere to the European Convention on Human Rights (ECHR).[11] A remedy is now provided by the insertion of a legal basis in Article 6 TEU stipulating that the EU 'shall accede' to the ECHR, thereby expressly conferring the competence to do so to the EU. The crucial question still left to be solved, especially after Opinion 2/13, is how to safeguard the autonomy of the EU legal order in this accession process.[12]

Mostly, however, the Lisbon Treaty does not mean to transfer new competence to the Union. Rather the catalogue of competence inserted in Articles 2 to 6 TFEU appears to a large extent to codify prior case law of the CJEU in a static manner. The Lisbon Treaty expressly lists the subject matters that fall under exclusive, shared or complementary competence of the Union. But it also goes further, as the Lisbon Treaty additionally spells out the different modalities, as well as consequences for the Member States, of the conferral of competence.[13]

---

[10] Case C-399/12 *Germany v Council*, Judgment, EU:C:2014:2258. For an analysis of the issues at stake in this case, see I Govaere, 'Novel Issues Pertaining to EU Member States' Membership of Other International Organisations: The *OIV* Case' in I Govaere, E Van Elsuwege, P Stanislas and S Lannon (eds), *The EU in the World, Essays in Honour of Marc Maresceau* (Leiden, Brill, 2014).

[11] Opinion 2/94, EU:C:1996:140.

[12] Article 6 TEU states the objective of accession to the ECHR yet does not determine the modalities to do so. The key issue is to safeguard the autonomy of the EU legal order in the process, see the negative opinion on the Draft Accession Agreement, Opinion 2/13, EU:C:2014:2454.

[13] For instance, Art 2 TFEU reads: '1. When the Treaties confer on the Union exclusive competence in a specific area, only the Union may legislate and adopt legally binding acts, the Member States being able to do so themselves only if so empowered by the Union or for the implementation of Union acts. 2. When the Treaties confer on the Union a competence shared with the Member States in a specific area, the Union and the Member States may legislate and adopt legally binding acts in that area. The Member States shall exercise their competence to the extent that the Union has not exercised its competence. The Member States shall again exercise their competence to the extent that the Union has decided to cease exercising its competence'.

The catalogue of competence thus provides some clarity and transparency which before was sometimes lacking. Unfortunately, in so doing it also creates a false sense of legal certainty as it leaves crucial issues regarding the principle of conferral untouched and unresolved. What, for instance, is the precise scope of the newly formulated Common Commercial Policy (CCP),[14] which is now expressly listed among the exclusive competences of the EU in Article 3(1) TFEU? How should the conferral of competence be formulated if an agreement relates to different policies, such as both the CCP and the internal market, which are listed respectively as exclusive and shared competence? Not surprisingly, such questions were already at the core of the early post-Lisbon case law of the CJEU in the *Daiichi Sankyo*[15] case, as well as the 'conditional access'[16] judgments.[17] The CJEU thus necessarily had to come up with new delineating criteria not expressly listed in the Lisbon Treaty to determine the precise legal basis of conferral of competence to the EU. As such, it clarified that the CCP relates to measures which 'specifically' relate to international trade. This was fulfilled in both cases as they concerned either 'external harmonisation' of intellectual property rights in the framework of TRIPS/WTO,[18] or the 'externalisation of the internal market *acquis*' for application in third countries.[19]

In spite of all the efforts made by the Member States to control the conferral of competence to the Union, it thus immediately became apparent with those first post-Lisbon cases that they did not manage to completely forego the role of the CJEU in interpreting the newly inserted catalogue of competence. However, in terms of modalities of conferral these were rather easy cases. The use of either legal basis, CCP or internal market, in any event implied a 'full' conferral of competence, thus simultaneously to both the EU and the autonomous EU legal order. Considered from a constitutional perspective[20] and maintaining inter-institutional balance, the stakes were surely important, but in retrospect not as high as they initially seemed. The above judgments were rapidly followed by more truly challenging cases in terms of conferral of competences post-Lisbon.

---

[14] Article 207 TFEU expressly opens up the scope of the CCP to include commercial aspects of intellectual property rights, services and foreign direct investments.

[15] Case C-414/11 *Daiichi Sankyo*, Judgment, EU:C:2013:520.

[16] Case C-137/12 *Commission v Council*, Judgment, EU:C:2013:675.

[17] See, *inter alia*, J Larik, 'No Mixed Feelings: The Post-Lisbon Common Commercial Policy in Daiichi Sankyo and Commission v. Council (Conditional Access Convention)' (2015) 52 *CML Rev* 779: L Ankersmit, 'The Scope of the Common Commercial Policy After Lisbon: The *Daiichi Sankyo* and *Conditional Access Services* Grand Chamber Judgments' (2014) 41 *Legal Issues of Economic Integration* 193.

[18] *Daiichi Sankyo* (n 15) paras 52–53. The contextual criterion seemed very important in the *Daiichi Sankyo* case, thus begging the question of the legal basis for so-called 'TRIPS+' provisions in bilateral agreements. On such TRIPS+ obligations, see the respective contributions: M Aleman, 'Impact of TRIPS-Plus Obligations in Economic Partnership and Free Trade Agreements on International IP Law', and S Nadde-Phlix, 'IP Protection in EU Free Trade Agreements vis-à-vis IP Negotiations in the WTO', both in J Drexl *et al* (eds), *EU Bilateral Trade Agreements and Intellectual Property: For Better or Worse?* (Heidelberg, Springer, 2014) 61 and 133, respectively.

[19] *Commission v Council* (n 16) paras 64–65.

[20] The CJEU consistently holds that the choice of legal basis has constitutional significance, see Opinion 2/00, EU:C:2001:664, para 5.

## B. Conferral of Competence: To Give or To Grab ?

A degree of complexity was already added in the cases where the Member States pointed out that they clearly meant to reserve competence to themselves by virtue of the Lisbon Treaty. Such was the firm position of the Council and the Member States in both the *Broadcasting Organisations* case[21] and Opinion 1/13.[22] In both instances, they argued that the Member States, as masters of the Treaties, had on purpose only expressly inserted the *ERTA* test of 'to affect internal measures or alter their scope' in Article 3(2) TFEU. In other words, they claimed that the Lisbon Treaty only partially codified prior implied powers case law of the CJEU. The intended effect was thus to lead to a reversal of prior case law of the CJEU in the International Labour Organization (ILO)[23] and Lugano Convention[24] Opinions which introduced the test of 'already covered to a large extent'.[25] It was spelled out to the CJEU that to reinstate the latter case law post-Lisbon would amount to an unlawful extension of the scope of Article 3(3) TFEU contrary to the principle of conferral.[26]

This argument fully exposes the underlying quest for control over the principle of conferral through the introduction and formulation of the catalogue of competence in the Lisbon Treaty. Is EU competence for the Member States to give, and if so also to freely take back, by virtue of the Treaties? Or is conferral of competence a concept of EU law so that the CJEU may firmly grab control in order to safeguard a uniform and binding interpretation for all the Member States alike?

It does not come as a total surprise that the CJEU was clearly not inclined to follow the Member States in a textual interpretation of the Treaty provisions. Instead, it again turned to its habitual purposive method of interpretation of the Treaties, whereby it interprets individual EU law provisions in the light of the objectives of the EU Treaties.[27] As such, it pointed out that the ILO and Lugano Convention developments in implied powers reasoning were not new and separate tests but

---

[21] Case C-114/12 *Commission v Council*, Judgment, EU:C:2014:2151.

[22] Opinion 1/13, EU:C:2014:2303.

[23] Opinion 2/91, EU:C:1993:106.

[24] Opinion 1/03, EU:C:2006:81.

[25] Opinion 1/03 enlarges this to include 'foreseeable developments' of EU law, see para 126: 'However, it is not necessary for the areas covered by the international agreement and the Community legislation to coincide fully. Where the test of "an area which is already covered to a large extent by Community rules" (Opinion 2/91, paragraphs 25 and 26) is to be applied, the assessment must be based not only on the scope of the rules in question but also on their nature and content. It is also necessary to take into account not only the current state of Community law in the area in question but also its future development, insofar as that is foreseeable at the time of that analysis (see, to that effect, Opinion 2/91, paragraph 25)'.

[26] *Commission v Council* (n 21) para 60.

[27] I have argued elsewhere that only a clear and express prohibition in the Treaties could limit the purposive method of interpretation, as the CJEU adopts a *pro-legem*, but not a *contra-legem* interpretation of the Treaties, see I Govaere, '"Setting the International Scene": EU External Competence and Procedures Post-Lisbon Revisited in the Light of ECJ Opinion 1/13' (2015) 52 *CML Rev* 1277.

rather interpretations of the original *ERTA* test, which could thus still be applied post-Lisbon.[28] At least for the sake of clarity as to who controls the principle of conferral, it is to be welcomed that the CJEU, contrary, for instance, to Advocate General Jääskinen in his view on Opinion 1/13,[29] did not additionally search for the intention of the drafters of the Lisbon Treaty in order to guide its conclusions *in casu*.[30] It also firmly rejected the reference to Protocol No 25 by pointing out that this protocol only applies to Article 2(2) TFEU in relation to the exercise of shared competence, and cannot serve to limit the conferral of exclusive competence to the EU by virtue of Article 3(2) TFEU.[31]

Yet, what is then the meaning of the principle of conferral of competence for those cases? Rather than making an abstract assessment on the basis of the Treaty provisions, the CJEU indicated that, to answer this crucial question, an assessment of the *ERTA* criteria need to be made *in concreto*, in the light of each case. In the words of the CJEU:

> That said, it is important to note that, since the European Union has only conferred powers, any competence, especially where it is exclusive, must have its basis in conclusions drawn from a specific analysis of the relationship between the envisaged international agreement and the EU law in force, from which it is clear that such an agreement is capable of affecting the common EU rules or of altering their scope (see, to that effect, Opinion 1/03, EU:C:2006:81, paragraph 124).[32]

This forceful statement is most likely meant to act as a counterweight to the generous application and interpretation of the *ERTA* test. It is nonetheless difficult to disagree with Alan Rosas that the reasoning in Opinion 1/13 creates the impression of a low threshold for concluding as to an *ERTA* effect,[33] and thus to the conferral of competence to the EU.

The same reasoning was already applied in the *Broadcasting Organisations* judgment. A bit more puzzling, however, considering that it concerns a structural principle of constitutional significance, is that the CJEU in the *Broadcasting Organisations* case then proceeded to point to the burden of proof specifically in relation to the principle of conferral:

> In accordance with the principle of conferral as laid down in Article 5(1) and (2) TEU, it is, for the purposes of such an analysis, for the party concerned to provide evidence

---

[28] For a detailed analysis in terms of implied powers reasoning, see ibid.

[29] Opinion 1/13, View of AG Jääskinen, EU:C:2014:2292, para 70.

[30] Yet note that in a very early post-Lisbon case, the CJEU did point to the intention of the drafters of the Treaties, see Case C-130/10 *European Parliament v Council (Financial Sanctions)* EU:C:2012:472, para 82: 'Nevertheless, the difference between Article 75 TFEU and Article 215 TFEU, so far as the Parliament's involvement is concerned, is the result of the choice made by the framers of the Treaty of Lisbon conferring a more limited role on the Parliament with regard to the Union's action under the CFSP'.

[31] *Commission v Council* (n 21) para 73.

[32] ibid para 74. Compare to Opinion 1/13 (n 22) para 74, which is very similar in formulation but with the added reference also to 'foreseeable developments' of EU law by reference to Opinion 1/03.

[33] A Rosas, 'EU External Relations: Exclusive Competence Revisited' (2015) 38 *Fordham International Law Journal* 1073, 1091.

to establish the exclusive nature of the external competence of the EU on which it seeks to rely.[34]

Does the CJEU mean to say that there is a burden of proof solely in relation to the exclusive nature of EU competence, or with respect to the application of the principle of conferral itself? And on who rests such a burden of proof? Should the Commission *in casu* provide all the necessary evidence, so as to avoid the conclusion that (exclusive) competence is not transferred to the EU? If so, to what extent is it then really up to the Council and the Member States to prove that the negotiations 'might also go beyond the EU *acquis*' to support their claim that (exclusive) competence has not been conferred, rather than for the Commission to prove the contrary?[35]

In spite of those questions, the key issue with this reference to the burden of proof lies elsewhere. It could be maintained that the application of such a crucial structural principle as the principle of conferral should not depend mainly or even exclusively on whether the EU institutions have done their homework sufficiently well. Could, or even should, it not be applied *ex officio* by the CJEU? Considering the similarity in reasoning of the CJEU in both cases, it is striking that Opinion 1/13, which was rendered about one month after the *Broadcasting Organisations* case, no longer mentions the burden of proof in relation to the principle of conferral. This may in part be due to the fact that here it concerned an advisory opinion rather than an adversary procedure, thereby clearly exposing the limits of the burden of proof approach adopted in the *Broadcasting Organisations* case. What those cases reveal, however, is that the CJEU has maintained the application of the principle of conferral firmly within its grasp also post-Lisbon. Yet in so doing, it appears to be struggling to ascertain the precise grounds for, and limits to, its exclusive jurisdiction.

# III. Special Modalities of Conferral

In post-Lisbon practice, not many cases openly address the issue of whether or not external power is at all conferred to the EU, in spite of the theoretical importance of the question. More often, cases expressly or impliedly raise the issue of the precise modalities of the conferral,[36] with the added difficulty in terms of possible crippled and/or split conferral of competence.

---

[34] *Commission v Council* (n 21) para 75.
[35] ibid para 95.
[36] See, eg, the cases discussed in the previous section.

## A. Crippled and Semi-crippled Conferral of Competence

Already before the Lisbon Treaty it was theoretically possible to determine a crippled conferral of competence, whereby competence would be conferred to the EU without the corresponding conferral to the autonomous legal system. Pre-Lisbon, both the CFSP and JHA pillars were to a large extent kept outside the scope of EU judicial and EU democratic control in favour of bundling such control at the level of the Member States. The practical effect thereof was, however, strongly mitigated by the clear statement in ex Article 47 TEU that the two EU pillars should not affect the European Community (EC) pillar. This allowed the CJEU to jealousy shield the external *acquis communautaire* against any unwarranted influence from those intergovernmental pillars.[37] Full conferral of competence to the EC was thus systematically favoured over a crippled conferral to the EU. The Lisbon Treaty has fundamentally altered this given.

### (i) Redressing Full and Crippled Competence

The Lisbon Treaty at first sight simplifies the system. It formally abolishes the pillar structure which leads to the incorporation of the former third pillar into the autonomous EU legal order.[38] But at the same time it re-inserts the CFSP as a 'horizontal pillar'[39] by stipulating in Article 24 TEU that '(t)he common foreign and security policy is subject to specific rules and procedures'. In essence, this implies that the intergovernmental approach still prevails for CFSP measures post-Lisbon, whereby also judicial and democratic control is largely kept at national level, thus outside the autonomous EU legal order.[40] With respect to CFSP, the major change in terms of conferral of competence is, however, to be found in Article 40 TEU which redrafts the former Article 47 TEU.[41] It is still stipulated that the CFSP shall

---

[37] See especially Case C-91/05 *Commission v Council (ECOWAS)*, Judgment, EU:C:2008:288. On this case, see, eg, B Van Vooren, 'EU–EC External Competences after the Small Arms Judgment' (2009) 14 *European Foreign Affairs Review* 7.

[38] See section III B (i) below.

[39] On this concept, see I Govaere, 'Multi-faceted Single Legal Personality and a Hidden Horizontal Pillar: EU External Relations Post-Lisbon (2010–2011) 13 *Cambridge Yearbook of European Legal Studies* 87.

[40] Article 24 TEU specifies: 'It shall be defined and implemented by the European Council and the Council acting unanimously, except where the Treaties provide otherwise. The adoption of legislative acts shall be excluded. The common foreign and security policy shall be put into effect by the High Representative of the Union for Foreign Affairs and Security Policy and by Member States, in accordance with the Treaties. The specific role of the European Parliament and of the Commission in this area is defined by the Treaties. The Court of Justice of the European Union shall not have jurisdiction with respect to these provisions, with the exception of its jurisdiction to monitor compliance with Article 40 of this Treaty and to review the legality of certain decisions as provided for by the second paragraph of Article 275 of the Treaty on the Functioning of the European Union'.

[41] Article 40 TEU (ex Art 47 TEU) reads: 'The implementation of the common foreign and security policy shall not affect the application of the procedures and the extent of the powers of the institutions laid down by the Treaties for the exercise of the Union competences referred to in Articles 3 to 6 of the Treaty on the Functioning of the European Union. Similarly, the implementation of the policies listed

not affect 'other external EU action' listed in the TFEU. But, importantly, a counterweight is added in the second paragraph stipulating that that 'other external EU action' may not affect the exercise of the Union competences under the CFSP.

In so doing, the Lisbon Treaty radically alters the prior approach as it removes the possibility to systematically favour full conferral over crippled conferral of competence.[42] This was clearly illustrated already by the very first post-Lisbon case, the *Financial Sanctions* case, relating to a dispute between the European Parliament and the Council on the proper legal basis to adopt restrictive measures against certain persons and entities associated with Osama bin Laden, the Al-Qaeda network and the Taliban.[43] The European Parliament had expressly drawn the CJEU's attention to the continuing crippled nature of conferral of competence by virtue of the CFSP post-Lisbon. In particular, the European Parliament evoked the consequences in terms of the level of exercise of democratic control in case the legal basis for a full conferral, Article 75 TFEU, was rejected in favour of Article 215 TFEU.[44] This instance is nonetheless special for it only presented features of 'semi-crippled conferral' as it concerned the adoption of financial sanctions which, even under the CFSP, exceptionally come under judicial control of the CJEU.[45] As such, the only issue at stake was whether democratic control could be kept at the level of the Member States whilst conferring competence to the EU and exclusive jurisdiction to the CJEU.

In line with the newly formulated Article 40 TEU, the CJEU firmly rejected the reasoning that the prospect of a full or (semi-)crippled conferral of competence should determine the legal basis withheld. The Court held that the fact that the European Parliament is only informed and not a co-legislator under CFSP cannot determine the choice of legal basis.[46] Instead, it agreed with the Council that 'it is not procedures that define the legal basis of a measure but the legal basis of a measure that determines the procedures to be followed in adopting that measure'.[47] The full importance of the renewed post-Lisbon setting in terms of conferral of competence was made clear by further underlining:

> [T]he difference between Article 75 TFEU and Article 215 TFEU, so far as the Parliament's involvement is concerned, is the result of the choice made by the framers of the Treaty of Lisbon conferring a more limited role on the Parliament with regard to the Union's action under the CFSP.[48]

in those Articles shall not affect the application of the procedures and the extent of the powers of the institutions laid down by the Treaties for the exercise of the Union competences under this Chapter'.

[42] See also A Dashwood, 'The Continuing Bipolarity of EU External Action' in I Govaere, E Van Elsuwege, P Stanislas and S Lannon (eds), *The EU in the World, Essays in Honour of Marc Maresceau* (Leiden, Brill, 2014) 3.

[43] *Financial Sanctions* (n 30).

[44] ibid, para 32.

[45] Art 275 TFEU.

[46] *Financial Sanctions* (n 30) paras 79–80.

[47] ibid para 80.

[48] ibid para 82.

This clearly shows that all the Treaty legal bases relating to external relations are now on an equal footing and should be assessed on their own merit.

### (ii) Mixed Legal Basis CFSP: Other External Action?

The above finding leads to the next question: if in a post-Lisbon setting full conferral of competence can no longer be systematically favoured over crippled conferral, is it then at all conceivable to determine a mixed legal basis of the CFSP and other EU external action? In other words, is it possible to combine full and crippled conferral of competence in relation to one and the same legal act? The common procedural provision for the conclusion of agreements inserted by the Lisbon Treaty, Article 218 TFEU, could perhaps seem to militate in favour of such a conclusion.[49] However, the *Financial Sanctions* case raises important considerations in this respect. The CJEU pointed to the absence of democratic control by the EU under the CFSP as compared to the full democratic control at EU level for other external action,[50] to conclude forcefully '(d)ifferences of that kind are such as to render those procedures incompatible'.[51] The CJEU proceeded unequivocally to spell out the consequences:

> It follows from the foregoing that, even if the contested regulation does pursue several objectives at the same time or have several components indissociably linked, without one's being secondary to the other, the differences in the procedures applicable under Articles 75 TFEU and 215(2) TFEU mean that it is not possible for the two provisions to be cumulated, one with the other, in order to serve as a twofold legal basis for a measure such as the contested regulation.[52]

If it is fundamentally incompatible to combine semi-crippled and full conferral of competence because of the different level of democratic control, then it would surely not be logical to allow for a mixed legal basis including a CFSP provision

---

[49] The fact that both the CFSP and 'other' external relations agreements are to be concluded on the basis of Art 218 TFEU seems to set this question apart from the procedural issue in relation to 'mixed agreements' concluded on behalf of both the EU and its Member States. In relation to the latter, see Case C-28/12 *Commission v Council (Mixed International Agreements)*, Judgment, EU:C:2015:282, see especially paras 47–53. At paras 49 and 50, the CJEU points in particular to the following: '(49) First, that decision in fact merges two different acts, namely, on the one hand, an act relating to the signing of the agreements at issue on behalf of the European Union and their provisional application by it and, on the other, an act relating to the provisional application of those agreements by the Member States, without it being possible to discern which act reflects the will of the Council and which the will of the Member States. (50) It follows that the Member States participated in the adoption of the act relating to the signing of the agreements at issue on behalf of the European Union and their provisional application by it although, under Article 218(5) TFEU, such an act must be adopted by the Council alone. Moreover, the Council was involved, as an EU institution, in the adoption of the act concerning the provisional application of those agreements by the Member States although such an act falls within the scope of, first of all, the internal law of each of those States and, then, international law.' For a comment, see C Flaesch-Mougin, (2015) *Revue Trimestrelle De Droit Européen* 617.

[50] *Financial Sanctions* (n 30) para 47.

[51] ibid para 48.

[52] ibid para 49.

other than Article 215 TFEU. A strong case can be made that truly crippled conferral under CFSP, whereby not only democratic control by the European Parliament but additionally all judicial control by the CJEU is excluded, can never go hand in hand with a finding of full conferral on the basis of other Treaty provisions. One and the same measure can hardly at the same time be within and outside the autonomous EU legal order. But such a conclusion would then entail that, instead, a clear and often difficult choice will need to be made between the CFSP and other EU external action as a legal basis where a measure has multiple objectives.

### (iii)  Centre of Gravity Test

This begs the question of what objective legal criteria could and should be used by the CJEU to determine the proper legal basis of the conferral. An easy answer is, of course, to point to the centre of gravity test to determine a full or crippled conferral of competence. But this is only half of the answer. The precise criteria to be applied to establish the gravity in each and every case may be less easy to pinpoint in a satisfactory manner. Again this was illustrated by the *Financial Sanctions* case. Here, the CJEU first invoked the centre of gravity test and proceeded to rule in favour of the CFSP as the sole legal basis. It held in essence that Article 215 TFEU provides for action to counter the threat of 'international' terrorism, in relation to persons in third countries.[53] This was held to be the case of the envisaged measure so that Article 75 TFEU, which should then be taken to refer to financial sanctions to counter threats 'internal' to the Area of Freedom, Security and Justice (AFSJ), was not withheld. Not surprisingly, much of the debate in legal doctrine has focused precisely on these criteria laid down by the CJEU,[54] as it seems especially difficult to isolate international from internal terrorism in practice.

The centre of gravity test was also put forward in the subsequent *Mauritius Agreement* case[55] which again opposed the European Parliament to the Council concerning a measure relating to both the CFSP and other external action of the EU. Yet, this time, the dispute did not concern the proper legal basis for the conferral of the competence as such. The European Parliament in fact expressly agreed with the use of the sole legal basis of Article 37 TEU to the extent that the other external relations objectives were merely incidental to the principle aim of the Agreement relating to the CFSP.[56] Instead, the European Parliament sought to

---

[53]  ibid paras 55–66.
[54]  See, eg, the respective contributions by C Hillion, 'Fighting Terrorism Through the Common Foreign and Security Policy' and J Czuczai, 'The Powers of the Council Concerning the Emergency of International Terrorism after the Judgment in Case C-130/10 Parliament v. Council' both in I Govaere and S Poli (eds), *EU Management of Global Emergencies: Legal Framework for Combating Threats and Crises* (Leiden, Brill, 2014) 75 and 97, respectively.
[55]  Case C-658/11 *European Parliament v Council (Mauritius Agreement)*, Judgment, EU:C:2014:2025. For a comment, see P Van Elsuwege, 'Securing the Institutional Balance in the Procedure for Concluding International Agreements: European Parliament v. Council (Pirate Transfer Agreement with Mauritius)' (2015) 52 *CML Rev* 1379.
[56]  *Mauritius Agreement* (n 55) paras 44–45.

alter the status of the Agreement from a crippled conferral to more of a full conferral through the backdoor of the unitary procedural provision for the conclusion of agreements, Article 218 TFEU.

## (iv) Reducing the Handicap

The argument of the European Parliament in the *Mauritius Agreement* case first of all went that considering the underlying multiple objectives of the Mauritius Agreement it did not constitute an 'agreement exclusively related to the CFSP', so that the Parliament should have been duly consulted pursuant to Article 218(6) TFEU.[57] The CJEU, however, rejected this interpretation by reiterating that the substantive legal basis of a measure determines the procedure to be followed, and not vice versa, with the additional clarification that this includes the procedures under Article 218(6) TFEU.[58] In other words, if the sole legal basis legitimately withheld exclusively confers a crippled competence to the EU, then the handicap in terms of EU level democratic procedures cannot be remedied by pointing to other incidental (full) competence nor to the common procedural provision for the conclusion of agreements.[59]

The second argument of the European Parliament was, however, more successful. The CJEU agreed that the Council had nonetheless infringed Article 218(10) TFEU by failing to immediately and fully inform the European Parliament at all stages of the procedure for negotiating and concluding the EU–Mauritius Agreement.[60] The CJEU refused to equate the European Parliament's exclusion

---

[57] Article 218(6) TFEU reads as follows: 'The Council, on a proposal by the negotiator, shall adopt a decision concluding the agreement. Except where agreements relate exclusively to the common foreign and security policy, the Council shall adopt the decision concluding the agreement: (a) after obtaining the consent of the European Parliament in the following cases: (i) association agreements; (ii) agreement on Union accession to the European Convention for the Protection of Human Rights and Fundamental Freedoms; (iii) agreements establishing a specific institutional framework by organising cooperation procedures; (iv) agreements with important budgetary implications for the Union; (v) agreements covering fields to which either the ordinary legislative procedure applies, or the special legislative procedure where consent by the European Parliament is required. The European Parliament and the Council may, in an urgent situation, agree upon a time-limit for consent; (b) after consulting the European Parliament in other cases. The European Parliament shall deliver its opinion within a time-limit which the Council may set depending on the urgency of the matter. In the absence of an opinion within that time-limit, the Council may act'.

[58] *Mauritius Agreement* (n 55) paras 57–58. The CJEU first reasoned in terms of symmetry in internal measures and international agreements, in compliance with the institutional balance, see also para 56.

[59] The CJEU further reasoned as follows in para 60: 'That interpretation is justified particularly in the light of the requirements relating to legal certainty. By anchoring the procedural legal basis to the substantive legal basis of a measure, this interpretation enables the applicable procedure to be determined on the basis of objective criteria that are amenable to judicial review, as noted in paragraph 43 of the present judgment. That ensures consistency, moreover, in the choice of legal bases for a measure. By contrast, the interpretation advocated by the Parliament would have the effect of introducing a degree of uncertainty and inconsistency into that choice, insofar as it would be liable to result in the application of different procedures to acts of EU law which have the same substantive legal basis'.

[60] *Mauritius Agreement* (n 55) paras 75–76.

from the procedures for negotiating and concluding a CFSP-based agreement with a total absence of a right of scrutiny. Instead, it pointed out that the Lisbon Treaty precisely enhanced the importance of the exercise, at EU level, of democratic scrutiny of EU external action by inserting this information obligation applicable to all the types of procedures listed in Article 218 TFEU, including the CFSP. Article 218(10) TFEU was held to be an essential procedural requirement, breach of which necessarily leads to the annulment of the contested decision.[61]

Very importantly, in so doing, the CJEU also forcefully claimed its own jurisdiction to fully interpret the common procedural provision of Article 218 TFEU. It firmly rejected the argument of the Council that, since the CJEU in principle has no jurisdiction to control the CFSP, it also has no jurisdiction to rule on the legality of a measure adopted on the basis of the CFSP. The CJEU pointed out that Articles 24(1) TEU and 275(1) TFEU introduce a derogation to the rule of general jurisdiction of the CJEU laid down in Article 19 TEU, so that, like all derogations, they 'must, therefore, be interpreted narrowly'.[62] The CJEU concluded that:

> [I]t cannot be argued that the scope of the limitation, by way of derogation, on the Court's jurisdiction envisaged in the final sentence of the second subparagraph of Article 24(1) TEU and in Article 275 TFEU goes so far as to preclude the Court from having jurisdiction to interpret and apply a provision such as Article 218 TFEU which does not fall within the CFSP, even though it lays down the procedure on the basis of which an act falling within the CFSP has been adopted.[63]

As a consequence, the CJEU may thus annul any decision, including exclusively CFSP measures, for breach of an essential procedural requirement listed in Article 218 TFEU. As a counterpart, this most likely entails that the CJEU would also claim jurisdiction to deliver a corresponding Advisory Opinion under Article 218(11) TFEU, not shying away from envisaged CFSP agreements. The recent statement by the CJEU that 'Article 218 TFEU constitutes, as regards the conclusion of international treaties, an autonomous and general provision of constitutional scope',[64] appears to be foreboding in this respect.

As a result of such case law, which deftly explores the potential of the unitary procedural provision of Article 218 TFEU, the CFSP thus becomes a bit less of a crippled competence than it was most likely intended to be by the Member States in the Lisbon Treaty. One may discern an echo of pre-Lisbon case law, notably in

---

[61] ibid paras 79–87. However, the CJEU added: 'It must be acknowledged that annulment of the contested decision without maintenance of its effects would be liable to hamper the conduct of operations carried out on the basis of the EU–Mauritius Agreement and, in particular, the full effectiveness of the prosecutions and trials of suspected pirates arrested by EUNAVFOR' (para 90).

[62] ibid para 70.

[63] ibid para 73.

[64] Case C-425/13 *Commission v Council (Negotiating Directives)*, Judgment, EU:C:2015:483, para 62. The main issue in this case concerned Art 218(4) TFEU and institutional balance.

the *Kadi* cases,[65] where the CJEU already firmly claimed jurisdiction to perform a legality control, including of CFSP related measures for respect of fundamental rights.[66] But as important as it may be, case law merely reduces and cannot totally overcome the initial handicap for the application of the autonomous EU legal order in CFSP matters written into the Lisbon Treaty. At best, it qualifies the degree of crippled conferral short of turning it into a full conferral.

## B. Split Conferral

A different problem is posed where most but not all of the Member States confer competence to the EU. Already prior to the Lisbon Treaty this was made possible by the insertion of the constructive abstention procedure as regards the CFSP.[67] A number of Member States may thus decide not to be bound by a CFSP measure but to allow the others to go ahead. For the latter, the conferral of powers takes place without the corresponding transfer to the autonomous EU legal order. Using a CFSP legal basis together with the constructive abstention procedure thus in fact amounts to a combined split crippled conferral which remains to a large extent outside the control of the CJEU.

### (i) Post-Lisbon Split Conferral

The novelty of the Lisbon Treaty lies in the fact that the former third pillar is abolished and fully incorporated into the autonomous EU legal order, thus in principle leading to a full conferral of competence to the EU. The difficulty lies, however, in the fact that the opt-outs for the United Kingdom, Ireland and Denmark have been expressly confirmed to apply in a post-Lisbon setting.[68] Triggering the

---

[65] Joined Cases C-402/05P and C-415/05P *Yassin Abdullah Kadi and Al Barakaat International Foundation v Council and Commission (Kadi I)*, Judgment, EU:C:2008:461 and Joined Cases C-584/10P, C-593/10P and C-595/1P *Commission and others v Yassin Abdullah Kadi (Kadi II)*, Judgment, EU:C:2013:518; I Govaere, 'The Importance of International Developments in the Case-law of the European Court of Justice: *Kadi* and the Autonomy of the EC Legal Order' in M Hiscock and W van Caenegem (eds), *The Internationalisation of Law: Legislation, Decision–Making, Practice and Education* (Cheltenham, Edward Elgar Publishing, 2010) 187. Much has been written about these cases, see the doctrine mentioned in S Poli and M Tzanou, 'The *Kadi* Rulings: A Survey of the Literature' (2009) 28 *Yearbook of European Law* 533; M Avbelj, F Fontanelli and G Martinico (eds), *Kadi on Trial: A Multifaceted Analysis of the Kadi Trial* (London, Routledge, 2014).

[66] Codified in Art 275(2) TFEU by the Lisbon Treaty.

[67] Article 31 TEU.

[68] See Protocols Nos 21 and 22, respectively. This should be read together with Declaration 65: 'Declaration by the United Kingdom of Great Britain and Northern Ireland on Article 75 of the Treaty on the Functioning of the European Union. The United Kingdom fully supports robust action with regard to adopting financial sanctions designed to prevent and combat terrorism and related activities. Therefore, the United Kingdom declares that it intends to exercise its right under Article 3 of the Protocol on the position of the United Kingdom and Ireland in respect of the area of freedom, security and justice to take part in the adoption of all proposals made under Article 75 of the Treaty on the Functioning of the European Union'.

opt-outs with respect to external measures relating to the Area of Freedom, Security and Justice therefore amount to a straightforward split conferral under the control of the CJEU. This has induced a novel line of questioning in terms of external relations competence which, however, is still in a rather embryonic state.[69]

The difficulty of coming to terms with those important variations of split conferral in a post-Lisbon era was not really acknowledged in the *Mauritius Agreement* case. Advocate General Bot did, however, expressly point to the necessity to delineate between the external action of (respectively) the EU as such, the Area of Freedom Security and Justice, and the CFSP but without analysing the different modalities of conferral involved.[70]

## (ii) Split or Full Conferral?

The issue of the split conferral was posed again in the *Philippines Agreement* case.[71] Whereas it was not disputed that a double legal basis, the CCP and development cooperation, was indicated *in casu* nor that the Agreement should be concluded in a mixed form, ie on behalf of the both the EU and the Member States, the addition of other legal bases was a source of conflict and institutional bickering. The CJEU in essence agreed with the Commission that development cooperation should be broadly interpreted so as to 'absorb' the provisions in the Agreement relating to transport and environment, but also re-admission of third country nationals.[72] In so doing, the CJEU downplayed the importance of the lack of conferral of competence by the United Kingdom, Ireland and Denmark by virtue of the opt-outs. Instead, it determined a full conferral to the EU by all the Member States under the development cooperation legal basis.

Contrary to the environment and transport chapters, the CJEU did acknowledge that the Agreement contained 'specific obligations' for the contracting parties as concerns re-admission of third country nationals. In particular, the CJEU pointed out that:

> [the] Republic of the Philippines and the Member States undertake therein to readmit
> their nationals who do not fulfil, or no longer fulfil, the conditions of entry or resi-
> dence on the territory of the other party, upon request by the latter and without undue
> delay once the nationality of those nationals has been established and due process

---

[69] See I Govaere and V Demedts, 'Quelle définition de l'"externe" en matière d'ELSJ? Le cadre et les enjeux' in C Flaesch-Mougin and LS Rossi (eds), *La dimension extérieure de l'espace de liberté, de sécurité et de justice de l'Union européenne après le traité de Lisbonne* (Brussels, Bruylant, 2013) 489; E Neframi, 'L'aspect externe de l'espace de liberté, de sécurité et de justice: quel respect des principes et objectifs de l'action extérieure de l'Union?' in ibid 510.

[70] Case C-658/11 *European Parliament v Council (Mauritius Agreement)*, Opinion of AG Bot, EU:C:2014:41, paras 106–8.

[71] Case C-377/12 *Commission v Council (Philippines Agreement)*, Judgment, EU:C:2014:1903.

[72] On this case, see M Broberg and R Holdgaard, 'Demarcating the Union's Development Cooperation Policy after Lisbon: Commission v. Council (Philippines PCFA)' (2015) 52 *CML Rev* 547.

carried out, and to provide their nationals with documents required for such purposes. They also agree to conclude an agreement governing admission and readmission as soon as possible.[73]

In spite of such clear and specific obligations pinpointed in the Agreement, the CJEU nonetheless justified the disregard of the opt-outs by reference to the absence of 'detailed' provisions for the implementation of the re-admission process. The fact that reference is made in the Agreement to the future conclusion of a readmissions agreement apparently served to support such a conclusion.[74] On this basis, the CJEU proceeded to state that:

> the provisions of the Framework Agreement relating to readmission of nationals of the contracting parties, to transport and to the environment do not contain obligations so extensive that they may be considered to constitute objectives distinct from those of development cooperation that are neither secondary nor indirect in relation to the latter objectives.[75]

This reasoning immediately triggers the question as to when 'specific' provisions on re-admission of third country nationals would be considered to be 'sufficiently detailed' and thus 'sufficiently extensive' so as to justify recourse to a split conferral legal basis.

## (iii) Mixed Legal Basis, Full and Split Conferral?

A crucial underlying issue is whether, and if so when, the CJEU would allow a combined use of a full and split conferral as legal bases. It cannot go unnoticed that in the *Philippines Agreement* case, the Commission had forcefully spelled out that, in particular, the addition of Article 79(3) TFEU as a legal basis would produce unwarranted legal effects, both internally and externally. The Commission had warned that such a legal basis would trigger the opt-outs under Protocols No 21 and No 22, thereby leading not only to incompatible procedures but also to uncertainty about the degree of exercise of the EU's competence under Articles 3(2) TFEU and 4(2) TFEU.[76] The Council had countered this argument

---

[73] *Philippines Agreement* (n 71) para 57.

[74] ibid para 58: 'Whilst Article 26(3) of the Framework Agreement does admittedly contain wording stating how requests for readmission are to be dealt with, the fact remains that, as is apparent from Article 26(2)(f), the readmission of persons residing without authorisation is included in Article 26 as one of the matters upon which cooperation on migration and development will have to focus, without it being covered at this stage by detailed provisions enabling its implementation, such as those contained in a readmission agreement. It cannot therefore be considered that Article 26 of the Framework Agreement prescribes in concrete terms the manner in which cooperation concerning readmission of nationals of the contracting parties is to be implemented, a conclusion which is reinforced by the commitment, in Article 26(4), to conclude a readmission agreement very soon'.

[75] ibid para 59.

[76] ibid para 22. Article 3(2) TEU stipulates: 'The Union shall offer its citizens an area of freedom, security and justice without internal frontiers, in which the free movement of persons is ensured in conjunction with appropriate measures with respect to external border controls, asylum, immigration and the prevention and combating of crime'. Article 4(2) TEU reads: 'The Union shall respect

by first of all reiterating the CJEU's statements in the above-mentioned 'crippled conferral' cases, namely that 'it is not procedures that define the legal basis of a measure but the legal basis of a measure that determines the procedures to be followed in adopting that measure'.[77] The Council also pointed out that the obligations of the various Member States may not vary all that much in practice, as the opted-out Member States may choose to opt in to a particular measure or to conclude similar obligations with the third country bilaterally. It is clear, however, that in the latter case they would only be bound by virtue of international law and not by virtue of EU law,[78] thus not resolving the unwarranted legal effect the Commission was referring to.

Subsequent case law has clarified that 'Protocol No 21 is not capable of having any effect whatsoever on the question of the correct legal basis for the adoption of the contested decision'.[79] At least, not in the sense that the United Kingdom could successfully claim the (additional) use of Article 79 TFEU as the correct legal basis for external measures as soon as it related to the situation of third country nationals. Already in the *EEA Agreement* and *Swiss Agreement*[80] cases, relating to social security for EEA and Swiss nationals respectively, the CJEU followed the interpretation of Advocate General Kokott,[81] whereby Article 79 TFEU was held to strictly relate to the development of external borders measures, in terms of border checks, asylum and migration.[82] This was held to be different from and even 'manifestly

---

the equality of Member States before the Treaties as well as their national identities, inherent in their fundamental structures, political and constitutional, inclusive of regional and local self-government. It shall respect their essential State functions, including ensuring the territorial integrity of the State, maintaining law and order and safeguarding national security. In particular, national security remains the sole responsibility of each Member State'.

[77] *Philippines Agreement* (n 71) para 31.

[78] This also follows from Recitals 2 and 3 in the Preamble to the contested decision in the *Philippines* case: '(2) The provisions of the [Framework] Agreement that fall within the scope of Part Three, Title V of the [TFEU] bind the United Kingdom and Ireland as separate Contracting Parties, and not as part of the European Union, unless the European Union together with the United Kingdom and/or Ireland have jointly notified the Republic of the Philippines that the United Kingdom or Ireland is bound as part of the European Union in accordance with the Protocol (No 21) on the position of the United Kingdom and Ireland in respect of the Area of Freedom, Security and Justice annexed to the [EU Treaty] and the [TFEU]. If the United Kingdom and/or Ireland cease(s) to be bound as part of the European Union in accordance with Article 4a of the Protocol (No 21), the European Union together with the United Kingdom and/or Ireland are to immediately inform the Republic of the Philippines of any change in their position in which case they are to remain bound by the provisions of the [Framework] Agreement in their own right. The same applies to Denmark in accordance with the Protocol (No 22) on the position of Denmark annexed to those Treaties. (3) Where the United Kingdom and/or Ireland has/have not provided the notification required under Article 3 of the Protocol (No 21) on the position of the United Kingdom and Ireland in respect of the Area of Freedom, Security and Justice, they do not take part in the adoption by the Council of this Decision to the extent that it covers provisions pursuant to Part Three, Title V of the [TFEU]. The same applies to Denmark in accordance with the Protocol (No 22) on the position of Denmark, annexed to the Treaty on European Union and the Treaty on the Functioning of the European Union'.

[79] Case C-81/13 *United Kingdom v Council (Turkey Agreement)*, Judgment, EU:C:2014:2449, para 37.

[80] Case C-656/11 *United Kingdom v Council (Swiss Agreement)*, Judgment, EU:C:2014:97.

[81] Case C-431/11 *United Kingdom v Council*, Opinion of AG Kokott, EU:C:2013:187, paras 39–41.

[82] Case C-431/11 *United Kingdom v Council*, Judgment, EU:C:2013:589, para 63.

irreconcilable'[83] with the objectives of the EEA Agreement, as the latter means to extend[84] internal market measures to the third countries concerned.[85] Full conferral of competence under Article 48 TFEU was therefore withheld rather than a split conferral on the basis of Article 79 TFEU.

Interestingly, however, in the European Economic Agreement (EEA) Agreement cases, the CJEU also plainly rejected the reasoning of the United Kingdom invoking the use of Article 79 TFEU for other similar decisions in relation to other third countries. It was spelled out that each act must be assessed on its own aim and content in order to establish the proper legal basis.[86] In theory, this would then imply that similar decisions relating to different Agreements could have a different legal basis and thus also entail different modalities in terms of conferral of competence. Such a reverse reasoning was subsequently invoked by the United Kingdom in the *Turkey Agreement* case, in order to justify a different outcome here and to accept Article 79 TFEU as the correct legal basis. The CJEU, however, rejected this conclusion by pointing out that besides the objectives and content, also the 'context' of a measure needs to be taken into account, in particular where it concerns an amendment of rules adopted under an existing agreement.[87] *In casu*, the measure was adopted in the context of the EEC–Turkey 1963 Association Agreement, constituting a further step in the objective to progressively secure free movement for workers between the European Union and Turkey under the Association Agreement.[88]

If the contextual setting was thus similar, the main difference was to be found in the different objective of the Turkey Association Agreement which falls short of the EEA Agreement objective to extend the internal market to the third country concerned. The CJEU therefore agreed with the United Kingdom that the contested decision could not legitimately be adopted exclusively on the basis of Article 48 TFEU.[89] But it disagreed that it was the split conferral legal basis of Article 79 TFEU that should be added. The CJEU conceded to the United Kingdom that:

> it is true that Article 79(2)(b) TFEU empowers the European Union to adopt measures defining the rights of third-country nationals residing legally in a Member State,

---

[83] ibid para 64.

[84] For a recent assessment of the functioning of the EEA agreement, see H Fredriksen, C Franklin, 'Of Pragmatism and Principles: The EEA Agreement 20 Years On' (2015) 52 *CML Rev* 629.

[85] *United Kingdom v Council* (n 82) para 58. The CJEU further pointed out that to allow the opt-outs to be triggered in such a case would lead to two parallel regimes for the coordination of social security systems (para 65). Also in *Swiss Agreement* (n 80), the CJEU pointed out that the EU extended the application of its legislation concerning coordination of social security systems to the Swiss Confederation, see paras 55–67.

[86] *United Kingdom v Council* (n 82) paras 66–67.

[87] *Turkey Agreement* (n 79) para 38. The CJEU referred in this respect to *United Kingdom v Council* (n 82) para 48, and *Swiss Agreement* (n 80) para 50.

[88] *Turkey Agreement* (n 79) paras 43–45.

[89] ibid para 59: 'As a rule, it is only in the sphere of the internal policies and actions of the European Union or of the external actions relating to third countries which can be placed on the same footing as Member State of the European Union, according to the case-law cited in paragraph 58 of this judgment, that Article 48 TFEU empowers the European Union to adopt measures in this area'.

including the conditions governing freedom of movement and of residence in other Member States[90]

only to immediately limit the scope of application to serve strictly the purposes of Article 79(1) TFEU in terms of the common immigration policy.[91] Instead, the CJEU held that the respect for the principle of conferral, which was at stake *in casu*, could be safeguarded by the addition of Article 217 TFEU which was also the legal basis for the initial Association Agreement. The latter legal basis provides full conferral of external competence to the EU in all the fields covered by the TFEU.

Neither of those cases thus allowed for a combined full and split conferral, instead the legal basis which led to a full conferral was systematically preferred by the CJEU. The context criterion might in practice serve to exclude the addition of a split conferral legal basis to any post-Lisbon measure adopted in the context of a pre-Lisbon agreement. Yet the *Philippines Agreement* case shows that it is also highly unlikely for the use of a double legal basis for conferral to become the standard procedure for post-Lisbon Agreements.

# IV. Conclusion

The Lisbon Treaty has triggered a renewed line of questioning with respect to the principle of conferral which goes to a large extent still unresolved. Certainly, the CJEU has firmly asserted its exclusive jurisdiction to interpret this crucial structural principle so as to determine whether or not competence is transferred to the EU in any given case. But it appears to be more difficult to come to terms with the various post-Lisbon modalities of conferral of powers to the EU and the variations in terms of full, crippled and split conferral.

The CJEU recurrently states that it is the legal basis of a measure that determines the procedures to be followed, not vice versa. Such a statement does not always appear to be consonant with the impression created by the outcome of post-Lisbon case law. The above analysis of the cases rendered so far seems to indicate a systematic preference for conferral of competence to the EU and the autonomous EU legal order alike, be it under full conferral or a semi-crippled conferral. This is in spite of Article 40 TEU, which redresses the balance between the CFSP and other external EU action. The handicap in terms of pure crippled conferral under the CFSP, whereby control by both the CJEU and the European Parliament is in principle excluded, is as much as possible reduced by deftly

---

[90] ibid para 41.
[91] ibid para 42: '[T]hat is to say for the purposes of the common immigration policy aimed at ensuring the efficient management of migration flows, fair treatment of third-country nationals residing legally in Member States, and the prevention of, and enhanced measures to combat, illegal immigration and trafficking in human beings'.

exploring the potential of the unitary procedural provision of Article 218 TFEU. It is most likely highly significant for future case law that the CJEU has recently labelled this procedural provision for the conclusion of agreements as 'an autonomous and general provision of constitutional scope'.

The post-Lisbon importance of possible split conferral scenarios has also been downplayed so far by the CJEU. To do so, it pointed to the absence of sufficiently detailed provisions to warrant a split conferral or to the objective or context of the agreement which could justify a full conferral of competence.

The question is what will be the outcome if such a reasoning is no longer convincingly possible. Could one at all envisage mixed legal bases combining full, split and/or crippled conferral? So far, the CJEU has managed to steer away from this thorny issue but it is bound to arise in this difficult post-Lisbon setting—it is only a matter of time.

# 5

# Subsidiarity as a Structural Principle Governing the use of EU External Competences

GEERT DE BAERE

## I. Introduction

The Preamble to the Treaty on European Union (TEU) notes the High Contracting Parties' resolve 'to continue the process of creating an ever closer union among the peoples of Europe, in which decisions are taken as closely as possible to the citizen in accordance with the principle of subsidiarity'.[1] That reflects the balancing act performed by the drafters of the Maastricht Treaty, in which the phrase first appeared: integration was and is to be deepened, but must not lead to undue centralisation or undercut the necessary proximity of government. This was made more concrete by the insertion of what is now Article 5(3), first subparagraph TEU, intended to arbitrate the tension between integration and proximity.[2] It contains the following definition of the principle of subsidiarity:

> Under the principle of subsidiarity, in areas which do not fall within its exclusive competence, the Union shall act only if and in so far as the objectives of the proposed action cannot be sufficiently achieved by the Member States, either at central level or at regional and local level, but can rather, by reason of the scale or effects of the proposed action, be better achieved at Union level.

Crucially, the principle of subsidiarity in Article 5(3) TEU is intended to decide whether the Union ought to exercise a certain competence that has been conferred on it, and not to decide whether certain competences ought to be conferred on it or should be reattributed to the Member States. Article 5(1) TEU is clear on that

---

[1] Thirteenth recital in the preamble to the TEU.
[2] K Lenaerts, 'The Principle of Subsidiarity and the Environment in the European Union: Keeping the Balance of Federalism' (1994) 17 *Fordham International Law Journal* 846, 847–48.

issue: 'The limits of Union competences are governed by the principle of conferral. The use of Union competences is governed by the principles of subsidiarity and proportionality'. While viewed more broadly, subsidiarity as a political theoretical principle can arguably inform both pre-constitutional reflections on the limits of EU competences (ie whether certain competences ought to be attributed to the Union) and constitutional analyses on the use of EU competences guided by Article 5(3) TEU,[3] this chapter only examines the latter aspect. It offers an interpretation of Article 5(3) TEU with a view to its application to external action.

As the European Court of Justice[4] has held, the interpretation of a provision of EU law requires that account be taken not only of its wording and objectives, but also of its context and EU law as a whole.[5] That implies that subsidiarity must be interpreted in light of the principles on which the Union is founded,[6] and which it upholds and promotes in the wider world.[7] In addition, an interpretation of subsidiarity should take into account the type of legal order the Union is. Notably, the Union pursues the values in Articles 2 and 3(5) TEU through a legal order organised along federal lines. Article 4 TEU provides the 'programme' for the Union's conception of federalism.[8] It provides that competences *not* conferred upon the Union remain with the Member States,[9] that the Union is under an obligation to respect the equality of Member States before the Treaties 'as well as their national identities',[10] and entrenches the mechanism to keep the federal construction together, in the form of the principle of sincere cooperation.[11]

The balancing act between subsidiarity and consistency against the background of these principles structurally determines the constitution of EU external action. In particular, the foundational principles of the Union legal order also play a crucial role in enhancing consistency by providing an overarching constitutional framework for EU external action, and for the EU in general, through a set of values that are to govern all EU action,[12] as well as a single set of principles

[3] A Herwig, 'Federalism, the EU and International Law: On the Possible (and Necessary) Role of Subsidiarity in Legitimate Multilevel Trade Governance' in E Cloots, G De Baere and S Sottiaux (eds), *Federalism in the European Union* (Oxford, Hart, 2012) 65, 73 and 81–82.

[4] Under the first paragraph of Art 19(1) TEU, the institution of the Court of Justice of the EU encompasses the Court of Justice (ECJ), the General Court (EGC) and specialised courts. The only court falling in the latter category, the Civil Service Tribunal, established in 2004, ceased to operate on 1 September 2016 after its jurisdiction was transferred to the EGC in the context of the reform of the EU's judicial structure.

[5] Case C-583/11P *Inuit Tapiriit Kanatami and others v Parliament and Council*, Judgment, EU:C:2013:625, para 50, referring to that effect to Case 283/81 *Cilfit and others*, Judgment, EU:C:1982:335, para 20.

[6] Art 2 TEU.

[7] Art 3(5) TEU.

[8] E Sharpston, 'Preface' in E Cloots, G De Baere and S Sottiaux (eds), *Federalism in the European Union* (Oxford, Hart, 2012) viii.

[9] Article 4(1) TEU.

[10] Article 4(2) TEU; *cf* E Cloots, *National Identity in EU Law* (Oxford, Oxford University Press, 2015).

[11] Article 4(3) TEU; *cf* G De Baere and T Roes, 'EU Loyalty as Good Faith' (2015) 64 *International and Comparative Law Quarterly* 829.

[12] Article 2 TEU.

and objectives for the entire field of EU external action.[13] The Union, through the Council and the Commission, assisted by the High Representative of the Union for Foreign Affairs and Security Policy (HR), must ensure consistency between the different areas of its external action and between these and its other policies.[14]

This chapter is structured in two main sections, respectively on subsidiarity as a structural principle governing the use of Union competences (II) and subsidiarity as a structural principle governing the use of Union external competences (III), flanked by the introduction (I) and conclusion (IV). Section II starts with an exploration of the interpretation and application of subsidiarity under Article 5(3) TEU (A), which is followed by an exploration of judicial review by the ECJ of compliance with subsidiarity (B). Section III first suggests that implied external competences may be regarded as an exercise in balancing the limits and the use of Union competences (A), which is followed by an exploration of non-dichotomous subsidiarity in non-exclusive external competences (B), and a preliminary mapping exercise of traces of subsidiarity in external action measures (C).

# II. Subsidiarity as a Structural Principle Governing the use of Union Competences

## A. Interpretation and Application

The principle of subsidiarity in Article 5(3) TEU is intended to decide whether the Union ought to exercise a certain competence that has been conferred on it:[15] it operates as a limit to be observed *intra vires*.[16] Put differently, it is not because the Union has been attributed a certain competence by the Member States (conferral), that it should necessarily exercise it instead of its Member States (subsidiarity).

Article 5(3) TEU takes as a starting point that the several levels of government in EU governance are in agreement on the objective to be reached.[17] Contesting the objectives themselves is a question of conferral: can the Union pursue these objectives within the limits of its current competences? The objective or objectives that the Union wishes to attain with any particular action are shaped by the Member States when negotiating or amending the Treaties and further developed by the Commission in proposals and again by the Member States through their representatives in the Council during the legislative process at Union level.

---

[13] Articles 3(5) and 21 TEU, and Art 205 TFEU; cf J Larik, *Foreign Policy Objectives in European Constitutional Law* (Oxford, Oxford University Press, 2015).

[14] Article 21(3), second subpara TEU.

[15] Article 5(1) TEU.

[16] Lenaerts, 'The Principle of Subsidiarity and the Environment in the European Union' (n 2) 849.

[17] G Davies, 'Subsidiarity: The Wrong Idea, in the Wrong Place, at the Wrong Time' (2006) 43 *CML Rev* 63, 78.

Subsequently, subsidiarity tests Union action against both a necessity and an added value criterion: the former requires EU institutions to assess whether the Member States have the necessary resources to attain the objectives by themselves or whether Union action is necessary, while the latter requires that the institutions provide evidence that, even if the Member States acting by themselves was a possible alternative, it is not viable, as it would harm other interests, and/or Union action would on balance have clear comparative advantages.[18] The two criteria are clearly closely interrelated and if a proposal meets the necessity criterion, it should logically also meet the added value criterion.[19]

Furthermore, the question whether an objective can be better achieved at Union level can be analysed from different angles. It may be that its optimal achievement requires the Union to lay down detailed measures, leaving only the application in particular instances to Member States. However, it is equally likely that the optimal achievement of an objective requires only a basic framework of rules at EU level, leaving Member States in charge of working out the details of the regulatory framework as well as its implementation and application.[20] In other words, deciding at what level action is required to attain EU objectives is closely connected to deciding on the intensity of EU action, which is governed by the principle of proportionality.[21]

Article 5(3), first subparagraph TEU requires the Union to comply with subsidiarity only in 'areas which do not fall within its exclusive competence'. It is in that regard crucial to distinguish subsidiarity from the determination of the nature (exclusive or not) of EU competence. For example, in *Unitary Patent*, Italy argued that enhanced cooperation for a unitary patent would not be possible as the establishment of such a patent could only be achieved at Union level and *hence* fell within exclusive EU competences. In response, Advocate General (AG) Bot rightly noted that the fact that the objectives cannot be achieved by the Member States is an argument for the *exercise* by the Union of its competence, but does not mean Union competence is *ipso facto exclusive*.[22]

The exclusion of subsidiarity from areas of exclusive competence is explained by the fact that it would be meaningless in the light of Article 2(1) of the Treaty on the Functioning of the European Union (TFEU),[23] which provides that when

---

[18] See, eg, Case C-58/08 *Vodafone and others*, Opinion of AG Poiares Maduro, EU:C:2009:596, para 34.

[19] See in that sense P Van Nuffel, 'The Protection of Member States' Regions Through the Subsidiarity Principle' in C Panara and A De Becker (eds), *The Role of the Regions in EU Governance* (Berlin, Springer-Verlag, 2011) 55, 61.

[20] P Craig, 'Subsidiarity: A Political and Legal Analysis' (2012) 50 *Journal of Common Market Studies* 72, 75 and 82v83.

[21] See G De Baere, '"Единство димногообразиието": Balancing Unity and Diversity in EU Competences through Subsidiarity, Proportionality and Flexibility' (2015) XII *Evropeiski praven pregled* 8.

[22] Joined Cases C-274/11 and C-295/11 *Spain and Italy v Council (Unitary Patent)*, Opinion of AG Bot, EU:C:2012:782, point 62.

[23] But see HM Government, *Review of the Balance of Competences between the United Kingdom and the European Union: Subsidiarity and Proportionality* (London, HMG, 2014) 60, para 2.46.

the Treaties confer on the Union exclusive competence in a specific area, 'only the Union may legislate and adopt legally binding acts, the Member States being able to do so themselves only if so empowered by the Union or for the implementation of Union acts'. In other words, with the exception of implementing measures, a reflection on what would be the most appropriate level to act is superfluous if that determination is made *a priori* in the Treaties.[24] An important question for EU external action nevertheless remains whether that inapplicability of subsidiarity only applies to the *a priori* exclusive competences in Article 3(1) TFEU, or also to competences that have become exclusive through the operation of Article 2(2) TFEU or externally through Article 3(2) TFEU.[25]

Union action will conflict with the principle of subsidiarity where it can be shown that the objective sought can be achieved just as much in all Member States either by individual action or by cooperation between Member States. However, given that Union action is invariably tested against Union objectives, such as the achievement of uniform or coherent rules or the equal treatment of EU citizens, the burden of proof for the Union is often easily discharged and the protection offered by subsidiarity suboptimal.[26] For example, once the ECJ has accepted that a certain measure is legitimately intended to improve the conditions for the establishment and functioning of the internal market and can therefore be adopted on the basis of Article 114 TFEU, the step to accepting that the objective can be better attained at Union level is small indeed.[27]

## B. Judicial Review

The ECJ's review of the Union's compliance with the principle of subsidiarity is as a rule careful and circumspect.[28] The Court likely takes the view that subsidiarity requires consideration of a multitude of complex factors for which it often does not possess the necessary legal tools. The answer to the question at what level of

[24] *cf* Lenaerts, 'The Principle of Subsidiarity and the Environment in the European Union' (n 2) 849.
[25] See section III B (i) below.
[26] K Lenaerts and P Van Nuffel, *EU Law*, 2nd edn (London, Sweet & Maxwell, 2011), paras 7-028 and 7-032. See, eg, the judgment in Case C-276/14 *Gmina Wrocław*, Judgment, EU:C:2015:635, para 41, concluding that EU action complied with subsidiarity: 'As is apparent from recital 65 in the preamble to the VAT Directive, the objective of that directive, namely to harmonise the laws of the Member States in order to establish a common system of VAT, can be better achieved at EU level'. Contrast with the fuller subsidiarity reasoning in the judgment in Case C-508/13 *Estonia v Parliament and Council*, Judgment, EU:C:2015:403, paras 44–55.
[27] See, eg, Case C-491/01 *British American Tobacco (Investments) and Imperial Tobacco*, Judgment, EU:C:2002:741, paras 180–83. See also the oral evidence by Dashwood in HC European Scrutiny Committee, *Thirty-third Report: Subsidiarity, National Parliaments and the Lisbon Treaty* (HC Report, 2007–2008, no 563, Ev 3. See nevertheless the subsidiarity analysis in the judgment in Case C-58/08 *Vodafone and others*, Judgment, EU:C:2010:321, paras 72–79.
[28] S Weatherill, 'Better Competence Monitoring' (2005) 30 *EL Rev* 23, 27–28 and 37. See the overview of the Court's substantive subsidiarity assessment in Van Nuffel, 'The Protection of Member States' Regions Through the Subsidiarity Principle' (n 19) 62–66.

government a policy should optimally be pursued is determined by a multifaceted set of considerations that are not easily converted into a legal formula that a court can apply.[29]

Furthermore, the number of serious cases brought on the basis of alleged non-compliance with subsidiarity is limited.[30] This may be explained by the fact that Member States wishing to challenge a Union action on the basis of subsidiarity must do so within the applicable time limits, which *de facto* implies that the action must be brought shortly after the adoption of the act. The Member State in question cannot be unaware of the fact that at least a qualified majority of the representatives of the Member States in the Council believed that action at Union level was indeed necessary.[31]

A fruitful avenue for the ECJ could be to focus its review further on procedural aspects of subsidiarity and proportionality,[32] in line with the abolition of the more qualitative criteria that the Subsidiarity and Proportionality Protocol entailed in its pre-Lisbon version. It could use the Impact Assessments (IAs) to help guide its analysis, as it did, for example, in *Vodafone*.[33] IAs require an explicit justification of Union action on the basis of subsidiarity.[34] The ECJ could use IAs in combination with the duty to give reasons in Article 296, second paragraph TFEU to scrutinise the arguments on the basis of which the Union introduced certain measures by

---

[29] G de Búrca, *Reappraising Subsidiarity's Significance after Amsterdam*, Harvard Jean Monnet Working Paper 7/1999, 10.

[30] With respect to actions brought by Member States, see, eg, Case C-84/94 *United Kingdom v Council (Working Time Directive)*, Judgment, EU:C:1996:431; Case C-233/94 *Germany v Parliament and Council (Deposit-Guarantee Schemes)*, Judgment, EU:C:1997:231; Case C-376/98 *Germany v Parliament and Council (Tobacco Advertising I)*, Judgment, EU:C:2000:544; Case C-377/98 *Netherlands v Parliament and Council (Biotechnological Inventions Directive)*, Judgment, EU:C:2001:523; Case C-110/03 *Belgium v Commission (State Aid for Employment)*, Judgment, EU:C:2005:223; Case C-176/09 *Luxembourg v Parliament and Council (Airport Charges Directive)*, Judgment, EU:C:2011:290; Case C-358/14 *Poland v Parliament and Council (Tobacco Products Directive)*, Judgment, EU:C:2016:323; Joined Cases C-643/15 and C-647/15 *Slovakia and Hungary v Council (Relocation Quotas Decision)*, Judgment, EU:C:2017:631.

[31] Craig, 'Subsidiarity' (n 20) 80–81 and 83. The ECJ's possibilities to monitor compliance with subsidiarity have been enhanced by the fact that it now has jurisdiction in actions on grounds of its infringement by a legislative act, brought in accordance with Art 263 TFEU by Member States, or 'notified by them in accordance with their legal order on behalf of their national Parliament or a chamber thereof': Art 8 of Protocol No 2 on the application of the principles of subsidiarity and proportionality [2016] OJ C202/206. See further P Craig, *The Lisbon Treaty: Law, Politics, and Treaty Reform* (Oxford, Oxford University Press, 2010) 186–87. Pursuant to the same provision in Protocol No 2, the Committee of the Regions may also bring such actions against legislative acts for the adoption of which the TFEU provides that it be consulted.

[32] See Craig, 'Subsidiarity' (n 20) 78.

[33] *Vodafone* (n 27) paras 5, 45, 55, 51–79. See also the similar approach in *Airport Charges Directive* (n 30).

[34] European Commission, *Commission Staff Working Document: Better Regulation Guidelines* (SWD(2017)350 19; European Commission, *Impact Assessment Guidelines* (SEC(2009)92), paras 2.1, 2.3, 5.2 and 7.2; *cf* HM Government (n 23) 74–78 and 92–93, paras 2.90–2.91 and 3.35–3.38, criticising the current institutional practice with respect to IAs as suboptimal, but making various suggestions for improvement.

directly looking at the justification put forward in the IA,[35] as suggested by AG Sharpston.[36] Scrutinising the appropriateness of the reasons is arguably the only practical route for the ECJ to supervise the respect of subsidiarity by the EU institutions. The duty to state reasons forces the political institutions to express their motivation with respect to subsidiarity, which will hopefully have as an effect that they think more thoroughly before acting at Union level.[37]

Nevertheless, the ECJ in the past has not always explored the full potential of the duty to state reasons in combination with subsidiarity.[38] In *Deposit-Guarantee Schemes*, the Court explicitly held that an express reference to subsidiarity was not required in the Preamble to a measure.[39] This also points at a paradox in the subsidiarity obligations for the EU institutions, even post-Lisbon: while draft legislative acts are to be clearly justified with regard to subsidiarity and proportionality,[40] there is regrettably no such explicit obligation with respect to the legislative act itself.[41]

Furthermore, useful though IAs may be, the obligation in Article 5 of Protocol No 2 that any draft legislative act 'should contain a detailed statement making it possible to appraise compliance with the principles of subsidiarity and proportionality', plainly means that a subsidiarity and proportionality justification in IAs only does not suffice. At least the explanatory memorandum of the proposal, and if adopted the Preamble to the measure, should contain such a detailed justification.[42] That is also important for the well functioning of the early warning mechanism involving national parliaments. Finally, the explanatory memorandum or the Preamble is a more straightforward place for interested members of the general public to look than IAs. In short, while taking IAs into account when exercising judicial review seems sensible, that does not mean that no subsidiarity justification should be given in the explanatory memorandum and the Preamble

---

[35] Craig, 'Subsidiarity' (n 20) 78.

[36] Case C-310/04 *Spain v Council*, Opinion of AG Sharpston, EU:C:2006:179, paras 82–96. The Court too held that the proportionality principle had been infringed, but did not base that conclusion on the absence of an IA. *cf* also P Craig, 'The ECJ and *Ultra Vires* Action: A Conceptual Analysis' (2011) 48 *CML Rev* 395, 427; X Groussot and S Bogojevic, 'Subsidiarity as a Procedural Safeguard of Federalism' in L Azoulai (ed), *The Question of Competence in the European Union* (Oxford, Oxford University Press, 2014) 234, 240–41.

[37] Lenaerts, 'The Principle of Subsidiarity and the Environment in the European Union' (n 2) 894. Article 5 of Protocol No 2 provides a number of further indications on how the institutions are supposed to comply with that duty.

[38] See, eg, *Working Time Directive* (n 30) para 91.

[39] *Deposit-Guarantee Schemes* (n 30) para 28.

[40] Article 5 of Protocol No 2.

[41] *cf* Van Nuffel, 'The Protection of Member States' Regions Through the Subsidiarity Principle' (n 19) 68.

[42] See also the *Joint Practical Guide of the European Parliament, the Council and the Commission for Persons Involved in the Drafting of European Union Legislation* (Luxembourg, Publications Office of the European Union, 2015), 34, para 10.15.1: 'When exercising their legislative powers, the institutions have regard to the principle of subsidiarity and state how they are doing so in the explanatory memorandum and, more succinctly, in the recitals'.

for the benefit of 'democratic scrutiny' in the broader sense. This chapter therefore contains a preliminary mapping of traces of subsidiarity in Preambles to EU external action measures.[43]

It is also worth noting that the limitation of the subsidiarity review to draft legislative measures can have the effect that infringements of subsidiarity by non-legislative measures go unnoticed.[44] That may be particularly problematic for EU external action, where non-legislative measures are habitually used. That is, of course, especially true for the Common Foreign and Security Policy (CFSP), where legislative measures are excluded.[45] That said, even though the monitoring mechanism may not apply to non-legislative acts, the Treaties contain no such limitation with respect to subsidiarity itself, contrary to what is the case regarding exclusive competences. Furthermore, the Treaties likewise do not limit the applicability of subsidiarity to new measures, and the Union is required to respect the principle also when it amends or implements existing measures.[46]

At any rate, judicial review is not the only manner in which EU competences are kept in check. As AG Poiares Maduro pointed out in his Opinion in *Vodafone*, the decision-making processes through which EU competences are exercised and the participation in those processes by Member States often constitute the most effective way of controlling Union competences.[47] It is only with the explicit consent of at least a qualified majority of the Member States' representatives in the Council, and *de facto* often by consensus, that Commission proposals are transformed into binding EU law.[48] Apart from the lack of judicially applicable standards, this is another reason why the Court should tread carefully when considering annulling a measure on the basis that it does not respect subsidiarity. The balancing required by the Court is not the crude 'EU versus Member State', but between the need to pursue an EU objective at EU level as interpreted by some Member States against that same need or the lack thereof as interpreted by the Member State(s) who brought the action.[49]

---

[43] See section III C below.

[44] Craig, *The Lisbon Treaty* (n 31) 185.

[45] Article 24 TEU.

[46] See in that sense Van Nuffel, 'The Protection of Member States' Regions Through the Subsidiarity Principle' (n 19) 57.

[47] Opinion in *Vodafone* (n 18) point 1.

[48] Weatherill, 'Better Competence Monitoring' (n 28) 25. *cf* Case C-507/13 *United Kingdom v Parliament and Council*, Opinion of AG Jääskinen, EU:C:2014:2394, point 103, taking the view that the procedural requirements relating to subsidiarity had been complied with as 'the European Parliament's proposals for amendments were intensively analysed and discussed within the preparatory bodies of the Council'. The United Kingdom subsequently withdrew its application and the case was removed from the register by Order of 9 December 2014, EU:C:2014:2481. See further on the role of the Council in ensuring the observance of subsidiarity: HM Government (n 23) 71, paras 2.78–2.79.

[49] *cf* Craig, 'Subsidiarity' (n 20) 83.

# III. Subsidiarity as a Structural Principle Governing the use of Union External Competences

## A. Balancing the Limits and Use of Union Competences: Implied External Competences

The doctrine of implied competences[50] is essentially based on a simple premise. As the International Court of Justice (ICJ) put it in *Reparation for Injuries*:

> Under international law, the Organization must be deemed to have those powers which, though not expressly provided in the Charter, are conferred upon it by necessary implication as being essential to the performance of its duties.[51]

A few years later, the ECJ in *Fédéchar* referred to:

> a rule of interpretation generally accepted in both international and national law according to which the rules laid down by an international treaty or a law presuppose the rules without which that treaty or law would have no meaning or could not be reasonably and usefully applied.[52]

The reasoning on which implied competences are based therefore appears akin to a subsidiarity assessment: given the objectives and tasks of the Union, is action needed at Union or Member State level or, more likely, both?

Implied competences are structurally part of the constitutional framework of EU external action, mostly due to the scattered and limited nature of explicitly conferred external competences.[53] The (extensive and meandering) ECJ case-law on implied external competences has now been codified in Article 216(1) TFEU.[54] That provision encompasses three principles, which can be seen as three separate grounds on the basis of which a subsidiarity test would point to the Union as the most appropriate level of action.

First, the Union 'may conclude an agreement with one or more third countries or international organisations ... where the conclusion of an agreement ... is likely to affect common rules or alter their scope'. This purports to codify the *ERTA* principle:[55] the Member States are not allowed to act internationally in a way that

---

[50] G De Baere, *Constitutional Principles of EU External Relations* (Oxford, Oxford University Press, 2008) 16–17.

[51] ICJ, *Reparation for Injuries Suffered in the Service of the United Nations* (Advisory Opinion) [1949] ICJ Rep 174, 182.

[52] Case 8/55 *Fédération Charbonnière de Belgique v High Authority of the ECSC*, Judgment, EU:C:1956:11, 292, 299.

[53] De Baere, *Constitutional Principles of EU External Relations* (n 50) 17–29.

[54] G De Baere, 'EU External Action' in C Barnard and S Peers (eds), *European Union Law*, 2nd edn (Oxford, Oxford University Press, 2017) 710, 717–20.

[55] Originating from Case 22/70 *Commission v Council (ERTA)*, Judgment, EU:C:1971:32. The ERTA judgment is authority for the existence of implied external competences on the basis of the existence of internal Union rules and for the acquisition of exclusive external competences on the same basis.

would affect existing EU law, because the situation cannot be remedied by merely disapplying the infringing rule. The Member States' level would therefore not be appropriate to take action, and their competence is consequently excluded. At this stage, it will be clear that external action is necessary, and the existence of EU competences is necessary to compensate for the Member States' inability to act.[56] As a result, the Union is the most appropriate level of action.

Secondly, the Union 'may conclude an agreement with one or more third countries or international organisations … where the conclusion of an agreement is necessary in order to achieve, within the framework of the Union's policies, one of the objectives referred to in the Treaties'. This codifies the 'complementarity principle'.[57] Once the Member States agreed to allocate the relevant internal competence explicitly to the Union in the Treaties, the type of policy necessitated corresponding Union external action. In other words, subsidiarity dictates that the Union level is the most appropriate to achieve the objective agreed upon by the Member States. Internal Union competences are supported by the corresponding external competences only when the latter are truly 'implicit' in the former. This is the case when the internal Union competences cannot reasonably be expected to be effectively exercised without the possibility for the Union to enter into international agreements with third countries on the same subject matter.

See Opinion 2/15 (EU-Singapore Free Trade Agreement) of 16 May 2017, EU:C:2017:376, paras 170–172: 'In paragraph 17 of [ERTA], the Court stated that, when the European Union adopts provisions laying down common rules, whatever form these may take, the Member States no longer have the right, acting individually or even collectively, to undertake obligations with third States which affect those rules […]. In line with that case-law, Article 216 TFEU grants to the EU competence to conclude, inter alia, any international agreement which "is likely to affect common rules or alter their scope". Under Article 3(2) TFEU, the competence of the European Union to conclude such an agreement is exclusive'. Compare Case C-114/12 Commission v Council ('Rights of Broadcasting Organisations'), Opinion of AG Sharpston, EU:C:2014:224, points 81–114.

   [56] The resulting EU competence is exclusive pursuant to Art 3(2) TFEU: see n 55.
   [57] A Dashwood, 'The Attribution of External Relations Competence' in A Dashwood and C Hillion (eds), *The General Law of EC External Relations* (London, Sweet & Maxwell, 2000) 115, 127–32. The complementarity principle as codified in Art 216(1) TFEU appears to be wider in scope than the case-law on which it is based: M Cremona, 'External Relations and External Competence of the European Union: The Emergence of an Integrated Policy' in P Craig and G de Búrca (eds), *The Evolution of EU Law*, 2nd edn (Oxford, Oxford University Press, 2011) 217, 225. See also Case C-600/14, Germany v Council, Opinion of AG Szpunar, EU:C:2017:296, point 101, arguing that the criterion of necessity 'could even be regarded as a simple declaratory confirmation of the principles of subsidiarity and proportionality'. See further Opinion 2/15 (n 55), paras 237–42, where the Court explicitly distinguished between necessity as a criterion for the existence of EU external competence and for its exclusivity (at paragraphs 237–242) albeit without explaining where precisely the distinction lay. Regarding exclusivity, the Court noted that the Commission had stated in its observations that the conclusion of an agreement concerning non-direct foreign investment did not appear 'necessary to enable the Union to exercise its internal competence', within the meaning of Article 3(2) TFEU, and that it followed that the EU does not have exclusive competence to conclude such an agreement. By contrast, the Court held that the conclusion of such an agreement was 'necessary in order to achieve, within the framework of the Union's policies, one of the objectives referred to in the Treaties', within the meaning of Article 216(1) TFEU. In particular, the Court pointed out that in the light of the fact that the free movement of capital and payments between Member States and third States, laid down in Article 63 TFEU, is not formally binding on third States, the conclusion of international agreements contributing to free movement on a reciprocal basis may be classified as necessary in order to achieve fully such free movement, which is one of the objectives of Title IV of Part Three TFEU.

Thirdly, Article 216(1) TFEU also lists the prima facie rather straightforward possibility for the Union to 'conclude an agreement with one or more third countries or international organisations ... where the conclusion of an agreement ... is provided for in a legally binding Union act', that is to say, in a Regulation, a Directive or a Decision.[58] The competence is implied in the sense that the Treaties themselves do not explicitly provide for an external counterpart to the explicitly conferred internal competence. However, a subsidiarity assessment by the representatives of the Member States in the Council, often in combination with the European Parliament, will have pointed to the Union as the most appropriate level to conclude an international agreement to complement the internal measure in question.

In any event, applying the doctrine of implied competences in the 'sovereignty-sensitive' area of EU external action requires caution. That is even more the case with respect to the CFSP, where the ECJ for the most part lacks jurisdiction.[59] Moreover, the CFSP attribution in Article 24(1) TEU is so broad that an application of the doctrine of implied competences implying all the competences needed for an effective CFSP would lead to an extensive grant of external action competences going far beyond what the EU Treaty permits.

A discrepancy might prima facie seem to exist between implied competences and conferral. However, while the Union only has those competences that have been conferred on it, this does not mean that it can only act on the external front when it has *explicitly* been granted the competence to do so. In that sense, the implied competences reasoning can be seen as an example of using the subsidiarity principle to determine the limits of Union external competence. However, the subsidiarity test regarding implied competences can only result in the Union being designated as the appropriate level if external action turns out to be necessary but remains within the limits of existing Union competences. If the subsidiarity test reveals that Union action is necessary but no competences can be implied, the Member States as Masters of the Treaties must redo the test. On that basis, they must decide whether pre-constitutional subsidiarity requires that the limits of Union competence are reconsidered, and perhaps more competences at Union level are necessary. Conversely, if the exercise of an explicitly attributed internal competence requires that

---

[58] Article 288 TFEU.

[59] Article 275 TFEU. The ECJ does have jurisdiction to monitor compliance with Art 40 TEU and to review, pursuant to Art 263, fourth para TFEU, the legality of decisions providing for restrictive measures against natural or legal persons. In Opinion 2/13 (Accession of the European Union to the ECHR) of 18 December 2014, EU:C:2014:2454, para 251, the Court held that it had 'not yet had the opportunity to define the extent to which its jurisdiction is limited in CFSP matters' as a result of these provisions. However, more recent cases have given the Court precisely that opportunity. See eg Case C-439/13 P *Elitaliana v Eulex Kosovo*, Judgment, EU:C:2015:753, para 42, and Case C-455/14 P *H v Council and Commission*, Judgment, EU:C:2016:569, para 40. Most notably, in Case C-72/15 *Rosneft*, Judgment, EU:C:2017:236, para 81, the Court held that TEU arts 19, 24, and 40, TFEU art 275, and art 47 of the Charter must be interpreted as meaning that the Court has jurisdiction to give preliminary rulings, under TFEU art 267, on the validity of an act adopted on the basis of provisions relating to the CFSP, provided that the request for a preliminary ruling relates either to the monitoring of that decision's compliance with TEU art 40, or to reviewing the legality of restrictive measures against natural or legal persons. See also Case C-72/15 *Rosneft*, Opinion of AG Wathelet, EU:C:2016:381, points 36–93.

the Union use its capacity to act internationally, the requisite external competence may be implied. In other words, the subsidiarity test regarding implied competences concerns the use of Union competence, and corresponds to Article 5(3) TEU.

## B. Beyond Either/or: Subsidiarity in Non-exclusive External Competences

### (i) Scope

Subsidiarity in Article 5(3) TEU applies to non-exclusive competences. That limitation is particularly salient for EU external action. The scope of subsidiarity therefore depends on how exclusive competences are defined, which has only been partly clarified by the Lisbon Treaty.[60]

Article 3 TFEU now lays down the main principles on when the Union is exclusively competent.[61] Article 3(1) TFEU lists five *a priori* exclusive competences:

(a)   customs union;
(b)   the establishing of the competition rules necessary for the functioning of the internal market;
(c)   monetary policy for the Member States whose currency is the euro;
(d)   the conservation of marine biological resources under the common fisheries policy;
(e)   common commercial policy.

Both the internal and the external aspects of these policies belong to the Union's exclusive competence. In addition, Article 3(2) TFEU provides for the Union to have exclusive competence 'for the conclusion of an international agreement when its conclusion is provided for in a legislative act of the Union or is necessary to enable the Union to exercise its internal competence, or insofar as its conclusion may affect common rules or alter their scope'.[62]

Is subsidiarity only inapplicable to the *a priori* exclusive competences listed in Article 3(1) TFEU, or also to competences that have become exclusive through the operation of Article 3(2) TFEU? Arguably, when a situation falls within one of the categories of Article 3(2) TFEU, such as when an internal legislative act provides for the conclusion of an international agreement by the Union, the exclusive competence flows directly from the application of Article 3(2) TFEU and

---

[60]   Craig, 'Subsidiarity' (n 20) 74. See also Case C-600/14, Opinion of AG Szpunar (n 57) point 118, noting that the principle of subsidiarity 'applies to the exercise of any shared competence, whether internal or external'.

[61]   See De Baere, 'EU External Action' (n 54) 720–24.

[62]   Article 3(2) TFEU. While it codifies ECJ case-law on exclusive external competences, the criteria listed are neither entirely clear nor sufficiently nuanced and hence in need of judicial clarification. The existing case-law on the nature of EU external competences therefore needs to be taken into account: see Case C-114/12 *Commission v Council*, Judgment, EU:C:2014:2151, paras 65–67. See also Case C-66/13 *Green Network*, Judgment, EU:C:2014:2399, paras 27–28.

a reflection on whether the Union or its Member States are the most appropriate level is bound to be meaningless. Once it has been determined that the situation falls under one of the instances that trigger exclusive external competence under Article 3(2) TFEU, the choice of the appropriate level follows automatically and inevitably points to the Union.

Nevertheless, Article 3(2) TFEU also provides that the Union will have exclusive competence for the conclusion of an international agreement 'insofar as its conclusion may affect common rules or alter their scope'. That reflects the possibility for an EU external competence to become exclusive through the exercise of an EU internal competence, so-called '*ERTA* exclusivity'. While once it has been determined that independent Member State international action would affect existing internal EU law, the exclusivity follows automatically from Article 3(2) TFEU, the Union does have a choice under Article 2(2) TFEU whether or not to exercise competences shared with the Member States. As the Court confirmed in Opinion 1/13,[63] the extent to which it exercises those internal competences crucially affects what scope for autonomous Member State external action remains. Once a policy field is entirely or largely covered by Union measures, the Union and its Member States have no choice but to leave the negotiation and conclusion of international agreements in that area to the Union, as Article 3(2) TFEU inevitably excludes the Member States. However, they do have the choice whether or not they will continue to regulate the area internally at Union level or to scale back Union involvement and reinstate the Member States' autonomous scope for action on the basis of Article 2(2) TFEU. Pursuant to Article 5(3) TEU, they are to make that choice in accordance with the subsidiarity principle. In that sense, even subsidiarity in Article 5(3) TEU can have a lateral impact on the limits of Union competences and hence on the division of competences between the Union and its Member States.[64]

Be that as it may, given that the category of exclusive EU competences is limited, and that in the absence of any indication to the contrary, Union competences must be regarded as non-exclusive,[65] subsidiarity applies in most areas of EU external competence.

*(ii) Subsidiarity in the Practice of Non-Exclusive Union Competences*

'Shared competences', as provided for by Articles 2(2) and 4 TFEU, can be exercised by the Member States to the extent that the Union has not exercised, or has

---

[63] Opinion 1/13 (Accession of third States to the Hague Convention) of 14 October 2014, EU:C:2014:2303, para 73. See also Green Network (n 62 above) para 31; and Opinion 3/15 (Marrakesh Treaty on access to published works) of 14 February 2017, EU:C:2017:114, para 107.

[64] *cf* on the pre-Lisbon situation: Lenaerts, 'The Principle of Subsidiarity and the Environment in the European Union' (n 2) 850.

[65] *cf* eg Case C-370/12 *Pringle*, Judgment, EU:C:2012:756, paras 120–21; and *Commission v Council* (n 62) para 75.

decided to cease exercising,[66] its competence.[67] Article 2(2) TFEU ties Member States' competences to the evolving exercise of EU competence over time.[68] The effect of this is often referred to as 'occupying the field' or, by analogy with US constitutional doctrine, 'pre-emption'.[69] It renders the corresponding EU external competence exclusive, and hence renders subsidiarity inapplicable. However, the mechanism is not universally applicable. This section discusses the structural presence of subsidiarity in how non-exclusive EU external action competences operate, taking minimum standards and the CFSP as examples. Furthermore, the mere fact that international treaties tend not to follow the division of competences between the Union and its Member States de facto leads to both of them acting together. That results in so-called mixed external action, which requires sincere cooperation. Both will also be examined below.

## (a) Minimum Standards

The Union has the competence to harmonise certain areas through minimum requirements, leaving the Member States free to adopt more stringent measures. The pre-constitutional subsidiarity test at the basis of this arrangement possibly involves considerations on sparking a race to the top rather than a race to the bottom, for example, in environmental protection.[70]

Nevertheless, when moving to the sphere of external action, the subsidiarity equation changes to take into account the involvement of other international legal actors. First, as the ECJ held in Opinion 1/03, the fact that both the Union rules and the international agreement in question lay down minimum standards 'may justify the conclusion that the [Union] rules are not affected, even if the [Union] rules and the provisions of the agreement cover the same area'.[71] The requirement that both the Union rules and the international agreement in question lay down minimum standards is necessary in order not to inhibit the development of Union law. If an international agreement concluded by a Member State lays down an absolute standard, and the Union subsequently decides to raise its minimum standards above the absolute standard of the agreement, a conflict may arise with inevitable consequences for the international responsibility of the Union and its

---

[66] See Declaration 18 in relation to the delimitation of competences [2016] OJ C202/344.

[67] On non-exclusive external competences, see further De Baere, 'EU External Action' (n 54) 726–29.

[68] The Member States' unease in that regard caused them to annex to the TEU and TFEU Protocol No 25 on the exercise of shared competence [2016] OJ C202/306.

[69] *cf* G De Baere and K Gutman, 'Federalism and International Relations in the European Union and the United States: A Comparative Outlook' in E Cloots, G De Baere and S Sottiaux (eds), *Federalism in the European Union* (Oxford, Hart, 2012) 131, 157–65. However, the Court has not generally adopted this term, and there is no academic consensus on its usage. Nevertheless, the term has on occasion been used, especially by Advocates General: see eg Opinion 2/15 (EU-Singapore Free Trade Agreement), Opinion of AG Sharpston, EU:C:2016:992, points 59, 61, and 73.

[70] See De Baere, *Constitutional Principles of EU External Relations* (n 50) 66 and the references cited there.

[71] Opinion 1/03 (New Lugano Convention), of 7 February 2006, EU:C:2006:81, paras 123 and 127. See also Opinion 2/91 (ILO Convention No 170), of 19 March 1993, EU:C:1993:106.

Member States. The Union is therefore the appropriate level of action in those circumstances. Secondly, the ECJ made clear in *PFOS* that while a Member State is free to adopt measures providing for a higher level of protection within its own jurisdiction, proposing such measures within the framework of an international agreement to which the Union is a party, which would imply that the Union may be bound by a more stringent measure with which it did not express its agreement, falls foul of the duty of sincere cooperation in Article 4(3) TEU.[72] That can be explained on the basis of a so-called 'all affected' subsidiarity reasoning, which requires that all those affected by a decision should have a say in it:[73] while measures restricted to a Member State's own jurisdiction only affect that Member State, measures at an international level by which the Union may be bound affect the Union in its entirety. It is therefore appropriate that such measures are not taken without the Union taking part in the decision.

## (b) CFSP

Whatever type of competence the CFSP may be,[74] it is not exclusive. Pursuant to Article 5(3) TEU, the principle of subsidiarity therefore applies.

Nevertheless, the application of subsidiarity to the CFSP has gained little attention. De Búrca has suggested a number of reasons for that apparent lack of interest. In particular, the CFSP's problem has traditionally been perceived as one of inadequate rather than excessive action. The 'dictate of restraint implicit in the subsidiarity principle' could therefore be unnecessary and even inappropriate.[75] However, while subsidiarity implies restraint, it also requires reflection on the appropriate level of action, which does not necessarily run counter to more adequate action at EU level. The view that discussions about effectiveness as a means of dividing power should be avoided in the sensitive area of foreign affairs[76] therefore seems over-cautious.

De Búrca also points out that CFSP legal instruments are very different from the 'harder' legal instruments in the rest of EU law and the idea of subsidiarity requiring 'softer' forms of law seems superfluous.[77] While the remark concerned pre-Lisbon joint actions and common positions,[78] it essentially remains valid under

---

[72] Case C-246/07 *Commission v Sweden (PFOS)*, Judgment, EU:C:2010:203, para 102.

[73] See N Barber, 'The Limited Modesty of Subsidiarity' (2005) 11 *European Law Journal* 308, 315–20. The 'all affected' reasoning is notoriously difficult to apply to measures having extraterritorial effect, including of course external action measures, but equally private international law: see A Mills, 'Private International Law and EU External Relations: Think Local Act Global, or Think Global Act Local?' (2016) 65 *International and Comparative Law Quarterly* 541.

[74] See De Baere, 'EU External Action' (n 54) 729.

[75] De Búrca, *Reappraising Subsidiarity's Significance after Amsterdam* (n 29) 28.

[76] See N Neuwahl, 'Foreign and Security Policy and the Implementation of the Requirement of "Consistency" under the Treaty on European Union' in D O'Keeffe and PM Twomey (eds), *Legal Issues of the Maastricht Treaty* (London, Wiley Chancery Law, 1994) 227, 237.

[77] De Búrca, *Reappraising Subsidiarity's Significance after Amsterdam* (n 29) 28.

[78] See ex Arts 12, 14–15 TEU.

the now sole CFSP legal instrument: Decisions.[79] Subsidiarity implies a proportionality assessment, and in that sense a reflection on the appropriate type of legal instrument. However, the 'spirit of subsidiarity' also requires that, where possible, less detailed and less regulative instruments be used. That requirement is firmly structurally embedded in the CFSP.

Indeed, subsidiarity is present in the entire CFSP decision-making process. Reading Articles 25 to 29 TEU, it seems clear that the entire system is based on the principle that the EU only takes action in CFSP matters when that would represent a clear advantage over Member State action.[80] Furthermore, the Member States remain in control of the decision-making process, which remains largely based on unanimity, rather than QMV.[81] The extension of QMV might have been one of the reasons Member States introduced a reasonableness filter in the form of subsidiarity into EU law. Given that such 'supranational' decision-making is largely absent, that filter function would arguably make little sense in the CFSP.[82]

The operation of subsidiarity in the CFSP can also not be seen independently of the scope of the CFSP. In particular, Article 24(1) TEU provides for the CFSP to cover *all* areas of foreign and security policy, which may give the impression that, vertically, a comprehensive transfer of competence from the Member States to the EU in foreign policy has happened, and that, horizontally, the Union can in principle take any external action under CFSP competences. Both impressions are erroneous.[83]

Answering the vertical competence question is not made easier by the absence of a list of criteria to determine when CFSP action is necessary, though the Member States' Ministers of Foreign Affairs did attempt to draw up such a list in 1992. The result ended up in a report without legal force, adopted by the European Council. They agreed that it is possible to list certain factors determining important common interests and that these and other factors should be taken into account in defining the issues and areas for joint action. The following criteria were put forward:[84]

— the geographical proximity of a given region or country;
— an important interest in the political and economic stability of a region or country;
— the existence of threats to the security interests of the Union.

---

[79] See Arts 25, 28–29 TEU.
[80] R Von Borries, 'Das Subsidiaritätsprinzip im Recht der Europäischen Union' (1994) *Europarecht* 286.
[81] De Búrca, *Reappraising Subsidiarity's Significance after Amsterdam* (n 29) 28.
[82] Von Borries, 'Das Subsidiaritätsprinzip im Recht der Europäischen Union' (n 80) 286.
[83] See De Baere, *Constitutional Principles of EU External Relations* (n 50) 106–8.
[84] *Report to the European Council in Lisbon on the Likely Development of the Common Foreign and Security Policy (CFSP) with a View to Identifying Areas Open to Joint Action vis-à-vis Particular Countries or Groups of Countries* (adopted by the European Council at Lisbon, 26–27 June 1992), para 12.

These criteria are essentially an attempt to apply subsidiarity to the CFSP. They seem fairly self-evident, not to say vapid. Arguably, the Member States declined to circumscribe the limits of CFSP competences more clearly as the entire CFSP is structurally set up to leave the Member States in control of the process and able to prevent the Union from 'running wild'. Their pre-constitutional subsidiarity reflection presumably resulted in the decision that for most elements of 'high politics' foreign policy, the Member State level is most appropriate. It would also arguably be impossible *a priori* to describe in detail all foreign policy actions that might be necessary to preserve peace and strengthen the security of the Union and international security.

## (c) Mixed External Action and Sincere Cooperation

'Mixed agreements'[85] include among their parties the Union and all or some of the Member States, and fall partly within Union competence and partly within Member State competence.[86] Their lack of clarity regarding the precise vertical division of competences makes mixed agreements suitable for enabling the Union to act internationally while keeping the competence situation sufficiently vague so as not to affect openly the Member States' external competences. Moreover, an overly precise determination of the respective competences of the Union and the Member States might 'freeze' the Union's competences and hinder its evolving constitutional order. That illustrates that external competence in a multi-level system such as the EU is rarely a matter of either the Union or the Member States having competence, but rather of establishing to what degree both have competence. Subsidiarity must therefore not be seen as restricting the analysis to the binary question of either the Union or the Member States acting. In that sense, it can function as a 'central and dynamic aspect' of the discussions between the Union and the Member States on what the appropriate level or levels of action are, and can form part of the constitutional practice of justification,[87] or indeed as a principle of 'cooperative federalism'.[88] Identifying the appropriate level of action often involves acknowledging the need for both levels to act with respect to certain aspects and to coordinate their action. As Advocate General Sharpston put it, 'the mixed agreement is itself a creature of pragmatic forces—a means of resolving the problems posed by the need for international agreements in a multi layered system'.[89]

---

[85] See De Baere, 'EU External Action' (n 54) 746–48.

[86] J Heliskoski, *Mixed Agreements as a Technique for Organizing the International Relations of the European Community and Its Member States* (The Hague, Kluwer Law International, 2001) 7. Further: C Hillion and P Koutrakos, *Mixed Agreements Revisited: The EU and Its Member States in the World* (Oxford, Hart, 2010). In Opinion 2/15 (n 55) para 29, the Court defined a mixed agreement simply as an agreement that has to be 'signed and concluded both by the European Union and by each of its Member States'.

[87] A Mills, 'Federalism in the European Union and the United States: Subsidiarity, Private Law and the Conflict of Laws' (2010) 32 *University of Pennsylvania Journal of International Law* 369, 382.

[88] R Schütze, *European Union Law* (Cambridge, Cambridge University Press, 2015) 253.

[89] C-240/09 *Lesoochranárske zoskupenie*, Opinion of AG Sharpston, EU:C:2010:436, point 56.

However, the dynamism and flexibility inherent in mixed agreements also have drawbacks, as was clear from the outset. Mixity was thoroughly discussed for the first time by the ECJ in Opinion 1/76.[90] The Court held that the part played by the then Community institutions in the bodies and organs set up by the agreement was 'extremely limited', and that all the most important functions were performed by the Member States.[91] It was also concerned that the applicable arrangements would become a model for future agreements, and that this would progressively and irreversibly undo the work of the Community.[92] The Court had thus spotted that the potential danger with mixed agreements lay in their tendency to tilt the balance of power to the advantage of the Member States as traditional subjects of international law, which in turn explains the attraction of mixed agreements for the Member States.[93] Timmermans has suggested that Opinion 1/76 should be read as confirming that when a proposed international agreement comes entirely within EU shared competences, specific reasons are needed to justify mixed external action.[94] Arguably, that reflection ought to be made on the basis of subsidiarity: does the optimal achievement of the objective of the international agreement and the Union's objective in concluding it require that the Union exercise its shared competence to cover the entire agreement, resulting in a sole Union agreement? Alternatively, does that optimal achievement require that the Union and its Member States conclude the agreement jointly, thus causing the Union only to exercise its shared competence over part of the agreement. If the objective is better achieved by the Union solely concluding the agreement, the insistence by the Member States to maintain the mixed character of the agreement may be considered as contrary to the principle of subsidiarity. Given that the unnecessary participation of the Member States in the conclusion of an international agreement may be making it more difficult or cumbersome for the Union to achieve its objectives, it may also be considered to violate the principle of loyalty or sincere cooperation as enshrined in Article 4(3) TEU,[95] which governs the resolution of such vertical competence conflicts with regard to internal as well as external competences.

Sincere cooperation is of great importance for the Union's external action and for its entire constitutional structure.[96] It requires the Union and the Member States to assist each other in full mutual respect in carrying out tasks that flow from

[90] Opinion 1/76 (Agreement on the establishment of a European Laying-up Fund for Inland Waterway Vessels) of 26 April 1977, EU:C:1977:63.

[91] ibid para 9.

[92] ibid para 14.

[93] cf M Cremona, 'The Doctrine of Exclusivity and the Position of Mixed Agreements in the External Relations of the European Community' (1982) 2 *OJLS* 393, 414.

[94] CWA Timmermans, 'Division of External Powers Between Community and Member States in the Field of Harmonization of National Law: A Case Study' in A Bleckmann, A Barav, JHJ Bourgeois and CWA Timmermans (eds), *Division of Powers Between the European Communities and Their Member States in the Field of External Relations* (Deventer, Kluwer, 1981) 20.

[95] cf P Eeckhout, *EU External Relations Law*, 2nd edn (Oxford, Oxford University Press, 2011) 216–17.

[96] See De Baere, 'EU External Action' (n 54) 748–49; and further De Baere and Roes, 'EU Loyalty as Good Faith' (n 11).

the Treaties. It is of general application and, in contrast with subsidiarity, does not depend on whether the Union competence concerned is exclusive.[97] Loyalty lies at the basis of the specific duty of cooperation in external action,[98] which in turn results from the requirement of unity in the Union's international representation.[99]

Crucially, and like subsidiarity, the duty of cooperation does not regulate the limits of EU competences, but their use.[100] Nevertheless, the ECJ has been steadily reinforcing loyalty's procedural obligations,[101] the strictures of which depend on the international context in which the Union and the Member States operate together. *PFOS* appears to indicate that if Member State action is likely to hinder, impede or otherwise affect Union external action, for example, by potentially committing the Union at international level, the Union must be involved and the Member States cannot act solely. Such action affects the Union in its entirety. It is therefore appropriate that such measures are not taken without the Union taking part in the decision. The duty of sincere cooperation must therefore be applied together with a non-dichotomous conception of subsidiarity in order to determine whether the Member States, the Union, or both are the appropriate level of action. In sum, when interpreted against the background of sincere cooperation, the apparent tension between subsidiarity and consistency can be mediated.

That can be illustrated by the manner in which subsidiarity is present in the implementation of EU external action. Union measures are, in the absence of specific provisions to the contrary, to be implemented by the Member States,[102] with due regard to sincere cooperation. This decentralised way of implementation, sometimes referred to as 'executive federalism',[103] can enhance the chances of measures achieving their effect. A general framework can thus be provided at EU level, while Member States provide local knowledge necessary for proper implementation.[104] That set-up accords with the spirit of subsidiarity. In internal matters, the Union's brand of 'executive federalism' operates on the basis that the Commission's role is intermediate and traditionally largely limited to the issuance of short-term regulations. The Member States are responsible for most implementation. By contrast, in ordinary EU external action the Commission generally plays a central role in 'on the ground' implementation. In the field of development cooperation, for example, the Commission actively oversees implementation. However, the Commission needs to coordinate in that regard with the HR, and the European External Action Service (EEAS) is to contribute to the programming

---

[97] *PFOS* (n 72) paras 69–71 and the case-law referred to therein.
[98] Ruling 1/78 [*Draft Convention of the IAEA*] of 14 November 1978, EU:C:1978:202, paras 33–34.
[99] Opinion 2/91 (n 71) para 36.
[100] See C Hillion, '*Tous pour un, un pour tous!* Coherence in the External Relations of the European Union' in M Cremona (ed), *Developments in EU External Relations Law* (Oxford, Oxford University Press, 2008) 10, 28.
[101] See, eg, Case C-459/03 *Commission v Ireland (Mox Plant)*, Judgment, EU:C:2006:345; Case C-266/03 *Commission v Luxembourg*, Judgment, EU:C:2005:341; Case C-433/03 *Commission v Germany*, Judgment, EU:C:2005:462; and *PFOS* (n 72).
[102] Article 291(1) TFEU.
[103] Lenaerts and Van Nuffel, *EU Law* (n 26) para 17-002; R Schütze, 'From Rome to Lisbon: "Executive Federalism" in the (New) European Union' (2010) 47 *CML Rev* 1385.
[104] See, eg, the common fisheries policy in HM Government (n 23) 58, para 2.38.

and management cycle for the relevant instruments. That said, the EEAS has a particular role in the programming, but the management of the Union's external cooperation programmes remains under the responsibility of the Commission, which implements the Union budget[105] and retains the authority over the operational credits.[106]

## C. Traces of Subsidiarity in External Action Measures

A preliminary examination of measures in the area of EU external action appears to indicate that, much as in EU law in general, subsidiarity, while in principle applicable, is somewhat hard to trace in specific actions taken by the Union or, if present, is only mentioned in a perfunctory manner. The tone was set in that regard from early on. For example, the Preamble to the Council Decision adopting a specific programme of research and technological development, including demonstration in the field of cooperation with third countries and international organisations, contains the following subsidiarity justification:

> Whereas the content of the fourth framework programme for Community RTD activities was established in accordance with the subsidiarity principle; whereas this specific programme specifies the content of the activities to be carried out in accordance with this principle in the area of cooperation with third countries and international organizations.[107]

That laconic style has remained essentially the same. Regulation 236/2014 is illustrative in that regard. The Preamble limits itself to the following standard formula:

> Since the objectives of this Regulation cannot be sufficiently achieved by the Member States but can rather, by reason of the scale and effects of the action, be better achieved at Union level, the Union may adopt measures, in accordance with the principle of subsidiarity as set out in Article 5 TEU. In accordance with the principle of proportionality, as set out in that Article, this Regulation does not go beyond what is necessary in order to achieve those objectives.[108]

Nevertheless, though few and far between, examples can also be found of more fully or at least differently reasoned subsidiarity justifications, as is illustrated by

---

[105] Article 317 TFEU.

[106] Article 9 of Council Decision 2010/427/EU of 26 July 2010 establishing the organisation and functioning of the EEAS [2010] OJ L201/30. See further on the EEAS–Commission relationship: J Wouters, G De Baere, B Van Vooren, K Raube, J Odermatt, T Ramopoulos, T Van den Sanden and Y Tanghe, *The Organisation and Functioning of the European External Action Service: Achievements, Challenges and Opportunities* (European Parliament, 2013) 46–57.

[107] Preamble to Council Decision 94/807/EC of 23 November 1994 adopting a specific programme of research and technological development, including demonstration in the field of cooperation with third countries and international organizations (1994 to 1998) [1994] OJ L334/109.

[108] Recital 21, Preamble to Regulation (EU) 236/2014 of the European Parliament and of the Council of 11 March 2014 laying down common rules and procedures for the implementation of the Union's instruments for financing external action [2014] OJ L77/95. See similar recitals in the Preambles to Regulations (EU) 231/2014, 232/2014 and 233/2014.

the Preamble to the Council Decision on the conclusion of the Convention for the protection of the marine environment of the north-east Atlantic, which provides:

> Whereas the Community has adopted measures in the area covered by the Convention and should therefore undertake international commitments in that area; whereas the Community's action is a necessary complement to that of the Member States directly concerned and its participation in the Convention would appear to comply with the principle of subsidiarity.[109]

That justification pertains ostensibly both to the existence (in the light of what would now be Article 216(1) TFEU) and to the exercise of EU competence (in the light of what is now Article 5(3) TEU). It therefore exemplifies what was said above on the intertwinement of the subsidiarity test and the test to establish the existence of implied external competences.

Subsidiarity has also featured in declarations of competence submitted by the Union upon accession to an international agreement or organisation. Notably, the declaration submitted by the then Community upon accession to the Hague Conference on Private International Law (HCPIL) notes:

> In areas which do not fall within its exclusive competence, the European Community shall take action, in accordance with the principle of subsidiarity, only if and insofar as the objectives of the proposed action cannot be sufficiently achieved by Member States and can therefore, by reason of the scale or effects of the proposed action, be better achieved by the European Community. Any action by the European Community shall not go beyond what is necessary to achieve the objectives.[110]

Whether that paragraph contributes to clarifying the division of competences between the Union and the Member States to other HCPIL members is doubtful.[111]

In addition, subsidiarity is sometimes mentioned not as an application of its specific incarnation in Article 5(3) TEU, but as part of an external policy goal. It can in that guise be found in a number of Association Council Decisions[112] or decisions establishing the EU position in such bodies.[113]

---

[109] Preamble to Council Decision 98/249/EC of 7 October 1997 on the conclusion of the Convention for the protection of the marine environment of the north-east Atlantic [1998] OJ L104/1.

[110] Declaration of competence of the European Community specifying the matters in respect of which competence has been transferred to it by its Member States Council, Annex II to Decision 2006/719/EC of 5 October 2006 on the accession of the Community to the Hague Conference on Private International Law [2006] OJ L297/1, para 3.

[111] *cf* P Koutrakos, *EU International Relations Law*, 2nd edn (Oxford, Hart, 2015) 176–77.

[112] See, eg, Art 1 of Decision 1/2012 of the EU–Montenegro Stabilisation and Association Council of 21 June 2011 amending Decision 1/2010 adopting the rules of procedure of the Stabilisation and Association Council, in view of setting up a Joint Consultative Committee between the European Economic and Social Committee and Montenegro's social partners and other civil society organisations and a Joint Consultative Committee between the Committee of the Regions of the European Union and Montenegrin local and regional authorities [2012] OJ L158/21, providing for dialogue and cooperation between the local and regional authorities in the EU and those in Montenegro, which is to be aimed, *inter alia*, at 'assisting Montenegrin local and regional authorities by means of information exchange on the practical implementation of the principle of subsidiarity in all aspects of life on local and regional level'.

[113] Sole Article of Council and Commission Decision 2013/489/EU (Euratom) of 22 July 2013 establishing the position to be taken on behalf of the European Union and the European Atomic Energy

Generally speaking, the style of subsidiarity justifications in EU external action measures remains troubling. In particular, while the token subsidiarity justifications in EU external action measures may in part be a symptom of a lack of rigour in that respect in EU law in general, it is worth asking the question whether EU external action is, at least from the perspective of the EU institutions, susceptible to passing the subsidiarity test with greater self-evidence than other areas of EU law. An example of that approach may be found in the judgment of the General Court (EGC) in *Ayadi*, which concerned the freezing of funds as part of a restrictive measures regime taken against persons and entities associated with Osama bin Laden, the Al-Qaeda network and the Taliban. In its judgment, the EGC held that the principle of subsidiarity could not 'be relied on in the sphere of application of Arts 60 TEC and 301 TEC [now Articles 75 and 215 TFEU], even on the assumption that it does not fall within the exclusive competence of the Community',[114] adding that:

> even assuming that the principle of subsidiarity finds application in circumstances such as those of this case, it is plain that the uniform implementation in the Member States of Security Council resolutions, which are binding on all members of the United Nations without distinction, can be better achieved at Community level than at national level.[115]

Finally, perhaps unsurprisingly, it is hard to track down specific references to subsidiarity in CFSP acts. That may be to a large extent explained by the fact that the 'spirit of subsidiarity' is part and parcel of CFSP decision-making. However, it is also tempting to conjecture that part of the reason resides in the fact that CFSP measures are excluded from scrutiny by national parliaments under the 'yellow and orange card' mechanism. That is so because the Protocol makes it plain that the mechanism applies to 'draft legislative acts',[116] while, the adoption of legislative acts is excluded in the CFSP.[117] Especially given the very limited role of the European Parliament in CFSP matters, the exclusion of proposals for CFSP acts from subsidiarity scrutiny by national parliaments is regrettable.

# IV. Conclusion

Subsidiarity as a constitutional principle governing the use of EU external competences, as laid down in Article 5(3) TEU, is unmistakeably structurally present

Community within the EU–Serbia Stabilisation and Association Council concerning a Decision of the EU–Serbia Stabilisation and Association Council adopting its rules of procedure [2013] OJ L278/1, providing for the identical set-up as in n 112 above.

[114] Case T-253/02 *Ayadi v Council*, Judgment, EU:T:2006:200, para 108.
[115] ibid para 112. The judgment was set aside by the ECJ on appeal, without ruling on the issue of subsidiarity: Joined Cases C-399/06P and C-403/06P *Hassan and Ayadi v Council and Commission*, Judgment, EU:C:2009:748.
[116] Article 3 of Protocol No 2.
[117] Article 24(1), second subpara TEU.

in EU external action. In particular, the essentially 'shared' character of most EU external action, requiring action both by the Member States and the Union, implies a conception of subsidiarity not limited to a binary either/or test, but allowing for the appropriate level of action to be the Member States, the Union, or—most commonly—the Member States and the Union acting in concert.

By emphasising sincere cooperation, the ECJ arguably embraces such a conception of non-exclusive competence not confined to external competences of the Member States and the Union in juxtaposition, but rather of a truly 'shared' competence, with regard to which the Union and the Member States need to cooperate and coordinate.[118] Nevertheless, such a conception of subsidiarity regarding the use of Union competences has no bearing on the limits of Union competences and hence on the division of competences between the Union and the Member States. As Advocate General La Pergola remarked: 'Coordination in fact requires that the bodies providing it should enjoy equal standing'.[119] That idea should also be structurally present in the ECJ's case-law, in particular in how compliance with subsidiarity is adjudged.

The most promising avenue to assess (judicially or otherwise) compliance with the subsidiarity principle is to focus on the procedural aspects of compliance in combination with the duty to state reasons. Nevertheless, the suboptimal manner in which subsidiarity justifications can be found in external action measures shows that there remains some distance to cover before the procedural manner for checking compliance with subsidiarity delivers on its promise. That remains the case as much (or more) in EU external action as in EU law as a whole.

Finally, given that the Union is to contribute to 'the strict observance and the development of international law',[120] a sound conception of EU subsidiarity must reject the competition between international and national or subnational levels. Instead, it should put forward a model of cooperation and assistance, transcending the dichotomy between the national or regional and international legal orders by including all levels of supra- and substate government in its analysis.[121] In that way, subsidiarity can coherently posit both that action should be taken at the most local level of government capable of achieving an objective (and hence put the burden of argument with attempts to centralise authority)[122] and that a more comprehensive body should intervene to the extent that the local level cannot sufficiently achieve an objective on its own. That presupposes the same non-binary conception of subsidiarity structurally ingrained in the Union's EU external action constitution.

---

[118] De Baere, *Constitutional Principles of EU External Relations* (n 50) 257.

[119] Case C-268/94 *Portugal v Council*, Opinion of AG La Pergola, EU:C:1996:207, point 19.

[120] Article 3(5) TEU.

[121] See regarding human rights: PG Carozza, 'Subsidiarity as a Structural Principle of International Human Rights Law' (2003) 97 *American Journal of International Law* 38, 65–68.

[122] A Føllesdal, 'The Principle of Subsidiarity as a Constitutional Principle in International Law' (2013) 2 *Global Constitutionalism* 37, 37–38.

# 6

# Conferral, Cooperation and Balance in the Institutional Framework of EU External Action

CHRISTOPHE HILLION

## I. Introduction

The European Union (EU) is equipped with an institutional framework to 'promote its values, advance its objectives, serve its interests, those of its citizens and those of its Member States and ensure the consistency, effectiveness and continuity of its policies and actions',[1] including on the external plane.[2] Several 'principles' structure the way this framework operates.[3] While each of the EU institutions 'shall act within the limits of the powers conferred on it in the Treaties, and in conformity with the procedures, conditions and objectives set out in them', they shall also 'practise mutual sincere cooperation'.[4]

Coined by the European Court of Justice as 'conferral', 'institutional balance' and 'cooperation',[5] the principles now enshrined in Article 13(2) of the Treaty on European Union have already been studied in the literature.[6] And yet their nature,

---

[1] Article 13(1) TEU.

[2] Articles 3(5) and 21(1–2) TEU.

[3] On the notion of 'structural principles' for the purpose of this study, see Marise Cremona, Chapter 1.

[4] Article 13(2) TEU.

[5] See eg Case C-409/13 *Council v Commission (Macro-Financial Assistance (MFA))*, Judgment, EU:C:2015:217, para 107.

[6] On conferral and institutional balance in particular: see, eg, G Guillermin, 'Le principe de l'équilibre institutionnel dans la jurisprudence de la CJCE' (1992) 119 *Journal du droit international* 319; S Prechal, 'Institutional Balance: A Fragile Principle with Uncertain Contents' in T Heukels, N Blokker and M Brus (eds), *The European Union After Amsterdam* (The Hague, Kluwer, 1998) 273; in P Craig and G de Búrca (eds), *The Evolution of EU Law* (Oxford, Oxford University Press, 1999) 55; K Lenaerts and A Verhoeven, 'Institutional Balance as a Guarantee for Democracy in EU Governance' in C Joerges and R Dehousse (eds), *Good Governance in the Internal Market* (Oxford, Oxford University Press, 2002) 35; JP Jacqué, 'The Principle of Institutional Balance' (2004) 41 *CML Rev* 383; P Craig, 'Institutions, Power and Institutional Balance' in P Craig and G de Búrca (eds), *The Evolution of EU Law*, 2nd edn (Oxford, Oxford University Press, 2011) 41; B Smulders and K Eisele, *Reflections on the Institutional Balance, the Community Method and the Interplay between Jurisdictions after Lisbon*, College of Europe Research Paper in Law 04/2012; M Chamon, 'The Institutional Balance, an Ill-fated Principle of EU Law' (2015) 21 *European Public Law* 371.

function and application remain fuzzy. Not only have their legal underpinnings evolved, the institutional system they govern and the constitutional context within which they apply have also changed, particularly following the entry into force of the Treaty of Lisbon.[7] Having codified part of the EU institutional *acquis*, the so-called 'Reform Treaty'[8] Thus altered the institutions' legal biotope, prompting novel interactions among them,[9] which have since then been catalysed by the crisis-management mode that has recently infused the EU decision-making process.[10]

This chapter therefore takes another look at these principles, especially as they operate in the context of the EU external action. Having examined their developing legal foundations and articulation (II), the analysis will turn to their application, in the light of the post-Lisbon case-law of the Court of Justice of the European Union (CJEU) (III). Through this essentially legal discussion, it will hopefully become clear that although they remain notionally distinct, the three principles have become increasingly interdependent in their definition and interwoven in their application. While the balance of powers remains primarily contingent on institutions' observance of the principle of conferral, it is also gradually more dependent on their mutual cooperation.

## II. Foundations and Articulation

The principles of conferral, institutional balance and cooperation have governed the operation of the EU institutional framework well before the Treaty of Lisbon brought them together in Article 13(2) TEU. This section traces their legal

---

[7] See, eg, M Dougan, 'The Treaty of Lisbon 2007: Winning Minds, Not Hearts' (2008) 45 *CML Rev* 617; P Van Elsuwege, 'EU External Action after the Collapse of the Pillar Structure: In Search of a New Balance Between Delimitation and Consistency' (2010) 47 *CML Rev* 987; JC Piris, *The Treaty of Lisbon* (Cambridge, Cambridge University Press, 2010); J Monar, 'The European Union's Institutional Balance of Power after the Treaty of Lisbon' in EB Irusta (ed), *The European Union after the Treaty of Lisbon: Visions of Leading Policy-makers, Academics and Journalists* (Luxembourg, Publications Office of the European Union, 2011) 60; T Christiansen, 'The European Union After the Lisbon Treaty: An Elusive "Institutional Balance"?' in A Biondi, P Eeckhout and S Ripley (eds), *EU Law After Lisbon* (Oxford, Oxford University Press, 2012) 228; S Blockmans and A Lazowski, 'Constitutional Foundations and EU Institutional Framework: Seven Years of Working with Lisbon Reform' in A Lazowski and S Blockmans (eds), *Research Handbook on EU Institutional Law* (Cheltenham, Edward Elgar, 2016) 13; M Chamon, 'Institutional Balance and Community Method in the Implementation of EU Legislation Following the Lisbon Treaty' (2016) 53 *CML Rev* 1501.

[8] See IGC 2007 Mandate, 11218/07 (26 June 2007).

[9] See, eg, Editorial Comments, 'The Post-Lisbon Institutional Package: Do Old Habits Die Hard?' (2010) 47 *CML Rev* 597; R Gosalbo Bono, 'The Organization of the External Relations of the European Union in the Treaty of Lisbon' in P Koutrakos (ed), *The European Union's External Relations a Year after Lisbon*, CLEER Working Papers 2011/3, 13; B Van Vooren and RA Wessel, *EU External Relations Law: Text, Cases and Materials* (Cambridge, Cambridge University Press, 2014).

[10] See, eg, the various contributions in M Dawson, H Enderlein and C Joerges (eds), *Beyond the Crisis: The Governance of Europe's Economic, Political, and Legal Transformation* (Oxford, Oxford University Press, 2015); M Dawson and F Witte, 'Constitutional Balance in the EU after the Euro Crisis' (2013) 76 *MLR* 817.

genealogy first by recalling how the Court of Justice initially articulated them by oblique references to the Treaties (A) and secondly, by deciphering their post-Lisbon formulation (B).

## A. Oblique Treaty Underpinnings

The treaty-based principle that institutions only act within the limits of their powers ('conferral')[11] underpins the principle of institutional balance. But the Court of Justice has progressively given the latter a broader content. The notion of *balance* entails that institutions have regard to the general 'role' each of them is deemed to play in the specific institutional system of the EU (i). The Court has in addition established a (complementary) inter-institutional duty to cooperate by reference to the Treaty-based obligation of sincere cooperation binding Member States (ii).

### (i) From Respect for Allocation of Powers to Institutional Balance

EU primary law does not explicitly refer to the notion of institutional balance.[12] Yet, the principle 'goes back a long way',[13] chiefly in the case-law of the European Court of Justice. In the early days of the European Coal and Steel Community (ECSC), the Court evoked a '*balance of powers* which is *characteristic* of the institutional structure of the Community' (emphasis added).[14] A hallmark of this structure is that its institutions have been endowed with distinct yet overlapping functions, representing different interests and constituencies,[15] and interacting differently at successive stages of policy-making in a manner that is partly at odds with the classic constitutional law notion of 'separation of powers'.[16] Yet, akin to the latter, the notion of 'balance' has primarily entailed that institutions could only act within the limits of their powers, subject to judicial control.[17]

---

[11] Though other formulations have been used for this principle, eg the 'principle of distribution of powers', see in Case C-660/13 *Council v Commission (Memorandum of Understanding)*, Opinion of AG Sharpston, EU:C:2015:787.

[12] The phrase was only mentioned in Protocol No 7 annexed to the Treaty of Amsterdam on the application of the principles of subsidiarity and proportionality, which states that '[t]he application of the principles of subsidiarity and proportionality shall respect the general provisions and objectives of the Treaty, particularly as regards … the institutional balance'.

[13] Jacqué, 'The Principle of Institutional Balance' (n 6) 383.

[14] Case 9/56 *Meroni*, Judgment, EU:C:1958:7.

[15] Further on this, see, eg, Lenaerts and Verhoeven, 'Institutional Balance as a Guarantee for Democracy in EU Governance' (n 6).

[16] See, eg, K Lenaerts, 'Some Reflections on the Separation of Powers in the European Community' (1991) 28 *CML Rev* 11; P Craig, *EU Administrative Law* (Oxford, Oxford University Press, 2006) 274; see also Case C-425/13 *Commission v Council*, Opinion of AG Wathelet, EU:C:2015:174, paras 102–3; Case C-282/10 *Dominguez*, Opinion of AG Trstenjak, EU:C:2011:559, paras 139–40.

[17] In Case 204/86 *Hellenic Republic v Council*, Judgment, Judgment, EU:C:1988:450 (1988), the Court emphasised (para 17) that 'the Community institutions possess a discretionary power which, however, is limited by the separation of powers, as laid down in the Treaty, between institutions.

That '[e]ach institution shall act within the limits of the powers conferred upon it by this Treaty' was indeed enshrined in Article 3 ECSC. It was replicated in Article 4(1) of the EEC Treaty, which subsequently became Article 7 EC included in Part 1 of the EC Treaty entitled 'Principles'. As a 'principle', conferral also governed the institutions' activities in the context of Community external relations. The Court of Justice thus annulled a contentious Commission's initiative de facto concluding an EC agreement with the United States of America, on the ground that only the Council was empowered to do so.[18] For the Court, the notion of balance is inherent in the distribution of powers among institutions, as envisaged by procedural arrangements set out in the Treaty. Hence, balance is primarily maintained if such distribution is respected, namely, if each institution acts within the limits of its powers, determined by reference to the powers of others.

The *relative* allocation of powers intrinsic to the notion of balance, found salient expressions in the litigation regarding the prerogatives of the European Parliament.[19] Safeguarding balance not only entailed enforcing the limits of each institutions' powers as set out in a particular procedure, but equally in consideration of a more systemic conception of each institution's 'role' in the EC institutional system. The Court's *Chernobyl* pronouncement typified this evolution:

> Those [Parliament's] prerogatives are one of the elements of the institutional balance created by the Treaties. The Treaties set up a system for distributing powers among the different Community institutions, assigning to each institution its own role in the institutional structure of the Community and the accomplishment of the tasks entrusted to the Community.

> Observance of the institutional balance means that each of the institutions must exercise its powers with due regard for the powers of the other institutions. It also requires that it should be possible to penalize any breach of that rule which may occur. ...

> The absence in the Treaties of any provision giving the Parliament the right to bring an action for annulment may constitute a procedural gap, but it cannot prevail over the fundamental interest in the maintenance and observance of the institutional balance laid down in the Treaties establishing the European Communities.[20]

The Court must therefore make sure that in the context of inter-institutional cooperation, the institutions do not ignore the rules of law and do not exercise their discretionary power in a manifestly wrong or arbitrary way'. See further JP Jacqué, 'Cours général de droit communautaire' in *Collected Courses of the Academy of European Law* (Dordrecht, Kluwer, 1990) vol 1, Book 1, 289.

[18] Case C-327/91 *France v Commission*, Judgment, EU:C:1994:305. The Court thus held that: '[Ex] 228 EEC [now Art 218 TFEU] constitutes, as regards the conclusion of treaties, an autonomous general provision, in that it confers specific powers on the Community institutions. *With a view to establishing a balance between those institutions*, it provides that agreements between the Community and one or more States are to be negotiated by the Commission and then concluded by the Council, after consulting the European Parliament where required by the Treaty. However, the power to conclude agreements is conferred on the Council "subject to the powers vested in the Commission in this field"' (emphasis added).

[19] Case 138/79 *Roquette Frères v Council*, Judgment, EU:C:1980:250, and Case 139/79 *Maizena GmbH v Council (Isoglucose)*, Judgment, EU:C:1980:249.

[20] Case C-70/88 *European Parliament v Council (Chernobyl)*, Judgment, EU:C:1990:217, paras 21, 22 and 26.

Having to act within the limits of its powers, an institution must equally *exercise* them having 'due regard' for the prerogatives of others, an obligation whose breach could be penalised. The Court thereby broadened the normative effect of the principle of institutional balance. It also pointed to a dynamic conception of power delimitation, informed by eg the evolving constitutional landscape within which each institution acts.[21]

In this broader conception of institutional balance, each institution's power is identified taking account of other institutions' powers in the context of a particular procedural arrangement, and more broadly in consideration of their 'role in the institutional structure of the [Union] and the accomplishment of the tasks entrusted to [it]'. The principle of conferral whereby limits of powers must be observed could thus be adjusted in consideration of 'the fundamental interest in the observance and maintenance of the institutional balance', the latter being invoked to fill a possible 'gap' in the functioning of the institutional system as a whole.[22] As will be shown below, it is that broader, if then more abstract and prescriptive notion of the 'role' of each institution that appears increasingly instrumental in the post-*Chernobyl* conception of the principle of institutional balance.

### (ii) From Member States' to Inter-institutional Duty of Sincere Cooperation

Akin to institutional balance, the principle of inter-institutional sincere cooperation had no express basis in EU primary law prior to the Lisbon Treaty. However, the EC Treaty and subsequently the Treaty on European Union (TEU) have included *specific* expressions of the institutions' duty to cooperate. For instance, pre-Lisbon Article 3 TEU foresaw that the Council and the Commission had to cooperate so as to ensure the consistency of EU external activities.

Moreover, the Court of Justice gradually articulated a *general* obligation of cooperation binding institutions. The Court began by reciprocating the primarily Member States' treaty-based obligation to cooperate with the Union in the fulfilment of its tasks. In a case in which Luxembourg contested a resolution of the European Parliament on the seat of the Community's institutions, European judges referred to '*mutual* duties of sincere cooperation, as embodied in particular in [then] Article 5 EEC',[23] a provision which, like Article 4 EEC on conferral, was included in Part 1 of the EEC Treaty, entitled 'Principles'. Having recalled Member States' duties to cooperate with institutions, the Court held that:

> in accordance with the above-mentioned mutual duties of sincere cooperation, the *decisions of the Parliament in turn must have regard to the power of the Governments of the*

---

[21] See also Case 294/83 *Parti écologiste 'Les Verts' v European Parliament*, Judgment, EU:C:1986:166. Further on this notion see, eg, Jacqué, 'The Principle of Institutional Balance' (n 6).

[22] Further on this point, see, eg, Chamon, 'The Institutional Balance, an Ill-fated Principle of EU Law' (n 6) and Craig, *EU Administrative Law* (n 16).

[23] Case 230/81 *Luxembourg v European Parliament*, Judgment, EU:C:1983:32.

*Member States* to determine the seat of the institutions and to the provisional decisions taken in the meantime. (emphasis added)[24]

The institutions' *mutual* duties of cooperation thus rested on the general principle of sincere cooperation, now enshrined in Article 4(3) TEU, even if textually the latter only bound the Member States. It is noticeable that the Court of Justice referred to the duty of sincere cooperation as the basis for an obligation for institutions to 'have regard to the power' of the Member States' governments. As noted earlier, the requirement that institutions have 'due regard' for each other's powers, was derived from the principle of institutional balance. That this obligation could also be an expression of the institutions' obligation of cooperation illustrates the close connection between institutional balance and sincere cooperation, which will be further discussed below.[25]

The Court of Justice also enunciated an obligation of cooperation *between institutions*. In the *Hellenic Republic v Council* case[26] relating to the 'compulsory' v 'non-compulsory' classification of a Community aid to Turkey, the Court relied on a Declaration on an 'inter-institutional dialogue' and conciliation procedure aimed at handling such complex matters to craft a specific inter-institutional duty of cooperation.[27] The complexity of the budgetary procedure, and the explicit institutions' commitments to cooperate, viewed as 'essential to the smooth operation of the Community', provided the normative grounds for the judicial acknowledgement of the duty of sincere cooperation binding institutions *inter se*. Indicating that the latter was an extension of the general duty of sincere cooperation, and elaborating upon the *Luxembourg* judgment cited above, the Court held that inter-institutional dialogue underpinning the budgetary procedure was 'subject to the *same mutual duties of sincere cooperation* which ... govern relations between the Member States and the Community institutions' (emphasis added).[28]

Indeed, the Court gradually generalised the inter-institutional duty of cooperation. Building on the above pronouncement, the *GSP* judgment[29] referred to an 'obligation to cooperate sincerely' which, *in casu*, obliged the European Parliament vis-à-vis the Council. The Parliament challenged a Council Regulation aimed at extending for another year the application of several Regulations 'applying generalized tariff preferences in respect of certain products originating in developing countries, and adding to the list of beneficiaries of such preferences'. The Parliament claimed that the Council breached an essential procedural requirement

---

[24] ibid para 38.
[25] See section II A (iii) below.
[26] *Hellenic Republic v Council* (n 17) paras 15–16.
[27] ibid.
[28] The mutual character of the Member States–EU principle of cooperation was reaffirmed in Case C-45/07 *Commission v Greece (IMO)*, Judgment, EU:C:2009:81. It is also more explicit in its post-Lisbon formulation, *viz.* Art 4(3) TEU, whose first sentence foresees that '[p]ursuant to the principle of sincere cooperation, the Union and the Member States shall, in full mutual respect, assist each other in carrying out tasks which flow from the Treaties'.
[29] Case C-65/93 *Parliament v Council (GSP)*, Judgment, EU:C:1995:91.

when adopting the regulation without waiting for its opinion. In its defence, the Council argued that the Parliament had failed to cooperate by not delivering its opinion on time for it to adopt the envisaged regulation, and thus to guarantee that the Generalised Scheme of Preferences (GSP) would continue to operate in favour of developing countries. The Court agreed with the Council, based on a reasoning worth recalling in full:

> [T]he Court has held that *inter-institutional dialogue*, on which the consultation procedure in particular is based, is subject to the *same mutual duties of sincere cooperation as those which govern relations between Member States and the Community institutions* (see Case 204/86 *Greece v Council* [1988] ECR 5323, paragraph 16).
>
> In this case, it is undisputed that the Council informed the President of the Parliament in its letter of 22 October 1992 of the need to adopt the contested regulation before the end of 1992, so as to enable it to enter into force on 1 January 1993. It is also undisputed that, having regard to the special relations between the Community and the developing countries and to the difficulties, both political and technical, which would result from an abrupt interruption in the application of generalized tariff preferences, that request was justified. ...
>
> [T]he documents before the Court show that, notwithstanding the assurances ... given to the Council, the Parliament decided ... to adjourn the plenary session ... without having debated the proposal for the regulation. It appears, moreover, that that decision was based on reasons wholly unconnected with the contested regulation and did not take into account the urgency of the procedure and the need to adopt the regulation before 1 January 1993.
>
> By adopting that course of action, *the Parliament failed to discharge its obligation to cooperate sincerely with the Council ...*
>
> In those circumstances, the Parliament is not entitled to complain of the Council's failure to await its opinion before adopting the contested regulation of 21 December 1992. *The essential procedural requirement of Parliamentary consultation was not complied with because of the Parliament's failure to discharge its obligation to cooperate sincerely with the Council.* (emphasis added)[30]

From a specific inter-institutional dialogue in the budgetary context, the Court thus articulated a more general binding 'obligation', irrespective of whether institutions expressed a prior commitment to cooperate.[31] It also confirmed that sincere cooperation between institutions entails the 'same mutual duties of sincere cooperation which ... govern relations between the Member States and the Community institutions', implicitly maintaining the connection with the Treaty basis of the principle of sincere cooperation.

---

[30] ibid paras 23–28.
[31] The Court's phraseology as to what cooperation entails in normative terms is not always consistent, as indeed with respect to the principle of cooperation based on Art 10 EC. Thus, in Case C-29/99 *Commission v Council*, Judgment, EU:C:2002:734, the Court refers to 'the *duty* of sincere cooperation between the institutions' by referring to the *GSP* case, while in the latter it talks about 'obligation'.

*In casu*, the Parliament's failure to provide its opinion for 'reasons wholly unconnected with the contested regulation' hampered the adoption of the regulation, thus jeopardising the Community development policy. For the Court, such misconduct amounted to the Parliament's failure to discharge its obligation to cooperate sincerely with the Council, a failure which entailed significant legal consequences. The European Parliament had thus forfeited its ability to exercise its consultative power, and the Council could lawfully proceed without waiting for the Parliament's opinion. It is noticeable, and understandable given the particular circumstances of the case, that the Court accepted that the Council could take, on its own authority, corrective measures to obviate the breach, in the sense that it did not have to use the Treaty mechanisms which could have allowed it to challenge the Parliament's failure.[32] It is all the more remarkable since the Court had hitherto developed a jurisprudence that was particularly supportive of the Parliament's prerogatives. The *GSP* case thus underscores the significance the Court attributed to inter-institutional cooperation.

In the light of the above, the purpose of the obligation of inter-institutional cooperation is seemingly twofold. First, it aims at preserving the integrity of the institutional framework and the institutional balance it establishes. Akin to the requirement of due regard stemming from the principle of institutional balance, the obligation of cooperation complements the principle of conferral to ensure that in exercising its powers, each institution acts in a way that does not undermine the power of others and thus preserves the Treaty-based institutional balance. The other purpose of sincere cooperation, which is linked to the previous one, is to ensure that the institutional framework fulfils its aims of assisting the Union in fulfilling its tasks. This means that the obligation of cooperation could be invoked against an institution on the ground that the latter action or inaction jeopardises the attainment of the Union's objectives or fails to facilitate the achievement of its tasks.[33] The *GSP* case thus indicates that the Parliament's inaction (ie failure to deliver its opinion to the Council on time) risked undermining the GSP system as such, which was an important element of the EU development policy. While the Court held that the 'Parliament failed to discharge its obligation to cooperate sincerely with the Council', this failure could also affect the Union as a whole, as indeed suggested by the Court's reference to 'the special relations between the Community and the developing countries and to the difficulties, both political and technical, which would result from an abrupt interruption in the application of generalized tariff preferences'.[34]

---

[32] *cf* Case 45/07 *Commission v Hellenic Republic*, Judgment, EU:C:2009:81, para 26.

[33] *cf* M Cremona, 'EU Treaty Making: A Test Case for Mutual Sincere Cooperation?' in J Czuczai and F Naert (eds), *The EU as a Global Actor: Bridging Legal Theory and Practice, Liber Amicorum in Honour of Ricardo Gosalbo Bono* (Leiden, Brill, 2017), and Case 28/12 *Commission v Council (Hybrid Act)*, Opinion of AG Tizzano, EU:C:2015:43.

[34] *GSP* (n 29) para 24.

## B.  Partial Codification by the Treaty of Lisbon

As discussed in the previous section, the Court of Justice elaborated the principles of institutional balance and inter-institutional cooperation relying on the treaty-based principles of conferral and obligation of sincere cooperation binding Member States, respectively. The Treaty of Lisbon partly codified these judge-made notions. In particular, Article 13(2) TEU elaborates the principle of conferral in a manner which may provide a more solid legal basis for the principle of institutional balance (i), while the provision codifies and arguably bolsters the institutions' obligation to cooperate (ii).

### (i)  Treaty 'Reflection' of the Principle of Institutional Balance

Despite the Treaties' enduring silence on the notion of institutional balance, the Court of Justice has reiterated its significance as a principle governing the EU's institutional framework. Indeed, as will become evident, its violation has been a recurrent plea in the post-Lisbon inter-institutional litigation in the field of external relations. In what has become a standard paragraph, the Court has thus held that:

> under Article 13(2) TEU, each institution is to act within the limits of the powers conferred on it in the Treaties, and in conformity with the procedures, conditions and objectives set out in them. *That provision reflects the principle of institutional balance,* characteristic of the institutional structure of the European Union, a principle *which requires that each of the institutions must exercise its powers with due regard for the powers of the other institutions.* (emphasis added)[35]

The existence of a '*principle* of institutional balance' has therefore been reaffirmed. The Court has also shed further light on its Treaty underpinnings, by linking it explicitly to the first sentence of Article 13(2) TEU and the principle of conferral it encapsulates. While the phrase 'reflects'[36] does not immediately entail that Article 13(2) TEU constitutes the very legal foundation of institutional balance,[37] the Court has nevertheless made this point clearer, at least occasionally, when considering that, akin to the principle of conferral, the principle of institutional balance is '*laid down* in Article 13(2) TEU' (emphasis added).[38]

---

[35]  *MFA* (n 5) para 64. See also eg, Case C-73/14 *Council v Commission (ITLOS)*, Judgment, EU:C:2015:663, para 61; Case C-425/13 *Commission v Council (ETS)*, Judgment, EU:C:2015:483, para 69; Case C-660/13 *Council v Commission (Memorandum of Understanding)*, Judgment, EU:C:2016:616, para 32.

[36]  Translated as '*traduit*' in the French version of Art 13(2) TEU.

[37]  In several judgments, the Court (and litigants) distinguishes the principle of conferral and/or Art 13(2) TEU, on the one hand, from the principle of institutional balance, on the other. See, eg, *ETS* (n 35); *Memorandum of Understanding* (n 35).

[38]  In its French version, para 95 of *MFA* (n 5) reads: '[P]rincipe d'attribution de compétences (…) principe de l'équilibre institutionnel, *consacrés* à l'article 13, paragraphe 2, TUE' (emphasis added): the plural form of the word '*consacrés*' confirms that the latter relates to both principles of conferral and institutional balance.

In substance, the first sentence of Article 13(2) TEU, which is held to reflect the principle of institutional balance, appears to combine the two slightly distinct pre-Lisbon provisions governing the operation of the institutional framework. In particular, it brings together the succinct dispensation of conferral enshrined in previous Article 7 EC,[39] and the pre-Lisbon Article 5 TEU (included in then Title I 'Common Provisions' TEU) according to which: '[the institutions] shall exercise their powers under the conditions and for the purposes provided for ... by the provisions of the [Treaties])'.

Article 13(2) TEU thus amalgamates several structural principles that govern the *demarcation* and the *exercise* of powers, respectively. Indeed, in referring to the institutions' duty to act 'in conformity with the procedures, conditions and objectives set out in them', the Treaty provision further spells out how institutions' powers ought to be envisaged, arguably in line with the broader requirement deriving from the principle of institutional balance previously articulated by the Court.

In particular, the first sentence allows for a contextual and dynamic conception of institutions' powers in the sense that the latter are determined not only by the static prescriptions of a specific 'procedure' laid down in a legal basis, but also in consideration of the 'conditions' and 'objectives set out *in them*', (emphasis added) *viz* the Treaties more generally. This phrasing arguably 'reflects' the requirement that each institution act with 'due regard' for the powers of others as envisaged in a procedure, but also in consideration of their role in the institutional system. Also, the reference to 'objectives set out in [the Treaties]' allows for a purposive approach to institutions' powers. It requires that each of their actions corresponds to the aims for which a power is conferred, and thus points to the requirement of effectiveness 'in the accomplishment of the tasks entrusted to the Union' evoked in the *Chernobyl* pronouncement,[40] and now envisaged in Article 13(1) TEU. Indeed, the most recent institutional balance case-law makes the connection with the *Chernobyl* jurisprudence more explicit. Hence, in its *Memorandum of Understanding* decision, the Court inserted a paragraph before the usual mantra on Article 13(2) TEU and institutional balance, according to which:

> It must be borne in mind ... that the Treaties set up a system allocating powers among the EU institutions, assigning to each institution its own role in the institutional structure of the Union and the accomplishment of the tasks entrusted to the Union (see, to that effect, judgment of 22 May 1990 in *Parliament v Council*, C-70/88, EU:C:1990:217, paragraph 21).[41]

While 'reflected' by the first sentence of Article 13(2) TEU, the principle of institutional balance also finds further legal articulation in Title III of the TEU, entitled

---

[39] See section I A (i) above.
[40] See, eg, the *GSP* case (n 29). Also in this regard, see the argument of the Council and intervening Member States in *ETS* (n 35) para 45.
[41] *Memorandum of Understanding* (n 35) para 31.

'Provisions on Institutions'. Drawing upon the defunct Constitutional Treaty, and inspired by the aim of simplification prescribed by the Laeken Declaration on the Future of the European Union,[42] this Title consists of an entirely new cluster of provisions on the EU institutional framework. Composed of seven articles including Article 13 TEU, Title III TEU enunciates the respective roles of most institutions envisaged in Article 13(1) TEU, as well as those of the High Representative for Foreign Affairs and Security Policy.[43] In spelling out the core functions of each institution, these provisions give further legal substance to what the Court referred to in *Chernobyl* as the 'system for distributing powers among the different [EU] institutions, assigning to each institution *its own role in the institutional structure* of the [Union] and the accomplishment of the tasks entrusted to the Union' (emphasis added). Title III thus fleshes out the notion of institutional balance.

The addition of new set of Treaty articles on institutions has unsurprisingly triggered a wave of litigation to clarify the intended clarification. Being themselves the object of inter-institutional strife,[44] the provisions of Title III TEU have also been used by litigants, and by the Court for (re)interpreting specific institutions' prerogatives. This has been particularly true in the context of the EU treaty-making procedure.

In the *ETS* case, for example,[45] the Commission contested various elements of the Council Decision authorising it to open negotiations with Australia for linking the latter's emissions trading system with that of the EU. It argued that the detailed procedural arrangements contained in the Council Decision and its Annex granted excessive powers to the Council and to the special committee foreseen by Article 218(4) TFEU, thereby encroaching on those the Treaties conferred on the Commission as negotiator. The latter thus claimed that the Council had infringed Article 13(2) TEU and the principle of institutional balance.

The Court of Justice began its analysis by mentioning Article 218(4) TFEU, considering that it 'constitute[d] the principal provision to be referred to for the purpose of demarcation of the powers conferred, respectively, on the Council and the special committee and on the Commission'. But it immediately added a reference to Article 17(1) TEU and to the Commission's responsibility to ensure the EU external representation that it foresees.[46] Its interpretation of the Commission's negotiating power under Article 218(4) TFEU thus seemingly took account of the latter's representative role as stipulated in Title III TEU. Indeed, the

---

[42] See Annexes to the Presidency Conclusions, Laeken, 14 and 15 December 2001.

[43] Title III thus covers the European Parliament (Art 14 TEU); European Council (Art 15); the Council (Art 16); the Commission (Art 17); the High Representative for Foreign Affairs and Security Policy (Art 18); and the Court of Justice (Art 19). A slight discrepancy is thus noticeable between the list of institutions included in Art 13(1) and the content of Title III TEU, also because it does not cover the European Central Bank or the Court of Auditors. See discussion in section II B below.

[44] See, eg, the interface between Arts 16 and 17 TEU in *ITLOS* (n 35), and the scope of Art 17 TEU in *Memorandum of Understanding* (n 35); see further below.

[45] *ETS* (n 35).

[46] ibid para 63.

subsequent analysis examined whether the contested Council Decision 'contain[ed] other provisions which, while being procedural in nature, [were] *liable to deny the negotiator the power which it is granted in Article 17(1) TEU*' (emphasis added).[47]

The *Mauritius* case provides another illustration of the significance of Title III TEU in the Court's interpretation of institutions' powers.[48] The European Parliament contested the legality of a Council Decision on the signing and conclusion of a Common Foreign and Security Policy (CFSP) agreement between the EU and the Republic of Mauritius. In particular, the Parliament claimed that 'by failing to inform it "immediately and fully" at all stages of the negotiations and of the conclusion of the ... Agreement, the Council infringed Article 218(10) TFEU', which allegedly applied to all EU agreements, including those falling within the CFSP.[49] The Council considered such plea inadmissible inasmuch as the impugned decision was a CFSP act falling outside the Court's limited jurisdiction in this area, as foreseen in Articles 24(1) TEU and 275(2) TFEU. Referring to Article 19 included in Title III TEU, the Court, however, responded to the Council claim as follows:

> [I]t is apparent from the final sentence of the second subparagraph of Article 24(1) TEU and the first paragraph of Article 275 TFEU that the Court does not, in principle, have jurisdiction with respect to the provisions relating to the CFSP or with respect to acts adopted on the basis of those provisions.

> Nevertheless, the final sentence of the second subparagraph of Article 24(1) TEU and the first paragraph of Article 275 TFEU introduce a *derogation from the rule of the general jurisdiction which Article 19 TEU confers on the Court* to ensure that in the interpretation and application of the Treaties the law is observed, and they must, therefore, be interpreted narrowly. (emphasis added)[50]

The judgment, and the subsequent *Tanzania* pronouncement concerning a similar EU CFSP agreement with Tanzania, also suggest, albeit less explicitly, that the Parliament's function set out in Title III TEU was considered when envisaging its right to be informed provided in Article 218(10) TFEU. The Court thus held that the aim of that information requirement was:

> inter alia, to ensure that the Parliament is in a position *to exercise democratic control over the European Union's external action* and, more specifically, to verify that the choice made of the legal basis for a decision on the conclusion of an agreement was made *with due regard to the powers of the Parliament*' (emphasis added)

adding that it allows it 'to exercise its own powers with full knowledge of the European Union's external action as a whole'.[51] The Court's terminology thus

---

[47] ibid para 79.
[48] Case C-658/11 *Parliament v Commission (Mauritius)*, Judgment, EU:C:2014:2025.
[49] ibid para 64.
[50] ibid paras 69–70.
[51] Case C-263/14 *Parliament v Council (Tanzania)*, Judgment, EU:C:2016:435.

partly echoed the terms of Article 14 TEU according to which the Parliament 'shall exercise functions of political control and consultation as laid down in the Treaties'. Indeed, in underlining that the information requirement of Article 218(10) TFEU was also a way to ensure 'due regard' to the Parliament's powers, the Court also indicated that it contributed to secure compliance with the principle of institutional balance.

The distribution of powers specific to a policy area, here the CFSP, and the expression of institutional balance encapsulated in related legal bases was interpreted in consideration of the general provisions of Title III TEU, and the essential *role* of each institution which they envisage. This is all the more remarkable here since the TEU otherwise requires that the integrity of the specific CFSP institutional arrangements be protected.[52]

The provisions of Title III TEU have been equally instrumental in interpreting the role of the institutions operating within the ordinary legislative procedure. Hence, in the *MFA* case,[53] the Court had to determine whether and how the Commission could withdraw a proposal for a regulation submitted to the Council and the Parliament, laying down general provisions for macro-financial assistance to third countries. The Court found that:

> The power of legislative initiative accorded to the Commission by Articles 17(2) TEU and 289 TFEU means that it is for the Commission to decide whether or not to submit a proposal for a legislative act, except in the situation, not material to the present case, where it would be obliged under EU law to submit such a proposal. By virtue of that power, if a proposal for a legislative act is submitted it is also for the Commission, which, in accordance with Article 17(1) TEU, is to promote the general interest of the European Union and take appropriate initiatives to that end, to determine the subject-matter, objective and content of that proposal.[54]

Title III TEU thus helped again in articulating the notion of institutional balance. As its provisions spell out the primary 'role' of each institution in the system of allocation of powers, it may influence the Court's interpretation of specific procedural arrangements and of the particular expression of institutional balance they may otherwise contain elsewhere in the Treaties, or indeed when there are no other specific provisions.[55]

The manner in which Title III TEU effectively inspires the Court's interpretation of other institutional provisions, however, remains ambiguous. While its location in the system of the Treaties grants it an important interpretative function for TEU provisions, it is nevertheless not ascribed any principled pre-eminence over specific institutional provisions located in the TFEU. Instead, the third indent of Article 1 TEU recalls that the two Treaties (*viz* TEU and TFEU) shall have the same legal value, while Article 40 TEU requires that the differentiation between

---

[52] Article 40(2) TEU; see discussion further below.
[53] *MFA* (n 5).
[54] ibid para 70.
[55] *Memorandum of Understanding* (n 35).

the institutional arrangements for exercising TFEU-based and CFSP competence, respectively, be observed.

The Court thereby enjoys a degree of discretion in articulating the interface between Title III TEU and specific TEU and TFEU- based procedures, and in turn in refining the functioning of the EU institutional system. Indeed, the emerging post-Lisbon case law discloses different possible approaches. Specific Treaty procedures associated with policy fields (eg CFSP) may operate as institutional *lex specialis*, with Title III TEU operating as *lex generalis*, the former in principle prevailing over the latter. Hence in the first post-Lisbon case involving inter-institutional disagreement in the field of external relations, namely the *Smart Sanction* case,[56] the Court showed deference to the Member States' constitutional choice to limit the role of the European Parliament in the context of the CFSP. The latter's procedural arrangements prevailed over the essential role the European Parliament had been endowed with in the general EU context. No reference was made to its general function of political control, let alone to the provisions of Article 14 TEU. Instead, the Court opined that:

> the difference between Article 75 TFEU and Article 215 TFEU, so far as the Parliament's involvement is concerned, is the result of the choice made by the framers of the Treaty of Lisbon conferring a more limited role on the Parliament with regard to the Union's action under the CFSP.[57]

But specific procedural arrangements may also be interpreted in the light of the 'general' distribution of powers that Title III TEU foresees,[58] or even be conceived as exception to the general institutional rules which this Title contains, and as such be interpreted restrictively. This is what the *Mauritius* pronouncement, mentioned earlier, suggests.[59] It will be recalled that the Court of Justice held that Article 19 TEU, enshrined in Title III TEU, establishes the principle of general jurisdiction of the Court of Justice within the EU legal order, to which the specific judicial arrangements of Article 24(1) TEU regarding the CFSP constitute a derogation.[60] The question could thus be raised as to whether the same logic could be applied, *mutatis mutandis*, with respect to other provisions contained in Title III TEU. Since Article 24(1) TEU similarly foresees a 'specific role of the European Parliament and of the Commission in this area', could the Court regard this as derogation to their general functions enshrined in Title III TEU, and thus to be understood restrictively? Or would this be incompatible with the stipulation

---

[56] Case C-130/10 *Parliament v Council (Smart Sanctions)*, Judgment, EU:C:2012:472.

[57] ibid para 82.

[58] See, eg, the argument of the Council in *Memorandum of Understanding*, mentioned in Sharpston's Opinion (n 11) para 91; she also refers to Arts 16 and 17 TEU, included in Title III, as containing 'the *general* distribution of powers' (emphasis added).

[59] See *Mauritius* (n 48) para 69 *et seq.*

[60] The rule has been confirmed since in Case C-455/14 P *H v Council and Commission*, Judgment, EU:C:2016:569, para 40.

of Article 40(2) TEU that the institutional and procedural integrity of the CFSP be preserved?[61]

The same *Mauritius* judgment gives a hint on this point. The Court found that the powers of the European Parliament, and notably that of democratic scrutiny via its right of information based on Article 218(10) TFEU, had to be observed also as regards the negotiation and conclusion of CFSP agreements despite the Treaty-based limitations on its role in this area. Acknowledging that the role which the Treaty of Lisbon has conferred on the Parliament in relation to the CFSP remains limited, the Court nevertheless held that:

> it cannot be inferred from that fact that despite its exclusion from the procedure for negotiating and concluding an agreement relating exclusively to the CFSP, the Parliament has no right of scrutiny in respect of that EU policy,

adding that:

> [o]n the contrary, it is precisely for that purpose that the information requirement laid down in Article 218(10) TFEU applies to any procedure for concluding an international agreement, including agreements relating exclusively to the CFSP.[62]

The Court did not restrict the application of Article 218(10) TFEU, as specific expression of the Parliament's general function of democratic control, by reference to other specific institutional arrangements applying to other stages of the EU treaty-making procedure, or to provisions set out in the CFSP chapter.

It further specified its approach in the subsequent *Tanzania* case, which seemingly took account of the European Parliament's circumscribed role in the field of CFSP. Having reiterated that the Parliament must be informed at all stages of the procedure, it then underlined that:

> the fact that its participation in the negotiation and conclusion of agreements falling exclusively within the scope of the CFSP is specifically excluded means that that information requirement does not extend to stages that are part of the internal preparatory process within the Council.[63]

In other words, the limited role of the Parliament in the CFSP field could still influence the scope of information it is entitled to obtain, and thus the democratic

---

[61] Article 17(1) TEU itself contains an exception to the general responsibility of the European Commission to represent the EU externally. This exception concerns, *inter alia*, the CFSP, the representation of the EU in this area being the responsibility of the President of the European Council and of the High Representative for Foreign Affairs and Security Policy, in accordance with other provisions of Title III (*viz* Art 15(5)(d) TEU, and Art 27(2) TEU). Given that it is Art 17 TEU itself that contains that exception, it could be wondered whether it would be understood restrictively along the same lines as for exceptions located elsewhere in the Treaties.

[62] *Mauritius* (n 48) paras 83–85. P Van Elsuwege, 'Securing the Institutional Balance in the Procedure for Concluding International Agreements: *European Parliament v. Council (Pirate Transfer Agreement with Mauritius)*' (2015) 52 *CML Rev* 1379.

[63] *Tanzania* (n 51) para 77; S Sánchez-Tabernero, 'Mitigating the Effects of Gravity in Competence Demarcation Through the Principle of Consistency: *Parliament v Council (Pirate-Transfer Agreement with Tanzania)*' (2017) 54 *CML Rev* 899.

scrutiny it exercises in that area.[64] The Court seemingly attempted to reconcile the *Smart Sanction* case-law in terms of respecting the choice of the Treaty drafters as regards the limited powers of the Parliament in the CFSP,[65] and the *Mauritius* approach whereby the Parliament must be able to exercise democratic control over the EU external action as a whole.[66]

That said, in considering that the Parliament's right of information 'does not extend to stages that are part of the internal preparatory process within the Council', the Court's approach could be understood as this: it is only access to information *outside* the formal procedure of Article 218 TFEU that is affected by the CFSP-based limitations of Article 24(1) TEU. Once the procedure is formally activated, triggering what the Court has otherwise called a 'closely circumscribed process of concerted action and consultation between institutions',[67] the obligation of paragraph 10 is fully applicable: the Parliament shall then be 'immediately and fully informed at *all stages of the procedure*', stages which the Court indeed spelled out in its pronouncement.[68] Another reading, namely, that the scope of the obligation of Article 218(10) TFEU *itself* should be adapted in consideration of Article 24(1) TEU, would be more difficult to support, and would certainly deserve more solid justification than the judgment offers as it would be a departure from its earlier *Mauritius* approach.[69] In particular, how can an obligation established by Article 218(10) TFEU, which unlike other elements of the procedure does not foresee any differentiation in its application in consideration of the policy context, be nevertheless modulated based on a provision belonging to the

---

[64] Indeed, a slight change in the formulation of the European Parliament's right to scrutiny is noticeable in the first quoted paragraph, compared to the *Mauritius* pronouncement: in the latter judgment, the Court considered that 'it cannot be inferred ... that the EP has *no* right of scrutiny', whereas it uses the phrase 'deprived of any' in *Tanzania*. In referring to 'any', the Court allows for a *degree* of scrutiny that might differ from the one exercised in other policy contexts, whereas the former formulation was more binary: it entailed that the Parliament had the right of scrutiny also in the CFSP field, which could be the same as in other fields.

[65] *Smart Sanctions* (n 56).

[66] *Tanzania* (n 51) para 70–71.

[67] See *ETS* (n 35) para 64.

[68] *Tanzania* (n 51) paras 75–76 (emphasis added). At para 76 of the judgment the Court indicated that 'with respect to the scope of the information obligation covered by that provision, it must be stated that the procedure for negotiating and concluding international agreements laid down in Article 218 TFEU includes, *inter alia*, the authorization to open negotiations, the definition of the negotiating directives, the nomination of the Union negotiator and, in some cases, the designation of a special committee, the completion of negotiations, the authorization to sign the agreement, where necessary, the decision on the provisional application of the agreement before its entry into force and the conclusion of the agreement'.

[69] In his Opinion in the *Mauritius* case, AG Bot had suggested to adjust the intensity of the information obligation depending on the Parliament's involvement in the procedure for the conclusion of international agreements. Hence, since the Parliament has no role in negotiation and conclusion of CFSP agreements, its right to information could consequently be more limited (C-658/11 *Parliament v Council*, Opinion of AG Bot, EU:C:2014:41, paras 142–45).

CFSP? This would indeed be difficult to reconcile with what the Court recalled earlier in the same judgment, that:

> the obligation, prescribed in Article 218(10) TFEU, to ensure that the Parliament is immediately and fully informed at all stages of the procedure for the conclusion of an international agreement also extends to the stages that precede the conclusion of such an agreement, and therefore covers, in particular, the negotiation phase.[70]

The foregoing indicates that, although it does not explicitly refer to the principle of institutional balance, the Treaty of Lisbon, as interpreted by the Court since, has consolidated its legal underpinnings, through a wider formulation of the principle of conferral from which it stems. The post-Lisbon EU primary law, which also includes the rationalisation of the decision- and treaty-making procedures,[71] and delegation of powers,[72] could also contribute to making the notion of institutional balance less abstract, and possibly less contestable than it used to be.[73] In particular, the provisions of Title III TEU, and the general institutional balance they incarnate, have already helped fulfil the gap-filling function that the Court ascribed to the notion of institutional balance in case of an 'absence in the Treaties of [a] provision [amounting to] a procedural gap'.[74]

A level of uncertainty nevertheless lingers as regards the impact of these legal developments considering the broader institutional context in which they are embedded. The recurrent degree of procedural specialisation *ratione materiae*, epitomised by the persistent 'bipolarity' of the EU external action,[75] may for

---

[70] *Tanzania* (n 51) para 75.

[71] The contribution of the Lisbon Treaty in further articulating of institutions' 'role' is particularly significant when considering the streamlining of decision-making procedures that the Treaty prompted. In introducing an *ordinary* legislative procedure, and in combining within the same provision the hitherto distinct EU and EC treaty-making procedures, the Treaty drafters formally reduced the diversity of expressions of institutional balance, to the benefit of a possibly simpler system of allocation of powers. As recalled by the Court in its *Tanzania* judgment (n 51): 'Article 218 TFEU, in order to satisfy the requirements of clarity, consistency and rationalisation, lays down a single procedure of general application concerning the negotiation and conclusion of international agreements by the European Union in all the fields of its activity, including the CFSP which, unlike other fields, is not subject to any special procedure'.

[72] PJ Kuijper, 'Commission's Right of Withdrawal of Proposals: Curtailment of the Commission's Right or Acceptance by the Court of the Commission's Long-standing Position?' (1 June 2015), http://acelg.blogactiv.eu/2015/06/01/commissions-right-of-withdrawal-of-proposals-curtailment-of-the-commissions-right-or-acceptance-by-the-court-of-the-commissions-long-standing-position/.

[73] See, eg, Prechal, 'Institutional Balance: A Fragile Principle with Uncertain Contents' (n 6) and Chamon, 'The Institutional Balance, an Ill-fated Principle of EU Law' (n 6).

[74] This gap-filling function of Title III TEU could be of particular importance in Case C-72/15 *Rosneft*, Opinion of AG Wathelet, EU:C:2016:381. The Court was asked to shed further light in its CFSP related jurisdiction, more particularly on the availability of the preliminary ruling procedure in the context of Art 275(2) TFEU. On this, see the intervention of CJEU President Koen Lenaerts, at the I.CON Conference 2016: https://youtu.be/WoCKg31jo3Y?list=PLljW4VOt-et-Qc1RnHMje6YBtu1bSOs8V.

[75] See A Dashwood, 'The Continuing Bipolarity of EU External Action' in I Govaere, E Lannon, P van Elsuwege and S Adam (eds), *The European Union in the World, Essays in Honour of Marc Maresceau* (Leiden, Martinus Nijhoff, 2014) 3.

instance weaken the added value of Title III TEU. Moreover, the reinforced role of the European Council,[76] the establishment of the hybrid High Representative for Foreign and Affairs and Security Policy–Vice-President of the Commission,[77] also included in Title III TEU, and that of the European External Action Service (EEAS)[78] which the Treaty of Lisbon introduced in EU primary law, have partly blurred the traditional power allocation which Title III purported to sharpen, particularly between the Commission and the Council. More than the multiplication of institutions itself, and the strengthening of the powers of some actors (eg the European Parliament),[79] the functions those new protagonists are deemed to play in the institutional system might challenge the classic tenets of institutional balance. In particular, one of their primary tasks is to foster the coordination in external policy-making, and thus to mitigate the effects of,[80] if not to transcend, power allocation in the name of coherence in the EU external action.[81] While such institutional developments might in principle facilitate institutional balance, the way inter-institutional arrangements have done in the past,[82] their very existence has paradoxically prompted new issues of power allocation.[83] The creation of hybrid functions and offices may thwart the maintenance of balance if these protagonists become themselves claimants in the allocation of powers within the system, prompting the question of whether, in turn, they should themselves be

---

[76] See, eg, Editorial Comments, 'An Ever Mighty European Council: Some Recent Institutional Developments' (2009) 46 *CML Rev* 1383; W Wessel, *The European Council* (Basingstoke, Palgrave, 2015).

[77] Article 18 TEU.

[78] Article 27(3) TEU.

[79] See, eg, contributions in P Koutrakos (ed), *The European Union's External Relations a Year after Lisbon*, CLEER Working Papers 2011/3.

[80] See Art 22 TEU as regards the European Council; Art 27(3) TEU and Art 2 of the 2010 Council Decision 2010/427/EU establishing the organisation and functioning of the European External Action Service [2010] OJ L201/30 ('EEAS Decision') as regards the EEAS. On the imperative of coherence and consistency, see, eg Mireia Estrada Canamares, Chapter 10.

[81] In particular, the creation of the EEAS has involved the amalgamation of hitherto separate Commission and Council services, and of their previously distinct tasks. See further S Blockmans and C Hillion (eds), *EEAS 2.0* (Stockholm, SIEPS/CEPS, 2013).

[82] See case-law discussed in section I A (i) above. According to Wathelet AG: 'The practice of forming interinstitutional agreements gives specific expression to the complementarity between [the principles of institutional balance and sincere cooperation] ... In areas where competence is shared between the three political institutions, an interinstitutional agreement is a means of establishing good practices, preventing disputes and, above all, preserving the institutional balance' (see Opinion in *ETS* (n 35) para 79).

[83] As the EEAS Decision indicates, the European External Action Service is a hybrid organ both in its composition and in terms of its functions: while it operates at the service of the HR-VP, it also has its own tasks. Thus, while it ought to ensure coherence and coordination in the EU external action, it may become part of inter-institutional bickering. A particular illustration relates to the negotiations of international agreements in the field of CFSP, in which the initiation can become an issue between the HR/EEAS and the Commission based on diverging understandings of the relevant provisions of Art 218(3) TFEU: it appears that the Commission submits recommendations to the Council whenever the envisaged agreement does not relate exclusively or principally to the CFSP, which means that CFSP matters in other agreements are covered by the Commission's recommendations without consultation of the HR/EEAS.

subject to the obligations deriving from the principles of Article 13(2) TEU.[84] It is indeed symptomatic that the 2010 Decision on the Organisation and Functioning of the EEAS contains a long article requiring the Service itself to cooperate with the institutions of the EU external action,[85] following the provision that establishes its tasks.[86]

## (ii) Codification and Articulation of the Inter-institutional Duty of Cooperation

In requiring that institutions 'practice mutual sincere cooperation', the second sentence of Article 13(2) TEU codifies the inter-institutional duty which the Court of Justice had previously articulated on the basis of Article 5 EEC/Article 10 EC. Its inclusion in the Treaty in Article 13(2) TEU, alongside the cardinal principles of conferral and institutional balance, also bolsters its significance as key principle of the EU institutional framework.

Most political institutions have indeed invoked it in inter-institutional litigation since the entry into force of the Treaty of Lisbon, usually in addition to the more conventional allegation of breaches of conferral and institutional balance. Even the Council, which is rarely in the position of applicant before the Court of Justice, has been a vocal advocate of sincere cooperation, referring to it in several institutional cases it instigated against the Commission.[87]

That no EU act has ever been annulled because of a breach of cooperation does not mean that the principle is legally and/or normatively weak. Article 13(2) TEU does not only codify the Court's case-law whereby institutions are bound by a 'obligation' of cooperation, which entails tangible legal consequences if ignored.[88] In stipulating that institutions '*shall practice* sincere cooperation', it also constitutes a specific inter-institutional application of the general principle of 'sincere cooperation' enshrined in Article 4(3) TEU, thereby confirming the Court's pre-Lisbon case law that it entails the '*same duties* of sincere cooperation as those which govern the relations between Member States and the [EU] institutions'. As a result, institutions must assist each other in carrying out tasks which flow from the Treaties, take any appropriate measure, general or particular, to ensure fulfilment of the obligations arising out of the Treaties or resulting from the acts of the institutions of the Union, and facilitate the achievement of the

---

[84] This will be discussed in the last section of this chapter.
[85] Article 3 EEAS Decision (n 80). Further, see Blockmans and Hillion, *EEAS 2.0* (n 81).
[86] Article 2 EEAS Decision (n 80).
[87] *MFA* (n 5); *ITLOS* (n 35); *Memorandum of Understanding* (n 35). The Council has also used the argument of cooperation to justify various arrangements which the Court eventually considered in breach of conferral and institutional balance (see the *ETS* and *Hybrid Act* judgments, discussed further below). The Commission also invoked the duty of cooperation against the Council, although less systematically (Case 28/12 *Commission v Council (Hybrid Act)*, Judgment, EU:C:2015:282), and so did the Parliament (Case C-48/14 *European Parliament v Council (Radioactive substances)*, Judgment, EU:C:2015:91).
[88] See *GSP* (n 29), and section I A (ii) above.

Union's tasks and refrain from any measure which could jeopardise the attainment of the Union's objectives.[89] It also implies that the obligations which the Court has derived from Article 4(3) TEU (and previously from Article 10 EC) are in principle applicable, *mutatis mutandis*, to inter-institutional relations.

Indeed, the case-law confirms that the principle of cooperation of Article 13(2) TEU is no less constraining than its Article 4(3) counterpart. The various cases in which the principle was invoked show that the Court performs a careful control of compliance with procedural obligations it has derived from sincere cooperation, and that are typical of those that it had articulated on the basis of Article 4(3) TEU. To be sure, the particular factual elements of the cases reveal that institutions tend to take the obligation to cooperate seriously in the functioning of the institutional framework.

In the *MFA* case, for example,[90] the Council argued, in addition to the alleged breach of the principles of conferral and institutional balance, that the Commission had infringed the principle of sincere cooperation when it decided to withdraw its proposal for a Council and Parliament Regulation laying down general provisions for macro-financial assistance (MFA) to third countries. The aim of the proposal was to grant EU MFA to third countries more effectively, and thus suggested conferring implementing powers to the Commission, instead of using the lengthier ordinary legislative procedure each time a MFA would be awarded. Sharing the view that the proposed decision-making would not involve sufficient political and democratic scrutiny, the Parliament and the Council, however, intended to retain the ordinary legislative procedure for each decision to grant MFA. Considering that this would distort its proposal, the Commission withdrew it before they could formally decide on it. The Council contended that the Commission *failed first to express any reservation or give warning* when the co-legislators adopted their positions on the proposal, and secondly, *failed to inform* them in good time of its intention to withdraw it, thereby preventing them from avoiding the planned withdrawal by amending their common approach. The Council also complained that the Commission rushed to withdraw its proposal on the very day the co-legislators were preparing to finalise an agreement leading to the adoption of the act.

Through a detailed analysis, the Court found that the Commission had not infringed the principle of cooperation. It noted that instead it '*sought to reach a solution*, which while safeguarding the objectives pursued by [its] proposal for a framework regulation in respect of MFA, *sought to take the concern of the Parliament and the Council into account*' (emphasis added). The Court also observed that as soon as it became evident that the co-legislators intended to maintain the ordinary legislative procedure for adopting MFA decisions, the Commission *mentioned at several meetings the possibility of withdrawal* of its proposal, and

---

[89] In this sense, see, eg, Opinion of AG Sharpston in *Memorandum of Understanding* (n 11).
[90] *MFA* (n 5).

the grounds for it. Documents relating to these meetings were relied on for the Court to establish that 'the co-legislators clearly perceived those warnings from the Commission'.[91]

The Court thereby assessed how the Commission interacted with the Parliament and the Council before deciding to withdraw its proposal to find out whether it had cooperated and how. It did not only verify that the procedural obligations of information and consultation were formally observed, it also ascertained that they were *genuinely* complied with. Hence, the Court paid particular attention to the fact the Commission gave consideration to the Council's views. In sum, the Court verifies that cooperation is 'practised' and that it is 'sincere'.

The *ITLOS* case provides further evidence of the post-Lisbon judicial articulation and control of the principle of cooperation.[92] The Council contested the Commission's decision to submit written observations to the International Tribunal of the Law of the Sea (ITLOS) without first obtaining its authorisation, in accordance with Article 218(9) TFEU, which in its views was applicable. Alongside the plea of a violation of the first sentence of Article 13(2) TEU, the Council argued that the Commission had breached the principle of cooperation on two levels: first, by making it impossible for the Council to adopt the decision under Article 218(9) TFEU to authorise the Commission to submit those observations, and secondly, by providing the Council, for information only, with less detailed documents during the preparation of the written statement, than the final document sent to the Tribunal. Having concluded that the procedure requiring Council prior authorisation (*viz* Article 218(9) TFEU) was *in casu* inapplicable, the Court underlined that pursuant to the principle of cooperation the Commission had an obligation to consult the Council before submitting its observations to the Tribunal. The obligation of consultation being established, the Court not only checked whether the Commission complied with it, but in line with its *MFA* approach, it also controlled *how*, and in particular how it took into consideration the Council's views so as to deal with the latter's claim.

Complementing that jurisprudence, the *ETS* judgment typifies how the Court relies on its case-law relating to Article 4(3) TEU to interpret Article 13(2) TEU. Not only are the procedural obligations deriving from sincere cooperation similar, their normative content may similarly vary depending on the degree to which the powers at hand are intertwined. The Court thus held that:

> In the context of those functions [stipulated in Article 218 TFEU], the Council and the Commission are nevertheless required to comply with the second sentence of Article 13(2) TEU, which states that '[t]he institutions shall practice mutual sincere cooperation'. *That cooperation is of particular importance for EU action at international level, as such action triggers a closely circumscribed process of concerted action and consultation between the EU institutions.* (emphasis added)[93]

---

[91] ibid paras 103–4.
[92] *ITLOS* (n 35).
[93] *ETS* (n 35) para 64.

This particular phraseology echoes the one which the Court has used in articulating the obligations deriving from Article 4(3) TEU in the context of mixed agreements, and in particular the notion that cooperation is all the more necessary in a particular context where EU and Member States competences are interlinked.[94] The use of the phrase 'concerted action' also resonates with the wording of the Court to justify more constraining procedural obligations based on Article 4(3) TEU: it was that very notion of 'concerted action' in the 2005 infringement proceedings that triggered

> if not a duty of abstention on the part of the Member States, at the very least a duty of close cooperation between the latter and the Community institutions in order to facilitate the achievement of the Community tasks and to ensure the coherence and consistency of the action and its international representation.[95]

It is that terminology which also led the Court to consider that a Member State, in certain circumstances, must refrain from exercising its competence, as it could 'compromise the principle of unity in the international representation of the Union and its Member States and weaken their negotiating power'.[96]

This embryonic case-law, to which the discussion will come back, briefly exemplifies how litigants have been invoking sincere cooperation and the rules of conduct binding institutions which they have derived therefrom. Inspired by their pleas, the Court has discretely articulated those rules, confirming their connection with the application of Article 4(3) TEU in external relations and their enforceability, while taking up the task of ascertaining through a meticulous scrutiny that they are genuinely complied with.

It may therefore be a matter of time and circumstances rather than of principle for the Court to find that an institution has breached of the principle of cooperation enshrined in Article 13(2) TEU.[97] The question will then be whether such an infringement possibly provides a basis for annulling the contested act. Indeed, as the emerging case-law indicates, the way to contest an institution's failure to

---

[94] See, eg, Opinion 1/94, EU:C:1994:384; Case C-459/03 *Commission v Ireland (Mox Plant)*, EU:C:2006:345. See further Joris Larik, Chapter 7; M Cremona, 'Defending the Community Interest: The Duties of Cooperation and Compliance' in M Cremona and B de Witte (eds), *EU Foreign Relations Law: Constitutional Fundamentals* (Oxford, Hart Publishing, 2008) 125; C Hillion, 'Mixity and Coherence in EU External Relations: The Significance of the "Duty of Cooperation"' in C Hillion and P Koutrakos (eds), *Mixed Agreements Revisited: The European Union and Its Member States in the World* (Oxford, Hart Publishing, 2010) 87.

[95] Case C-433/03 *Commission v Germany*, Judgment, EU:C:2005:462, para 66.

[96] See Case C-246/07 *Commission v Sweden (PFOs)*, Judgment, EU:C:2010:203; M Cremona, 'Case C-246/07, Commission v. Sweden (PFOS), Judgment of the Court of Justice (Grand Chamber) of 20 April 2010' (2011) 48 *CML Rev* 1639; A Casteleiro and J Larik, 'The Duty to Remain Silent: Limitless Loyalty in EU External Relations?' (2011) *EL Rev* 524.

[97] It should be recalled that it was only in 2005 that the Court of Justice established that a Member State violated EC law based on the sole breach of sincere cooperation enshrined in Art 10 EC, even if the later had been a principle of EC primary law from the outset. Until then, a violation of Art 10 EC was invoked as a complementary point to the primary plea that a Member State had breached specific EC primary and/or secondary rules.

cooperate is, akin to breaches of conferral and institutional balance principles, through the annulment procedure (Article 263 TFEU). In order for such a claim to be successful in inter-institutional settings, the Court would have to be convinced that a breach of sincere cooperation does correspond to one of the grounds mentioned in Article 263 TFEU, eg an infringement of an 'essential procedural requirement', or in any event an 'infringement of the Treaties or any rule of law relating to its application'. The applicant could also opt for the failure to act procedure (Article 265 TFEU), based on the argument that not cooperating amounts to such a failure, in infringement of the Treaties.

Does the fact that judicial means to enforce Article 13(2) TEU differ from those applicable to Article 4(3) TEU (ie no enforcement mechanism based on Articles 258-260 TFEU) entail that the principle of cooperation is less constraining for institutions than for Member States? Arguably, the terms of Article 13(2) TEU seem to point to the opposite direction, referring as they do to the institutions' obligation to 'practise' sincere cooperation, suggesting an even more compelling obligation than under Article 4(3) TEU. On the other hand, the question can still be asked as to whether the Court would be as assertive in enforcing cooperation in relation to institutions as it has been in relation to Member States. It has indeed been noticed that in the Member States–EU interface, the judiciary has been less prone to enforce the duty against institutions.[98]

The *Memorandum of Understanding* case could have provided an opportunity for the Court of Justice to shed further light on this question of enforceability. The Council challenged a decision of the Commission on the signature of an addendum to the EU–Switzerland Memorandum of Understanding on a Swiss financial contribution to the new EU Member States, which the Commission took on the basis of Article 17 TEU. The Council claimed that the Commission could not do so solely on the basis of its power of representation that Article 17 TEU recognises, and that it impinged on the Council's policy-making powers foreseen in Article 16 TEU. It also argued that by its conduct the Commission had breached the principle of sincere cooperation. Being only authorised to negotiate the 2013 addendum, it had failed to seek the Council's authorisation before signing it, and to inform it of its intention to sign the addendum without such an authorisation. The Council further submitted that the Commission had breached the principle of unity in the Union's external representation, deriving from the duty of sincere cooperation, by involving Switzerland in an inter-institutional disagreement.[99]

In the event, the Court opined that the Commission did not have the power to sign the agreement at hand, and annulled the contentious decision. It thereby did not have to examine whether the principle of sincere cooperation had been observed or not. Advocate General Sharpston by contrast did. In her Opinion, she noted that the Commission only informed the Council on the day of the adoption

---

[98] In this respect, see the Court's decision in *IMO* (n 28).
[99] *Memorandum of Understanding* (n 35).

of its decision, and considered that '[b]y acting in such a manner and not informing the Council beforehand, [it] rendered the principle of sincere cooperation ineffective and made it impossible for the Council to contribute (if it wished to do so)'. Importantly for the present discussion, she however added that the Council failed to show 'that this infringement vitiated the contested decision, in particular by affecting its content and form, and [was] therefore sufficient to justify annulling the contested decision'. Conversely, she admitted that the conduct prior to the adoption of a contested act could be contrary to the principle of sincere cooperation and affect its content or form, which 'in appropriate circumstances … [could] be a proper basis for annulling an act'.[100] Sharpston thus recognised, albeit cautiously, that violation of the obligation to cooperate may be 'a proper basis for annulling' the contested act, though 'in appropriate circumstances' and provided the applicant shows that the infringement vitiated the act, in particular by 'affecting its content or form'. This prerequisite would indeed prevent excessive formalism, and filter out cases where failure to consult would have no implications whatever on the content or form of the act.

It remains to be seen whether the Court will deem such a burden of proof warranted. In its *Mauritius* and *Tanzania* decisions discussed above,[101] the Court considered that the Council's failure to inform the Parliament, admittedly in breach of an obligation explicitly set out by Article 218(10) TFEU, was a basis for annulment of the Council Decision on the conclusion of the CFSP agreement, regardless of whether that breach had an impact on the content and/or form of the contested act. The information requirement had to be enforced regardless, considering the aims that it pursues, and which the Court underlined.[102] Indeed, the condition that the infringement vitiated the act, in particular by 'affecting its content or form', would hardly be relevant in these circumstances given that the Parliament does not have that power of influence on such a CFSP act. It is thus arguable that the breach of the principle of sincere cooperation, which typically encompasses obligations of information, be in principle a basis for annulment without the applicant having to demonstrate that the failure to inform had any impact on the content or form of the impugned act. The alternative position would significantly diminish the effectiveness of the duty, and would arguably be at odds with its recent constitutionalisation alongside the principle of conferral, and with the pre-Lisbon case-law recalled earlier.[103]

---

[100] Opinion of Sharpston AG in *Memorandum of Understanding* (n 11) paras 135–38.
[101] *Mauritius* (n 48); *Tanzania* (n 51).
[102] See *Tanzania* (n 51) paras 71–72.
[103] The Court recognised in the *GSP* case that failure of cooperation entails legal consequences, *in casu* the Council was entitled to act without waiting for the European Parliament's opinion, regardless of whether the Parliament's failure affected the content or the form of the act. In this context, it could also be recalled that in the 2005 infringement cases against Member States on the ground that they had infringed their obligation of cooperation under Art 10 EC (Art 4(3) TEU), the Commission did not have to show how their actions had a particular impact on the Community undertakings. The Court considered that their *very conduct* did not facilitate the Community undertaking, and as such breached the principle of sincere cooperation (see Case C-266/03 *Commission v Luxembourg*,

Indeed, while codified as legal requirement governing the institutional framework in Article 13(2) TEU, the principle of sincere cooperation also finds other specific expressions in the area of external relations. For example, like the pre-Lisbon Article 3 TEU, Article 21(3) TEU foresees that:

> The Union shall ensure consistency between the different areas of its external action and between these and its other policies. The Council and the Commission, assisted by the High Representative of the Union for Foreign Affairs and Security Policy, shall ensure that consistency *and shall cooperate to that effect.* (emphasis added)

The requirement of cooperation has equally generated specific arrangements envisaged as having legally binding effect. This is particularly the case of inter-institutional agreements, adopted post-Lisbon on the basis of Article 295 TFEU,[104] and which the Court of Justice has generally considered to be legally binding.[105] And while Article 295 TFEU is the legal basis for such cooperation arrangements, the Court has also recognised that cooperation can be organised otherwise.[106] It has indeed been wondered whether an agreement concluded only by two institutions would be legally acceptable. The Commission and the European Parliament agreed such an arrangement, which the Council Legal Service (CSL) considered problematic.[107] It notably held that the establishment of a special partnership between the Parliament and the Commission was not envisaged in the Treaties, and ran against the principle of sincere cooperation as per Article 13(2) TEU. The envisaged 'Partnership' contained several Commission's commitments, eg to increase Parliament's access to confidential documents related to international negotiations, to take account of the Parliament's views in the negotiations, and to facilitate participation of its members as observers in all relevant meetings prior and after negotiations. The CLS recalled that neither an inter-institutional agreement, nor institutions themselves could modify the allocation of powers under Treaties, in that it would violate the principle of institutional balance, thus raising the question of how the structural principles are deemed to interact, which is the subject of the next section of this discussion.

---

Judgment, EU:C:2005:341, and Case C-433/03 *Commission v Germany*, Judgment, EU:C:2005:462). Based on the notions that the principle of Art 13(2) TEU entails the same duties as under Art 4(3) TEU, a failure to comply should arguably entail equivalent legal effects.

[104] According to Art 295 TFEU: 'The European Parliament, the Council and the Commission shall consult each other and by common agreement make arrangements for their cooperation. To that end, they may, in compliance with the Treaties, conclude inter-institutional agreements which may be of a binding nature'.

[105] Case C-40/10 *Commission v Council*, Judgment, EU:C:2010:713, para 80, and before: *Hellenic Republic v Council* (n 17).

[106] For instance, that legal basis 'does not prevent the Council from being able to set out, in a decision authorising negotiation [of an EU agreement based on Art 218 TFEU], the arrangements relating to the information which the Commission must provide to it periodically throughout the negotiating process for the conclusion of an international agreement by the European Union', ETS (n 35) para 72.

[107] Avis du service juridique: projet d'accord-cadre sur les relations entre le Parlement européen et la Commission, Doc 12964/10 (30 August 2010). See A Rosas and L Armati, EU *Constitutional Law: An Introduction* (Oxford, Hart Publishing, 2012).

# III. Interactions and Application

That the three principles of conferral, institutional balance and sincere cooperation are 'laid down'[108] in one single provision is a legal novelty which the Treaty
of Lisbon introduced.[109] This second section discusses some of the implications
of this combined formulation, in the light of the subsequent case-law of the
European Court of Justice. In particular, it examines how the principles of Article
13(2) TEU are deemed to *interact* in structuring the institutional framework of the
EU external action (A),[110] and *how far* they are meant to apply (B).

## A. Complementary Application of the Three Principles

The post-Lisbon inter-institutional litigation shows that applicants often contest
the defendant's power to take the impugned measure by referring to the principles
of conferral and institutional balance, before claiming the violation of the principle of sincere cooperation to dispute the way that contested power was exercised.
This is also the way the Court generally structures its judgments. More particularly, the case-law shows that the principles of conferral and institutional balance
are in principle dealt with together (i), and that the principle of sincere cooperation is deemed to operate in the framework of conferred powers (ii). Various
pronouncements however indicate, admittedly less conspicuously, that the specific
requirement deriving from the principle of institutional balance, and particularly
that institutions have due regard for each other's powers, and the procedural
imperatives stemming from the principle of sincere cooperation, significantly
overlap (iii).

### (i) Conferral and Institutional Balance

The principles of conferral and institutional balance are referred to as distinct
principles, and yet they continue to be invoked as elements of the same plea.
Occasionally presented as a principle 'laid down in Article 13(2) TEU' alongside conferral, or sometimes mentioned separately from Article 13(2) TEU
altogether,[111] the principle of institutional balance is deemed to generate its own

---

[108]  *MFA* (n 5).
[109]  This combination finds its origins in Art I-19(2) of the defunct Constitutional Treaty, and previously in Art 18(3) of the Draft Constitution prepared by the European Convention, whereby: 'Each
Institution shall act within the limits of the powers conferred on it in the Constitution, and in conformity with the procedures and conditions set out in it. The Institutions shall practice full mutual
cooperation'.
[110]  Partly replicating the litigation of interactions between the principles of conferral and cooperation in the interface between Member States and the EU.
[111]  Litigants and the Court have adopted varying formulations, *cf MFA* (n 5) and *ETS* (n 35).

'requirement', distinct from those associated with conferral. To recall the Court's standard formula:

> [U]nder Article 13(2) TEU, each institution is to act within the limits of the powers conferred on it in the Treaties, and in conformity with the procedures, conditions and objectives set out in them. *That provision reflects the principle of institutional balance, characteristic of the institutional structure of the European Union, a principle which requires that each of the institutions must exercise its powers with due regard for the powers of the other institutions.* (emphasis added)[112]

This paragraph gives an indication of how the two principles interact, and how they should be approached in operational terms. Thus, when faced with the argument that an institution has breached the principle enshrined in the first sentence of Article 13(2) TEU and the principle of institutional balance, the Court *first* verifies whether the Treaties do confer the claimed power. This is how the analysis proceeded in the *MFA* case: based on Article 17(2) TEU in conjunction with Articles 289 and 293 TFEU, the Court found that the Commission 'ha[d] the power, as long as the Council has not acted to alter its proposal or even, if need be, withdraw it'.[113] Also, in the *ETS* case, it recognised that Article 218(2) and (4) TFEU allowed the Council to require from the Commission that it regularly report to it in writing on the outcome of the negotiations, while in *ITLOS*, it admitted that Article 335 TFEU provided a basis for the Commission power to represent the EU before the international Tribunal. Conversely, the Court found in the later *Memorandum of Understanding* judgment, that the Commission did not have 'the right, by virtue of its power of external representation under Article 17(1) TEU, to sign a non-binding agreement resulting from negotiations conducted with a third country', and annulled the impugned Commission's Decision.[114]

If the Court finds that the contested power does *not* exist, it need not go any further,[115] since it is meaningless to examine whether the institution exercised an unlawfully usurped power in conformity with the behavioural requirements of Article 13(2) TEU. This is also why in inter-institutional cases, a breach of the principle of conferral in itself entails infringement of the principle of institutional balance, dependent as it is on the observance of the treaty-based distribution of powers. Conversely, and despite the close connection between the principles of conferral and institutional balance, acknowledging the existence of a particular power ought not immediately to entail compliance with the principle of institutional balance, let alone that of sincere cooperation.

Even if the *'very* existence'[116] of a power is acknowledged because a legal basis confers it, the Court still has to determine as part of its compliance control of

---

[112] *MFA* (n 5) para 64; *ITLOS* (n 35) para 61; *ETS* (n 35) para 69; *Memorandum of Understanding* (n 35) para 32.
[113] *MFA* (n 5) para 74.
[114] *Memorandum of Understanding* (n 35) para 38.
[115] ibid.
[116] See *MFA* (n 5).

the principle of conferral whether the institution acted within the *limits* of that power, once these have been identified. Such limits may be deduced from the legal basis conferring the power at hand, and the procedure envisaged therein, as well as the 'conditions' and 'objectives' set out in the Treaties, pursuant to Article 13(2) TEU.

The *Hybrid Act* case illustrates how the Court of Justice ascertains that the limits of a power are respected for the purpose of conferral, without having to assess the compliance with the principle of institutional balance as such.[117] The case concerned a dispute between the Commission and the Council on the limits of the latter's powers in the context of the EU treaty-making procedure, following its adoption together with the 'Member States' representatives meeting in the Council', of a decision on the signature of a mixed agreement. The Commission was not disputing the way the Council acted by reference to its powers. Rather, the Court was asked to establish whether the impugned hybrid decision had been adopted in compliance with the provisions of Article 218(2), (5) and (8) TFEU, and particularly within the limits of the Council's power they foresee, in line with the requirement of Article 13(2) TEU.

The Court held that under Article 218 TFEU the Council was empowered *alone* to adopt the decision authorising the signature and provisional application of the agreements involved insofar as they concerned the EU. This power did not allow it to modify the terms of the EU treaty-making procedure so as to permit the Member States (themselves bound under EU law not to interfere with the procedure of Article 218 TFEU) to participate in the adoption of an act relating to the signing and provisional application of agreements *on behalf of the EU*. Nor was the Council able to combine 'without distinction elements falling within the decision-making process specific to the Council and elements of an intergovernmental nature',[118] thereby merging the rule of Article 218(8) that the decision is to be adopted by qualified majority voting, with the required consensus of the Member States' representatives.

The Court thereby enforced the limits of the Council's power as they derived from Article 218 TFEU itself, regardless of other institutions' powers in the procedure. Those were not directly affected here given that the case related to the modalities of the signature of a mixed agreement, and thus to the relationship between the EU and Member States. Ascertaining compliance with the principle of conferral of Article 13(2) TEU here did not relate directly to the principle of institutional balance. It is noticeable that, in its analysis, the Court nevertheless used a terminology that is reminiscent of that of balance when underlining that:

> [t]he contracting parties to a mixed agreement concluded with third countries are, first, the European Union and, second, the Member States. When such an agreement is negotiated and concluded, each of those parties must act within the framework of the

---

[117] *Hybrid Act* (n 87).
[118] ibid para 51.

competences which it has *while respecting the competences of any other contracting party.* (emphasis added)

Hence, while acting within the limits of a power is a *sine qua non* for an institution to comply with the principle of conferral, the scope of its action is also delimited by the competences of other protagonists in the situation at hand, a notion that is emblematic of the language of balance of powers,[119] though here between institutions and Member States.

Inter-institutional litigation confirms that setting the limits of an institution's power for the purpose of conferral also entails consideration of the powers other institutions enjoy in the procedure at hand, and possibly of their role within the broader institutional framework spelled out in Title III TEU. In the *ETS* case, for example, the Court acknowledged that the power of the Council to define the directives of negotiation under Article 218(2) and (4) TFEU included the power to set out a detailed negotiation procedure imposing obligations of reporting on the Commission, also in consideration of the latter's power to represent the Union under Article 17(1) TEU. Conversely, empowering the special committee to set out detailed negotiating positions with the intention to bind the Commission as negotiator, was regarded as exceeding the limits of the Council's power conferred by Article 218(4) TFEU. The powers of the Commission as set out in Article 218 TFEU, and enshrined in Article 17(1) TEU, helped identify the limits to the Council's power.

Once respect for the principle of conferral is established, the analysis ought to verify compliance with the specific requirement which the Court has derived from the principle of institutional balance, and which it has recalled time and again in the post-Lisbon case-law, namely, that the institution exercised it with due regard for the powers of other institutions. Here the question is no longer whether its action has *encroached* upon the powers of others, thus violating the treaty-based limits of its own in breach of the principle of conferral. Instead, it is whether in exercising its power, the institution did consider the prerogatives of other institutions, and the interests they represent in the institutional framework, so as not to *negatively affect* their position, and thus whether it exercised its conferred power

---

[119] As flagged up in section I A above, the Court had used this terminology in dealing with interactions between the institutions and the Member States' governments in *Luxembourg v Parliament* (n 23). The Court thus underlined that: 'It must nevertheless be emphasized that when the governments of the Member States make provisional decisions they must, in accordance with the rule imposing on Member States and the Community institutions mutual duties of sincere cooperation, as embodied in particular in Article 5 of the EEC Treaty, *have regard to the power of the Parliament* to determine its internal organization. They must ensure that such decisions *do not impede the due functioning of the Parliament*. (38) Furthermore the Parliament is authorized, pursuant to the power to determine its own internal organization given to it by Article 25 of the ECSC Treaty, Article 142 of the EEC Treaty and Article 112 of the EAEC Treaty, to adopt appropriate measures to ensure the due functioning and conduct of its proceedings. However, in accordance with the above-mentioned mutual duties of sincere cooperation, the *decisions of the Parliament in turn must have regard to the power of the governments of the Member States* to determine the seat of the institutions and to the provisional decisions taken in the meantime' (paras 37–38) (emphasis added).

within *limits*, albeit of a different order. These limits derive from considerations of *effectiveness* of other institutions' prerogatives in the situation at hand, and of their 'role in the institutional structure of the Union and the accomplishment of the tasks entrusted to the Union'.[120]

The *MFA* case illustrates that it is perhaps at this juncture that the interface between the principles of conferral and institutional balance, and their operationalisation, is in practice far less clear. Having confirmed the 'very existence' of the withdrawal power, the Court turned to the 'scope and limits' of that power. One is well established: the Commission can only decide to withdraw if the Council itself has not yet acted. The Court also posited that the withdrawal power does not '*confer* upon [the Commission] a right of veto in the conduct of the legislative process, a right which would be contrary to the principles of conferral and institutional balance' (emphasis added).[121]

In order to determine whether the withdrawal decision at hand amounted to such veto, the Court set out several requirements: the Commission 'must state to the Parliament and the Council the grounds for the withdrawal, which, in the event of challenge, have to be supported by cogent evidence or arguments'.[122] These grounds must be capable, in substance, of justifying the withdrawal of the proposal. In this regard, the Court then held that:

> It must be accepted that, where an amendment planned by the Parliament and the Council distorts the proposal for a legislative act in a manner which prevents achievement of the objectives pursued by the proposal and which, therefore, deprives it of its raison d'être, the Commission is entitled to withdraw it.

In sum, the Commission would act within the limits of its withdrawal power if the co-legislators *distorted* its proposal.[123] Its *entitlement* to exercise its power is thus dependent on the conduct of the other involved institutions, but also contingent on that of the Commission too. The Court thus added that the latter:

> may, however, do so [ie decide to withdraw its proposal] only after having due regard, in the spirit of sincere cooperation which, pursuant to Article 13(2) TEU, must govern relations between EU institutions in the context of the ordinary legislative procedure … to the concerns of the Parliament and the Council underlying their intention to amend that proposal.[124]

To establish 'whether the arguments put forward by the Commission in this instance support[ed] the grounds relied upon by it in support of the contested decision', the Court examined in detail the aim of the Commission's proposal and

---

[120] *Chernobyl* (n 20) para 21; see also *Memorandum of Understanding* (n 35) para 31.
[121] *MFA* (n 5) para 74.
[122] ibid para 76.
[123] On the background to this doctrine, see Kuijper, 'Commission's Right of Withdrawal of Proposals' (n 72).
[124] *MFA* (n 5) para 83.

position taken thereon by the co-legislators. The grounds the Commission invoked being capable of justifying its course of action the Court concluded that its:

> decision ... to withdraw the proposal for a framework regulation in the light of such considerations *did not infringe the principle of conferral of powers or the principle of institutional balance, laid down in Article 13(2) TEU.* (emphasis added)[125]

The Court therefore not only admitted that the Commission had acted within the limits of its powers, its action also complied with the principle of institutional balance. What is remarkable, however, is that, at this point, the Court had hardly discussed whether the Commission had acted with 'due regard' for the powers of the co-legislators, as it suggested it would by referring earlier to its standard formula on the principle of institutional balance. In effect, the only discussion of due regard in that part of the analysis rather concerned, albeit implicitly, the behaviours of the co-legislators vis-à-vis the Commission. In establishing whether they had distorted the proposal of the Commission, the Court de facto examined whether, although acting within the formal limits of their powers, the co-legislators exceeded the *limits* associated with the exercise of their legislative powers, thus entitling the Commission to withdraw its proposal and thus stop the decision-making process.

The approach of the Court indicates that while conceptually distinct and entailing specific requirements, the two principles remain deeply intertwined, if not confused, in operational terms. Indeed, it is difficult to decipher how the respective principles effectively structure the judicial enquiry, and how to determine where the control of compliance with the principle of conferral stops, and where the analysis relating to the principle of institutional balance really begins.[126]

To be sure, most post-Lisbon judgments show a recurrent conflation of conferral and institutional balance in operational terms. In the *ETS* case, the Court held that the impugned Council act 'complie[d] with the obligation laid down in Article 13(2) TEU that each institution is to act within the limits of the powers conferred on it by the Treaties',[127] adding in the following paragraph, and without further explanation that '*[l]ikewise*, that provision of the contested decision *does not in any way infringe* the principle of institutional balance' (emphasis added).[128] The absence of reasoning to substantiate this conclusion is remarkable considering the Court's definitive language. Indeed, the Court followed the same approach later in the judgment, in relation to another aspect of the contested decision. Having found that 'the Council infringed the obligation laid down in Article 13(2) TEU to act within the limits of the powers conferred on it by Article 218(2) to (4) TFEU', it then held in the subsequent paragraph that '*[i]n doing so*, the Council

---

[125] ibid para 95.

[126] T Tridimas, *The General Principles of EU Law* (Oxford, Oxford University Press, 2006) 2.

[127] It is noticeable that the Court does not refer here to the second part of the first sentence of Art 13(2) TEU which sets out the duty to conform to the procedure, conditions and objective of the treaties.

[128] *ETS* (n 35) paras 70–71.

*also* infringed the principle of institutional balance' (emphasis added),[129] again without further explanation. The language ('likewise', 'in doing so') thereby suggests an automaticity between respect for/or violation of the first sentence of Article 13(2) TEU and in particular the principle of conferral (first part of the first sentence), on the one hand, and observance/infringement of the principle of institutional balance, on the other.[130] But the lack of explanation adds support to the claim that the principle of institutional balance is easy short-hand for the principle of conferral.[131]

As much as it is logical that a breach of the principle of institutional balance may derive from a violation of that of conferral from which it stems, and might not therefore deserve specific analysis,[132] the opposite is less obvious. Although acting within the formal limits of a power and in conformity with the procedure, conditions and objectives set out in the treaties, and thus in line with the requirement of Article 13(2) TEU, an institution may still, in principle, infringe the principle of institutional balance, understood as the specific requirement of due regard for the powers of other institutions. And since the Court formally continues to refer to conferral and institutional balance as two distinct principles, one would expect that such distinction be further operationalised in its analysis.[133]

Admittedly, such requirement may also amount to establishing the institution's observance of the very *limits* of its powers, in line with the stipulation of Article 13(2) TEU. In that, the apparent conflation of conferral and institutional balance in the Court's analysis would be understandable. However, even if due regard revolves around the notion of limits of institutions' actions, as does conferral, the limits of a power may not necessarily be similarly located in a particular situation, whether analysed from the viewpoint of conferral, or from that of institutional balance, given that the latter touches upon the exercise of a particular power. As suggested earlier, limits may be defined by reference to the procedure setting out the power, and the conditions and objectives set out in the treaties, whereas the limits for the purpose of institutional balance also relate to how far an institution can *exercise* that established power in a particular situation without undermining other institutions' prerogatives in the context of that action, and considering their role in the institutional framework more generally.

Perhaps the reason behind this lingering mixture in the Court's approach to conferral and institutional balance lies in the fact that ascertaining that an institution had due regard for the powers of others entails a more complex, more

---

[129] ibid paras 91–92.

[130] The Court reiterates the distinction in para 84 of the judgment. Institutions too make such direct connection between conferral and institutional balance in their pleadings before the Court. See, eg, the arguments of the Commission in the case at hand. In the same vein, the Council and intervening Member States also argued in the *MFA* case, that 'the Commission *exceeded the powers conferred* upon it by the Treaties *and in so doing, undermined the institutional balance*, as the Treaties do not give it the power to withdraw a legislative proposal in circumstances such as those' (emphasis added).

[131] See Chamon, 'The Institutional Balance, an Ill-Fated Principle of EU Law?' (n 6).

[132] See, eg, *Memorandum of Understanding* (n 35).

[133] See in this respect the Council argumentation in eg the *ETS* case (n 35).

intrusive, and thus more sensitive Court control, compared to policing the limits of a power based on an interpretation of treaty provisions. The latter is a binary legal assessment (*viz* does the institution have a power or not?), whereas the former is a matter of degree, which entails more judicial scrutiny of the behaviour of the institution in exercising its lawful powers.

After all, as an EU institution, the Court is equally bound by the principles of Article 13(2) TEU. Articulating a specific test to control compliance with the principle of institutional balance could display too clearly the degree to which it may adjust the treaty-based demarcation of powers by reference to the general and still ambivalent notion of institutional balance. Keeping the latter closely associated, if not confused with the principle of conferral, instead embeds it firmly in, and thus shows deference to the primary allocation of powers envisaged by the *constituants*.

## (ii) Conferral and Cooperation

Article 13(2) TEU refers in the first sentence to the principle that institutions must act within the limits of their powers, while the requirement that they practise sincere cooperation is set out in the second sentence. This sequenced formulation not only reflects the way the principles are deemed to operate, namely, that power has to be ascertained first, and then the principle governing its exercise applies. Conferral is also the primary principle structuring the functioning of the EU institutional framework.

The case-law confirms this pre-eminence. The Court found that the allocation of powers could not be altered by the application of the principle of cooperation, adding that:

> Under Article 13(2) TEU, [EU] institutions are to practise mutual sincere cooperation. That sincere cooperation, however, is *exercised within the limits of the powers conferred by the Treaties on each institution*. The obligation resulting from Article 13(2) TEU is therefore *not such as to change those powers*. (emphasis added)[134]

That the general requirement of sincere cooperation cannot in principle alter the allocation of powers was also made clear in the above-mentioned *Hybrid Act* pronouncement. The Commission considered that the Council had breached its 'duty' of cooperation when adopting, together with the representatives of the Member States' governments, the impugned hybrid decision to sign a mixed agreement. The Commission considered that pursuant to this duty, the Council 'should have performed its functions in such a way as not to weaken the institutional framework of the [EU] by permitting Member States to be involved in the carrying out of a procedure concerning exclusively the Council'.[135] In its defence, the Council argued that the adoption of the contentious decision was 'the very embodiment of the obligation of close cooperation' binding the EU and the Member States, adding that the decision was not only consistent with the objective

---

[134] *eg ITLOS* (n 87) para 84.
[135] *Hybrid Act* (n 87) para 34.

of unity in the international representation of the EU, usually associated with the duty of cooperation, it also 'guarante[ed], promote[d] and strengthen[ed] that objective, by setting out the common position of the EU and its Member States'.[136]

As mentioned above, the Court did not consider the Commission's argument that the Council had breached its duty of sincere cooperation. Instead, it approached the case solely through the prism of the first sentence of Article 13(2) TEU, including the duty to conform to the procedures, conditions and objectives set out in the Treaties. It nevertheless responded to the Council's claim that the hybrid decision was a reflection of the duty of cooperation. While acknowledging the latter's importance between the EU and the Member States, it nevertheless underlined that 'that principle [could not] justify the Council setting itself free from compliance with the procedural rules and voting arrangements laid down in Article 218 TFEU'.[137] The Council thus failed to convince the Court that a joint EU–Member States' decision to sign and provisionally implement a mixed agreement, deviating from the procedural requirements of Article 218 TFEU, was justifiable in the name of the duty of cooperation between the EU and the Member States.[138] In other words, the argument of cooperation could not be relied upon to alter the treaty-based power allocation.

This approach resonates with the general stance the Court of Justice took in the early *Hellenic Republic* case, whereby:

> [It] must ... make sure that in the context of the inter-institutional cooperation the institutions do not ignore the rules of law and do not exercise their discretionary powers in a manifestly wrong and arbitrary way.[139]

In the same vein, the Court has rejected the use of the principle of sincere cooperation to contest *the effects* of the treaty-based demarcation of powers. Thus, in the *ITLOS* case, the Council and various Member States argued that the Commission had breached the principle of cooperation because it had failed to submit a proposal to the Council for a decision establishing the EU position before ITLOS contrary to the requirement set out in Article 218(9) TFEU, thereby making it impossible for the Council to adopt such a decision. By not submitting a proposal, the argument went, the Commission also failed to fulfil its obligation, under Article 17(1) TEU, to take appropriate initiatives to promote the general interest of the European Union, a failure which in turn made it impossible for the Council to carry out the functions conferred on it by Article 16(1) TEU. In response, the Court recalled that sincere cooperation is exercised within the confines of the powers the Treaties confer on each institution, and that the obligation resulting from it could not be such as to change those powers. It concluded that:

> In the present case, the main argument put forward by the Council ... in the context of the second plea in law is based on the premise that the determination of the content

---

[136] ibid para 36.
[137] ibid para 55.
[138] See also Case C-114/12 *Commission v Council*, Opinion of AG Sharpston, EU:C:2014:224, para 195.
[139] *Hellenic Republic v Council* (n 17) para 17.

of the written statement submitted on behalf of the European Union to ITLOS ... fell within the competence of the Council pursuant to Article 218(9) TFEU or the second sentence of Article 16(1) TEU. That was not the case, however, as can be seen from the examination of the first plea in law. Accordingly, it cannot be claimed that the Commission failed to fulfil its obligation of sincere cooperation by not taking the initiatives entailed in the application of those two provisions.[140]

In sum, as the principle of sincere cooperation is deemed to apply only within the limits of institutions' prerogatives, it cannot itself be a source of a new power, ie beyond those that the Treaties confer.

Having said this, obligations associated with the duty of cooperation may have a significant impact on an institution's power: they constrain the way it is exercised, and can even condition the institution's very ability to exercise it. Moreover, constraints on an institution's exercise of its power may entail corresponding rights for other institutions. In other words, the interface between conferral and sincere cooperation is more nuanced than the above discussion suggests.

The Court made clear that the requirement of cooperation is particularly significant where the allocation of powers among institutions is complex, and thus difficult to operate in practice.[141] It thereby ascribed a *corrective* function to the principle of cooperation, to help prevent disputes on allocation of powers.[142] It has indeed been noted that 'the principle of sincere cooperation makes it possible to resolve the uncertainties arising from "grey areas" of the Treaties, such as the uncertainty surrounding the manner in which the [Commission's] power to withdraw [a legislative proposal] may be exercised'.[143]

To be sure, the lack of cooperation may conversely entail *a loss of the right to exercise* allocated powers. Hence, in the *GSP* case, the European Parliament's failure to comply with its obligation of sincere cooperation vis-à-vis the Council undermined its ability to exercise its consultative power. The Court admitted that the Council was entitled to adopt the impugned decision without waiting for the Parliament's opinion. The Parliament had forfeited its consultative power by putting the EU policy at risk.[144]

While in principle, it cannot alter the allocation of powers as such, the principle of cooperation may nevertheless affect the very ability of an institution to exercise its powers in a particular situation. It contributes to keeping the institutional balance by preventing an institution from misusing or abusing its power, thereby preserving the integrity of a procedure and the functions of the other institutions

---

[140] See *ITLOS* (n 35). In the *Memorandum of Understanding* case too, the Council argued that the Commission had failed to cooperate based on the claim that it proceeded with the signature of the addendum to the MoU with Switzerland despite the Council's objection that it was encroaching on its powers. See AG Sharpston's Opinion in *Memorandum of Understanding* (n 11) para 133. In the same vein, see *Parliament v Council* (n 87) para 58.

[141] See *Hellenic Republic v Council* (n 17) para 15.

[142] ibid.

[143] See Case C-409/13 *Council v Commission (MFA)*, AG Jääskinen, EU:C:2014:2470, para 98.

[144] This approach could be related to the Court's approach in *PFOs* (n 96).

therein, as well as the purpose for which that procedure is established. The respective operations of the principles of conferral and institutional balance are therefore deeply intertwined.

In this regard, the Court has articulated obligations deriving from the principle of cooperation which not only constrain but condition the exercise of a power. In the *ITLOS* case, for example, it acknowledged the Commission's power to submit observations to the international Tribunal without it infringing the Council's powers under Articles 218 TFEU and 16 TEU. However, it underlined that:

> the principle of sincere cooperation *requires the Commission to consult the Council beforehand* if it intends to express positions on behalf of the European Union before an international court. (emphasis added)[145]

In other words, the very ability of the Commission to exercise its acknowledged power was contingent on its prior compliance with the obligation of cooperation with the Council.

As discussed earlier, the Court indeed examined what the Commission did before presenting the EU position to the tribunal to find out whether it had effectively cooperated. It did not only assess whether the Commission had formally cooperated, eg by way of communicating with the Council, it also inspected the manner in which the Commission complied with its obligation to consult, by examining how it interacted with the Council. In the event, the Court held (para 87):

> In the present case, the Commission complied with that obligation ... prior to submitting the written statement on behalf of the European Union to ITLOS in Case No 21, the *Commission sent the Council the working document* of 22 October 2013, which was *revised several times* up until 26 November 2013 *in order to take account of the views expressed* within the FISH and COMAR groups. The Council's claim that the Commission did not sincerely cooperate in the preparation of the content of that written statement is therefore incorrect. (emphasis added)

It is unclear whether the list of the Commission's *conducts* which the Court evoked as evidence of cooperation amounts to a list of procedural requirements which would *all* have to be fulfilled for the principle of cooperation effectively to be observed. Thus, beyond mere communication, was the Commission bound to revise the content of its document to take account of the observations made by the Council committees, and if so, how far? What if the Commission did not revise its document because eg of a substantive disagreement with the Council's views? Given its formulation as an 'obligation' deriving from the principle of cooperation,[146] the Commission's failure to consult, or indeed failure to consult properly, would in principle amount to a violation of the principle of cooperation which, if construed as an 'essential procedural requirement', could then vitiate the legality of the decision, and in turn lead to its annulment.

---

[145] *ITLOS* (n 35) para 86.
[146] ibid para 87.

This would be all the more remarkable since the Court established a procedural obligation, *viz consultation*, that was more constraining than the one which the Commission had envisaged, namely, a mere duty of information. The Court did not explain why such an obligation should be preferred in this instance, but simply considered that the Commission complied with it anyway. In the event, while the Council lost on its first plea, it nevertheless won on the second one, by way of acquiring a right to be consulted in instances where the Commission submits positions of the Union before an international judicial body, outside the context of Article 218(9) TEU.

In the *MFA* case too, the Court of Justice examined the 'events concerning the work that preceded the adoption of the contested decision'[147] and the behaviour of the Commission in this context, to find out whether as contended by the Council it had failed to cooperate. In essence, the Court verified that the Council and Parliament were properly informed of the Commission's intention, in due time, and that that information had been effectively received by the co-legislators. It also noted the degree to which the Commission strove to find a solution, taking account of their different positions, while preserving the main objective of the initiative, as if to show that withdrawal was the last resort.[148] Though less explicitly than in the *ITLOS* judgment, the Court's pronouncement in *MFA* does indicate that the Commission was bound by various procedural obligations conditioning its ability to exercise its power to withdraw. The Court had indeed emphasised before engaging with its meticulous analysis that, while entitled to withdraw its proposal, the Commission:

> may only do so after having due regard in the spirit of sincere cooperation which, pursuant to Article 13(2) TEU, must govern relations between EU institutions in the context of the ordinary legislative procedure ... to the concerns of the Parliament and the Council underlying their intention to amend that proposal.

Turning to the Commission's actual behaviour, the Court also mentioned the content of the compromise solution it proposed as part of its assessment of whether and how the concerns of the co-legislators had been considered.

While this is presented as evidence of the Commission's cooperative attitude vis-à-vis the other institutions in this instance, it could again be read as an indication of what the Court would be controlling for the purpose of establishing whether the principle of cooperation has been duly observed, and in turn a hint at what the Court requires for a particular power to be lawfully exercised, more generally. There is arguably a prescriptive dimension to the Court's extensive verification. In other words, the Commission will likely have to consider these elements next time it intends to withdrawal a proposal. Its very ability to exercise that power could be questioned if those behavioural obligations were not observed.[149]

---

[147] *MFA* (n 5) para 61, which sums up the Commission's response to the alleged breach of the principle of cooperation.

[148] ibid paras 100–4.

[149] On the feedback effect of the Court's findings, see A Stone Sweet, *Governing with Judges: Constitutional Politics in Europe* (Oxford, Oxford University Press, 2000).

That said, it may be wondered whether the Court would have annulled the decision solely on the basis of non-observance of the principle of cooperation. As suggested in the previous section, there are grounds to argue that, in principle, failure to cooperate in the exercise of a power vitiates the legality of that exercise. Moreover, in practice, annulment of the withdrawal decision in *MFA* could have meant that the proposal would have been restored, which the Commission in the end would have still been able to withdraw, though after having properly complied with its principle of cooperation, since the Court had already accepted the justification for doing so. Similarly in the *ITLOS* case, an annulment of the Commission's initiative based on a breach of sincere cooperation could have been meaningless if in the meantime, the international Tribunal would have used the Commission's statement in its own proceedings.

To be sure, the principle of sincere cooperation appears to influence the exercise of allocated power in another way. As in the *Hybrid Act* case,[150] the Council and some intervening Member States attempted in the *ETS* case to justify the content of the impugned decision on the negotiation of the agreement by referring to the principle of cooperation. They submitted (partly successfully) that the power to address negotiating directives to the Commission included 'the power to specify the procedural requirements for negotiation *in order to ensure sincere cooperation between the institutions, enshrined in Article 13(2) TEU*, and compliance with the institutional balance' (emphasis added).[151] The principle of cooperation was thus invoked as a justification for the way the Council exercised its power, and the Court was receptive to the argument. Having recalled the terms of Article 218 TFEU, and those of Article 17(1) TEU, it held that:

> In the context of th[eir] functions [in the framework of Article 218], the Council and the Commission are nevertheless required to comply with the second sentence of Article 13(2) TEU, which states that '[t]he institutions shall practice mutual sincere cooperation'. That cooperation is of particular importance for EU action at international level, as such action triggers a closely circumscribed process of concerted action and consultation between the EU institutions.

> Furthermore, Article 218(4) TFEU provides that, when the Council has designated a special committee, the negotiations must be conducted in consultation with that committee.

> In those circumstances, which correspond to the present case, *the Commission must provide the special committee with all the information necessary for it to monitor the progress of the negotiations*, such as, in particular, the general aims announced and the positions taken by the other parties throughout the negotiations. *It is only in this way that the special committee is in a position to formulate opinions and advice relating to the negotiations.*

> Having regard to the various functions of the institutions in the negotiation and conclusion of the agreements referred to in Article 218 TFEU, *the Commission can be required to provide that information to the Council as well. It is expedient for the Council to possess that*

---

[150] *Hybrid Act* (n 87).
[151] *ETS* (n 35) para 47.

*information in order to have clear knowledge of the course of the negotiations concerning the preparation of a draft agreement that will be submitted to it for approval.*

Consequently, the obligation set out in the second sentence of Article 2 of the contested decision, which provides that 'the Commission shall report in writing to the Council on the outcome of the negotiations after each negotiating session and, in any event, at least quarterly', must be regarded as in conformity with Article 218(2) and (4) TFEU. (emphasis added)[152]

The Court did not refer to the principle of sincere cooperation for the purpose of establishing whether it had been breached—understandably so, given that the applicant, namely the Commission, had not itself argued that it had been infringed. Instead, the Court relied upon the said principle to frame its interpretation of the 'functions' of the special committee and the Council in the context of Article 218 TFEU, and to articulate the ensuing Commission's responsibilities in relation to them. The Court was thus sensitive to the argument of efficiency of the procedure, and of the different functions therein, in line with the requirements of the principle of sincere cooperation. Invoked as the aim of a particular course of action, the principle of sincere cooperation could thus help articulate further the demarcation and the exercise of power. For, here, the Court ultimately acknowledged that the Council could require the Commission to act the way it did in the impugned decision.

The foregoing casts light on the interplay between the principle of conferral and that of cooperation. Although it applies *within* the system of allocation of powers, the principle of sincere cooperation does influence the latter's operation. The Court has elaborated a list of obligations stemming from the cooperation principle that constrain, if not condition, the institutions' ability to exercise their powers, and how the two principles should relate to one another more generally. Moreover, it has been accepted that sincere cooperation might be used to construe the scope of institutions' powers, so as to ensure the latter's full effectiveness.

This elaboration of obligations based on the principle of cooperation and the ensuing compliance control that the Court methodically performs, find a normative basis in the notion that institutions shall '*practice* mutual sincere cooperation'. Moreover, the introduction of Title III TEU which, as argued above incarnates the principle of institutional balance, might in practice inspire the articulation of this second-order layer of institutions' rights and responsibilities, supplementing the treaty-based distribution of powers. Indeed, these additional obligations arguably dovetail with the requirement of 'due regard' deriving from the principle of institutional balance, as discussed in the next section.

What remains unclear is the degree to which these judge-made duties may affect the operation of the institutional framework. In particular, it remains to be seen whether failure to comply with an obligation deriving from the principle of cooperation could in itself lead to a possible annulment of the act, or whether the

---

[152] ibid paras 64–68.

Court might be less formalistic and accept that an act adopted in compliance with the principles of conferral and institutional balance should be maintained. Arguably, this could be contingent on the specific circumstances of the case (ie what would be the implications of annulment), but also on the degree of articulation of the procedural obligation at play in the case at hand, and the principle that it expresses, whether democracy or efficiency in the operation of the system.[153] It may equally depend on how confident the Court feels to do so, bound as it is too by the principles of Article 13(2) TEU.[154]

### (iii)  Overlapping Institutional Balance and Cooperation

Having discussed the interactions between the principles of conferral and of institutional balance, on the one hand, and between the latter and that of sincere cooperation, on the other, this section turns to the interface between the principle of sincere cooperation and that of institutional balance. As mentioned earlier, the latter has a dual facet: it reflects the principle enshrined in the first sentence of Article 13(2) TEU, and it also requires that institutions exercise their powers with due regard for those of others. As the relationship between the principle of cooperation and the first facet of institutional balance has already been touched upon, the following will focus on the connection between the latter's second facet and the second sentence of Article 13(2) TEU.

The preceding discussion may already have made it apparent that in some respects, both principles operate on the same terrain. They equally govern the *exercise* of conferred powers, and they both entail obligations of a procedural nature that constrain the conduct of institutions.[155] In both cases, these obligations have been articulated by the Court, which has also exercised a scrupulous compliance control with a view to ensuring the effectiveness of each institution's function in the system and of the institutional framework more generally to ensure that it fulfils its purposes envisaged in Article 13(1) TEU. Both principles of institutional balance and of sincere cooperation play a complementary function to that of the principle of conferral, and the treaty-based system of power allocation it is aimed to preserve.

The case-law suggests that, for practical purposes, the Court occasionally considers these principles together. The *MFA* judgment is a case in point.[156] Following a classic approach, the Council had distinguished its plea relating to conferral and institutional balance from the one concerning the principle of sincere cooperation, and at first sight the distinction is replicated in the Court's

---

[153] See in this regard, how the Court characterises the obligation of information enshrined in Art 218(19) TFEU in its *Mauritius* judgment (n 48) para 80.

[154] See further T Horsley, 'Reflections on the Role of the Court of Justice as the "Motor" of European Integration: *Legal* Limits to Judicial Lawmaking' (2013) 50 *CML Rev* 931.

[155] As mentioned, the Court's earlier case-law already displayed connections between sincere cooperation and the requirement of due regard; see, eg, *Luxembourg v Parliament* (n 23).

[156] For an earlier illustration, see *Hellenic Republic v Council* (n 17) paras 15–16.

analysis. Thus, in the first part of its judgment, the Court essentially established whether the Commission had a power to withdraw and its limits.[157] The concluding paragraphs indeed confirmed that until that point, the Court had assessed the Commission's observance of the principles of conferral and of institutional balance.[158] Then, the subsequent analysis seemingly turned to the question of sincere cooperation.[159]

Upon a closer look, however, several elements of the twofold structure of the judgment appear. First, the Court began its general analysis by positing that it was 'appropriate to examine [the Council's pleas] together',[160] then referring to Article 13(2) TEU without distinguishing between its first and second sentences. Thus, it mentioned the principle of conferral that 'reflects' the principle of institutional balance,[161] while the following paragraph recalled that Article 13(2) provides 'in addition' that EU institutions are to practise mutual sincere cooperation. The analysis is thus framed by reference to Article 13(2) TEU as a whole.[162]

Secondly, and following from the first point, the Court's assessment in the first part of whether the principle of institutional balance was observed used the language of sincere cooperation. In particular, when examining the grounds invoked by the Commission to justify its decision to withdraw, which is seemingly part of checking that the principles of conferral and institutional balance have been respected, the Court held that the Commission could exercise its power to withdraw:

> *only after having due regard, in the spirit of sincere cooperation which, pursuant to Article 13(2) TEU,* must govern the relations between institutions in the context of the ordinary legislative procedure ... *to the concerns of the European Parliament and the Council underlying their intention to amend that proposal.* (emphasis added)[163]

The condition set by the Court for the Commission to exercise its withdrawal power therefore brings together the notions of due regard, characteristic of the principle of institutional balance although relating here to the 'concerns' of other institutions rather than to their 'powers', and that of sincere cooperation, albeit expressed here in terms of 'spirit' rather than 'principle'.[164] In the event, the conclusion of this part is limited to acknowledging compliance with the principles of conferral and institutional balance; the Court's mixed references to the two sets of principles in its analysis. The combination of the languages of institutional

---

[157] *MFA* (n 5) paras 68–76.
[158] ibid paras 95 and 97.
[159] ibid paras 98 et seq.
[160] ibid para 63.
[161] ibid para 64.
[162] The Commission seemingly suggested the same approach, as summarised in ibid para 32.
[163] ibid para 83.
[164] Incidentally, it is indeed noticeable that the Court refers to Art 13(2) TEU generally, in which both principles are 'laid down', rather than to its second sentence where the principle of sincere cooperation is located.

balance and of cooperation is indeed noticeable in the paragraph that precedes
that conclusion:

> It follows from the analysis set out in paragraphs 85 to 93 of the present judgment that
> the Commission was entitled to consider that the amendment planned by the Parliament
> and the Council so far as concerns Article 7 of the proposal for a framework regula-
> tion *was liable to distort that proposal*, on the essential issue of the procedure for grant-
> ing MFA, *in a way which would have prevented the objectives pursued by the Commission
> through the proposal from being achieved* and which, therefore, would have deprived the
> proposal of its *raison d'être*. (emphasis added)[165]

The notion that the co-legislators acted 'in a way which would have prevented
the objectives' of the Commission 'being achieved' could be read as an indication
that the Parliament and the Council may have failed to exercise their co-legislative
function with due regard for the powers of the Commission which, as recalled in
an earlier paragraph, 'is to promote the general interest of the European Union
and take appropriate initiatives to that end'.[166] But arguably it could also be read
as a breach of the principle of mutual sincere cooperation of Article 13(2) TEU, if
read in conjunction with Article 4(3) TEU. Sincere cooperation entails that institutions, 'in full mutual respect, assist each other in carrying out tasks which flow
from the Treaties' and 'facilitate the achievement of the Union's tasks and refrain
from any measure which could jeopardise the attainment of the Union's objectives'. The operation of the principles of institutional balance and of sincere cooperation, respectively, thus appear to overlap.

    While the language of sincere cooperation is visible in the Court's analysis relat-
ing to institutional balance, the opposite is also true. Although it had concluded at
the end of the first part of the judgment that the Commission had complied with
the principles of conferral and institutional balance, the Court actually tackled the
question of whether the Commission had 'due regard ... to the concerns' of the
co-legislators in the second part of its analysis, devoted to establishing whether the
principle of sincere cooperation had been observed. Thus, it emphasised that 'faced
with the common concern of the Parliament and the Council ... the Commission
strove to reconcile the respective positions of the institutions concerned',[167] before
spelling out in detail the tenets of the proposed compromise. One of the principles
the Court recalled to frame its examination of whether withdrawal was justified
and whether institutional balance was respected, was in effect handled in the part
of the judgment that relates to the question of whether the Commission cooperated with the other institutions.

    Comparing the analysis that addresses the question of compliance with institu-
tional balance, with that concerning sincere cooperation, shows that the latter is in
various ways a continuation of the evaluation of the institutions' conduct before

---

[165] *MFA* (n 5) para 94.
[166] ibid para 70.
[167] ibid para 101.

the decision was taken, for the purpose of ascertaining whether the requirement of due regard was fulfilled. What differs is that in the second part of the analysis,[168] the Court focused on the behaviour of the Commission, whereas the previous part mainly concerned that of the Council and the European Parliament in exercising their co-legislative powers. In particular, one relates to the content of the proposal and the way the Parliament and the Council distorted it, thereby entitling the Commission to decide to withdraw, whereas the other concerns the response of the Commission to the said conducts of the co-legislators at various points of the procedure. In other words, once the 'very power' to withdraw was established, the remainder of the Court's analysis concerned the framework for its legitimate exercise, in consideration of the essential functions of the institutions involved in the ordinary legislative procedure, and the ability of the institutional framework to assist the Union fulfilling its aims, *in casu* to ensure an effective and coherent EU external assistance.[169]

The subsequent *ETS* pronouncement further illustrates the combination of the respective languages of institutional balance and sincere cooperation in the Court's case-law. Having first established the negotiating power of the Commission, the rest of the judgment is almost entirely concentrated on the modalities of its exercise in relation to the special committee foreseen in Article 218(4) TFEU and to the Council. It should be recalled that, in this case, the Commission did not invoke the principle of cooperation, it was rather the Council that referred to it as a motive behind the impugned decision. This may partly explain how the principle was then referred to in the judgment.

Indeed, the way the invoked principles practically structure the Court's reasoning is not manifest, leaving instead the impression that they are considered and applied together. The analysis begins with a reminder of the procedure of Article 218 TFEU and the Commission's general negotiating power under Article 17(1) TEU. It then mentions the principle of sincere cooperation before, seemingly, proceeding with its analysis of the procedural arrangements of Article 218 TFEU, and the institutional balance they foresee, to acknowledge in the event the conformity of the Council Decision with Article 218(2) and (4) TFEU.[170] So if this part of the analysis was indeed aimed at establishing whether the principles of conferral and institutional balance had been observed, one may question the relevance of the reference to the principle of sincere cooperation, unless the latter too has a function in establishing that institutional balance is observed.

The Court held that, in exercising the powers it enjoys under Article 218(2) and (4) TFEU, the Commission may be required to provide all the necessary information to a special committee established by the Council in order for that committee to monitor the progress of the negotiations. To support this, the Court seemingly

---

[168] ibid, following para 97.
[169] See, eg, ibid, paras 85, 91 and 93.
[170] See section I above.

relies both on the duty to practise mutual sincere cooperation, which constrains institutions 'in the context of their functions', and on Article 218(4) TEU that specifically foresees that when the Council establishes a special committee, 'the negotiations must be conducted in consultation with that committee'. In addition, and perhaps more importantly for the present discussion, it considers that '[h]aving regard to the various functions of the institutions in the negotiation and conclusion of the agreements referred to in Article 218', 'the Commission *can be required to provide that information* to the Council as well' (emphasis added). In the words of the Court:

> It is *expedient* for the Council to possess that information in order to have clear knowledge of the course of the negotiations concerning the preparation of a draft agreement that will be submitted to it for its approval. (emphasis added)

This leads to the conclusion that the Council's requests do not constitute an encroachment on the Commission's power, but rather an expression of the latter's responsibility in the exercise of its negotiating powers to help the Council fully fulfil its own functions, at other stages of the procedure.

Yet it is not clear from the reasoning whether the legal underpinnings of the above dictum is the principle of sincere cooperation mentioned a couple of paragraphs earlier, or whether those are the terms of Article 218(4) TFEU, or both. The use of the word 'expedient' suggests a connection with sincere cooperation. For the point is not that the Council is legally empowered to request information from the Commission, akin to the special committee, rather the Court's formulation points to an argument of effectiveness of the overall procedure, and in turn the fulfilment of Union tasks.[171]

Incidentally, the tight connection between power allocation, cooperation and institutional balance was also evident in the pleas of some of the intervening governments. Thus, the power to address negotiating directives to the Commission included 'the power to specify the procedural requirements for negotiation in order to *ensure sincere cooperation between the institutions, enshrined in Article 13(2) TEU, and compliance with the institutional balance*' (emphasis added). The exercise of the Council power to adopt directives of negotiation could thus serve the purpose of cooperation *and* balance, illustrating that the former is in effect a key factor for the latter: institutional balance cannot be maintained without a degree of cooperation between institutions.

---

[171] The judicial conflation of institutional balance and cooperation considerations, by way of a purposive interpretation of the respective actors' roles in the procedure, is particularly visible in the following paragraphs: 'Since the Council is empowered to designate a special committee and the Commission is required to conduct the negotiations "in consultation with" that committee under Article 218(4) TFEU, the Commission must inform the committee of all aspects of the negotiations *in order that it may be properly consulted. It is only in this way that the special committee is in a position to formulate opinions and advice relating to the positions that the Commission must adopt in the negotiations.* That being so, Article 218(4) TFEU must be interpreted as empowering the Council to set out, in the negotiating directives, procedural arrangements governing the process for the provision of information, for communication and for consultation between the special committee and the Commission, *as such rules meet the objective of ensuring proper cooperation at the internal level*': ETS (n 35) paras 77–78 (emphasis added).

Indeed, it may be wondered, in the light of the foregoing discussion, whether institutional balance is a self-standing principle structuring the operation of the institutional framework, or whether in the end its maintenance is a derivative of institutions' compliance with both the principles of conferral and cooperation enshrined in Article 13(2) TEU. Reflecting conferral, institutional balance involves the *negative* obligation that institutions refrain from abusing their powers and encroaching upon the powers of others,[172] and the *positive* requirement that they pay due regard to those of others in the form of engagement to ensure the latter's effectiveness, which arguably is underpinned by the obligation to practise cooperation.

The question can then be asked whether institutional balance and sincere cooperation should continue to be approached as distinct principles structuring the operation of the EU institutional framework. In the light of the case-law, such distinction appears impractical. The requirement of due regard stemming from the principle of institutional balance is an expression of sincere cooperation,[173] itself a contribution to institutional balance, alongside observance of the principle of conferral, which it supplements. This is not to suggest that in operational terms verifying that the principle of institutional balance is complied with should be severed from controlling respect for conferral, and instead be addressed together with the principle of sincere cooperation. This is rather to propose that the institutional balance be conceived as a meta-principle whose observance is function of the institutions' adherence to *both* principles of conferral and cooperation, enshrined in Article 13(2) TEU. Institutional balance straddles the classic distinction between the principles governing the existence of powers, and those concerning the exercise of such powers. *Balance* not only presupposes plurality and allocation, it also requires cooperative interactions between the different power holders.

## B. A Broadly Construed Scope of Application?

Having examined how the principles of Article 13(2) TEU operate and interact, this last section briefly discusses their scope of application. In particular, it questions whether they apply to institutions irrespective of the area of EU law in which they intervene (i), it then envisages what institutional actors are bound by those principles (ii).

### (i) Application to All Institutions' Activities

The general question to be addressed here is whether the recurrent procedural differentiation which characterises the EU external action has any impact on the

---

[172] Lenaerts and Verhoeven, 'Institutional Balance as a Guarantee for Democracy in EU Governance' (n 6).
[173] See in this regard *Luxembourg v European Parliament* (n 23).

application of the principles of Article 13(2) TEU, and if so how. In particular, do those principles bind the EU institutional framework differently depending on whether it operates within the TFEU or CFSP environment?

As mentioned at the outset of this discussion, Article 13(1) TEU establishes an institutional framework for the Union to 'promote its values, advance its objectives, serve its interests ... and ensure the consistency, effectiveness and continuity of its policies and actions'. Having cited the institutions that formally constitute such a framework, the same Article then stipulates in its second paragraph that each of them is to 'act within the limits of the powers conferred on it by the *Treaties*, and in conformity with the procedures, conditions and objectives *set out in them*' (emphasis added). Article 13 TEU is thus deemed to establish an institutional framework for the whole Union, and to govern the allocation and exercise of powers of its constitutive institutions in the contexts of both TFEU and TEU, including the CFSP, to fulfil the general aims of Article 13(1) TEU.[174]

Indeed, Article 13 is the first provision of Title III TEU. Keystone of the Union's institutional edifice, it spearheads Articles that spell out the essential role of EU institutions, including in the context of the CFSP. For example, Article 14 TEU on the European Parliament refers to powers that are of relevance for the EU external action whether based on the TEU or the TFEU: while its legislative role is limited to the non-CFSP context given that the CFSP excludes legislative acts, its budgetary function nevertheless concerns the whole EU budget, including the budgetary aspects of the CFSP. The same holds true as regards its function of political control, as the Court confirmed.[175] Similarly, Article 16 TEU articulates the general policy-making functions of the Council applicable in the contexts of both the TEU, and of the TFEU.[176]

The general terms of Title III TEU therefore support the claim that the principles of Article 13(2) TEU structure all actions of, and interactions between, all institutions, in the framework of all EU activities in the TEU and TFEU contexts, and thus including the CFSP. Arguably, this contention is not contradicted by the equal legal value of the TEU (institutional) provisions and those of the TFEU.[177] The TFEU provisions, including those on institutions, do not intend to establish alternative rules governing the institutional framework of Title III TEU, but rather to articulate them, in line with the purpose of the TFEU which is, pursuant to Article 1(1) to 'organise ... the functioning of the Union and determines the areas of, delimitation of, and arrangements for exercising its competences'.[178]

---

[174] The Preamble to the post-Lisbon TEU still refers to the notion of 'single institutional framework': 'DESIRING to enhance further the democratic and efficient functioning of the institutions so as to enable them better to carry out, within a single institutional framework, the tasks entrusted to them'. Earlier TEU provisions on the Union's institutional framework also referred to the 'single institutional framework', to indicate that the Union, despite its pillar architecture, had one set of institutions.

[175] See *Mauritius* (n 48), and *Tanzania* (n 51).

[176] Article 15(6)(d) TEU, which concerns the President of the European Council, confirms that Title III covers CFSP related powers.

[177] Article 1(3) TEU and Art 1(2) TFEU.

[178] Indeed, several provisions of Title I of Part 6 TFEU contain cross-references to the provisions of Title III TEU.

Nor is it contradicted by the provisions of Article 40(2) TEU which require that the arrangements specific to the CFSP be preserved. The CFSP characteristics which these provisions aim at protecting are of an institutional and procedural nature. Article 24(1) TEU thus foresees that:

> the implementation of the policies listed in [Articles 3 to 6 TFEU, which spell out EU competences except for the CFSP competence] shall not affect the application of the *procedures and the extent of the powers of the institutions* laid down by the Treaties for the exercise of the Union competences under [the CFSP] Chapter. (emphasis added)

The *principles* governing the EU institutional framework are thus not precluded from applying to institutions operating in the context of the CFSP, on the contrary. In effect, the principle established by Article 40(2) TEU is a specific reiteration of Article 13(2) TEU, in that it sets out the requirement that the distinct procedures of the CFSP, the powers of institutions they foresee, and thus the institutional balance they encapsulate, must be respected.

The Court of Justice's pronouncements in the *Mauritius* and *Tanzania* cases provide additional support for the notion that the principles of Article 13(2) TEU structure the whole functioning of the institutional framework.[179] The Court made clear that while concluding a CFSP agreement based on Article 37 TEU, the Council remained equally bound to respect the right of the Parliament to be informed at all stages of the negotiation and conclusion of the agreement, in line with the procedural requirement of Article 218(10) TFEU.

More generally, the Court has indicated on several occasions that the obligation of cooperation binding institutions *inter se* entails the same mutual duties as those governing relations between the Member States and the Union.[180] As the principle of sincere cooperation based on Article 4(3) TEU binds Member States even when exercising their own competences,[181] or indeed when acting in the context of the CFSP,[182] it is arguable that, by implication, the duty of cooperation equally compels institutions, whatever the nature of the power (CFSP or otherwise) which they exercise.

In sum, both the Treaties and the case-law point to a general application of the principles of conferral, institutional balance and sincere cooperation, irrespective of the recurrent 'bipolarity' of the EU external action. Admittedly, this does not automatically entail that they may be equally enforced. Given its limited jurisdiction over CFSP provisions, the Court of Justice is unable to control whether, for instance, the Council acted in breach of the institutional requirement of a CFSP legal basis and encroached upon the powers of another institution involved in the procedure at hand. Only if the Council ignored the limits of its CFSP-based powers and infringed the principle of Article 40(1) TEU could action before the Court

---

[179] *Mauritius* (n 48), and *Tanzania* (n 51).
[180] See discussion in section I A above.
[181] *Commission v Luxembourg* (n 103) para 58; *Commission v Germany* (n 103) para 64; *PFOs* (n 96) para 71.
[182] See Hillion, 'Mixity and Coherence' (n 94).

be contemplated,[183] or if one managed to convince the Court that the breach of a CFSP procedural requirement would amount to a violation of the principle of conferral under Article 13(2) TEU. That said, such a breach is unlikely to occur in the context of a CFSP procedure in view of the fact that, except for the treaty-making procedure of Article 218 TFEU, the arrangements for adopting CFSP acts may, in addition to the Council, only involve the European Council, its President and/or the High Representative. The CFSP is based on a more restricted allocation of powers, between fewer and interrelated protagonists, entailing a simpler expression of institutional balance, whose maintenance is, as a result, less dependent on compliance with the principles of Article 13(2) TEU. The differentiation in terms of their enforcement is therefore of limited practical significance.

Beyond the 'bipolarity' of the EU external action, new institutional developments may also raise questions as to the reach of the principles of Article 13(2) TEU and their enforcement. EU institutions have increasingly used informal instruments, both autonomous, eg agendas, consensus, strategies, action plans, and contractual, eg memoranda of understanding, non-binding international arrangements, statements, that are usually crafted in an equally ad hoc fashion. The use of such instruments has been particularly conspicuous in the development of the EU external action through eg enlargement and neighbourhood policies.[184] In these contexts, Member States as such, or through the European Council, have endowed institutions with new roles, prompting new inter-institutional interactions. But informalism has also flourished in the wake of several crises afflicting the EU, eg as regards migration.[185]

The 2016 'EU–Turkey Statement' by the members of the European Council and their Turkish counterpart is a case in point.[186] Its formulation exhibits the intention of the parties to establish reciprocal rights and obligations characteristic of international agreements, as well as the involvement of EU actors for its implementation.[187] One could have therefore expected that such arrangement be negotiated and concluded in the framework of Article 218 TFEU, and thus in line with the principles of Article 13(2) TEU, particularly in view of the recent

---

[183] See *Tanzania* (n 51).

[184] See Ilaria Vianello, Chapter 9; also M Maresceau, 'Pre-accession' in M Cremona (ed), *The Enlargement of the European Union* (Oxford, Oxford University Press, 2003) 9; M Cremona, 'The European Neighbourhood Policy: More than a Partnership' in M Cremona (ed), *Developments in EU External Relations Law* (Oxford, Oxford University Press, 2008) 244; C Hillion, 'The EU's Neighbourhood Policy towards Eastern Europe' in A Dashwood and M Maresceau (eds), *Law and Practice of EU External Relations: Salient Features of a Changing Landscape* (Cambridge, Cambridge University Press, 2008) 309.

[185] On this see, eg, D Thym, 'The "Refugee Crisis" as a Challenge of Legal Design and Institutional Legitimacy' (2016) 53 *CML Rev* 1545.

[186] See http://europa.eu/rapid/press-release_MEMO-16-963_en.htm. See also the 'Joint Way Forward on migration issues between Afghanistan and the EU', https://eeas.europa.eu/sites/eeas/files/eu_afghanistan_joint_way_forward_on_migration_issues.pdf.

[187] ibid. cp the surprising Orders of the General Court in Case T-192/16, *NF* v. *European Council*, Order, EU:T:2017:128; Case T-193/16, *NG* v. *European Council*, Order, EU:T:2017:129; and Case T-257/16, *NM* v. *European Council*, Order, EU:T:2017:130; currently under appeal:

case-law of the Court of Justice on the applicability of this procedure.[188] It is also surprising that neither the Commission nor the European Parliament found such an arrangement contestable, given their traditional scrupulousness in being involved wherever legally warranted, but also in view of the contentious content of the Statement from the viewpoint of European and international protection of fundamental rights.[189]

Recourse to such informal arrangements, justified by political expediency, may upset the normal functioning of the institutional framework, and the application of the principles that structure it. Establishing the detailed implications of these phenomena for the application of the principles would deserve a far more elaborate discussion than can be undertaken here. The following remarks only flag up what the case-law and the practice suggest about the possible application of the principles to more informal settings, and show that an attempt is being made to circumscribe the corrosive effects of ad hoc arrangements for the EU legal order, and indeed to (re)assert the canons of Article 13(2) TEU.

The Court has thus considered that the non-legally binding nature of an instrument does not mean that it can be adopted without regard to the treaty-based distribution of powers. Nor indeed does it prevent judicial control to verify that the latter is respected. Thus, in the *Memorandum of Understanding* case, the Court confirmed that the conclusion of a non-binding agreement required observance of the basic tenets of the distribution of powers, as articulated in the provisions of Title III TEU:

> [T]he Commission cannot be regarded as having the right, by virtue of its power of external representation under Article 17(1) TEU, to sign a non-binding agreement resulting from negotiations conducted with a third country.

> The decision concerning the signing of an agreement with a third country covering an area for which the Union is competent—irrespective of whether or not that agreement is binding—requires an assessment to be made, in compliance with strategic guidelines laid down by the European Council and the principles and objectives of the Union's external action laid down in Article 21(1) and (2) TEU, of the Union's interests in the context of its relations with the third country concerned, and the divergent interests arising in those relations to be reconciled.

> Therefore, a decision concerning the signature of a non-binding agreement such as the agreement at issue in the present case is one of the measures by which the Union's

---

[188] See, eg, Case C-399/12 *Germany v Council (OIV)*, Judgment, EU:C:2014:2258; further, I Govaere 'Novel Issues Pertaining to EU Member States Membership of Other International Organisations: The *OIV* Case' in I Govaere, E Lannon, P van Elsuwege and S Adam (eds), *The European Union in the World, Essays in Honour of Marc Maresceau* (Leiden, Martinus Nijhoff, 2014) 225.

[189] See further E Cannizzaro, 'Disintegration through Law' (2016) 1 *European Papers* 3; S Peers, 'The Final EU/Turkey Refugee Deal: A Legal Assessment', http://eulawanalysis.blogspot.no/2016/03/the-final-euturkey-refugee-deal-legal.html. O Corten and M Dony, 'Accord politique ou juridique: Quelle est la nature du « machin » conclu entre l'UE et la Turquie en matière d'asile ?' in EU Immigration and Asylum Law and Policy, 10 June 2016, http://eumigrationlawblog.eu/accord-politique-ou-juridique-quelle-est-la-nature-du-machin-conclu-entre-lue-et-la-turquie-en-matiere-dasile/.

policy is made and its external action planned for the purpose of the second sentence of Article 16(1) and the third subparagraph of Article 16(6) TEU.[190]

Institutions' recourse to non-binding instruments is thus legally accepted if the basic requirements of the EU constitutional framework in general, and the institutional principles of Article 13(2) TEU in particular, are respected.

This appears to be the case in institutional practice too. The treaty-based distribution of powers has, for instance, pervaded the elaboration and implementation of ad hoc policy frameworks such as neighbourhood and enlargement policies. While the Treaty-makers have partly constitutionalised the neighbourhood policy,[191] Member States have involved the High Representative for Foreign Affairs and Security Policy in the pre-accession monitoring of the candidate states, alongside the Commission which until the entry into force of the Lisbon Treaty had operated on its own on this terrain. The negotiating frameworks with Serbia and Montenegro thus envisage that:

> In the field of CFSP, the High Representative is responsible, in close liaison with the Member States, and the Commission where appropriate, for screening, making proposals in the negotiations and reporting regularly to the Council.[192]

Indeed, the Court's seminal pronouncement in the *Pringle* case indicates that even *outside* the framework of the Union, institutions' actions remained governed by the principles structuring the institutional framework.[193] The Court was asked to rule on 'whether the allocation, by [the Treaty establishing the European Stability Mechanism (ESM)], of new tasks to the Commission, the European Central Bank and the Court [was] compatible with their powers as defined in the Treaties'. In the section of its analysis devoted to the 'interpretation of Article 13 TEU', the Court held that:

> [I]t is apparent from the case-law of the Court that the Member States are entitled, in areas which do not fall under the exclusive competence of the Union, to entrust tasks to the institutions, outside the framework of the Union, such as the task of coordinating a collective action undertaken by the Member States or managing financial assistance (see *Parliament v Council and Commission*, paragraphs 16, 20 and 22, and *Parliament v Council*, paragraphs 26, 34 and 41), *provided that those tasks do not alter the essential character of the powers conferred on those institutions by the EU and FEU Treaties* (see, inter alia, Opinion 1/92 [1992] ECR I-2821, paragraphs 32 and 41; Opinion 1/00 [2002]

---

[190] *Memorandum of Understanding* (n 35) paras 38–40. The Court has indeed construed the scope of application of Treaty procedures broadly enough: see *OIV* (n 188).

[191] Article 8 TEU.

[192] Conference on Accession to the European Union, Serbia, *General EU Position: Ministerial Meeting Opening the Intergovernmental Conference on the Accession of Serbia to the European Union* (Brussels, 21 January 2014) para 20, available at http://ec.europa.eu/neighbourhood-enlargement/countries/detailed-country-information/serbia_en.

[193] Case C-370/12 *Pringle*, Judgment, EU:C:2012:756. See further B de Witte and T Beukers, 'The Court of Justice Approves the Creation of the European Stability Mechanism Outside the EU Legal Order: *Pringle*' (2013) 50 *CML Rev* 805.

ECR I-3493, paragraph 20; and Opinion 1/09 [2011] ECR I-1137, paragraph 75). (emphasis added)[194]

Member States' freedom to endow institutions with additional tasks can thus be limited by reference to Article 13 TEU. In particular, in requiring that the '*essential character* of the powers conferred on the institutions' (emphasis added) should not be altered, the Court upholds the applicability of a fundamental aspect of the principle of conferral, and indirectly of institutional balance. Admittedly, the required observance of the principles of Article 13 TEU is limited in two ways. First, Member States are required to preserve only the 'essential character of [institutions'] powers', and secondly, to protect the core powers only of those institutions entrusted with additional tasks, not explicitly those that are *not* mentioned in the arrangement at hand, like the European Parliament, even though its powers, eg of political control, could be affected, in turn upsetting the institutional balance. This, at least, is a possible interpretation of the Court's reference to '*those* tasks' and '*those* institutions'.

On this reading, respect for the terms of Article 13 TEU in the situation of institutions being entrusted with 'peripheral' tasks would not require 'due regard' for other institutions powers deriving from the principle of institutional balance, and more generally consideration of each institution's 'role in the institutional structure' of the Union. The Court would thereby defer to the Member States' wish and accept that they can bring institutions out of their original constitutional biotope, and thus from the scope of application of the structural principles which normally govern their actions.

However, another reading is possible. In effect, the Court of Justice says little about whether those institutions that are endowed with peripheral tasks are bound or not by those principles. In effect, the Court only deals here with the constraints on Member States, deriving from Article 13 TEU, when they establish those tasks, but not with the constraints on institutions themselves. It may thus be contended that, in performing their additional tasks, the institutions concerned remain bound by the general principles that govern their actions, including due regard for the powers of others and sincere cooperation.

The Treaty on Stability, Coordination and Governance (TSCG),[195] concluded outside the framework of the Treaty framework, provides some support to the claim that institutions are compelled by the cardinal principles structuring the operation of the institutional framework, even when acting outside the Treaty framework. Hence, the Preamble to the TSCG stipulates that:

> when reviewing and monitoring the budgetary commitments under this Treaty, the European Commission will act *within the framework of its powers, as provided by the Treaty on the Functioning of the European Union*, in particular Articles 121, 126 and 136 thereof; (emphasis added)

---

[194] *Pringle* (n 193) para 158.
[195] See www.consilium.europa.eu/en/european-council/euro-summit/. Further, House of Commons European Scrutiny Committee, Treaty on Stability, Coordination and Governance: Impact on the Eurozone and the Rule of Law, HC 1817, 3 April 2012.

while Article 2 foresees that:

1. This Treaty shall be applied and interpreted by the Contracting Parties *in conformity with the Treaties on which the European Union is founded, in particular Article 4(3) of the Treaty on European Union, and with European Union law*, including procedural law whenever the adoption of secondary legislation is required.

2. This *Treaty shall apply insofar as it is compatible with the Treaties on which the European Union is founded and with European Union law*. It shall not encroach upon the competence of the Union to act in the area of the economic union. (emphasis added)

Article 7 also underscores that the contracting parties fully respect the procedural requirements of the Treaties on which the European Union is founded.

In sum, while Member States are entitled to entrust EU institutions with additional tasks, insofar as the latter do not alter the 'essential character of [institutions'] powers', the institutions' performance of these tasks appears to remain governed by the principles structuring the EU institutional framework, in line with the requirements of the rule of law. This would suggest that the scope of application *ratione materiae* of the principles of Article 13(2) TEU should not be construed narrowly, and this is arguably true of their application *ratione personae*.

## (ii) Principles Binding Institutions, All Institutions, but Only Institutions?

Successive reforms have modified the institutional balance established by the Treaties, first, by conferring new powers on existing institutions, particularly the European Parliament,[196] and secondly, by expanding the list of formal EU institutions,[197] the recent institutionalisation of the European Council being a case in point.[198] As this list grows, the scope of application of the principles of conferral, institutional balance and cooperation mechanically widens and, as the distribution of powers evolves, so do the requirements that observance of these principles entails.

Potentially adding to the sophistication of the principles' application, the EU institutional framework includes more protagonists than those which Article 13(1) TEU mentions. In particular, the EU external action system involves several offices, agencies and bodies,[199] the most emblematic of which is the European

---

[196] See on this, see P Koutrakos (ed), *The European Union's External Relations a Year after Lisbon*, CLEER Working Papers 2011/3.

[197] On these institutional developments, see literature mentioned above nn 7 and 9.

[198] Article 13(1) TEU. As such, the European Council is bound by the principles of institutional balance and cooperation, something that might not be evident in the recent UK related negotiations, forcing the Commission to commit to new legislative initiatives to cater for the demands of one of its members. See *Pringle* (n 193) para 31. On the stronger influence of the European Council, see further Editorial Comments, 'An Ever Mighty European Council' (n 76).

[199] Specifically on agencies, see M Everson and E Vos, 'European Agencies: What about Institutional Balance?' in A Lazowski and S Blockmans (eds), *Research Handbook on EU Institutional Law* (Cheltenham, Edward Elgar, 2016) 139. More generally, P Craig and G de Búrca (eds), *The Evolution of EU Law*, 2nd edn (Oxford, Oxford University Press, 2011) 61.

External Action Service (EEAS), headed by the High Representative for Foreign Affairs and Security Policy–Vice-President of the European Commission.[200] This development begs the question of whether and if so, how the principles apply to these additional actors.

Located in the second paragraph of Article 13 TEU, immediately after the formal list of EU institutions, the principles of conferral, institutional balance and cooperation could arguably bind only those very institutions. However, Treaty provisions, secondary legislation, as well as the case-law of the Court of Justice indicate that their application *ratione personae* may be more broadly conceived, notably because formally the treaty-based system of distribution of powers which they govern is itself broader than the list of Article 13(1) TEU indicates.

For example, while Article 17(1) TEU stipulates that the Commission ensures the EU's external *representation*, it is however the responsibility of the President of the European Council and of the High Representative, respectively, in the field of CFSP.[201] Similarly, Article 218 TFEU entrusts the High Representative (HR) with specific functions in the EU treaty-making procedure, whenever the latter is used for the negotiation and conclusion of CFSP agreements. In particular, Article 218(3) TFEU foresees that where the agreement envisaged relates exclusively or principally to the CFSP, the HR should submit (assisted by the EEAS) recommendations to the Council, which shall adopt a decision authorising the opening of negotiations, and depending on the subject of the agreement envisaged, the Council then nominates the Union negotiator or the head of the Union's negotiating team, which can mean the HR if the agreement concerns the CFSP. To use the Court's terminology, Article 218 TFEU therefore establishes 'a balance of power between institutions' which,[202] when the procedure is used for a CFSP agreement, includes the HR.[203] In effect, the latter is entrusted with powers which the Commission exercises in the context of the same procedure when the agreement does not concern the CFSP, powers which are governed by the principles of Article 13(2) TEU.

These two examples show that the Treaties implicate entities from outside the formal list of Article 13(1) TEU in the 'system allocating powers among the EU institutions, assigning to each institution its own role in the institutional structure of the Union and the accomplishment of the tasks entrusted to the Union'.[204] Key provisions on the HR and on the President of the European Council are indeed included in Title III of the TEU, alongside those on other institutions (except for

---

[200] Article 27(3) TEU, and EEAS Decision (n 80).

[201] Articles 15(6) and 27 TEU.

[202] See, eg, *ETS* (n 35) para 62.

[203] The same holds true as regards the operation of Art 218(9) TFEU on the initiative to suspend agreement.

[204] *Memorandum of Understanding* (n 35) para 31, referring to *Chernobyl* (n 20) para 21, discussed earlier. In this regard, see E Paasivirta, 'The External Representation after Lisbon: New Rules, a New Era?' in P Koutrakos (ed), *The European Union's External Relations a Year after Lisbon*, CLEER Working Papers 2011/3, 39; see also the various contributions in S Blockmans and RA Wessel (eds), *Principles and Practices of EU External Representation*, CLEER Working Papers 5/2012.

the European Central Bank), and as such part of the institutional balance it incarnates, as contended above. The notion of institutional framework should therefore not be understood too restrictively for the purpose of the application of the principles of Article 13(2) TEU.

Indeed, while these entities are included in the EU system of allocation of powers, they are also addressees and beneficiaries of various cooperation obligations, envisaged as specific expressions of the second sentence of Article 13(2) TEU. For example, according to Article 15(6) TEU, the President of the European Council '(b) shall ensure the preparation and continuity of the work of the European Council *in cooperation with the President of the Commission*, and on the basis of the work of the General Affairs Council' (emphasis added). Conversely, the President of the European Commission is bound to cooperate with the President of the European Council.[205] Moreover the duty to cooperate to ensure consistency between the different areas of the EU external action and between these and its other policies explicitly binds the Commission and the Council. But Article 21(3) TEU also foresees that, in this context, they shall be assisted by the High Representative of the Union for Foreign Affairs and Security Policy, responsible too to ensure the consistency of the Union's external action, pursuant to Article 18(4) TEU.

Being included in the system of distribution of powers, the President of the European Council and the High Representative should as a result be bound by the principles that govern that system too. Considering the rule of law on which the Union is founded, it would be problematic if the Treaties endowed entities with formal rights, responsibilities, functions or tasks—all of which could indeed be encapsulated in a broadly construed notion of 'powers' for the purpose of Article 13(2) TEU—without subjecting them to the principles that govern the existence and exercise of such powers.

To be sure, indication of the inclusion of these entities within the scope of application of the principles of Article 13(2) TEU can be found in the case-law. Addressing the European Parliament's claim that the Council had failed to comply with its obligation to inform it in accordance with Article 218(10) TFEU, the Court found in the *Tanzania* case that:

> The Court must, at the outset, reject the Council's argument that the obligation to inform the Parliament of the conduct of negotiations is the responsibility of the High Representative and not that of the Council itself. Since Article 218(2) TFEU provides that it is for the Council to authorize the opening of negotiations, to adopt negotiating directives, and to authorize the signing and conclusion of the agreements, it follows that it is *also* incumbent on the Council, not least in the context of agreements exclusively concerning the CFSP, to ensure that the obligation laid down by Article 218(10) TFEU is fulfilled. (emphasis added)[206]

---

[205] This duty of mutual cooperation has been reiterated in the European Council Rules of Procedure. See Art 3 of European Council Decision 2009/882/EU of 1 December 2009 adopting its Rules of Procedure [2009] OJ L325/51; and Editorial Comments, 'The Post-Lisbon Institutional Package: Do Old Habits Die Hard?' (2010) 47 *CML Rev* 597.

[206] *Tanzania* (n 51) para 73.

If the obligation to inform the European Parliament in this context is 'also' incumbent on the Council, the Court then implies that the High Representative mentioned earlier in the paragraph is equally bound by that obligation. This, in turn, confirms that the HR is included in the 'balance between [the] institutions' envisaged by Article 218 TEU, at least for the negotiation and conclusion of CFSP agreements and that, as a result, the principles underpinning this balance should apply to her too.[207] If that is true, some of the Commission's rights and obligations in the context of Article 218 TFEU, as spelled out by the Court of Justice,[208] could also be of significance for the HR when exercising her functions.[209] In the same vein, the case-law articulating the representation powers of the Commission could be of relevance in delimiting the equivalent powers of the HR and of the President of the European Council.[210]

In sum, the case-law provides some support for the claim that the principles of Article 13(2) TEU have a wider scope of application *ratione personae* than that intimated by the terms of Article 13(1) TEU.[211] The question can nonetheless be raised as to whether the application also concerns entities that are not covered by Title III TEU, such as agencies, bodies and other committees. A full discussion of this question would deserve more space than this chapter allows.[212] Suffice to mention two judgments that indicate that the canons of Article 13(2) TEU have relevance for these entities too.

First, the *ETS* case suggests that the application of the principles of Article 13(2) TEU pervades interactions between institutions and *committees*.[213] In its judgment, the Court indicated that the Commission had to consult the 'special committee', which the Council may designate under Article 218(4) TFEU, so that this committee effectively performs its functions in that procedure.

---

[207] Though practically difficult in view of her institutional position vis-à-vis the Council and the Commission, one could imagine that where the EU agreement envisaged does not relate exclusively to the TFEU, but also covers CFSP matters, the HR (and the EEAS) would have a case against the Commission if the latter submitted recommendations to the Council for the entire agreement, without the HR (and the EEAS) being involved.

[208] As articulated in, eg, the Court's *ITLOS* and *Memorandum of Understanding* judgments (n 35).

[209] If the HR *qua* negotiator of CFSP agreement is bound, alongside the Council, to provide information to the European Parliament so it may fulfil its consistency related function, it may be argued that the Commission too, *qua* negotiator of non-CFSP EU agreements, is bound by the same obligation.

[210] See, eg, the Court's findings in the *ITLOS* and *Memorandum of Understanding* cases (n 35).

[211] The *Tanzania* judgment (n 51) underlines the importance of cooperation with the European Parliament too, in particular through Art 218(10) TFEU for the purpose of ensuring the consistency of the EU external action (para 72): '[T]he European Union must ensure, in accordance with Article 21(3) TEU, consistency between the different areas of its external action, and *the duty to inform which the other institutions owe to the Parliament under Article 218(10) TFEU contributes to ensuring the coherence and consistency of that action*' (emphasis added). (See, by analogy, as regards the cooperation between the EU institutions and the Member States, *Commission v Luxembourg* (n 103) para 60; Opinion 1/08, EU:C:2009:739, para 136; *PFOs* (n 96) para 75.) The duty of cooperation enshrined in Art 21(3) TEU therefore applies more widely than explicitly foreseen in the provision itself. See further Sánchez-Tabernero, 'Mitigating the Effects of Gravity in Competence Demarcation' (n 63).

[212] See, eg, Everson and Vos, 'European Agencies' (n 199).

[213] This ties in with the discussion on comitology and institutional balance, see further eg Chamon, 'Institutional Balance and Community Method in the Implementation of EU Legislation Following the Lisbon Treaty' (n 7).

In particular, it requested the Commission to provide it with all the information necessary for it to monitor the progress of the negotiations, adding that it was only in this way that the special committee would be in a position to formulate opinions and advice relating to the negotiations.[214] Later in the judgment, the Court also examined whether, as the Council had envisaged in the contested decision, the special committee was entitled to establish detailed negotiating positions of the Union, including before each negotiating session. On this point, the Court, however, found that:

> It is contrary to Article 218(4) TFEU for the positions established by the special committee or, as the case may be, the Council itself to be binding in this way.

> First, the two elements referred [of the impugned Council decision] confer upon the special committee the task of establishing detailed negotiating positions of the European Union, a task which goes beyond the consultative function assigned to it by that provision.

> Secondly, whilst it is true that Article 218(4) TFEU authorises the Council to draw up negotiating directives, it does not, on the other hand, contrary to what Section A of the Annex to the contested decision provides in the second sentence of paragraph 1, invest that institution with the power to impose 'detailed negotiating positions' on the negotiator.

> It follows that, by including those elements in the negotiating directives, the Council infringed the obligation laid down by Article 13(2) TEU to act within the limits of the powers conferred on it by Article 218(2) to (4) TFEU.[215]

Admittedly, it was the Council not the special Committee that violated the principle of conferral by exceeding the limits of its powers under Article 218(4) TFEU. The judgment nevertheless casts light on the consultative 'function' of the special committee, as well as its limits, and thus more generally on the institutional balance established by Article 218(4) TFEU of which this committee is part. This is significant not only for the Council in the context of the procedure at hand, but also for the special committee's future interactions with the Commission.

Secondly, the *ESMA* judgment shows how the Court uses the language of allocation of powers when dealing with activities of agencies, bodies and offices. The case concerned the powers of the European Securities and Markets Authority (ESMA), some of which were contested by the UK government, notably on the ground that they breached the principles relating to the delegation of powers laid down in the so-called *Meroni* doctrine.[216] The Court disagreed and underlined

---

[214] See *ETS* (n 35) para 66. At para 77, the Court reiterated that 'Since the Council is empowered to designate a special committee and the Commission *is required* to conduct the negotiations "in consultation with" that committee under Art 218(4) TFEU, the Commission *must* inform the committee of all aspects of the negotiations in order that it may be properly consulted. It is only in this way that the special committee is in a position to formulate opinions and advice relating to the positions that the Commission must adopt in the negotiations' (emphasis added).

[215] ibid paras 88–91.

[216] Case C-270/12 *United Kingdom v Council and Parliament*, Judgment, EU:C:2014:18.

that the powers available to ESMA were 'precisely delineated and amenable to judicial review in the light of the objectives established by the delegating authority'. It added more generally that:

> [W]hile the treaties do not contain any provision to the effect *that powers may be conferred on a Union body, office or agency, a number of provisions in the FEU Treaty none the less presuppose that such a possibility exists.*
>
> Under Article 263 TFEU, the Union bodies whose acts may be subject to judicial review by the Court include the 'bodies, offices' and 'agencies' of the Union. The rules governing actions for failure to act are applicable to those bodies pursuant to Article 265 TFEU. Article 267 TFEU provides that the courts and tribunals of the Member States may refer questions concerning the validity and interpretation of the acts of such bodies to the Court. Such acts may also be the subject of a plea of illegality pursuant to Article 277 TFEU.
>
> Those judicial review mechanisms apply to the bodies, offices and agencies established by the EU legislature which were given powers to adopt measures that are legally binding on natural or legal persons in specific areas, such as the European Chemicals Agency, the European Medicines Agency, the Office for Harmonisation in the Internal Market (Trade Marks and Designs), the Community Plant Variety Office and the European Aviation Safety Agency. (emphasis added)[217]

If the TFEU presupposes the possibility that 'powers may be conferred on a Union body, office or agency' notably because they can be brought to the Court, it also assumes that the principles that govern conferral and exercise of those powers apply *mutatis mutandis*. As suggested in the last paragraph above, the specific characteristics and functions of the entity, for instance, whether it has the power to adopt legally binding measures, determine the actual relevance and modalities of application of those principles.

In sum, the Treaties, secondary law and the case-law indicate that whether part of the formal institutional framework of Article 13(1) TEU or not, entities operating in the EU context and endowed with a particular function are not immune from the application of the fundamental principles governing the existence and the exercise of that power, enshrined in Article 13(2) TEU. These entities cannot act beyond the limits of their functions, nor can they act or fail to act in a manner that would impede the effectiveness of the institutional framework.

# IV. Conclusion

This chapter examined the foundations and application of three key principles structuring the institutional framework of the EU external action: conferral, institutional balance and sincere cooperation. Incrementally articulated by the Court

---

[217] ibid paras 79–80.

of Justice, these principles now share a common legal foundation in Article 13(2) TEU, and in turn an equivalent constitutional significance.

Studying their application in the case-law, it became evident that the said principles are highly interdependent in their definition and operation. While observance of the principle of conferral remains fundamental to the maintenance of institutional balance, the latter is also increasingly contingent, legally and practically, on compliance with the principle of cooperation. Enjoying discretion on this terrain, the Court has indeed buttressed the significance of cooperation by articulating binding duties that constrain the manner in which institutions exercise their powers. These duties supplement the treaty-based distribution of powers; they also contribute to a thicker conception of institutional balance, whereby the essential role of institutions is safeguarded in all operations of the institutional framework, ultimately to ensure that it legitimately and effectively fulfils its tasks, as envisaged by Article 13(1) TEU.

This case-law echoes the cooperation jurisprudence that the Court has developed in the context of Member States–EU interactions on the international plane, which in turn raises the question of possible broader commonalities between the principles structuring the interactions between the EU and its Member States on the international plane, and those governing inter-institutional relations. Hence, beyond the apparent parallel application of the principles governing the existence and exercise of powers,[218] additional connections could be made between, eg the principle of coherence and that of institutional balance. In effect, their observance similarly hinges on compliance with other key principles structuring the functioning of the legal order, *viz* respect for the treaty-based demarcation of powers, and with the duties to cooperate in the exercise of these powers, thereby inferring a possible multi-level set-up of principles structuring the overall system of EU external relations.

---

[218] It is also remarkable that in both cases, the Treaty of Lisbon combined these principles in the same provision. Thus, Art 4(1) TEU establishes the principle of conferral, while Art 4(3) TEU spells out the principle of sincere cooperation.

# 7

# *Pars Pro Toto*: The Member States' Obligations of Sincere Cooperation, Solidarity and Unity

JORIS LARIK

## I. Introduction

In 1936, the United States Supreme Court noted in its *Curtiss-Wright* decision, which addressed the extent of powers of the federal executive branch in foreign relations, that:

> It is important to bear in mind that we are here dealing not alone with an authority vested in the President by an exertion of legislative power, but with such an authority plus the very delicate, plenary and exclusive power of the President as the sole organ of the federal government in the field of international relations.[1]

This would become known as the 'sole organ' doctrine,[2] which expresses the extensive powers of the US President in foreign relations. Hence, constitutionally speaking, federalism in the United States is a mainly internal characteristic, which is not mirrored in the conduct of its foreign affairs and international representation. The 'sole organ' doctrine, consequently, can be considered the fundamental structural principle governing US external relations. Also, other internationally important powers with federal systems, such as India and Brazil, have a similar set-up.[3]

---

[1] *United States v Curtiss-Wright Export Corp*, 299 US 304, 320 (1936).

[2] The term 'sole organ' has its origins as far back as 1800, when Chief Justice Marshall noted in a speech to the US Congress: 'The President is the sole organ of the nation in its external relations, and its sole representative with foreign nations'. Cited in *United States v Curtiss-Wright Export Corp* (n 1) 319; see also L Henkin, *Foreign Affairs and the US Constitution*, 2nd edn (Oxford, Clarendon Press, 1996) 41–45.

[3] See for India, Constitution of India, arts 73, 245(2) and 253, Sch. 7 paras 1 and 10–21; further P Chandrasekhara Rao, *The Indian Constitution and International Law* (Dordrecht, Martinus Nijhoff, 1994) 5, 12–14; see for Brazil, Constitution of Brazil, arts 49(I), (II), 84(VII), (VIII). For an example of a formerly centralised and subsequently 'devolved' state retaining sole responsibility for the conduct of its foreign relations, see Constitution of Spain, s 149.

In the European Union, in contrast, there is nothing coming close to a 'sole organ' in its external relations. Instead, Eric Stein's finding in 1986 that 'there is no evidence that an organ equipped with centralized diplomacy and other requisite instrumentalities will emerge in the foreseeable future in Europe' still holds true today.[4] Within the EU, there exist a number of organs with a prominent role in external representation, with especially the Commission and European Council Presidents existing in a parallel relationship marked by uncertainty as to who is paramount.[5] Moreover, all the Member States continue to exist alongside each other and the European Union on the international stage.

It is this latter aspect of the 'polyphonic nature of the Union's external action'[6] on which the present chapter focuses. In the absence of a 'sole organ' in EU external relations, the oft-invoked coherence of its external action is to be ensured through other means and mechanisms.[7] Regarding the relationship between the Member States and the Union, this is best encapsulated by the principles of sincere cooperation and mutual solidarity, an important expression of which is the 'unity in the international representation of the Union'. As this chapter will expound, these represent relational structural principles of EU external relations law *par excellence*,[8] in that they are essential for the smooth articulation and carrying out of the EU's external action by structuring the interaction between the Member States and the Union on the international stage. They help to steer the individual foreign policies of the Member States into a common direction, ie that of the Union's interest and in pursuit of its foreign policy objectives. Member States, regardless of the area of EU competence or policy, and regardless of whether the Union acts alongside them internationally or not, are to operate as parts of the coherent whole of EU external relations—as a *pars pro toto*.

In order to approach and unpack the concepts of sincere cooperation and mutual solidarity as 'structural principles' of EU external relations law, the chapter proceeds as follows. First, it puts the EU's situation in comparative perspective, noting that while it is not the only system of 'foreign affairs federalism',[9]

---

[4] E Stein, 'Towards a European Foreign Policy? The European Foreign Affairs System from the Perspective of the United States Constitution' in M Cappelletti, M Seccombe and JHH Weiler (eds), *Integration Through Law: Europe and the American Federal Experience* (Berlin, Walter de Gruyter, 1986) vol I, Book 3, 3, 82.

[5] See further on this horizontal dimension of international representation and sincere cooperation Christophe Hillion, Chapter 6.

[6] C Hillion, 'Mixity and Coherence in EU External Relations: The Significance of the "Duty of Cooperation"' in C Hillion and P Koutrakos (eds), *Mixed Agreements Revisited: The EU and Its Member States in the World* (Oxford, Hart Publishing, 2010) 87.

[7] See on the concept of coherence as a legal principle and its different meanings M Cremona, 'Coherence in European Union Foreign Relations Law' in P Koutrakos (ed), *European Foreign Policy: Legal and Political Perspectives* (Cheltenham, Edward Elgar, 2011) 55; and C Hillion, '*Tous pour un, un pour tous!* Coherence in the External Relations of the European Union' in M Cremona (ed), *Developments in EU External Relations Law* (Oxford, Oxford University Press, 2008) 10.

[8] See on the concept of relational structural principles Marise Cremona, Chapter 1.

[9] Calling the duty of cooperation a 'federal principle', G De Baere, *Constitutional Principles of EU External Relations* (Oxford, Oxford University Press, 2008) 253; similarly, using the term 'federative principle', M Zuleeg, 'The Advantages of the European Constitution' in A von Bogdandy and J Bast (eds), *Principles of European Constitutional Law*, 2nd edn (Oxford, Hart Publishing, 2010) 763, 774–75.

it continues to stand out from both states and other regional organisations. The main parts of the chapter address the content and manifestations of these principles as regards the constraints on Member State behaviour on the international stage, and subsequently the limits of these duties and retained 'autonomous' or 'sovereign' powers of the Member States as international actors.

## II. The European Union and its Member States: A Special Relationship

Although not a common phenomenon, expressions of federalism in a polity's external relations are not a feature unique to the European Union. Other examples of this include federal states such as Germany, Belgium and Switzerland, in which the constituent units retain the power to act internationally.[10] However, compared to these systems, which allow for a measure of international representation of the entities below the federal level, the EU's approach stands out for two main reasons. First, the ultimate responsibility and decision-making power is not automatically located at the federal level; secondly, the extent to which the constituent units remain active and competent surpasses that of any other constituent state. These two characteristics can be illustrated by comparison with the foreign relations federalism present in Germany, Austria and Belgium, respectively.

Certain federal systems grant not only rights of internal consultation when the federation is negotiating international agreements, but also treaty-making powers to the subnational entities themselves. This is the case for the constitutions of Germany, Belgium and Austria. The German Constitution states as the general rule that '[r]elations with foreign states shall be conducted by the Federation',[11] and that the federation has 'exclusive power to legislate' in the area of 'foreign affairs and defence'.[12] However, in the case that the conclusion of a treaty affects 'the special circumstances of a Land, that Land shall be consulted in a timely manner'.[13] In addition, regardless of the legislative competences of the federation, '[i]nsofar as the Länder have power to legislate, they may conclude treaties with

---

[10] See also D Criekemans, 'Regional Sub-State Diplomacy from a Comparative Perspective: Quebec, Scotland, Bavaria, Catalonia, Wallonia and Flanders' (2010) 5 *Hague Journal of Diplomacy* 37; R Schütze, 'Federalism and Foreign Affairs: Mixity as an (Inter)national Phenomenon' in C Hillion and P Koutrakos (eds), *Mixed Agreements Revisited: The EU and Its Member States in the World* (Oxford, Hart Publishing, 2010) 57; E Cannizzaro, 'Unity and Pluralism in the EU's Foreign Relations Power' in C Barnard (ed), *The Fundamentals of EU Law Revisited: Assessing the Impact of the Constitutional Debate* (Oxford, Oxford University Press, 2007) 193, 195–201; and earlier JHH Weiler, 'The External Legal Relations of Non-Unitary Actors: Mixity and the Federal Principle' in D O'Keeffe and H Schermers (eds), *Mixed Agreements* (Deventer, Kluwer Law and Taxation, 1983) 35.

[11] Basic Law of Germany, art 32(1).

[12] ibid art 73(1), para 1.

[13] ibid art 32(2).

foreign states with the consent of the Federal Government'.[14] However, this practice is rather limited. Instead, it is the Federal Republic of Germany, not the Free State of Bavaria or the city-state of Hamburg (in its self-declared capacity as 'intermediary between all continents and peoples of the world'[15]), which concludes politically salient treaties, which is represented at the United Nations and NATO,[16] and which sends troops and warships on international peace and security missions.[17] Nonetheless, the Länder and the Bund are bound together in a relationship of 'federal loyalty', or *Bundestreue*, which according to German jurists represents a structural principle.[18]

Similarly, under the Austrian constitution, the Länder also retain certain treaty-making powers.[19] They can '[i]n matters within their own sphere of competence ... conclude treaties with states, or their constituent states, bordering on Austria'.[20] However, the Länder are both under an obligation to inform, and more importantly, require prior consent of the federal government before such agreements can be concluded. Such consent is deemed to have been given 'if the Federal Government, within eight weeks from the day that the request has reached the Federal Chancellery, has not communicated to the Land Governor that the consent is denied'.[21] However, the federal executive reserves the right to revoke treaties concluded by the Länder,[22] or to assume competence to ensure compliance with such treaties if the Land fails to do so.[23]

A particularly complex case is Belgium, which encapsulates next to the federal state not only regions (Flanders, Wallonia, and Brussels) but also linguistic communities (Flemish, French-speaking and German-speaking) with powers in external relations.[24] As a general rule, the Belgian Constitution provides that:

---

[14] ibid art 32(3). See further, C Calliess, 'Auswärtige Gewalt' in J Isensee and P Kirchhof (eds), *Handbuch des Staatsrechts der Bundesrepublik Deutschland*, 3rd edn (Heidelberg, CF Müller, 2006) vol IV, 589, 620–26; and U Fastenrath, *Kompetenzverteilung im Bereich der ausgewärtigen Gewalt* (Munich, CH Beck, 1986) 140–47. According to an understanding between the federation and the Länder of 1957 (the *Lindauer Abkommen*), the federation can also conclude treaties touching on the legislative powers of the Länder while providing for the involvement of the Länder in the negotiation and after obtaining their consent. See in detail, B Hartung, *Die Praxis des Lindauer Abkommens* (Cologne, Heymanns, 1984).

[15] First recital of the Preamble to the Constitution of Hamburg.

[16] Fastenrath, *Kompetenzverteilung im Bereich der ausgewärtigen Gewalt* (n 14) 153, notes that politically significant international organisations usually cover matters going beyond the legislative powers of the Länder, thus requiring federal action.

[17] See F Kirchhof, 'Verteidigung und Bundeswehr' in J Isensee and P Kirchhof (eds), *Handbuch des Staatsrechts der Bundesrepublik Deutschland*, 3rd edn (Heidelberg, CF Müller, 2006) vol IV, 633, 649–60.

[18] W Geiger, 'Die wechselseitge Treuepflicht von Bund und Ländern' in A Süsterhenn (ed), *Föderalistische Ordnung* (Koblenz, Rhenania Verlag, 1961) 113, 114; extensively on the concept H Bauer, *Die Bundestreue: Zugleich ein Beitrag zur Dogmatik des Bundesstaatsrechts und zur Rechtsverhältnislehre* (Tübingen, Mohr Siebeck, 1992).

[19] As a curious side note, the Constitution also provides for treaties between Länder and, to a certain extent, between Länder and the federation, to which '[t]he principles of the International Law of Treaties are to be applied'. Federal Constitutional Law of Austria, art 15a(3).

[20] ibid art 16(1).

[21] ibid art 16(2).

[22] ibid art 16(3).

[23] ibid art 16(4).

[24] See also S Paquin, 'Federalism and Compliance with International Agreements: Belgium and Canada Compared' (2010) 5 *Hague Journal of Diplomacy* 173, 184–92 on Belgium.

[t]he King directs international relations, notwithstanding the competence of Communities and Regions to regulate international cooperation, including the concluding of treaties, for those matters that fall within their competences in pursuance of or by virtue of the Constitution.[25]

In terms of international cooperation, the parliaments of the Flemish and French-speaking Communities, respectively, regulate through federate law 'cooperation between the Communities, as well as international cooperation, including the concluding of treaties'[26] in matters of culture and certain matters of education.

The treaty-making arrangement in the Belgian Constitution replicates this division of competences. Generally, '[t]he King concludes treaties',[27] with the exception of those 'regarding matters that fall within the competence'[28] of the parliaments of the regions and communities, which will be concluded by their respective governments. Federal treaties 'take effect only after they have received the approval of the Parliament [of the Federation]'.[29] Specific rules have to be adopted by law for the conclusion of treaties by the regions and communities and 'of the treaties that do not exclusively concern matters falling within the competence of the Regions or Communities'.[30] Denunciation of non-federal treaties is carried out by the King with the agreement of the regional and community governments, with special rules having to be adopted to regulate cases of disagreement.[31] However, in the interest of complying with international legal obligations, a rule of substitution similar to the one in Austria applies. The Belgian Constitution provides that '[i]n order to ensure the observance of international or supranational obligations' the federal executive and legislative branches can, 'provided that the conditions stipulated by the law are met, temporarily replace' the regional and community governments and parliaments.[32] Otherwise put, in order to ensure compliance with duties under international law, it is possible to lock the subnational external actors back into the 'black box' of the state as the unit ultimately responsible on the international stage.

By contrast, in EU external relations, as aptly put by Enzo Cannizzaro, neither the Union nor its Member States possess 'the plenitude of the foreign relations power, which is instead deeply segmented in a plurality of actors, objectives and decision-making procedures'.[33] This also sets the Union apart from other regional organisations. In these cases, the organisation and the respective Member States also co-exist internationally, with the organisation having typically powers of its own in terms of external representation and treaty-making. However, in contrast to the EU, the

---

[25] Constitution of Belgium, art 167(1).
[26] ibid art 127(1) No 3 read together with Nos 1 and 2; see art 128 for 'person-related matters'.
[27] ibid art 167(2).
[28] ibid art 167(3).
[29] ibid art 167(2).
[30] ibid art 167(4).
[31] ibid art 167(5).
[32] ibid art 169, read together with arts 36, 37, 115 and 127.
[33] Cannizzaro, 'Unity and Pluralism in the EU's Foreign Relations Power' (n 10) 194; see also B Van Vooren, *EU External Relations Law and the European Neighbourhood Policy: A Paradigm for Coherence* (London, Routledge, 2012) 11–56 for a concise account of the legal history of fragmentation and coherence in EU external relations.

ultimate decision-making power and autonomy as regards politically salient matters in international relations remains with the member countries, with the international action of other regional organisations per se remaining rather technical in nature.[34]

The Union remains an international actor of conferred powers across different policy areas, but also the Member States retain 'only limited capacity to act on the international plane because of the European integration system in which they take part'.[35] Consequently, to borrow Bruno de Witte's expression, both the Union and the Member States have become 'strange subjects' of international law.[36] To the contrary, hardly anybody would consider Germany, Austria and Belgium as 'strange subjects' of international law in view of the fact that their respective Länder, regions and communities assume not only a role in the making of certain treaties concluded by the federation but also when they enter into certain international agreements with other countries. By the same token, hardly anybody would consider Malaysia or Argentina 'strange subjects' due to the fact that they are members of the Association of Southeast Asian Nations (ASEAN) and the Union of South American Nations (UNASUR), respectively. What makes Germany, Austria, Belgium and the other Member States 'strange', instead, is their very special relationship with each other and with the EU as a whole, and the way this relationship is structured in their interactions with external parties, including third countries and international organisations.

In sum, while in the cases of 'foreign affairs federalism' referred to here, general ideas of solidarity among constituent units are supplemented by strong federal prerogatives such as prior consent and substitution to ensure ultimate compliance in the cases mentioned, and where the actual competences and scope of action of these units remains limited, similar elements are missing in the case of the EU. At the same time, powers have been conferred on it to a much larger degree than is the case with any other regional organisation. Sincere cooperation and mutual solidarity, hence, assume a more important role in ensuring unified, coherent external action within this markedly polyphonic structure, and particularly in view of the parallel presence of the Union and the Member States on the international stage.

## III. Origin and Content

Loyal cooperation and solidarity have a long history in European law, with legal provisions obliging the Member States to work together to achieve the Communities' and later the Union's objectives being enshrined already in the

---

[34] See, eg, M Cremona *et al, ASEAN's External Agreements: Law, Practice and the Quest for Collective Action* (Cambridge, Cambridge University Press, 2015) 57 and 130–33.

[35] B de Witte, 'The Emergence of a European System of Public International Law: The EU and Its Member States as Strange Subjects' in J Wouters, A Nollkaemper and E de Wet (eds), *The Europeanisation of International Law: The Status of International Law in the EU and its Member States* (The Hague, TMC Asser Press, 2008) 39.

[36] ibid.

founding Treaties.[37] Subsequently, these provisions have been applied and interpreted in a series of judgments of the Court of Justice of the European Union
(CJEU), including in the area of external relations. Scholarship, in turn, has taken
a keen interest in the different ways in which Member State action on the international stage can be constrained by the duty of sincere cooperation, known
pre-Lisbon as the principle of loyal cooperation.[38] Before turning to the main
manifestations of its application in practice, it is useful to recall the central provision in question, Article 4(3) of the Treaty on European Union (TEU):

> Pursuant to the principle of sincere cooperation, the Union and the Member States shall,
> in full mutual respect, assist each other in carrying out tasks which flow from the Treaties.
>
> The Member States shall take any appropriate measure, general or particular, to ensure
> fulfilment of the obligations arising out of the Treaties or resulting from the acts of the
> institutions of the Union.
>
> The Member States shall facilitate the achievement of the Union's tasks and refrain from
> any measure which could jeopardise the attainment of the Union's objectives.[39]

This entails, according to condensed formulation used in the case-law of the CJEU,
that the Member States and their authorities:

> must take any appropriate measure, general or particular, to ensure fulfilment of the
> obligations arising out of the Treaties or resulting from the acts of the institutions of the
> European Union and refrain from any measure which could jeopardise the attainment of
> the European Union's objectives.[40]

These duties are part of overarching provisions in the TEU, and therefore applicable to all of the Union's external policies. Mutual solidarity is evoked, moreover,
specifically in the context of 'a terrorist attack or … a natural or man-made disaster', in which case the 'Union and its Member States shall act jointly in a spirit
of solidarity'.[41] This provision is part of the policies and instruments of EU external action as laid out in the Treaty on the Functioning of the European Union
(TFEU). According to its implementing decision, all main political institutions
of the EU are involved, with the Council being entrusted with 'the political and

---

[37] See, for the earliest rendition, Art 86 of the European Coal and Steel Community (ECSC) Treaty;
see further G De Baere and T Roes, 'EU Loyalty as Good Faith' (2015) 64 *ICLQ* 829, 830–34; and
M Klamert, *The Principle of Loyalty in EU Law* (Oxford, Oxford University Press, 2014) 9–11.

[38] See, eg, A Hatje, *Loyalität als Rechtsprinzip der Europäischen Union* (Baden-Baden, Nomos,
2001); S Hyett, 'The Duty of Cooperation: A Flexible Concept' in A Dashwood and C Hillion (eds),
*The General Law of EC External Relations* (London, Sweet & Maxwell, 2000); E Neframi, 'The Duty of
Loyalty: Rethinking Its Scope through its Application in the Field of EU External Relations' (2010) 47
*CML Rev* 323; Klamert, ibid n 37.

[39] Article 4(3) TEU. The pre-Lisbon version of this provision could be found in Art 10 EC: 'Member
States shall take all appropriate measures, whether general or particular, to ensure fulfilment of the
obligations arising out of this Treaty or resulting from action taken by the institutions of the Community. They shall facilitate the achievement of the Community's tasks.'

[40] Case C-518/11 *UPC Nederland BV*, Judgment, EU:C:2013:709, para 59 and the case-law cited
there.

[41] Article 222(1) TFEU.

strategic direction of the Union response to the invocation of the solidarity clause, taking full account of the Commission's and the [High Representative]'s competences'.[42] As per Article 5(5) of the same decision '[t]he Presidency of the Council will inform the President of the European Council and the President of the European Parliament of the invocation of the solidarity clause and of any major developments'.

In the sphere of the Common Foreign and Security Policy (CFSP), loyalty and cooperation are evoked in strong terms in Article 24(3) TEU:

> The Member States shall support the Union's external and security policy actively and unreservedly in a spirit of loyalty and mutual solidarity and shall comply with the Union's action in this area.
>
> The Member States shall work together to enhance and develop their mutual political solidarity. They shall refrain from any action which is contrary to the interests of the Union or likely to impair its effectiveness as a cohesive force in international relations.[43]

Furthermore, with specific regard to the CFSP, duties of consultation and coordination applying to the Member States are spelled out,[44] in particular concerning actions within international organisations and at international conferences,[45] including the UN Security Council,[46] and pertaining to the diplomatic and consular missions of the Member States.[47]

In addition, within the framework of the Common Security and Defence Policy (CSDP), an integral part of the CFSP, Member States are called upon to coordinate and collaborate, by making 'civilian and military capabilities available to the Union for the implementation of the common security and defence policy' and by progressively improving their military capabilities.[48] In addition, as a specific expression of mutual solidarity in defence matters among the Member States— with no mention of the EU and its institutions—the TEU post-Lisbon also contains an 'obligation of aid and assistance by all the means in their power' in case of an armed attack.[49] This provision, rather than the solidarity clause contained in Article 222 TFEU, was invoked for the first time in November 2015 by France following the terrorist attacks in Paris.[50]

In addition to these provisions from the EU Treaties, there exists also the principle of the unity in the international representation of the Union. The latter originated from a transplant of the duty of cooperation found in the European Atomic

---

[42] Council Decision 2014/415/EU of 24 June 2014 on the arrangements for the implementation by the Union of the solidarity clause [2014] OJ L192/53, Article 5(1).

[43] Article 24(3) TEU.

[44] Article 32 TEU.

[45] Article 34 TEU.

[46] Article 34(2), second and third subparas TEU.

[47] Article 35 TEU.

[48] Article 42(3) TEU.

[49] Article 42(7) TEU.

[50] Council of the European Union, Outcome of the 3426th Council Meeting, Foreign Affairs, Brussels, 16 and 17 November 2015, 14120/15 (OR en), Presse 69, PR CO 6, at 6.

Energy Community (EAEC) Treaty to the EEC by the CJEU,[51] and appears in particular in the case-law concerning the implementation of mixed agreements.[52] Only as recently as the *PFOS* case, the Court referred to it as a 'principle' rather than a mere 'requirement'.[53] Doubt may be cast upon whether it is a self-standing principle. The Court has never made recourse to it in its own right, but always in combination with the duty of cooperation. As the Advocate General emphasised in his Opinion in the *PFOS* case '[t]he unity of international representation of the Community and its Member States does not have an independent value; it is merely an expression of the duty of loyal cooperation under Article 10 EC'.[54] Hence, it can be seen as one aspect of the structural principles of sincere cooperation and solidarity as regards the EU Member States.

# IV. Extent and Main Manifestations

In assessing the legal bearing and consequences of the duty of sincere cooperation and mutual solidarity as regards the Member States, it is important to distinguish these terms from non-legal concepts of loyalty, cooperation and solidarity.[55] Being applicable to virtually any external relations challenge the EU and its Member States are facing, such concepts tend to be evoked regularly in the political arena and used in policy documents.[56] However, this tells us little about the value of this as a *legal* principle.

As a preliminary note, one could consider whether all the references to sincere cooperation and solidarity in the Treaties qualify as legal principles, not least given that Article 24 TEU sandwiches the rather aspirational formulation of developing

---

[51] Opinion 2/91, EU:C:1993:106, para 36: 'This duty of cooperation, to which attention was drawn in the context of the EAEC Treaty, must also apply in the context of the EEC Treaty since it results from the requirement of unity in the international representation of the Community'. The Court refers explicitly there to Ruling 1/78, EU:C:1978:202. See also Hillion, 'Mixity and Coherence in EU External Relations' (n 6) 89.

[52] Opinion 2/91 (n 51) para 36; Opinion 1/94, EU:C:1994:384, para 106; and Opinion 2/00, EU:C:2001:664, para 18. See further P van Elsuwege and H Merket, 'The Role of the Court of Justice in Ensuring the Unity of the EU's External Representation' in S Blockmans and R Wessel (eds), *Principles and Practices of EU External Representation, CLEER Working Paper* 2012/5, 37, 43.

[53] Case C-246/07 *Commission v Sweden (PFOS)*, Judgment, EU:C:2010:203, para 104; as noted by A Thies, 'Shared Competence and the EU Member States' Obligation to Refrain from Unilateral External Action: PFOS and Beyond' in J Díez-Hochleitner *et al* (eds), *Recent Trends in the Case Law of the Court of Justice of the European Union (2008–2011)* (Las Rozas, La Ley, 2012) 703, 721.

[54] Case C-246/07 *Commission v Sweden (PFOS)*, Opinion of AG Poiares Maduro, EU:C:2009:589, para 37.

[55] Hatje, *Loyalität als Rechtsprinzip der Europäischen Union* (n 38) 15–18.

[56] See for one prominent example J-C Juncker, 'State of the Union 2015: Time for Honesty, Unity and Solidarity', Strasbourg, 9 September 2015, SPEECH/15/561, where the President of the European Commission repeatedly evoked 'solidarity' among the Member States in the refugee crisis, and stressed the need to 'show the world the strength that comes from uniting and the strategic interest in acting together', be it in the context of the conflict in Ukraine or in leading efforts to tackle climate change.

'mutual *political* solidarity'[57] between more rigid constructions such as those stating that the 'Member States *shall support* the Union's external and security policy actively and *unreservedly* in a spirit of loyalty'[58] and '*shall refrain from any action* which is contrary to the interests of the Union or likely to impair its effectiveness as a cohesive force in international relations'.[59]

Since all these references to sincere cooperation and solidarity are codified in the EU Treaties, they have to be regarded as legally binding provisions, more precisely as part and parcel of the primary law of the EU. Terms such as sincere cooperation, solidarity and unity encompass the same idea and represent legally binding norms in EU law, regardless of where they are placed in the Treaties. However, the questions remain, first, to what extent these legal duties incumbent on the Member States fall under the jurisdiction of the CJEU, and if so, to what extent they are justiciable and with what consequences. To this end, the following sections will address, first, the three main dimensions in which these duties manifest themselves in the case-law of the CJEU vis-à-vis the Member States, following an order of a decreasing degree of justiciability. These three dimensions are (A) the capacity of Member States to conclude international agreements on their own and implement treaties to which they are parties; (B) their autonomy in voting in international organisations; and (C) more long-term processes of socialisation. Subsequently, the analysis turns to the limits of these duties when being relied on in court.

## A. International Treaty-making and Implementation

The legal implications of the duty of sincere cooperation (and pre-Lisbon the duty of 'loyal cooperation') for the international dealings of the Member States became apparent first in the context of their ability to conclude international agreements in cases where this would affect the Union's (and previously the Community's) position.

This concerns the *Inland Waterway* cases, in which the European Commission had received a mandate from the Council to negotiate a set of international agreements on the Community's behalf.[60] Member States, which after that point continued to negotiate and move towards the conclusion of agreements in their own name with these same external partners on the same subject matter, as the Court found, were in violation of their loyalty obligations towards the Community:

> The adoption of a decision authorising the Commission to negotiate ... requires ... if not a duty of abstention on the part of the Member States, at the very least a duty of close cooperation between the latter and the Community institutions in order to facilitate the

---

[57] Article 24(3), second subpara TEU (emphasis added).
[58] Article 24(3), first subpara TEU (emphasis added).
[59] Article 24(3), second subpara TEU (emphasis added).
[60] Case C-266/03 *Commission v Luxembourg (Inland Waterway)*, Judgment, EU:C:2005:341; and C-433/03 *Commission v Germany (Inland Waterway)*, Judgment, EU:C:2005:462.

achievement of the Community tasks and to ensure the coherence and consistency of the action and its international representation.[61]

More recently, the CJEU has also found that 'hybrid decisions' to conclude international agreement, ie decisions adopted 'by both the Council and the Representatives of the Governments of the Member States meeting within the Council',[62] can violate the duty of sincere cooperation, though it framed this as a matter of inter-institutional loyalty rather than one in the relationship between the Union and Member States.[63]

Once a treaty is concluded, the duty of sincere cooperation applies also to its implementation by the Member States. This includes cases where the Union cannot be a party and has to act 'through the medium of the Member States',[64] and to which end the latter need to cooperate closely. It applies also in the case of so-called mixed agreements, ie agreements to which both the Union and (some of) the Member States are parties. While earlier case-law may suggest that the delimitation of the respective spheres of competence in such mixed agreements, as applied to the subject matter of the treaty, would have sufficed,[65] later judgments make clear that the duty extends beyond that, covering also areas which are still within the remit of Member State competence,[66] or which are only partially covered by EU legislation.[67] Implementing these treaties in full then becomes an obligation of EU law on the Member States. Failing in this implementation, vice versa, would not only constitute a violation of international legal obligations of the Member States, but also a breach of their duty of sincere cooperation within the EU.

## B. Voting in International Organisations

In addition to the issues of concluding and implementing international agreements, the duty of sincere cooperation has a significant impact on the actions of the Member States in international organisations.[68] Next to a general duty to inform and cooperate,[69] there are circumstances in which a Member State has to act in a certain way in order to further the Union's interests, and others in which it is precluded from exercising its voting rights in what it perceives to be its own interest if this would be at odds with the Union's interests.

---

[61] *Commission v Germany (Inland Waterway)* (n 60) para 66.
[62] Case C-28/12 *Commission v Council (Air Transport Agreement)*, Judgment, EU:C:2015:282, para 6.
[63] ibid para 53, where the CJEU finds a violation, among others, of Art 13(2) TEU.
[64] Opinion 2/91 (n 51) para 37.
[65] Ruling 1/78 (n 51) para 36.
[66] Case C-13/00 *Commission v Ireland (Berne Convention)*, Judgment, EU:C:2002:184.
[67] Case C-239/03 *Commission v France (Étang de Berre)*, Judgment, EU:C:2004:598. See further Neframi, 'The Duty of Loyalty' (n 38) 331–37.
[68] See also I Govaere, 'Novel Issues Pertaining to EU Member States Membership of Other International Organizations: The *OIV* Case' in I Govaere *et al* (eds), *The European Union in the World, Essays in Honour of Marc Maresceau* (Leiden, Martinus Nijhoff, 2014) 225, 228–32.
[69] Opinion 1/94 (n 52) para 19.

Also here, this applies to situations where the Union is competent, but precluded from becoming a member of the organisation in question due to rules in the international (institutional) legal sphere. Such scenarios are possible, given that it is up to each organisation, in accordance with its founding charter, to determine which entities can be a member. If those are only states, the EU has to rely on its Member States, and indeed their sincere cooperation. This is the case, for instance, with the International Labour Organization (ILO) and the International Maritime Organization (IMO). In the case of the ILO, the CJEU concluded that:

> although, under the ILO Constitution, the Community cannot itself conclude Convention No 170, its external competence may, if necessary, be exercised through the medium of the Member States acting jointly in the Community's interest.[70]

In the case of the IMO, a Member State had made a proposal within this forum in an area of exclusive EU competence. Even though that same Member State had attempted to obtain the Union's sanction to this end, the Court found it in violation of its loyalty obligations for making the proposal at the IMO on its own.[71]

As later case-law shows, this also applies to areas of shared competence and where the EU is present alongside the Member States, as long as there is a perceivable 'Union position' which is being undercut by Member State behaviour on the international stage. Such positions can take various forms, ranging from formalised Council Decisions, which require an identified and proper legal basis,[72] to looser kinds of 'concerted common strategies'.[73] The latter case took place against the backdrop of the Persistent Organic Pollutants Review Committee established by the Stockholm Convention on Persistent Organic Pollutants, to which both the EU and its Member States are parties.[74] The contentious issue in this case was the fact that Sweden had 'submitted in its name and on its own behalf a proposal' to the Convention's Secretariat to add a certain substance (perfluoroctane sulfonate, abbreviated as PFOS, by which the case is also known as a shorthand) to Annex A of the StockholmConvention,[75] while deliberations were still ongoing within the EU on the possible future inclusion of the substance. Not only did the CJEU find that, by this unilateral proposal in an area of shared competence, Sweden 'dissociated itself from a concerted common strategy within the Council'[76] and thereby violated its loyalty obligations, it also noted the negative consequences this can entail for a coherent message of the Union and the Member States in this mixed setting. This, according to the CJEU, would result in:

> a situation ... likely to compromise the principle of unity in the international representation of the Union and its Member States and weaken their negotiating power with regard to the other parties to the Convention concerned.[77]

---

[70] Opinion 2/91 (n 51) para 5.
[71] C-45/07 *Commission v Greece (IMO)*, Judgment, EU:C:2009:81, para 23.
[72] Case C-370/07 *Commission v Council (CITES)*, Judgment, EU:C:2009:590.
[73] *PFOS* (n 53) para 91.
[74] ibid paras 13 and 19.
[75] ibid para 40.
[76] ibid para 91.
[77] ibid para 104.

Hence, also where exercising "'their share" of shared competence',[78] and even when contemplating using their vote as members of international institutions, the Member States have to respect the duty of sincere cooperation towards the EU. Under international law, they might be entitled to speak up, but as EU Members they might have to remain silent if this 'could jeopardise the attainment of the Union's objectives'.[79]

## C. Beyond Legally Justiciable Duties

While Member States' actions with regard to international agreements as well as within international organisations concern legal acts on the international stage, or at the very least acts which may set in motion procedures which eventually can produce international legal repercussions for the EU and its Member States, obligations of sincere cooperation and solidarity reach further than that. They are overarching principles in the relations between the Union and its Member States and apply to all matters of foreign policy, including the realms covered by the CFSP and CSDP.[80]

However, due to the continuing 'bipolarity' in EU external relations,[81] and with it the exclusion of the Court's jurisdiction from most of the CFSP,[82] case-law on sincere cooperation in the 'non-TFEU' policy domain is lacking. However, this does not mean that the duty of sincere cooperation (or here rather 'mutual solidarity') does not apply. Ever since the *Centro-Com* judgment it has become evident that the CJEU does not give the Member States an entirely free hand as soon as they are acting in the domain of foreign and security policy.[83] They remain bound by their other EU membership obligations, including the respect of EU law in its entirety, the pursuit of non-CFSP related Union objectives,[84] and sincere cooperation in general.[85]

Hence, even if not justiciable by the CJEU, in any 'heterarchical' setting,[86] and *a fortiori* in the foreign affairs domain, it is then incumbent upon the other organs

---

[78] A Delgado Casteleiro and J Larik, 'The Duty to Remain Silent: Limitless Loyalty in EU External Relations?' (2011) 36 *EL Rev* 522, 538.

[79] Article 4(3), third subpara TEU.

[80] Note Art 24(1), first subpara TEU, which states that the 'Union's competence in matters of common foreign and security policy shall cover all areas of foreign policy and all questions relating to the Union's security'.

[81] A Dashwood, 'The Continuing Bipolarity of EU External Action' in I Govaere *et al* (eds), *The European Union in the World, Essays in Honour of Marc Maresceau* (Leiden, Martinus Nijhoff, 2014) 3.

[82] Art 24(1), first subpara TEU; Art 275 TFEU.

[83] Case C-124/95 *Centro-Com*, Judgment, EU:C:1997:8.

[84] C Hillion and R Wessel, 'Restraining External Competences of EU Member States under CFSP' in M Cremona and B de Witte (eds), *EU Foreign Relations Law: Constitutional Fundamentals* (Oxford, Hart Publishing, 2008) 79, 91–96.

[85] C Hillion, 'A Powerless Court? The European Court of Justice and the CFSP' in M Cremona and A Thies (eds), *The European Court of Justice and External Relations: Constitutional Challenges* (Oxford, Hart Publishing, 2014) 47.

[86] D Halberstam, 'Constitutional Heterarchy: The Centrality of Conflict in the European Union and the United States' in J Dunoff and J Trachtman (eds), *Ruling the World? Constitutionalism, International Law and Global Governance* (Cambridge, Cambridge University Press, 2009) 326.

of the EU to monitor and enforce this duty within their scope of action and with the means at their disposal. This could be done not only by the European Commission as the 'guardian of the Treaties', but arguably with more legitimacy also by the European Parliament through political oversight and pressure. Procedural rules, such as its right to information and consultation, in turn, have been shown to be judicially enforceable also in the CFSP/CSDP domain.[87] The CJEU stressed in the *EU–Mauritius Agreement* judgment that specific requirements to inform the European Parliament regarding the negotiation and conclusion of international agreements under Article 218(10) TFEU, including in the context of the intergovernmental CFSP, were an expression of the 'exercise of democratic scrutiny of the European Union's external action'.[88] In this vein, Article 218(10) TFEU can be seen as a specific expression of sincere cooperation, not least given that information and consultation have long been established as integral parts of duties of loyalty and cooperation.[89] Articles 4(3) and 24 TEU can then be regarded as establishing a general mandate also for the Parliament to monitor that the Member States, acting through the Council or in their own name, indeed live up to the spirit of loyalty across all of the EU's external policies, to encourage them to do so using the means at its disposal, and where necessary to bring cases to the CJEU to the extent that the latter can exercise jurisdiction.

Regarding the duty of sincere cooperation and solidarity more broadly, it is important to look beyond the immediate court case at hand and consider also what some legal scholars call the 'expressive function' of the law, which posits that the law and judgments do not only induce a change in behaviour and a change in perception of actors' behaviour through imposing legal sanctions, but already by positing a consensus on what is considered legally appropriate and normatively desirable.[90] Applying this to the domain of EU external action, the references to sincere cooperation, solidarity and unity used in court judgments, as well as inter-institutional and EU–Member State interaction, are prone to lead to processes described by social scientists as 'socialisation', or more particularly the 'Europeanisation' of foreign policy.[91] While CJEU pronouncements are certainly important precedents, sincere cooperation and mutual solidarity are not won or lost in the courtroom, but structure the relations between the Member States and the Union through continuous practice and an emerging culture of European composite

---

[87] Case C-658/11 *Parliament v Council (EU–Mauritius Agreement)*, Judgment, EU:C:2014:2025.

[88] ibid para 79.

[89] Case 141/78 *France v United Kingdom*, Judgment, EU:C:1979:22, paras 8–9 also later Case C-459/03 *Commission v Ireland (Mox Plant)*, Judgment, EU:C:2006:345, para 179; and Case C-29/14 *Commission v Poland*, Judgment, EU:C:2015:379, paras 32–33.

[90] See C Sunstein, 'On the Expressive Function of Law' (1996) 144 *University of Pennsylvania Law Review* 2012; and A Geisinger, 'A Belief Change Theory of Expressive Law' (2002) 88 *Iowa Law Review* 35.

[91] R Wong, 'The Europeanization of Foreign Policy' in C Hill and M Smith (eds), *International Relations and the European Union*, 2nd edn (Oxford, Oxford University Press, 2011) 149.

actorness and identity on the international stage, the polyphonic nature and legal complexity of EU external relations notwithstanding.

## V. Limits of Cooperation and Solidarity

Given the set of CJEU judgments condemning Member States for acts on the international stage in various settings and regarding both areas of exclusive and shared competence, the questions might be raised: in terms of a legal obligation, where do sincere cooperation and loyalty end? To what extent are the Member States autonomous international actors, unencumbered by their duties resulting from EU membership?

The *OIV* case in particular would arguably have served to establish clear limits to the constraints on the Member States. As noted above, in *PFOS*, the CJEU made clear that the fact that a shared competence is at hand rather than exclusive competence does not diminish the applicability of the duty of sincere cooperation in mixed settings, meaning that the Member States could not speak up in a way that would have undermined a Union position. The *OIV* case concerned a non-mixed setting in the sense that the EU was absent, and a subject matter that, according to the complaining Member State, was shared.[92]

In the *OIV* case, Germany challenged a decision of the Council, which established the position to be adopted on behalf of the Union within the International Organisation of Vine and Wine (known by its French abbreviation OIV). Most but not all of the EU Member States are members of the OIV, but not the EU.[93] The contested decision was adopted by qualified majority, with Germany having voted against it,[94] based on Article 218(9) TFEU. Germany argued that while the 'action of the Member States in the bodies of international organisations set up by international agreements of the Member States is ... coordinated in accordance with the principle of sincere cooperation laid down in Article 4(3) TEU',[95] Article 218(9) TFEU 'in accordance with its wording, scheme, drafting history and function ... is not applicable to agreements concluded by the Member States, but only to international agreements concluded by the European Union itself'.[96] However, with the Court's judgment in October 2014, the limits of loyalty remain elusive. The CJEU confirmed the applicability of Article 218(9) TFEU to situations where the Union is not present. While mentioning neither exclusivity nor the duty

---

[92] Germany referred to the common agricultural policy as referred to in Art 4(2)(d) TFEU, Case C-399/12 *Germany v Council (OIV)*, Judgment, EU:C:2014:2258, para 34.

[93] ibid para 5.

[94] ibid para 18.

[95] Case C-399/12 *Germany v Council (OIV)*, Opinion of AG Cruz Villalón, EU:C:2014:289, para 22.

[96] ibid.

of sincere cooperation explicitly, the Court noted that the case concerned 'an area which is regulated for the most part by the EU legislature'[97] and that, therefore:

> the fact that the European Union did not take part in the international agreement in question does not prevent it from exercising that competence by establishing, through its institutions, a position to be adopted on its behalf in the body set up by that agreement, in particular through the Member States which are party to that agreement acting jointly in its interest.[98]

Moreover, given that the CJEU considered the recommendations emanating from the OIV of being 'capable of decisively influencing the content of the legislation adopted by the EU legislature',[99] it concluded that the EU was indeed 'entitled to establish a position to be adopted on its behalf'[100] at the OIV, thereby dismissing Germany's claim.

This results in the situation where even where the Member States are full members of an international organisation, based on a treaty they concluded in their own name, and even in situations where the EU is not present, they may be prevented from submitting their own proposals and be obliged to defend a Union position they opposed within the Council.

In contrast, attempts by the Member States to use the duty of sincere cooperation as an argument in their favour, such as relying on 'mutual trust' as an escape from having to verify sensitive information in targeted sanction cases, have remained unsuccessful.[101] Only if there is a more specific obligation which covers the same violation would the CJEU deem the duty of sincere cooperation inapplicable,[102] but that can only be regarded as being of little solace to the Member States.

The principles of sincere cooperation, loyalty and unity are thus of a wide application, with the exact limits yet to be clarified by the Court. However, there are certain caveats which are already clearly visible from the wording and structure of the Treaties, as well as from a practical perspective, which show that this principle is not entirely limitless. Therefore, in the following sections, three 'red lines' will be drawn regarding the extent of these duties for the Member States, (A) one of a principled nature (constitutional identity); (B) one of a procedural nature

---

[97] *OIV* (n 92) para 51.

[98] ibid para 52.

[99] ibid para 63.

[100] ibid para 64.

[101] Case C-280/12P *Council v Fulmen and Fereydoun Mahmoudian*, Judgment, EU:C:2013:775, para 44. For an example of an organisation subject to targeted sanction unsuccessfully relying on the duty of sincere cooperation, see Joined Cases T-208/11 and T-508/11 *Liberation Tigers of Tamil Eelam (LTTE) v Council*, Judgment, EU:T:2014:885, paras 131–35.

[102] Case C-60/13 *Commission v United Kingdom*, Judgment, EU:C:2014:219, para 61: 'Lastly, as regards the infringement of Article 4(3) TEU, also relied on by the Commission, there are no grounds for holding that the United Kingdom has failed to fulfil the general obligations under that provision, which is separate from the established failure to fulfil the more specific obligations incumbent upon that Member State under [Article 8 of Decision 2000/597 and Articles 2, 6, 9, 10 and 11 of Regulation No 1150/2000]'.

(internal voting rights); and (C) a third one of a pragmatic nature ('sheering out of line', or 'doing it anyway').

## A. Constitutional Identity and International Actorness

A new explicit limit to the duties of sincere cooperation, solidarity and unity—and in fact European integration at large—can be found post-Lisbon in the paragraph directly preceding Article 4(3) TEU:

> The Union shall respect the equality of Member States before the Treaties as well as their national identities, inherent in their fundamental structures, political and constitutional, inclusive of regional and local self-government. It shall respect their essential State functions, including ensuring the territorial integrity of the State, maintaining law and order and safeguarding national security. In particular, national security remains the sole responsibility of each Member State.[103]

Also EU foreign policy is hence to be pursued in a manner consistent with this particular structural principle, ie the protection of the constitutional identity of the Member States and the respect for their essential functions. The jurisdiction of the Court of Justice extends over this provision. Invoking constitutional identity can aid in the justification of proportionate restrictions of an individual right (also under EU law) in the pursuit of policies that are aimed at preserving this identity.[104] It could be argued that it applies to limiting loyalty obligations towards the Union in the foreign relations domain as well.

This would fit with a general theme of sensitivity on the part of the Member States not to be fully overshadowed by the Union internationally.[105] This is reflected in a number of specific provisions and documents, such as the stipulations on shared external competences. For example, while the Treaties acknowledge that the EU shall have the competence to carry out policies in the areas of development and humanitarian aid, they also note that 'the exercise of that competence shall not result in Member States being prevented from exercising theirs'.[106]

In addition, the Member States made sure to attach Declarations Nos 13 and 14 to the Lisbon Treaty concerning the CFSP. Declaration No 13 stresses that Treaty provisions on the CFSP, including those on mutual political solidarity, 'do not affect the responsibilities of the Member States, as they currently exist, for the formulation and conduct of their foreign policy nor of their national representation in third

---

[103] Article 4(2) TEU. Prior to Lisbon, Art 6(3) TEU (Nice version) had already included a provision stating merely that '[t]he Union shall respect the national identities of its Member States'. See extensively F-X Millet, *L'Union européenne et l'identité constitutionnelle des États membres* (Paris, LGDJ, 2013).

[104] Case C-208/09 *Sayn-Wittgenstein*, Judgment, EU:C:2010:806; see further A von Bogdandy and S Schill, 'Overcoming Absolute Primacy: Respect for National Identity under the Lisbon Treaty' (2011) 48 *CML Rev* 1417, 1422–25.

[105] See also J Larik, *Foreign Policy Objectives in European Constitutional Law* (Oxford, Oxford University Press, 2016) 176.

[106] Article 4(4) TFEU.

countries and international organisations'.[107] Moreover, it states that the Union and the Member States 'remain bound by the provisions of the Charter of the United Nations and, in particular, by the primary responsibility of the Security Council and of its Members for the maintenance of international peace and security'.[108] Declaration No 14 furthermore 'notes that the provisions covering the Common Foreign and Security Policy do not give new powers to the Commission to initiate decisions nor do they increase the role of the European Parliament'.[109] In essence, the Declarations affirm that despite progressing European integration, the autonomy of the Member States as international actors, as well as their preferences in security and defence policy (such as neutrality, collective security and collective defence) are to be preserved.

Together, these can be seen as safeguards by the Member States that the EU will not entirely eclipse them as actors on the international stage, stressing that there remain situations in which they continue to act as autonomous subjects of international law. From the point of view of Westphalian international law, these are the Member States' remnants of 'normalcy'[110] as otherwise 'strange subjects' from an external perspective.

There is no simple way to determine which are the elements pertaining to a Member State's constitutional identity. According to von Bogdandy and Schill, a strong indicator for being part of the latter category is the special entrenchment of certain norms within the constitution,[111] such as the so-called 'eternity clause' (*Ewigkeitsklausel*) in the German Basic Law,[112] or the article in the Spanish Constitution which imposes a particularly burdensome procedure in instances where certain parts of the constitution were to be affected by amendment.[113] These concern provisions on the form of government, state sovereignty, state aims and the rule of law.

To which extent this is directly linked to Member States' foreign policies will require a case-by-case analysis. In Germany, for instance, the 'eternity clause' covers only Articles 1 and 10 of the Basic Law. By contrast, Article 23 on European integration and Article 24 on international cooperation are not protected by it. Article 1(2), on the other hand, which stresses the universal validity of human dignity and its indispensability for world peace, is. From this point of view, Germany would be 'eternally' mandated by its Constitution to also promote human dignity in its foreign relations. As part of its 'constitutional identity' this would be a feature that the Union would have to respect.

---

[107] Declaration concerning the Common Foreign and Security Policy (Declaration No 13) annexed to the Final Act of the Intergovernmental Conference which adopted the Treaty of Lisbon, para 1.

[108] ibid para 3.

[109] Declaration concerning the Common Foreign and Security Policy (Declaration No 14) annexed to the Final Act of the Intergovernmental Conference which adopted the Treaty of Lisbon, para 2.

[110] V Epping, 'Völkerrechtssubjekte' in K Ipsen (ed), *Völkerrecht*, 5th edn (Munich, CH Beck, 2004) 55, 59, who calls the state the 'normal subject of international law' (*Normalperson des Völkerrechts*).

[111] von Bogdandy and Schill, 'Overcoming Absolute Primacy' (n 104) 1432.

[112] Basic Law of Germany, art 79(3).

[113] Constitution of Spain, art 168.

In the case of Spain, Article 168 of its Constitution covers Article 56(1) and its reference to 'the nations of [Spain's] historical community', in relation to which the King of Spain will represent the country.[114] Following this benchmark, this provision could be considered part of Spain's constitutional identity and commands deference in terms of loyalty obligations.

Austrian permanent neutrality,[115] to give another example from the foreign policy domain, is deemed in the literature not to represent a 'leading constitutional principle' (*leitendes Verfassungsprinzip*), since it has not been introduced by referendum and can be dropped from the constitutional law without the need for such.[116] This would militate against considering it as part of Austrian constitutional identity and therefore as a grounds for derogation from obligations stemming from EU Membership.

Hence, such exceptions would only apply in rather limited, in all likelihood extreme, cases. Nevertheless, at least in theory, where actions in a Member State's foreign policy can be convincingly framed as a direct expression of its constitutional identity, and where loyalty to the EU and its 'common positions' would inevitably lead to infringing that identity, this could arguably trump its loyalty obligations towards the Union. Given that after *IMO*, *PFOS* and *OIV*, the extent and scope of loyalty obligations continues to expand unabatedly in the Court's case-law, the day might yet come when Member States fall back on this principled line of defence.

## B. Internal Voting Rights

Moving on from the more abstract idea of constitutional identity, the most powerful tool for the Member States to avoid situations in which their duties of sincere cooperation and solidarity as EU members are at odds with their own interests remains the exercise of their voting rights within the EU institutions. As Van Vooren aptly put it, 'the "vertical" interests of the Member States will be felt horizontally through the Council'.[117]

Within the internal political space of the Union, Member States are virtually free to vote as they like—or rather, as their internal politics demand—and to avoid the emergence of decisions being adopted against their will and having to defend them afterwards internationally, as happened in the *OIV* case. This finds its strongest expression in the domain of the CFSP/CSDP due to the prevailing rule

---

[114] ibid art 56(1), in Part II of the Constitution on 'the Crown'.

[115] Federal Constitutional Law of Austria, art 9a(1), read together with the Austrian Constitutional Law of 26 October 1955, the so-called 'Neutrality Law' (*Neutralitätsgesetz*). The latter is a document of constitutional rank but which is not incorporated into the main Federal Constitutional Law of Austria.

[116] G Lienbacher, 'Ausgewählte Rechtsfragen der Anwendung des Vertrages von Lissabon in Österreich' in W Hummer and W Obwexer (eds), *Der Vertrag von Lissabon* (Baden-Baden, Nomos, 2009) 427, 435–38.

[117] Van Vooren, *EU External Relations Law and the European Neighbourhood* Policy (n 33) 71.

of unanimity and the diminished influence of other Union institutions.[118] This was also identified as part of the reasoning why France opted to invoke the mutual defence clause of Article 42(7) TEU rather than the solidarity clause of Article 222 TFEU in the wake of the terrorist attacks in Paris in November 2015. According to the outcome document of the Foreign Affairs Council, France requested 'bilateral discussions' with the other Member States.[119] According to the, High Representative, '[n]o formal decision or conclusion by the Council will be required to implement' Article 42(7) TEU, as this concerned 'not a CSDP operation, but an activation of *bilateral* aid and assistance'.[120] In this particular expression of solidarity, Union institutions and procedures can be deliberately left on the side-lines.[121]

From the perspective of a Member State aiming to avoid scrutiny of its loyalty obligations, remaining within the scope of the intergovernmental CFSP, to the extent that this is legally permitted under Article 40 TEU,[122] seems in any event more promising protection than pointing fingers at the EU institutions for not living up to their respective and corresponding duties of cooperation. As the *IMO* case showed, this is no excuse for the Member States,[123] and would have been difficult to enforce as it would require determining the violation of a positive obligation (failure to act) on the part of these institutions.[124]

This raises the question to which extent the duty of sincere cooperation applies already in the process of finding a common position within the EU. While there are some signs that it might marginally apply, for all practical purposes the EU cannot force its Members to vote a certain way within its own organs.

As to its general application, Advocate General Tesauro in the *Hermès* case hinted at an obligation for the Member States to 'endeavour to adopt a common position'.[125] However, no duty to adopt a particular voting behaviour within the EU can be derived from this as far as internal fora are concerned. It would be difficult, indeed highly problematic from the point of view of legitimacy and conferral, to maintain that the duty of sincere cooperation applied fully within the internal organs of the Union in the same way as in external fora, as this is

---

[118] Article 24(1), second subpara TEU.

[119] Council of the European Union (n 50) 6.

[120] ibid 6 (emphasis added).

[121] See also J Valero, *France "at War" Inaugurates EU's Mutual Defence Clause* (17 November 2015), available at www.euractiv.com/sections/global-europe/france-war-inaugurates-eus-mutual-defence-clause-319531, who observes: 'The French president was careful to call for article 42.7 [TEU] instead of the article 222 of the [TFEU] (the so-called "solidarity clause"). While the latter paves the way for a greater involvement of the EU institutions, the former is rather an intergovernmental solution that allows Paris to play a greater role'.

[122] According to Art 40(1) TEU, the implementation of the CFSP 'shall not affect the application of the procedures and the extent of the powers of the institutions laid down by the Treaties for the exercise of the Union competences' and policies as laid down on the TFEU, and vice versa (Art 40(2) TEU). The CJEU has jurisdiction to monitor respect for this division and the use of the proper legal basis by the Union institutions (Art 24(1), second subpara TEU).

[123] *IMO* (n 71) para 26.

[124] M Cremona, 'Extending the Reach of the *AETR* Principle: Comment on *Commission v Greece* (C-45/07)' (2009) 34 *EL Rev* 754, 765–66.

[125] Case C-53/96 *Hermès International*, Opinion of Advocate General Tesauro, EU:C:1997:539, para 21. The Court, however, did not pick up the cooperation argument in its judgment, Case C-53/96 *Hermès International*, Judgment, EU:C:1998:292.

the 'policy space' in which different options are deliberated upon and common positions are being developed, and in which the CJEU is reluctant to intervene judicially.[126] The Council, after all, can be seen as the site for the pursuit of the various national interests of the Member States, which contributes to the process of elaborating a Union position, and which the duty of sincere cooperation will protect afterwards from being undermined through deviating actions on the international stage by the Member States.[127] Only in extreme cases of total obstruction ('empty chair') might one speak of violations of the duty in the internal dimension,[128] although in such cases, another legal avenue could become available as well, ie the procedure under Article 7 TEU for cases in which a Member State commits a 'serious breach' of the EU's values as enshrined in Article 2 TEU. Since this procedure comes with its own sanctions in the form of suspension of voting rights,[129] it may be more attractive in terms of enforcement.[130]

For the most part, Member States remain doubly protected in the sphere of the CFSP/CSDP, with an internal veto power as well as the aforementioned lack of jurisdiction of the Court to rule on external violations of the duty of sincere cooperation. In other external policies, as the *OIV* and *PFOS* cases showed, respectively, Member States can be outvoted due to qualified majority voting being applicable, or should have waited until the internal EU process in finding a common strategy was concluded (and subsequently adhere to the common strategy). Hence, in those cases it will depend on the negotiations and coalition-building skills of each Member State to avoid decisions it disagrees with emerging from within the internal 'policy space'. Once such common position are deemed to exist, however, the duty of sincere cooperation obliges the Member States to defend them in the external arena.

## C. 'Sheering Out of Line' and 'Disloyalty by Proxy'

Lastly, beyond constitutional identity and internal voting rights, one could consider the duties of sincere cooperation and mutual solidarity incumbent upon the Member States from a more pragmatic point of view. This contrasts the 'law in the

---

[126] M Cremona, 'A Reticent Court? Policy Objectives and the Court of Justice' in M Cremona and A Thies (eds), *The European Court of Justice and External Relations Law: Constitutional Challenges* (Oxford, Hart Publishing, 2014) 15.

[127] R Post, 'Constructing the European Polity: *ERTA* and the *Open Skies* Judgements' in M Poiares Maduro and L Azoulai (eds), *The Past and Future of EU Law: The Classics of EU Law Revisited on the 50th Anniversary of the Rome Treaty* (Oxford, Hart Publishing, 2010) 234, 238.

[128] In this sense, A von Bogdandy and S Schill, 'Artikel 4 EUV' in E Grabitz, M Hilf and M Nettesheim (eds), *Das Recht der Europäischen Union*, loose-leaf, 41st supplement (Munich, CH Beck, 2010), marginal no 105, stressing that the Council is the site for the pursuit of the national interest, from which subsequently a Union position can emerge. However, they regard extreme cases such as obstruction of the functioning of an organ as such, for instance through an 'empty chair' policy, as a violation of the duty of cooperation.

[129] Article 7(3) TEU.

[130] See further D Kochenov and L Pech, 'Monitoring and Enforcement of the Rule of Law in the EU: Rhetoric and Reality' (2015) 11 *European Constitutional Law Review* 512.

Treaties' with the 'law in action' in EU external relations. In a sort of cost-benefit-analysis, it is conceivable that a Member State would violate these obligations in a particular scenario where it considers that acting on its foreign policy imperatives at the detriment of common Union positions is worth the ensuing damage.

This is less an argument of legality than it is one of enforcement. Generally, judgments of the CJEU are complied with, even in the absence of fines or stronger sanctions.[131] In the case of external relations, the possibility of sanctions by the CJEU is already limited. The violations of the duty of sincere cooperation established by the CJEU in the judgments referred to in this chapter are all of a declaratory nature.

The threshold to 'sheer out of line' can be deemed as even lower in the CFSP/CSDP domain given that lack of judicial control by the CJEU, although as argued above, political oversight in the domain of foreign policy by the European Parliament may compensate for this. But even where the CJEU has jurisdiction and finds violations of the duty of sincere cooperation by the Member States, the only immediate legal consequence is limited to the judgment itself declaring an infringement of the Treaties. In the case of international treaties being negotiated by Member States, they can be considered to be legally barred from pursuing these projects further, and *a fortiori* from concluding such treaties, once the Court has determined that this violates their loyalty obligations towards the Union, as in an *Inland Waterway* scenario. More difficult, if not impossible to remedy, are situations of the *IMO* and *PFOS* type, where the 'damage', from the Union's point of view, has already been done by the errant Member State by voting in a particular way or submitting a proposal ('setting in motion the procedure') at the international stage. Where setting such a procedure in motion is seen as imperative by a Member State, it may be incentivised to 'do it anyway' and violate its loyalty obligations by creating accomplished facts.

In addition, one could consider various ways to circumvent loyalty obligations by acting through proxies. The violations in *IMO* and *PFOS* concerned overt Member State acts on record within international fora. However, if, for instance, the Swedish government in the *PFOS* context had simply called its Norwegian or Canadian colleagues (which are both also parties to the Stockholm Convention) and 'advised' them to submit the exact same proposal that Sweden was prohibited from submitting due to its EU Membership, it is highly doubtful whether such an act of informal diplomacy, setting in motion the same procedure, would also have resulted in violation of the duty of sincere cooperation by Sweden. Practically speaking, it is even more doubtful how such an instance of 'disloyalty by proxy' could be detected and adjudicated.

Of course, this concerned individual, hypothetical cases and stands in contrast to the more long-term perspectives of progressive 'socialisation' based on the structural principles of EU external action noted in the previous section. But as

---

[131] See also M Cremona, 'Introduction' in M Cremona (ed), *Compliance and the Enforcement of EU Law* (Oxford, Oxford University Press, 2012) xxxix, who notes also that the duty of sincere cooperation of Art 4(3) TEU is at 'the basis of all compliance proceedings' (xl).

a recurring pattern of behaviour (insofar as it can be ascertained), breaching the duty of sincere cooperation and disrupting the unity in the EU's international representation undermine trust among the Member States and thus tarnish and devalue the 'policy space' within the Union. If it proved to be systematic, sanctions might be considered, as with internal obstruction, in the form of suspension of voting rights under Article 7 TEU for a serious breach of the EU's values. However, as this has not yet materialised in the internal sphere (for instance, with regard to the policies of the Hungarian and Polish governments) it remains a very open question to what extent it could be applied to the external relations domain, as it requires a political decision, not a judicial one, in order to ensure loyalty and unity by this particular instrument.[132]

# VI. Conclusion

Having addressed the unique nature, content, main manifestations and limitations of the duties of sincere cooperation, solidarity and unity on the Member States as structural principles of the law of EU external relations, the following three main conclusions can be drawn.

First, while 'foreign affairs federalism' is not a unique feature of the EU, it does stand out from other international actors in that it occupies a middle ground in which neither the Union nor the Member States have the upper hand. Unlike federal states, there is no rule of substitution, by which the constituent units can be eclipsed by the federation if necessary. At the same time, unlike other regional organisations, the common institutions are not weak and easily domineered or side-lined by the 'Masters of the Treaties'. Neither Member States nor the Union eclipse each other on the international stage. Rather, each exists in the penumbra of the other. Hence, sincere cooperation, solidarity and unity assume a particularly important role in ensuring coherence and effectiveness in the EU's polyphonic and complex system of external relations.

Secondly, the balance between the Union and the Member States has been tilted in the case-law of the CJEU in favour of the Union. Today, there exists a string of cases in which the duty of sincere cooperation was successfully invoked to constrain Member States' actions on the international stage, but not vice versa. In particular, their role as erstwhile autonomous members of (other) international organisations, and with that their discretion in exercising their voting rights within such organisations, are considerably conditioned. Attempts to counter

---

[132] According to Art 7(1), subpara 1 TEU, what is required to set the procedure in motion is 'a reasoned proposal by one third of the Member States, by the European Parliament or by the European Commission' following which the Council 'acting by a majority of four fifths of its members after obtaining the consent of the European Parliament, may determine that there is a clear risk of a serious breach by a Member State of the values referred to in Article 2 [TEU]'.

this trend by pointing fingers at disloyal behaviour of EU institutions or other possible legal infringements have proven unsuccessful. In an increasing set of situations, Member States will have to act as the medium for the interests of a larger structure—as *a pars pro tota Unione*—feeding also into more long-term processes of the 'Europeanisation' of foreign policy as framed by the structural principles of EU external relations.

Thirdly, it remains equally important to think about the limits of loyalty, which seem to become ever more distant. Considerations of constitutional identity, now an explicit part of the Treaties, may prove a last line of defence. However, it will be of only very limited use, as the Member State would have to, first, rely on the very narrow scope of elements belonging to such a category and, secondly, prove that a certain act committed internationally was absolutely necessary in defence of their identity. Moreover, it raises the question why the same result could not be achieved by acting first within and then *through* the Union and utilising its 'politics of scale'.[133] This may not only prove politically beneficial, but would be legally on the safe side. Unlike the external sphere, within the internal 'policy space' of the Union, Member States are free to vote as they please and pursue their own preferences and interests unhindered by loyalty concerns, save perhaps for patterns of manifest obstruction. While in the CFSP/CSDP domain, they are protected by unanimity from decisions emerging which they might not want to defend internationally, in the other policy areas they will have to rely on their negotiating skills to avoid being overruled within the Council. Once such common positions have emerged, however, the duty of sincere cooperation bars the Member States from undermining them in the external sphere and obliges them to defend them even—or especially—in situations where the EU can be directly represented by its own institutions. Nevertheless, practically speaking, scenarios remain conceivable in which more clandestine modes of circumventing the duty of sincere cooperation may be employed externally, for instance acting through like-minded proxies, even though this may not offer the same scale effects as acting through the Union.

In sum, Article 4(3) TEU on sincere cooperation has proven a powerful legal tool for moulding the many voices of EU external action into a more coherent whole—perhaps not by always creating more harmony but in some cases by silencing those trying to sing a different tune. The same cannot be said for the expressions of mutual solidarity obtaining in the CFSP/CSDP area, over which the Court of Justice has no jurisdiction, while new expressions of solidarity post-Lisbon such as the solidarity and mutual defence clauses are only beginning to be explored as political tools and legal norms. However, and regardless of jurisdiction and policy area, loyalty among the many parts of EU external action will not be won in the courtroom in Luxembourg alone. These cases are important benchmarks

---

[133] R Ginsberg, *Foreign Policy Actions of the European Community: The Politics of Scale* (London, Adamantine Press, 1989).

for the international behaviour of the Member States, and part of larger processes of contestation and socialisation. Together, the Member States agreed as 'Masters of the Treaties' to 'facilitate the achievement of the Union's tasks and refrain from any measure which could jeopardise the attainment of the Union's objectives',[134] among which are ambitious goals such as 'the sustainable development of the Earth'[135] and to 'promote an international system based on stronger multilateral cooperation and good global governance'.[136] The duties of sincere cooperation, mutual solidarity and unity serve as a constant reminder to strive to achieve these together and in concert, and to structure the composite external action of the Union accordingly. For while there is no 'sole organ', there is a sole direction for the many parts of EU external action.

---

[134] Article 4(3), third subpara TEU.
[135] Article 3(5) TEU.
[136] Article 21(2)(h) TEU.

# 8

# The Principle of Transparency in EU External Relations Law: Does Diplomatic Secrecy Stand a Chance of Surviving the Age of Twitter?

PÄIVI LEINO

## I. Secrecy as a Paradigm in Foreign Relations

Agatha Christie's classic *The Secret of Chimneys*, first published in 1925, offers many insights into the classic running of international diplomacy. Lord Caterham reluctantly agrees to host a weekend party at his mansion, Chimneys. The plot builds on a political scheme aiming at restoring the monarchy in Herzoslovakia while placing access to the newly discovered oil in the hands of a British syndicate. The securing of these objectives involves a number of stolen letters, a lost manuscript that could result in a diplomatic crisis if placed in the wrong hands, a corpse to be moved in order to be discovered by the police at a more suitable spot, the killing of Prince Michael, the presumed heir to the throne of Herzoslovakia, a stolen diamond, and towards the end, a happy marriage. The tension builds on the understanding that certain diplomatic secrets must remain confidential at any cost. But the presumption is also that secrecy is achievable: there is one set of letters and one manuscript, and the price of silence is one dead man in the library, ultimately putting the matter at rest.

Maintaining diplomatic secrecy is a much more complicated business today. Contacts with foreigners are no longer that exotic, and national legislation is increasingly created in supranational and international settings. Also, the understanding of what should be considered secret has changed. Consequently, access to information concerning international negotiations has become highly topical also in the EU. Calls for greater transparency have in recent years been heard, eg in the context of the United States Treasury Department financial messaging data to prevent and combat terrorism and terrorist financing (the so-called SWIFT Agreement) rejected by the European Parliament in 2010; the Anti-Counterfeiting Trade

Agreement (ACTA), also rejected by the European Parliament two years later; and more recently, the Transatlantic Trade and Investment Partnership (TTIP), a trade agreement which is currently being negotiated between the European Union and the United States. In the twentieth century, most democracies, including the EU, have developed codes on public access and for classifying documents. However, since then we have moved to an age dominated by Twitter, and the urge to share every pathetic detail of everyone's life on Twitter, an urge equally shared by Commissioners, Prime Ministers and Foreign Ministers. Following episodes like 'Wikileaks', the relevant question would seem to be whether, today, all of these rules are becoming seriously outdated.

In this chapter, after a brief introduction to secrecy as the foreign relations paradigm, I will first discuss how the EU has attempted to strike the balance between secrecy and transparency through rules on public access and classification of sensitive documents. Alongside a Treaty-based access to documents regime, the EU also has a regime for protecting and handling classified information. This regime does not have a clear 'constitutional' basis, but has so far been adopted under Article 240(3) TFEU, the legal basis for the Council Rules of Procedure.[1] This is a regime that continues to be opposed by the European Parliament, but is defended by the Council as appropriate and absolutely necessary. Following this, I will explain how the EU Court has addressed this issue in its recent jurisprudence. This case-law also witnesses a changing paradigm to a certain extent, and circles around whether the applicable procedure (legislative or not) is decisive on defining the level of openness, or whether these choices should be made more on the basis of the substance of the future agreement. The recent debates illustrate how transparency has both an inter-institutional dimension, a party access dimension, and a more general 'fundamental rights' dimension relating to a general 'right to know'. My own interest relates more to the last of these, even if the two other situations will also be briefly discussed. I will close with a couple of more general remarks on the recent debates concerning the TTIP negotiations and the helpful contributions of the new European Ombudsman to these debates.

Secrecy in the area of international relations has been an exceptionally strong paradigm. Aurélien Colson has traced the emergence of secrecy as the uncontested norm for international relations to a time after the Renaissance, when relations between sovereign states concentrated in the hands of a select few Princes, creating a 'shadow paradigm' as the natural realm of negotiation.[2] Colson argues that while secrecy created an imperative for the Ambassador to protect his own secrets, it simultaneously also turned him into an *espion honorable* in order to gain access

---

[1] Council Decision 2013/488/EU on the security rules for protecting EU classified information [2013] OJ L274/1. For a defence of these solutions, see D Galloway, 'Classifying Secrets in the EU' (2014) 52 *Journal of Common Market Studies* 668.

[2] A Colson, *The Ambassador, Between Light and Shade: The Emergency of Secrecy as the Norm of International Negotiation*, ESSE Research Center Working Papers DR 07023 (November 2007).

to the information he needed in order to fulfil his own security function. In this way, spying also contributed to reinforcing the secrecy paradigm: '[S]uch was the fear of espionage that each party multiplied the precautions he took to preserve his secrets, which in turn encouraged the recourse to agents used to discover them'.[3] Foreign affairs have been characterised by secret deals and treaties, and the 'long-standing convention on the sacrosanct diplomatic pouch'.[4] And keeping in mind that these accounts largely consisted of handwritten copies, it was relatively easy to keep them concealed. Secrets were primarily stolen for tactical reasons, in order to buttress national secrecy or political advantage, and not only for the interest of a general 'right to know', as the case might be today.

Towards the end of the First World War, in 1918, United States President Woodrow Wilson discussed the question of secret diplomacy in the first one of his 'Fourteen Points'. He declared that '[o]pen covenants of peace, openly arrived at, after which there shall be no private international understandings of any kind but diplomacy shall proceed always frankly and in the public view'. While an attractive thought, secrecy soon won over the ideology of openness. *Oppenheim's International Law* (fifth edition edited by Professor Lauterpacht in 1937), provides several chapters that are of interest for the current study, in particular those relating to diplomatic envoys and the process of negotiation. The latter process is described as follows:

> The Law of Nations does not prescribe any particular form in which international negotiations must be conducted. Such negotiations may, therefore, take place viva voce, or through the exchange of written representations and arguments, or both. The more important negotiations are regularly conducted through the diplomatic exchange of written communications, as only in this way can misunderstandings be avoided, which easily arise during viva voce negotiations. Of the greatest importance are the negotiations which take place through congresses and conferences.[5]

The question of transparency or secrecy of such negotiations is not discussed, but the matter is briefly touched upon in the context of explaining the position of diplomatic envoys:

> Privileges due to diplomatic envoys, apart from ceremonial honours, have reference to their inviolability and to their so-called extraterritoriality … It is equally clear that if their full and free intercourse with their home States through letters, telegrams, and couriers were liable to interference, the objects of their mission could not be fulfilled. In this case it would be impossible for them to send independent and secret reports to, or receive similar instructions from, their home States.[6]

---

[3] ibid 15.
[4] M Macmillan, *A Short History of Secrecy* (2011), *Foreign Policy*, available at www.foreignpolicy.com/articles/2011/02/22/a_short_history_of_secrecy.
[5] L Oppenheim, *International Law: A Treatise*, 5th edn (H Lauterpacht (ed), London, Longmans, 1937) 685, para 481.
[6] ibid 615, para 385.

What is of the greatest interest in this account, though, is what the textbook does *not* enlarge upon. The fact that international negotiations must be conducted in secrecy seems so settled in 1937 that there is no reason to discuss the matter in any detail. A similar approach is adopted by the 1961 Vienna Convention on Diplomatic Relations,[7] which continues to be the main instrument regulating the exercise of old-fashioned diplomatic relations between states and pre-dates the modern running of day-to-day business between states.

## II. EU Transparency Regime and Secrecy

The EU transparency regime is much newer but has nevertheless noble foundations. It builds on Article 1 of the Treaty on European Union (TEU), which celebrates the new stage in the process of creating an ever closer union among the peoples of Europe, and emphasises that, in this Union, decisions are taken as openly as possible. Article 15 of the Treaty on the Functioning of the European Union (TFEU) then further elaborates on the principle of transparency and provides a legal basis for Regulation 1049/2001 on access to documents. Since the Treaty of Lisbon, Article 15 TFEU specifically emphasises the need to guarantee openness in the context of procedures that lead to the adoption of a legislative act.

Regulation 1049/2001 is the Act that defines in greater detail the 'principles, conditions and limits on grounds of public or private interest' that govern the right of public access to documents held by the EU institutions, 'in such a way as to ensure the widest possible access to documents'. The Regulation applies to 'all documents held by an institution, that is to say, documents drawn up or received by it and in its possession, in all areas of activity of the European Union' (Article 2(3)). The Regulation has not been updated since the entry into force of the Treaty of Lisbon, but it still acknowledges the need to grant even 'wider access' to:

> documents in cases where the institutions are acting in their legislative capacity … while at the same time preserving the effectiveness of the institutions' decision-making process. Such documents should be made directly accessible to the greatest possible extent.[8]

The Regulation includes no rules on either party access or inter-institutional access, but has been frequently used for both purposes.

---

[7] Vienna Convention on Diplomatic Relations (entered into force 24 April 1964) 500 UNTS 95.

[8] There are a number of significant questions that under the Lisbon rules fall outside the scope of legislative matters, and subsequently come under another transparency regime, in particular as far as the Council is concerned. Under Art 8(1) of the Council Rules of Procedure, 'internal measures, administrative or budgetary acts, acts concerning inter-institutional or international relations or non-binding acts (such as conclusions, recommendations or resolutions)' are defined as non-legislative even when 'legally binding in or for the Member States', and thus constitute an exception to open Council sessions.

The most relevant exception for international relations is included in Article 4(1)(a) of the Regulation, which establishes that:

[t]he institutions shall refuse access to a document where disclosure would undermine the protection of ... the public interest as regards ... international relations.

Unlike the exceptions under Article 4(2) of the Regulation, the exceptions under Article 4(1) include no 'public interest' test, which requires the institution to balance the possible harm following from disclosure with the public interest relating to it, and consider whether access could still be granted despite some harm to the protected interests. Under the international relations exceptions, the existence of harm is enough to deny access. This strengthens the understanding that tricky international negotiations are hard to conduct in public, and that they should, as the main rule, remain confidential if any evidence of possible harm can be identified.

While Regulation 1049/2001 in principle covers all documents irrespective of their subject matter, certain documents are subject to specific procedural rules. Under Article 2(5), '[s]ensitive documents as defined in Article 9(1) shall be subject to special treatment'.[9] Article 9(1–4) of the Regulation lays down more detailed rules concerning treatment granted to these documents within the EU institutions. The key principle is that sensitive documents can only be released with the consent of their originator.

The question of whether the practice of classifying documents affects public access[10] has been subject to inter-institutional disagreement. The General Court addressed this question more specifically in the first *Sison* cases,[11] and the Court of Justice of the European Union (CJEU) later upheld its arguments. The relevant question from the public access point of view has been what the effect of a possible classification of a document has when public access is considered. The intention behind the special procedural rules of the Regulation governing the treatment of sensitive documents was not to exclude such documents from the scope of the duty to carry out a concrete and individual examination of requested documents, but rather to provide for a framework within which such an examination may be carried out. Keeping in mind that Article 9 of Regulation 1049/2001 does not address the question of which documents should be classified or whether access should be granted but merely regulates the procedure for handling those documents that have been classified within the institutions,[12] the answer should be

---

[9] For a discussion of the background of Art 9, see J Heliskoski and P Leino, 'Darkness at the Break of Noon: The Case Law on Regulation No 1049/2001 on Access to Documents' (2006) 43 *CML Rev* 735.

[10] For a description of the development of security rules in the EU, see, eg, D Curtin, 'Official Secrets and the Negotiation of International Agreements: Is the EU Executive Unbound?' (2013) 50 *CML Rev* 423.

[11] Joined Cases T-110/03, T-150/03 and T-405/03 *Sison v Council*, Judgment, EU:T:2005:143, paras 59–60.

[12] See also Case C-576/12P *Ivan Jurašinović v Council*, Judgment, EU:C:2013:777, paras 38–41.

relatively clear. However, there have been persistent fears, in particular in the European Parliament, that documents are being stamped too easily, especially by the Council, and that a classification has the automatic consequence of denying access without serious consideration of the substance of the document and the possible harm of disclosure. In addition, the Parliament has criticised the fact that rules having a clear effect on public access established by the Treaties are decided unilaterally by the Council.[13]

This approach has never received support in the Council and the Commission. Instead, the Council has recently revised its own rules of classification,[14] which build on the assumption that not only the Member States' administrations, but also the Commission and the European External Action Service (EEAS) are committed to applying the same or equivalent standards. Agreements have also been concluded with third countries and other international organisations for the handling of classified information.[15] The relevant Council Decision includes no references to Regulation 1049/2001. The relevant point seems to be that the EU system includes currently no substantive internal control or oversight within the executive to combat over-classification.[16] Subsequently, it is difficult to ascertain whether the practice of classifying documents affects the level of openness, directly or indirectly, and this should of course in itself already be a matter for some concern.

There is little case-law on this question. The General Court's early ruling in *Sison v Council*[17] does little to drive away these fears and also illustrates the party access dimension of this case-law.[18] The dispute in *Sison v Council* involved three separate actions for annulment of Council Decisions whereby the applicant had been refused access to documents relating to three successive Council Decisions (of 21 January, 27 February and 2 October 2003) implementing Article 2(3) of the Council Regulation on specific restrictive measures directed against certain persons and entities with a view to combating terrorism. Each of the decisions adopted pursuant to the Regulation had included the applicant in the list of persons whose funds and financial assets were to be frozen. The applicant challenged the Council Decision refusing him access to the documents that had led the Council to adopt Decision 2002/848/EC and refusing disclosure of the identity of the states which had provided the Council with certain documents in that connection.

---

[13] See, eg, European Parliament Resolution of 14 September 2011 on public access to documents (Rule 104(7)) for the years 2009–2010 (2010/2294(INI)).

[14] See Council Decision 2013/488/EU of 23 September 2013 on the security rules for protecting EU classified information [2013] OJ L274/1. Of particular relevance for international relations is Annex VI, which includes specific provisions on the exchange of classified information with third states and international organisations.

[15] See, eg, Council Decision 2005/481/CFSP of 13 June 2005 concerning the conclusion of the Agreement between the European Union and Ukraine on the security procedures for the exchange of classified information [2005] OJ L172/83.

[16] Curtin, 'Official Secrets and the Negotiation of International Agreements' (n 10).

[17] *Sison v Council* (n 11).

[18] C- 266/05P *Sison v Council*, Judgment, EU:C:2007:75.

Mr Sison argued, among other things, that in adopting the contested Decision the Council had not conducted a concrete assessment of the requested information and failed to inform the applicant properly about the reasons behind its decisions. In its ruling, the CJEU confirmed that in applying the public interest exceptions under Article 4(1) of the Regulation, the institution enjoys wide discretion in determining whether disclosure of documents harms the sensitive and essential interests protected under that provision. Whether the documents contributed to the adoption of a legislative act did not affect the interpretation of Article 4(1). The main lesson to be drawn from *Sison v Council* is that no reasoning running into the details can legitimately be expected from an institution in the case of sensitive documents. It seems that hardly any reasoning going into the substance was necessary on the Council's part. In fact, a few magic phrases such as 'fight against international terrorism' and 'involvement of third states' seemed to be enough to satisfy the Court.[19]

It seems to follow from the Court's reasoning that, in the case of sensitive documents, such an individual examination of the requested document is deemed to have taken place each time the specific procedure under Article 9 governing the treatment of sensitive documents has been followed. A sufficient degree of concrete assessment of the requested information was demonstrated, first, by the existence of a specific procedure for considering requests for access to 'sensitive documents', under which both the officials authorised for that purpose and the delegations of the Member States were able to examine the documents in question and to express their views on their disclosure. The General Court required no proof of substantive examination of such documents, or any reasoning containing many details. Instead, general references to the objectives of the instrument were regarded as sufficient, as was a reference to 'the involvement of third states in the fight against terrorism'. For the denial of partial access to the requested documents it was sufficient for the Council to refer to the fact that the documents concerned were covered in their entirety by the relevant exceptions. Regarding, finally, the refusal to disclose the identity of the third states that had provided the Council with certain documents, a reference to the rule in Article 9(3) of the Regulation and to the opposition of the states concerned to any disclosure of their identity was considered adequate for the purpose of stating the reasons.

The European Parliament has consistently raised concerns about the classification regime, even if it has needed to adopt internal rules, also by means of administrative rules, on handling of confidential information in order to gain access to information from other institutions.[20] The practice of classified information and 'closed evidence' is also spreading to the CJEU, and likely to be introduced in its new Rules of Procedure in the near future. The Parliament's calls have

---

[19] See Heliskoski and Leino, 'Darkness at the Break of Noon' (n 9) which concerned the CFI ruling, which the CJEU later upheld.

[20] See Decision 2011/C 190/02 of the Bureau of the European Parliament of 6 June 2011 concerning the rules governing the treatment of confidential information by the European Parliament.

been strengthened by the entry into force of the Treaty of Lisbon. In the Hautala and Sargentini Report of 2011[21] the Parliament stressed that 'Article 9 of Regulation (EC) No 1049/2001 on sensitive documents is a compromise that no longer reflects the new constitutional and legal obligations after the Lisbon Treaty' and that classification has a direct bearing on citizens' right of access to documents. The Report questioned the basis of the current system of classification, which should be replaced by common rules of classification in the form of a Regulation, and pointed out how the current system is prone to over-classification. In particular, the Parliament called on the Council to grant Parliament full access to classified documents connected with international agreements.[22] The fears relating to a culture of secrecy and over-classification are shared even by academics, who have expressed concerns about the effect of rules on originator control and the process of derivative classification causing secrecy to multiply and then result in over-classification.[23]

The European Parliament's approach to classification rules being beyond democratic control was followed in its 2011 Legislative Resolution on the reform of Regulation 1049/2011,[24] which proposes adding a new Article 3a to the Regulation, including a procedure for the classification and declassification of documents. The provision would also aim at regulating the question of when a document is to be classified, and the meaning of different classifications ('EU TOP SECRET', 'EU SECRET', 'EU CONFIDENTIAL', and 'EU RESTRICTED'). In particular, the Parliament argued:

> International agreements dealing with the sharing of confidential information concluded on behalf of the Union shall not give any right to a third country or international organisation to prevent the European Parliament from having access to that confidential information.

The post-Lisbon institutional framework for international relations also includes the European External Action Service.[25] Article 11 of the EEAS Decision establishes that the EEAS is to apply Regulation 1049/2001, and that the High Representative is to decide on the relevant implementing rules.[26] So far, the EEAS has adopted two reports relating to the implementation of the Regulation, illustrating that there has been wide interest in documents held by the EEAS, with a considerable part of the requests coming from the academic sector. More than 70 per cent

---

[21] European Parliament Resolution of 14 September 2011 (n 13).

[22] ibid paras 9–12.

[23] Most notably, see D Curtin's 'Top Secret Europe', Inaugural Lecture published by the University of Amsterdam (2011).

[24] European Parliament Legislative Resolution of 15 December 2011 on the proposal for a Regulation of the European Parliament and of the Council regarding public access to European Parliament, Council and Commission documents (recast) (COM(2008)0229—C6-0184/2008—2008/0090(COD)).

[25] See Council Decision 2010/427/EU of 26 July 2010 establishing the organisation and functioning of the European External Action Service [2010] OJ L201/30.

[26] Decision 2011/C 243/08 of the High Representative of 19 July 2011 on the rules regarding access to documents [2011] OJ C243/16.

of the requests received a positive reply. Negative replies were mainly justified with reference to the exceptions relating to public security, defence and military matters, international relations, the privacy and integrity of the individual, or the 'space to think' exception.[27] Article 10(1) of the EEAS Decision lays down a series of security obligations for the EEAS:

> The High Representative shall, after consulting the Committee referred to in point 3 of Section I of Part II of the Annex to Council Decision 2001/264/EC of 19 March 2001 adopting the Council's security regulations (1), decide on the security rules for the EEAS and take all appropriate measures in order to ensure that the EEAS manages effectively the risks to its staff, physical assets and information, and that it fulfils its duty of care and responsibilities in this regard. Such rules shall apply to all EEAS staff, and all staff in Union Delegations, regardless of their administrative status or origin.

So far, the EEAS has spoken much more about secrecy than transparency—perhaps linked to recent reports on how Brussels has 'more spy activity than almost any other city in the world', with hundreds of foreign intelligence officers and agents being placed there to gain access to EU information in various policy fields, and not only traditional security issues.[28] In her statements, the first High Representative stressed the 'need for the EEAS to have a highly developed security culture, in particular for staff in EU delegations',[29] and the possibilities of 'quiet diplomacy', which she linked to the possibility of acting without full publicity, which can sometimes be more effective.[30] However, such a technique (if it indeed is one invoked by the EEAS) remains unstudied and lacks a clear definition.[31] Based on the Reports on the implementation of Regulation 1049/2001 by the EEAS, none of the negative decisions of the EEAS have been appealed so far. Therefore, there is so far little external insight as to whether and how the EEAS adds to the transparency dimension of external relations.

## III. Recent Case-Law on Transparency in External Relations

While the public access rules contained in Regulation 1049/2001 have not changed after the Treaty of Lisbon (despite two proposals to this effect by the Commission

---

[27] See EEAS, *Report on Access to Documents for the Years 2011 and 2012*, EEAS(2013)1141825 (Brussels, 13 May 2013); EEAS, *Report on Access to Documents for 2013*, EEAS(2014)2244316 (Brussels, 23 June 2014).
[28] See 'Intelligence Chief: EU Capital is 'Spy Capital', *EUobserver*, 17 September 2012, available at http://euobserver.com/secret_ue/117553.
[29] See *Report by the High Representative to the European Parliament, the Council and the Commission* (22 December 2011) para 36.
[30] See B Barton and P Quinn, 'Making EU Diplomacy Work: Treaty Changes, Political Will and the "Quiet Diplomacy" Strategy' in P Quinn (ed), *Making European Diplomacy Work: Can the EEAS Deliver?*, College of Europe, EU Diplomacy Paper 08/2011.
[31] ibid.

in 2008 and 2011), changes in the Treaty framework and subsequent case-law have emphasised the division between legislative and non-legislative documents. The most crucial question in determining the scope of access has therefore become whether the documents relate to a legislative procedure, in which case, following the Court's interpretation in cases like *Turco* and *Access Info Europe*, the main rule is full access already while the procedure is pending—something that the institutions are struggling with.[32] At the same time, it has become tempting for the institutions to argue that where the document does *not* relate to a legislative procedure (which is the case with most documents relating to international relations) then the principle of openness has less relevance. The simplistic division into legislative and non-legislative documents made on procedural grounds has been challenged several times before the courts. The key question has related to international agreements that are likely to produce comparable legal effects in the EU legal order as those created by legislative acts. In this way, the emphasis originally intended as a positive one has in fact also received negative connotations, reflecting the difficulties involved in creating 'positive discrimination' in a regime that already builds on 'widest possible access'. This is the balance that the CJEU has been trying to address in its recent case-law concerning the interpretation of the international relations exception.

Secondly, several of the cases relating to the implementation of the international relations exception relate to the growing case-law on sanctions and party access. In addition to the *Sison* case discussed above, for example, the famous *Kadi* saga illustrates the question of whether the people suspected of terrorism have the right to know why they are being listed.[33] Questions of fair process have also been visible in relation to documents originating in the EU missions in the Former Yugoslavia.[34] Despite the specific mention in Article 41(2)(b) of everyone's right to access their own file, there is no comprehensive EU legislation ensuring that this right can be properly exercised.[35]

Finally, institutional politics are particularly visible in the post-Lisbon case law on access to documents relating to international relations. The recent cases illustrate the difference between two forms of access. Public access under Regulation 1049/2001 is granted on a universal basis: if access to a document is granted based on an individual application, it is simultaneously made available to the public at large and comes without conditions concerning the use of the information contained. The applicant does not need to state any grounds for her application, since

---

[32] P Leino, *Transparency, Participation and EU Institutional Practice: An Inquiry into the Limits of the "Widest Possible"*, EUI Working Papers LAW.2014/3.

[33] On the *Kadi* saga, see P Leino, '"In Principle the Full Review": What Justice for Mr Kadi?' in R Liivoja and J Petman (eds), *International Law-making, Essays in Honour of Jan Klabbers* (Abingdon, Routledge, 2013) 225.

[34] See, eg, *Jurašinović v Council* (n 12).

[35] See P Leino, 'Efficiency, Citizens and Administrative Culture: The Politics of Good Administration in the EU' (2014) 20 *European Public Law* 681.

access is granted on a universal 'right to know' basis. Inter-institutional access (by the European Parliament) has been particularly topical post-Lisbon,[36] noting the new powers of the European Parliament in the conclusion of international agreements under Article 218 TFEU and the fact that it is usually not involved in the negotiations, and thus has access to considerably less information than the Commission, and to a lesser extent, the Council.[37] At the same time, the Parliament has traditionally not been too keen to undertake serious confidentiality obligations,[38] and its legal avenues for gaining access to information have subsequently been limited. Inter-institutional access belongs in principle under a different regime, can be granted for a particular purpose and be linked to confidentiality requirements.[39]

The questions relating to the reach of the access regime relating to legislative matters and inter-institutional access are present in two of the recent cases, which are appeals brought by Sophie In't Veld MEP in her personal capacity against the Council under Regulation 1049/2001 for public access to documents relating to pending negotiations on agreements where the flow of information to the European Parliament, its Committees and their rapporteurs had been less than satisfactory and it was felt that this lack of information had prevented the Parliament from exercising its powers of consent under Article 218 TFEU.

The first case concerned a Council Legal Service opinion on the proposed legal basis of the draft Council Decision to authorise the Commission to launch negotiations for the SWIFT agreement.[40] The requested document thus related clearly to the EU internal deliberations and contained legal advice concerning the choice of legal basis and EU competence. In't Veld received partial access, with the Council invoking the international relations exception quoted above, and the exception relating to court proceedings and legal advice, since in the Council's view, disclosure 'would reveal to the public information relating to certain provisions in the envisaged Agreement … and, consequently, would negatively impact on the [European Union]'s negotiating position and would also damage the climate of confidence in the on-going negotiations'. In the Council's view this 'sensitive issue, which has an impact on the powers of the European Parliament in the conclusion of the Agreement, has been [the] subject of divergent positions between

[36] For a discussion, see also Curtin, 'Official Secrets and the Negotiation of International Agreements' (n 10).

[37] R Passos, 'The European Union's External Relations a Year after Lisbon: A First Evaluation from the European Parliament' in P Koutrakos (ed), *The European Union's External Relations a Year after Lisbon*, CLEER Working Papers 2011/3.

[38] On the organisation of access to classified information, see also V Abazi, 'The Future of Europol's Parliamentary Oversight: A Great Leap Forward?' (2014) 15 *German Law Journal* 1121, 1140–41.

[39] See the Inter-institutional Agreement between the European Parliament and the Council concerning the forwarding to and handling by the European Parliament of classified information held by the Council on matters other than those in the area of the common foreign and security policy [2013] OJ C353E/156.

[40] Case T-529/09 *Sophie In't Veld v Council supported by the Commission (In't Veld No 1)*, Judgment, EU:T:2012:215.

the institutions'. In those circumstances, '[d]ivulgation of the contents of the requested document would undermine the protection of legal advice, since it would make known to the public an internal opinion of the Legal Service, intended only for the members of the Council within the context of the Council's preliminary discussions on the envisaged Agreement'. Furthermore, the Council 'concluded that the protection of its internal legal advice relating to a draft international Agreement ... outweighs the public interest in disclosure'.[41] The Council lost the case in General Court and appealed to the CJEU, which delivered its ruling in July 2014,[42] dismissing the Council appeal in its entirety.

Both courts rejected the Council's arguments concerning the sensitivity of its legal advice in a similar way as when the Council presented them in the legislative context. In fact, the CJEU relied in its ruling quite heavily on the general findings, such as the 'three-stage-test' to be used when determining whether access can be granted,[43] in its *Turco* and *Access Info Europe* case-law, which relate specifically to legislative documents. The General Court also stressed that the risk that the 'disclosure of legal advice relating to a decision-making process could give rise to doubts concerning the lawfulness of the adopted acts is not sufficient to constitute a threat to the protection of legal advice' was 'in principle, transposable to the field of the international activity of the European Union, because the decision-making process in that area is not exempt from the application of the principle of transparency' (para 76). Both Courts acknowledged that the considerations relating to citizen participation and the legitimacy of administration are of a particular relevance where the Council is acting in its legislative capacity. However, the General Court stressed that the importance of transparency could not 'be ruled out in international affairs, especially where a decision authorising the opening of negotiations involves an international agreement which may have an impact on an area of the European Union's legislative activity' (para 89). The General Court particularly emphasised the substance of the envisaged agreement, which concerned the processing and exchange of information in the context of police cooperation, with potential effects on the protection of personal data, which is a fundamental right, and something that the Council was obliged to consider when establishing whether the general interest relating to greater transparency justified the full or wider disclosure of the requested document (para 92). The CJEU confirmed that the fact that a document does not relate to a legislative procedure does not entail that no examination would be necessary, keeping in mind that the non-legislative activity of the institutions also falls under the scope of the Regulation.

The General Court also considered specifically the effect of the ongoing procedure for concluding the international agreement and established that this was

---

[41] Paragraphs 10 and 15 of the contested Council Decision.
[42] Case C-350/12P *Council v Sophie In't Veld*, Judgment, EU:C:2014:2039.
[43] ibid para 96.

not conclusive in ascertaining whether an overriding public interest justifying disclosure existed (para 101):

Indeed, the public interest in the transparency of the decision-making process would become meaningless if, as the Commission proposes, it were to be taken into account only in those cases where the decision-making process has come to an end.

The fact that the substance of the document had been partially reproduced in a public European Parliament resolution was recognised by the CJEU, which found it appropriate to take this fact into account when considering harm to international relations. The fact that earlier disclosure had been unlawful was not relevant for this evaluation (para 60). In conclusion, both Courts stressed the importance of protecting those elements that could reveal the strategic objectives pursued by the EU in the negotiations, but established that outside these parts, the Council had not demonstrated how, 'specifically and actually', harm to the public interest in the field of international relations existed.[44] Council Document 11788/2014 considering the ruling of the CJEU is not a public document, so it cannot be ascertained how the Council interpreted the outcome of the case. However, the document requested by Ms In't Veld is partially accessible through the Council register, with access being granted to the first two and a half pages of the legal service opinion, and the rest remaining secret. Is the assumption, then, that no further measures were needed to comply with the Court's ruling?

The second case brought by Ms In't Veld concerned a Commission Decision to refuse access to certain documents relating to the famous draft international Anti-Counterfeiting Trade Agreement,[45] which the European Parliament later refused to give its consent to and criticised for a lack of transparency in the negotiation process.[46] A particular characteristic of the case related to the agreement among the various negotiating partners that matters would remain confidential, and whether the Commission in fact had the right to consent to such a solution, keeping in mind the transparency obligations it has under the Treaties. This question has been raised both before the General Court and the European Ombudsman.

The appeal by Ms In't Veld in this case related more clearly to documents produced during the international stage of negotiations and not merely internal decision-making within the EU. Consequently, the General Court proved more responsive to the Commission's concerns. Following the *Sison* line, the General Court emphasised the 'particularly sensitive and essential nature of the interests'

---

[44] Even AG Sharpston suggested the Court should reject the Council's appeal, stressing that in her view it should not be determinative whether an institution acts in a legislative, executive or administrative capacity. Instead, the key factor is the need to conduct a careful and objective assessment and provide a detailed and specific reasoning. See Case C-350/12P *Council v Sophie In't Veld*, Opinion of AG Sharpston, EU:C:2014:88.

[45] Case T-301/10 *Sophie In't Veld v Commission (In't Veld No 2)*, Judgment, EU:T:2013:135.

[46] See European Parliament Written Declaration 12/2010 on the lack of a transparent process for the Anti-Counterfeiting Trade Agreement (ACTA) and potentially objectionable content, 8 March 2010.

relating to international relations, which gives the decisions on access 'a complex and delicate nature which calls for the exercise of particular care' and presumes 'some discretion' (para 108). The Court did not address the appropriateness of confidentiality agreements, but accepted that the confidentiality commitment had not been specifically invoked by the Commission, that its refusal had been legally based on Article 4(1)(a), and that the disclosure of EU positions in international negotiations could indeed damage the protection of the public interest as regards international relations. This could happen by indirectly disclosing the positions of other parties to the negotiations. Alternatively, the EU positions are (para 125):

> by definition, subject to change depending on the course of those negotiations, and on concessions and compromises made in that context by the various stakeholders. As has already been noted, the formulation of negotiating positions may involve a number of tactical considerations of the negotiators, including the European Union itself. In that context, it is possible that the disclosure by the European Union, to the public, of its own negotiating positions, even though the negotiating positions of the other parties remain secret, could, in practice, have a negative effect on the negotiating position of the European Union.

The Court also held that the unilateral disclosure of positions by one party may be likely to seriously undermine the mutual trust which is essential to the effectiveness of negotiations, the maintenance of which is a very delicate exercise in the context of international relations (para 126). Finally, since the international relations exception was mandatory and thus involved no public interest test, 'any argument based on an overriding public interest in disclosure must be rejected as ineffective' (para 131). The ruling in *In't Veld (No 2)* is extremely detailed, following the Court's examination of the requested documents and ruling on the parts that the Council should have handed out.[47] The decision was not appealed. Still, sensitivity to revealing negotiating positions of other parties in the ACTA context has also been shared by the European Ombudsman, when assessing access to ACTA documents:

> The Ombudsman shares the Council's opinion that releasing the documents in question, which reveal the negotiating position of the US and Japan, would be highly likely to be detrimental to the EU's relations with those countries. The Ombudsman also agrees that, as further argued by the Council, it is likely that such disclosure would have a negative [e]ffect on the climate of confidence in the on-going negotiations, and that it would hamper open and constructive co-operation.[48]

---

[47] The Court annulled the Commission Decision of 4 May 2010 (reference SG.E.3/HP/psi—Ares(2010)234950), insofar as it refused to grant access to documents 21 and 25 of the list annexed to that Decision and to the following redactions made on other documents of that list: document 45, page 2, under the heading 'Participants', second paragraph, last sentence; document 47, page 1, under 'Participants' second paragraph, last sentence; document 47, page 2, under '1. Digital Environment (including Internet)', second paragraph, last sentence; document 48, page 2, the paragraph under Section 4, end of sentence.

[48] Decision of the European Ombudsman closing his inquiry into Complaint 90/2009/(JD)OV against the Council of the European Union, para 33.

While the ACTA story has been most discussed from the point of view of the European Parliament defending the right to know and holding the Commission and Council accountable for their actions, it is of interest that even the Parliament's own transparency policy in relation to the negotiations has also been scrutinised by the European Ombudsman following complaints by 28 digital civil rights associations[49] who claimed that in refusing to grant full access to the negotiation documents that the Parliament had in its possession, largely received from the Commission based on the Framework Agreement between the two institutions,[50] it failed to act in line with the legitimate and reasonable expectation that the Parliament would live up to its past declarations on transparency in the ACTA process. In that context, the Parliament's defence follows very closely the line taken by the Council and Commission in other cases. While the Ombudsman accepted the Parliament's arguments at large, he was more critical about the confidentiality agreement than the General Court. While the Ombudsman noted that the Parliament had not signed the confidentiality agreement itself, Regulation 1049/2001 requires the institutions to assess each document in a concrete manner. Therefore, while he did not go as far as to state that no such commitments should ever be given, 'careful consideration should be given to the temporal and material scope of such agreements, particularly in cases where the issue will be submitted to the EU's legislative bodies for ratification' (para 60). Such commitments could not be made after the submission of the agreement to the legislature for the purpose of ratification. In any case, 'serious consideration should be given by any EU body that makes such a commitment to ensure that it does not undermine the principles essential to a democratic EU that underpin the *Turco* case-law' (para 62).

The third and final case involving an international agreement was brought by Professor Besselink concerning a draft negotiating mandate, the draft Council Decision authorising the Commission to negotiate the EU Accession Agreement to the European Convention on Human Rights (ECHR),[51] a matter which (according to the applicant, and it is difficult to disagree) was of a constitutional nature and also supported by the freedom of expression provision in the Charter. The General Court declared these points inadmissible since they had, in its view, been presented in an 'extremely laconic and summary way' preventing the Court from exercising its power of review. Even if the argument concerning constitutional nature were approved, the Court argued, the question was irrelevant, since the question addressed by the Council Decision was not whether the Union will accede to the ECHR, but the applicable procedure and strategic objectives. As to its contents, the document fell under the international relations exception.

---

[49] Decision of the European Ombudsman in his inquiry into Complaint 2393/2011/RA against the European Parliament.

[50] Framework Agreement on relations between the European Parliament and the European Commission [2010] OJ L304/47.

[51] Case T-331/11 *Leonard Besselink v Council*, Judgment, EU:T:2013:419.

The Court found that the Council had interpreted the said exception too broadly. It could not be used to justify a refusal to make public the negotiation directives, which concerned the protocols to which the EU was seeking to accede, especially since the matter was not subject to negotiations and the contents of the said directives had been communicated to the EU's negotiating partners. But the Court accepted that even if some parts of the other negotiating directives had been published, their precise content had not been previously disclosed, and could have been exploited by the EU's negotiating partners, thus establishing a risk to the EU's international relations. The Court did not discuss the fact that, unlike in the ACTA case described above, the EU's negotiating partner, the Council of Europe, had in fact been exceptionally open and placed all its negotiating directives on the Internet, which should have had some effect on the need to maintain a climate of confidence. But the Court did establish that those parts of the directives which merely referred to the principles that should govern the relevant negotiations, such as those contained in Article 6(2) TEU and Protocol No 8, or the list of questions to be addressed in the negotiations, should have been made public.

The Court left the identification of these parts to the Council itself, and the Council eventually came to the conclusion in January 2014 that 'at the present point in time, the applicant may have access to document 9689/10 in its entirety'. Formally, this was justified with the 'passing of time and of the fact that a draft Agreement on the Accession of the European Union to the ECHR has now been agreed at negotiators' level'.[52] Exceptionally, the Council thus decided to be sensible and not embarrass itself with yet another appeal. The mandate is now publicly available in the Council register, and anyone interested may try to identify the parts which might have fulfilled the criteria established by the Court. The document also highlights the general nature of many negotiating directives. This leaves the Commission to make the substantive choices, and should raise significant accountability issues in the context of international negotiations—issues that require democratic oversight at both EU and national levels. Transparency in external relations often appears more as an exercise in ensuring accountability than one relating to citizen participation as such.

As regards the recent case-law on transparency relating to international agreements, some conclusions can be drawn. So far, the claims relating to the need to protect legal advice as a part of the EU internal decision-making have not proved successful. Both the Council and the Commission have seen the international relations exception as a wide one, following the rationale that secrecy makes better decisions, both in internal and external affairs.[53] The Court has shown sensitivity to these claims and acknowledged that a certain discretion in applying the exception exists, but also as a rule established that the institutions have implemented the provision too broadly, in particular in *In't Veld (No 1)* and *Besselink*.

---

[52] Council Decision 5022/1 of 16 January 2014.
[53] D Curtin, 'Judging EU Secrecy' (2012) 2 *Cahiers de Droit Européen* 459, 471.

Finally, an important feature of this jurisprudence concerns the substance of all of the relevant agreements. They are fundamentally important international agreements that have implications for the life of individual citizens, which should have implications for the applicable transparency requirements. A key element in the recent jurisprudence is the General Court's recognition that even if international relations do not fall under legislative matters, transparency still has a function and its requirements must be taken into account. These cases have also demonstrated that international relations should not as a policy field be treated as a categorical exception, and that there are matters where, despite the fact that they formally fall under international relations, it should be possible to take into account the public interest relating to transparency, especially if the possible harm of disclosure seems limited or rather hypothetical.

As regards the two *In't Veld* cases, the Court has properly treated them as public access requests: after all, they were made under the Regulation 1049/2001 regime. Consequently, the position of Ms In't Veld in the Parliament does not seem to have affected the outcome much. More recently there has been case-law addressing more specifically the obligation to 'inform the Parliament immediately and fully' under the Article 218 TFEU procedure. The recent case involving the EU–Mauritius Agreement on the transfer of suspected pirates[54] concerned, first, the interpretation of Article 218(6) and the possible need of the Council to obtain the European Parliament's consent. The Court pointed out that while the provision 'covers three types of procedure for concluding international agreements, each one prescribing a different role for the Parliament', these differences were without prejudice 'to its right to be immediately and fully informed at all stages of the procedure, in accordance with Article 218(10) TFEU'.[55] The choice between the different procedures reflects the symmetry established by Article 218(6) TFEU between the procedures involved in adopting internal and external measures and the need to maintain institutional balance.[56] The CJEU established that while the Council could conclude the agreement without the consent or consultation of the Parliament, it could not do so without informing the European Parliament; a procedural stage that was necessary:

> to ensure that the Parliament is in a position to exercise democratic scrutiny of the European Union's external action and, more specifically, to verify that its powers are respected precisely in consequence of the choice of legal basis for a decision concluding an agreement.[57]

Another case relating to a similar agreement between the EU and Tanzania is pending; in that one, the Parliament is, however, also claiming that the agreement includes provisions falling under judicial cooperation in criminal matters

---

[54] Case C-658/1 *European Parliament v Council*, Judgment, EU:C:2014:2025.
[55] ibid para 54.
[56] ibid para 56.
[57] ibid para 79.

and police cooperation, involving matters that in the internal field would be regulated under the ordinary legislative procedure.[58] This new case-law suggests that the question of institutional access now seems to be moving to a more appropriate arena involving the interpretation of Article 218 TFEU instead of Regulation 1049/2001, where it more properly belongs. At the same time, the consequences of the case-law on Article 218 TFEU might have implications for the case-law on Regulation 1049/2001 and vice versa.

The most topical issue relating to access to documents concerns the Transatlantic Trade and Investment Partnership (TTIP). As with the ACTA negotiations earlier, the need to ensure transparency has been rather high on the agenda, visible for example in the 150,000 replies received through the Commission online consultation on the agreement. The question meriting recent attention has related to whether the negotiation mandate given by the Council to the Commission in the beginning of the negotiations, together with a number of other key documents relating to the process, would be made public or not. Numerous non-governmental organisations (NGOs), including Corporate Europe Observatory (CEO), have stressed how transparency in the negotiations needs to be ensured, since the TTIP will impact domestic regulations, standards and safeguards both in the United States and the EU, and future choices in permanent regulatory cooperation, including future possibilities to regulate a wide scope of matters falling under the future treaty. Ultimately, the CEO argues, a failure to commit to more openness in TTIP negotiations will not only result in growing public opposition to the TTIP as a whole, but also creates a real risk of a biased and flawed agreement.[59]

Following a number of complaints, the European Ombudsman opened an own-initiative inquiry into the matter, and sent a letter in July 2014 on the matter to both the Council and the Commission.[60] In her letters, the Ombudsman raised the significant public interest relating to the TTIP negotiations based on the potential impact of the agreement on the lives of citizens and stressed the importance of enabling the public to follow the progress of negotiations and contribute to shaping their outcome. The Ombudsman noted that despite numerous requests, the negotiating directives had not been legally made publicly available by the Commission or the Council, even if they in fact were easily available on the Internet. The Ombudsman noted the significant delays by the Commission in replying to numerous and broad-ranging requests for public access to documents relating to the TTIP, privileged access that the Commission had granted to certain stakeholders and the unauthorised disclosure of many TTIP documents. In relation to the Commission, the Ombudsman recommended a proactive approach to transparency, including setting up a comprehensive register of TTIP documents and improving the transparency of its relations with privileged stakeholders.

---

[58] Case 263/14 *European Parliament v Council*, Judgment, EU:C:2016:435.

[59] See the Corporate Europe Observatory website, http://corporateeurope.org/international-trade.

[60] See the letters addressed to the Council of the EU and the European Commission requesting an opinion in the European Ombudsman's own-initiative inquiry (OI/11/2014/MMN) concerning transparency and public participation in relation to the Transatlantic Trade and Investment Partnership (TTIP) negotiations, dated 29 July 2014 and available on the Ombudsman's website.

In relation to the Council, the Ombudsman argued that the directives as such were of a high level of generality, and that in her analysis, public disclosure of the directives, over a year after their adoption, would no longer damage public interest as regards international relations; after all, the EU can be assumed to have communicated to the United States and other third countries what it believes should be negotiated upon in the TTIP context. The Ombudsman set three criteria for evaluating harm in this context: disclosure would not:

(i)   damage mutual trust between the negotiators;
(ii)  inhibit the development of free and effective discussions in the context of the negotiations; and/or
(iii) reveal strategic elements of the negotiations either to the other negotiating party or to third parties.

The Ombudsman stressed that each access case should be decided on its own merits and invited the Council to consider proactively publishing the document in question: 'By doing so, it would help promote public trust, which is a key element in ensuring the eventual success of the negotiations'. With respect to the TTIP mandate, the Council finally agreed to declassify and make the mandate publicly available on 9 October 2014.[61] But this was too late, since the continued classification of the document had already become embarrassing. In November 2014, more than 250 NGOs from around Europe brought a case before the CJEU against the Commission concerning lack of transparency in the TTIP negotiations and the Commission's reluctance to see the citizen initiative being used in the context of trade negotiations. Whether the Court ever rules on this case might even be of lesser importance compared to the fundamental dissatisfaction in the running of external relations that it symbolises. In March 2015, the Council agreed to declassify the mandate given to the Commission two years earlier, in March 2013, to negotiate an international agreement on trade in services, as a response to 'a growing public interest in this plurilateral agreement'.[62] Following the events, one wonders whether at some point the institutions would be ready to see that the time has come to reconsider the limits of secrecy in international relations.

# IV.   Time for a New Paradigm?

The balancing between open and secret diplomacy illustrates how access to information is fundamentally about power. This is particularly visible in the

---

[61] See the directives for the negotiation of the Transatlantic Trade and Investment Partnership between the European Union and the United States of America, Doc No 11103/13, now fully accessible in the Council public register of documents.

[62] See Council Press Release, available at www.consilium.europa.eu/en/press/press-releases/2015/03/150310-trade-services-agreement-negotiating-mandate-made-public/. See also Council Doc 6891/13 ADD 1 DCL 1.

institutional politics of the European Parliament. While spies are not yet extinct, it seems that their focus is no longer on traditional international issues or national secrecy, but their interest in what takes place in Brussels relates to most areas in which the EU is run. As far as legislative matters are concerned, life should be easy for the simple spy: most stages of the process should take place in the open and even when not, secrecy seems next to impossible to guarantee. Even the most confidential documents now spread between institutions, representations, lobbyists and civil society by simply pressing 'send'. There is hardly any document in Brussels that one could not get hold of by knowing the right people. External relations are in many ways a similar process of regulation as the internal legislative one. The external relations business just takes place in another forum and might effectively dictate the EU legislative agenda and choices for some time to come.

Following these events, what can one say about the state of transparency in external relations law? The TTIP issue follows a rather consistent pattern of the Council having an illusion of believing that it can control the flow of information based on a rather strict understanding of its transparency obligations, before being forced to give up at the stage of a Court ruling, or when civil society pressure grows too difficult to handle, with the European Parliament joining the civil society in preaching the virtues of openness and accountability, in an orgy of institutional power games. These episodes do no favours for the legitimacy of Council or Commission decision-making.

As far as the Court's case-law is considered, one can make at least a number of preliminary remarks. First, while the Treaty-based transparency regime builds on the distinction between legislative and other matters, the Court seems to be some distance from making a categorical distinction. Similarly, the Court is developing a more nuanced case-law when compared to *Sison*, and focusing more on the need to demonstrate that harm is real and not merely hypothetical, which is more in line with the general principles of transparency. The Court has also avoided the creation of general presumptions of secrecy, which are regrettably spreading in many other key EU policy areas, in the area of international relations.[63] Consequently, international relations are not treated as a block exemption. EU internal discussions relating to international agreements, for example, do not merit automatic protection, but the current interpretation shared by the Court and the Ombudsman is more focused on the international negotiation stage, and on eventual strategic interests, in particular the need to protect the negotiating positions of other parties. In deciding on the degree of transparency, the substance of the agreement might also be of some relevance. The relevant question might be whether the Court is in fact introducing a distinction in international relations between agreements that are deemed 'fundamental' and of impact to individual citizens, and agreements that do not have these features, and how such

---

[63] See P Leino, 'Just a Little Sunshine in the Rain: The 2010 Case Law of the European Court of Justice on Access to Documents' (2011) 48 *CML Rev* 1215.

a distinction would relate to the scope of openness regarding international agreements. Attempting to decide on the degree of transparency based on a clear category (multilateral-bilateral agreements) is not a workable solution. At the same time, many multilateral agreements might today have a regulatory approach and as such compare well with the adoption of internal legislation. The Ombudsman's criticism concerning confidentiality agreements is timely and well-placed. The practice of signing up to confidentiality commitments is rather wide-spread, and it is certainly problematic if individual civil servants see it as their task to set aside the transparency obligations that flow from the EU Treaties.

The key word in the area of external relations might thus be 'strategic'. In the internal sphere, it would probably be institutional efficiency, with an overwhelming institutional preference for privileging the virtues of efficiency over any other value of good administration, such as openness and participation.[64] At the same time, it is not obvious that the function of transparency and openness in external relations would be any different from its general function in EU decision-making, as the legislature has defined it in the Preamble to Regulation 1049/2001:

> Openness enables citizens to participate more closely in the decision-making process and guarantees that the administration enjoys greater legitimacy and is more effective and more accountable to the citizen in a democratic system. Openness contributes to strengthening the principles of democracy and respect for fundamental rights.

It is exactly this angle that has been repeatedly voiced by civil society organisations in the contexts of recent core EU international negotiations. The rationale on openness and transparency should not be too focused on accountability or deliberation when legislative acts are adopted, but speak to a corresponding need for public involvement in many international affairs. In a global world, key agreements have a direct impact on individuals and their rights, and it should be a point of open discussion how these agreements are made and to what extent the rights of individuals are being balanced against other interests.

As the international relations exception is currently drafted, its formulation does not formally enable the consideration of public interest in openness. The legal avenue for enabling the consideration of public interest in granting access would seem to be rather simple. In the context of the reform process of the Regulation, the Parliament has voiced the possibility of introducing the public interest test into all the exceptions, and the recent jurisprudence demonstrates that this might indeed be a good idea. Similar experiences also exist from the other Article 4(1) exceptions, in particular relating to the protection of privacy and personal integrity.[65] However, it is not certain that this will have very clear outcomes. In Court jurisprudence, the 'overriding public interest' being referred to in the

---

[64] See P Leino, 'Efficiency, Citizens and Administrative Culture: The Politics of Good Administration in the EU' (2014) 20 *European Public Law* 681.

[65] See, eg T-82/09 *Dennekamp v Parliament*, Judgment, EU:T:2011:688.

Regulation has in fact remained a ghost concept and largely undefined:[66] it is difficult to identify a case where the Court would have been convinced about the existence of such an interest, either in relation to the environment[67] or the use of public funds, which would both appear as rather obvious candidates. Similarly, the Council has recently failed to see that there would be a public interest in information concerning the protection of the climate being made public; the Council refused to see 'how access to the requested document would impact the policies in this field' and concluded that 'the applicant has not demonstrated that an overriding public interest in disclosure exists'.[68]

Political scientists argue that we are witnessing the entry of a new era of politics in society, which has changed the way in which political participation takes place, challenging the state and existing institutional arrangements.[69] Against this background, it is evident that the institutional mindset prevailing in the Council and the Commission is out of date. In particular, there are some negotiation processes that are of interest more than others, and where civil society pressure also channelled through the European Parliament and the European Ombudsman has been enough to make the two conservative institutions look seriously odd when they are trying to defend the secrecy of documents that have long been in the public domain. NGOs also have a hard time understanding why these mandates would need to be secret. For example, Corporate Europe Observatory's response to the Ombudsman's consultation on transparency in the negotiations over the TTIP lists a significant number of international negotiating fora where greater transparency is routinely exercised.[70] In its reply, CEO demonstrates how openness leads to better results, because secrecy plays into the hands of the more resourceful and well-connected actors, most notably private corporations and their lobby groups, which creates a real risk that negotiations will lead to biased results. Transparency also allows outside experts to stay informed about the negotiations and provide essential analysis, improving the quality of the substance of the agreement and addressing substantive concerns. Finally, openness decreases the public distrust in the negotiations and enables negotiators to be held to account, leading to more legitimate results.

*The Secret of Chimneys*, quoted at the beginning of the chapter, ends with the secret remaining a secret. But as Anthony Cade, the young adventurer who in

---

[66] For a discussion, see D Adamski, 'Approximating a Workable Compromise on Access to Official Documents: The 2011 Developments in the European Courts' (2012) 49 *CML Rev* 521.

[67] See Joined Cases C-514/11P and C-605/11P *LPN and Finland v Commission*, Judgment, EU:C:2013:738, paras 91–93.

[68] For the application, see http://register.consilium.europa.eu/pdf/en/12/st13/st13306-re02.en12.pdf.

[69] On a discussion on these developments, see, eg, T Forsberg and T Raunio (eds), *Politiikan muutos* (Vastapaino, Tampere, 2014).

[70] These include the World Trade Organization (WTO), the United Nations Framework Convention on Climate Change (UNFCCC), the World Intellectual Property Organization (WIPO) and the bodies under the Aarhus Convention. See http://corporateeurope.org/international-trade/2014/10/ttip-talks-ceo-response-ombudsman-consultation-transparency.

fact turns out to be Prince Nicholas, the lost Prince of Herzoslovakia, points out, whether the secret actually remained secret was actually not that important: 'it is just a pile of dull reminiscences by an insufferably dull politician. Nothing racy or indiscreet at all!'[71] In our context, the solution does not seem to lie so much in the attempts to turn back the clock, or punish those making the information available, but in recognising that times have changed, and automatic secrecy regimes are something from the past.[72] Instead, greater transparency demands a much more sophisticated and proactive approach than those recently demonstrated by the key EU institutions. Choosing one's battles would be a clever approach, which would also increase confidence in the choices being made on justifiable grounds— something which none of the examples discussed in this chapter will contribute to. And when strong grounds for refusing access do not exist, just let it go.

---

[71] According to the Agatha Christie Graphic Novels adaptation of *The Secret of Chimneys*, adapted by Francois Rivière (London, HarperCollins, 2007).

[72] A similar finding would also seem to apply to another traditional secrecy regime, namely that relating to financial stability and monetary policy. See the European Central Bank (ECB) saga on a 'secret' exchange of letters between the President of the ECB and the Irish Minister for Finance, declassified on 6 November 2014 following leaks and public debate, and now available at the website of the ECB.

# 9

# The Rule of Law as a Relational Principle Structuring the Union's Action Towards its External Partners

ILARIA VIANELLO

## I. Introduction

The Treaty of Lisbon makes clear that the Union, when acting on the international scene, must not only promote the principles that inspired its own creation, among which the rule of law, but must also respect them in the development and implementation of its external action. Although, on the one hand, this statement does not seem to cast any doubt as to the legal obligation that the Union is required to respect, on the other, it becomes essential to understand concretely what this general statement implies. Is it only a piece of wishful thinking? Is it just a nice statement showing that the Union aims to behave like an exemplary normative actor in the world? If, on the contrary, this statement is to be taken seriously, a number of fundamental questions arise: Is it a legal norm? If so, what does it mean to respect the rule of law when the Union acts externally? Does the rule of law change meaning when operationalised in the Union's external domain? What are the means to enforce it? Is it possible to state that the current regulatory framework respects the rule of law?

The obligation to respect the rule of law when the Union acts externally is here demanding that the framework of external action (not the substantive content of the policies!) should abide by certain principles. The focus is here on the external dimension of the EU external action—meaning the Union's conduct on the international plane.[1] Analysing whether the Union respects the rule of law when acting externally means to disentangle the numerous external activities[2] and

---

[1] For an analysis on the role of principles as benchmark for lawfulness in the internal dimension of EU foreign affairs, see A Thies, 'General Principles in the Development of EU External Relations Law' in M Cremona and A Thies (eds), *The European Court of Justice and External Relations Law: Constitutional Challenges* (Oxford, Hart Publishing, 2014) 139, 147.

[2] Varying from Commission Communications on the development of a policy, to Council Decisions suspending aid, to human rights impact assessments, etc.

evaluate whether they respect the principles mandated by the rule of law. The content of the principles giving effect to the rule of law internally might need to be rethought and moulded in order to meet the demands of the external domain.[3] Moreover, the obligation implies the restructuring of the relations between the Union and those 'outside' its legal system; it requires redefining the actorness of the EU in its relations with its external partners as well as the actorness of the partners themselves.[4] The commitment to respect of the rule of law when the Union acts externally has the capability of acknowledging that the action of the Union in the international arena does not come without consequences, particularly when addressed to third countries or to third country citizens.

The purpose of this chapter is to establish that the Union is under an obligation to respect the rule of law as a structural principle in its external action and to explain what this obligation entails. With this aim in mind the chapter will proceed as follows. First, it will analyse the legal sources conducive to determining that the rule of law is a legal norm that needs to be respected when the Union acts externally. Secondly, by starting from the internal definition of the rule of law it will suggest what it means to respect the rule of law externally by highlighting the main differences between its internal and external application. Thirdly and finally, it will exemplify a new methodological approach aimed at operationalising the respect of the rule of law externally from mere utopian achievement to effective framework for analysis.

## II. Obligation to Respect the Rule of Law
## when EU Acts Externally

In order to determine whether we can talk of the rule of law as a legal norm guiding the external relations of the Union, the argument will proceed as follows. The first section will look at the meaning of the new Lisbon Treaty Articles which make a clear reference to the rule of law in the context of external relations; and secondly, by using the Court of Justice of the European Union (CJEU or 'the Court') case law and the European Ombudsman decisions, it will stress how the rule of law is a principle that needs to be respected internally as well as externally.

### A. Obligation in the Treaties

The Treaties of the European Union seem to be rather straightforward in establishing the obligation on the Union to respect the rule of law when acting externally. The most significant Articles will be analysed below.

---

[3] This process will here be called 'operationalisation of the rule of law externally'.
[4] As Sartre puts forward, man makes himself by acting in the world.

> Article 3(5) TEU: In its relations with the wider world, the *Union shall uphold* and promote *its values*. (emphasis added)

The values to which Article 3(5) of the Treaty on European Union (TEU) refers are the ones listed in Article 2, among which the rule of law. The Union under this Article is not only required to promote the rule of law, but is also required to uphold it in its relation to the wider world. Even if it is easy to denigrate such idealistic ambition, yet it is a fundamental Treaty provision formulated in mandatory terms: *shall* uphold.[5]

> Article 21(1) TEU: *The Union's action on the international scene shall be guided* by the principles which have inspired its own creation, development and enlargement, and which it seeks to advance in the wider world: democracy, the *rule of law*, the universality and indivisibility of human rights and fundamental freedoms, respect for human dignity, the principles of equality and solidarity, and respect for the principles of the United Nations Charter and international law. (emphasis added)

> Article 21(3) TEU: The *Union shall respect the principles* and pursue the objectives set out in *paragraphs 1 and 2 in the development and implementation of the different areas of the Union's external action* covered by this Title and by Part Five of the Treaty. (emphasis added)

Article 21 TEU is probably the most significant Article. Differently from Article 3(5) TEU, Article 21 TEU uses the term 'principles' rather than 'values'. Even if it is doubtful that those responsible for the terminological variation between 'values' and 'principles' in the Treaties intended to introduce a theoretical distinction, it is still remarkable that while in Article 2 TEU the rule of law is defined as a value, in Article 21 TEU it is defined as a principle. Values have a more indeterminate configuration and can be seen as part of the cultural patrimony or common heritage of Europe, whereas legal principles possess a more defined structure which makes them more suitable for the creation of legal rules.[6] Most importantly, Article 21(3) TEU makes a clear link between the respect of the principles and the development and implementation of the Union's external action. Again, in this Article also the provision is formulated in mandatory terms: *shall* respect.

The respect of the rule of law, in the development and implementation of the different areas of Union external action is not only a principle that limits the action of the Union; it is also an objective. The Union, according to Article 21(2) TEU, shall define and pursue common policies and actions in order to:

> Article 21(2)(b) TEU: consolidate and support democracy, *the rule of law*, human rights and the principles of international law. (emphasis added)

---

[5] P Eeckout, 'A Normative Basis for EU External Relations? Protecting Internal Values Beyond the Single Market' in M Krajewski (ed), *Services of General Interest Beyond the Single Market: External and International Law Dimensions* (The Hague, Asser Press, 2015) 219.

[6] L Pech, 'A Union Founded on the Rule of Law: Meaning and Reality of the Rule of Law as a Constitutional Principle of EU Law' (2010) 6 *European Constitutional Law Review* 359, 366; M Fernández Esteban, *The Rule of Law in the European Constitution* (The Hague, Kluwer Law International, 1999) 40–41.

Article 21(2)(h) TEU: promote an international system based on stronger multilateral cooperation and *good global governance*.[7] (emphasis added)

The fact that the rule of law is also an objective that the Union needs to pursue in its relation with the outer world simply strengthens the claim that the Union needs to respect the rule of law when interacting with third states. The conjunction of objectives and principles does not undermine the distinction between the rule of law as a principle and as an objective to be pursued.[8]

## B. Obligation in the Case-law of the CJEU and the European Ombudsman

In its very famous *Les Verts* judgment, the CJEU already back in 1986 referred to the European Community as a 'a community based on the rule of law'[9] to the extent that neither the Member States nor the Community's institutions could avoid review of the conformity of their acts with the Community's 'constitutional character'.[10] Subsequently, in its Opinion 1/91, by contrasting the EEA agreement with the Community legal order, the Court stated that:

[T]he *EEC Treaty*, albeit concluded in the form of an international agreement, none the less *constitutes the constitutional charter of a Community based on the rule of law*.[11] (emphasis added)

There seems to be widespread consensus among scholars that the rule of law has increasingly become an overarching and primary principle of Union constitutional law. Van Bogdandy concludes in his article on the founding principles of EU law that the 'values' listed in Article 2 TEU (among which the rule of law) can be understood as 'constitutional principles and a constitutional legal discourse based thereon is viable both from a theoretical and technical legal point of view'.[12] Pech is of the opinion that Article 2 TEU ultimately clarifies that the Union is 'founded on' the rule of law and that this is a foundational principle of constitutional value.[13] If the rule of law is to be understood as a legal principle having constitutional value in the EU polity, the latter should be upheld as to its actions having both an external as well as an internal dimension. This assumption of legal unity of EU law can also be justified

---

[7] Good global governance from a legal perspective has been increasingly the subject of research of the new emerging Global Administrative Law project which in its essence is a rule of law project. It aims at constitutionalising transnational public administration by binding it to general principles of administrative law rooted deeply in the rule of law. F Schuppert, 'New Modes of Governance and the Rule of Law' in M Zürn, A Nollkaemper and R Peerenboom (eds), *Rule of Law Dynamics: In an Era of International and Transnational Governance* (Cambridge, Cambridge University Press, 2012) 90, 103.

[8] A Von Bogdandy, 'Founding Principles of EU Law: A Theoretical and Doctrinal Sketch' (2010) 16 *European Law Journal* 95, 107.

[9] Case 294/83 *Les Verts v Parliament*, Judgment, EU:C:1986:166, para 23.

[10] Pech, 'A Union Founded on the Rule of Law' (n 6) 359.

[11] Opinion 1/91, EU:C:1991:490, para 21.

[12] Von Bogdandy, 'Founding Principles of EU Law' (n 8) 111.

[13] L Pech, *The Rule of Law as a Constitutional Principle of the European Union*, Jean Monnet Working Paper 04/09.

in light of the growing importance of guaranteeing coherence in the Union's action.[14] With the entry into force of the Treaty of Lisbon, significant emphasis has been put on the importance of guaranteeing consistency between the Union's policies and activities.[15] Therefore, guaranteeing coherence between the respect of the rule of law externally as well as internally seems to be in line with the new Lisbon Treaty focus. Next to coherence, a possible parallelism can be drawn with the 'principle of complementarity' suggested by Dashwood and Heliskoski in the context of exclusive and implied external competences.[16] The internal and external action do not run in parallel with each other, on the contrary, they complement one another.[17] The respect of the rule of law in developing and implementing the Union's external action complements the role of the rule of law as a constitutional principle in the Union legal order. The respect of the rule of law externally must be read in the context of the unity, coherence and complementarity of the Union legal order.[18]

The CJEU seems to be of the same view. In both *Kadi I* and *Kadi II*, it stressed the importance of reviewing any community measure in light of fundamental rights in order to ensure consistency with the expression 'a Community based on the rule of law'.[19] The expression 'Union based on the rule of law' instead of 'Community based on the rule of law' was for the first time used in the *E & F* case.[20]

---

[14] Von Bogdandy, 'Founding Principles of EU Law' (n 8) 109.

[15] Some significant examples: Art 7 TFEU: 'The Union shall ensure *consistency* between its policies and activities, taking all of its objectives into account and in accordance with the principle of conferral of powers'; Art 13(1) TEU: 'The Union shall have an institutional framework which shall aim to promote its values, advance its objectives, serve its interests, those of its citizens and those of the Member States, and ensure the *consistency*, effectiveness and continuity of its policies and actions'; Art 21(3) TEU: 'The Union shall ensure *consistency* between the different areas of its external action and between these and its other policies. The Council and the Commission, assisted by the High Representative of the Union for Foreign Affairs and Security Policy, shall ensure that *consistency* and shall cooperate to that effect'; Art 256(2), (3) TFEU: 'Decisions given by the General Court under this paragraph may exceptionally be subject to review by the Court of Justice, under the conditions and within the limits laid down by the Statute, where there is a serious risk of the *unity* or *consistency* of Union law being affected … Decisions given by the General Court on questions referred for a preliminary ruling may exceptionally be subject to review by the Court of Justice, under the conditions and within the limits laid down by the Statute, where there is a serious risk of the *unity* or *consistency* of Union law being affected' (all emphasis added).

[16] A Dashwood and J Heliskoski, 'The Classic Authorities Revisited' in A Dashwood and C Hillion (eds), *The General Law of EC External Relations* (London, Sweet and Maxwell, 2000) 3, 13.

[17] The principle of complementarity has been recently affirmed by the CJEU in Case C-658/11 *Parliament v Council*, Judgment, EU:C:2014:2025, paras 55–57.

[18] Eeckout in one of his recent works clearly stated '[t]he EU is required to act externally according to its own constitutionally determined normative basis: i.e. its values'. Eeckout, 'A Normative Basis for EU External Relations?' (n 5); see also E Herlin-Karnell, 'EU Values and the Shaping of the International Legal Context' in D Kochenov and F Amtenbrink (eds), *The European Union's Shaping of the International Legal Order* (Cambridge, Cambridge University Press, 2014) 89, 97.

[19] By no means may EU measures challenge 'the principles that form part of the very foundations of the EU legal order'. Cases C-402/05P and C-415/05P *Kadi and Al Barakaat International Foundation v Council and Commission*, Judgment, EU:C:2008:461, para 304.

[20] '[T]he European Union is based on the rule of law and the acts of its institutions are subject to review by the Court of their compatibility with EU law and, in particular, with the Treaty on the Functioning of the European Union and the general principles of law.' Case C-550/09 *E & F*, Judgment, EU:C:2010:382, para 44.

This new expression seems to reinforce the idea that the rule of law is a constitutional principle covering all actions of the Union and not only the ones under the old Community pillar. The Court in the *Air Transport* case reinforced the role of Article 3(5) TEU as obliging the Union to respect the Union's values when acting externally.

> Under Article 3(5) TEU, the European Union is to contribute to the strict observance and the development of international law. Consequently, *when it adopts an act, it is bound to observe international law* in its entirety.[21] (emphasis added)

If the Court could make the link between the Union's obligation to contribute to the strict observance and the development of international law and the Union's obligation to observe international law when adopting an act, it would be very difficult to argue that the same link could not be established under the same article between the Union obligation to uphold its values (among which the rule of law) and the Union's obligation to respect them when adopting an act.

Finally, on 26 March 2015, the European Ombudsman adopted a draft recommendation to the European Commission stating that the latter's refusal to carry out a human rights impact assessment constitutes an instance of maladministration. The Ombudsman is of the view that it would be in the spirit of Article 21(1), (2) TEU to carry out a human rights impact assessment.[22] The European Ombudsman underlines the duty on the side of the EU to respect its values—in this instance human rights—in the way in which it interacts with the outer world.

In light of the analysis so far conducted, there can be little argument as to the validity of the Union's obligation to respect the rule of law as a legal norm structuring the Union's external action. Even under the premise of uniform validity of the principle internally and externally, the question still arises as to whether this corresponds to a uniform meaning.[23] In order to construct the features that the rule of law assumes externally it seems reasonable to use as a starting point the meaning that the rule of law has when operating internally.

## III. What Does it Mean to Respect the Rule of Law when the EU Acts Externally?

Before entering in the specificities of the external domain, the next section will first briefly summarise what it entails to respect the rule of law in the EU internal legal order.

---

[21] Case C-366/10 *Air Transport Association of America v Secretary of State for Energy and Climate Change*, Judgment, EU:C:2011:864, para 101.

[22] Draft Recommendation of 26 March 2015 of the European Ombudsman on complaint 1409/2014/JN against the European Commission, para 24.

[23] Von Bogdandy, 'Founding Principles of EU Law' (n 8) 109.

## A. From the Internal Meaning ...

The Union constitutes a polity governed by the rule of law, meaning that the exercise of public power is subject to or regulated by a set of substantive and procedural standards. The CJEU has been able over the years to Europeanise the rule of law by using as starting point the legal traditions of the Member States.[24] In paraphrasing the famous *Les Verts* judgment, it seems possible to state that the Community was held to comply with the rule of law because it allegedly offered a comprehensive set of legal remedies and procedures with the aim of ensuring that its institutions, including Member States, adopt measures in conformity with EU law; and that natural and legal persons are able to challenge (directly or indirectly) the legality of any act which affects their Community rights. A remarkable development of the Court's more recent case-law lies in linking explicitly the rule of law to the respect by the Union of more substantive requirements, ie general principles.[25] General principles derive from the rule of law and their respect gives effect to the latter.[26]

The main meaning of the rule of law as achieved at the level of the Union can be defined as an organisational principle from which more concrete legal principles can be derived, with the objective of limiting the exercise of public power.[27] The principles deriving from the rule of law refer primarily to the relationship between the individual and the public authority, but may also be relied upon by Member States and Union institutions.[28] The same rule of law mandates that legal remedies

---

[24] T Tridimas, *The General Principles of EU Law*, 2nd edn (Oxford, Oxford University Press, 2006) 5–6; A Arnull, 'The Rule of Law in the European Union' in A Arnull and D Wincott (eds), *Accountability and Legitimacy in the European Union* (Oxford, Oxford University Press, 2002) 239, 254; Pech, 'A Union Founded on the Rule of Law' (n 6) 365.

[25] 'The European Community is a ... Community based on the rule of law in which its institutions are subject to judicial review of the compatibility of its acts with the Treaty and with the general principles of law which include fundamental rights.' Case C-50/00P *Unión de Pequeños Agricultores v Council*, Judgment, EU:C:2002:462, para 38. Compliance with general principles, including fundamental rights, goes back to *Internationale Handelsgesellschaft*. However, in that case the CJEU did not make an explicit link to the respect of the rule of law. See Case 11/70 *Internationale Handelsgesellschaft v Einfuhr und Vorratsstelle Getreide*, Judgment, EU:C:1970:114.

[26] Advocate General Sharpston in her Opinion in *Paul Miles and others v European Schools* stated that by upholding important principles of Community law, the Community ensures that it remains one that is based on the rule of law. 'I respectfully applaud the Court's willingness, in *Zwartveld*, to have regard to the teleology of the Treaties and to insist on its jurisdiction to uphold important principles of Community law, thereby ensuring that the European Communities continued to be a "Community based on the rule of law"'. Case C-196/09 *Paul Miles and others v European Schools*, Opinion of AG Sharpston, EU:C:2011:388, para 71.

[27] Comparative studies on the Member States' definition of the rule of law and the recent Commission Communication on the rule of law offer a coherent definition to the one provided by the CJEU. See also R Grote, 'Rule of Law, rechtsstaat and état de droit' in C Starck (ed), *Constitutionalism, Universalism and Democracy: A Comparative Analysis* (Baden-Baden, Nomos, 1999) 269, 305; M Krygier, 'Rule of Law' in M Rosenfeld and A Sajò (eds), *The Oxford Handbook of Comparative Constitutional Law* (Oxford, Oxford University Press, 2012) 233; Communication from the Commission to the European Parliament and the Council, *A New Framework to Strengthen the Rule of Law*, COM(2014)158 final/2 and its respective Annex I.

[28] Tridimas, *The General Principles of EU Law* (n 24) 4.

and procedures should be available in order to makes sure that the power stays within the defined boundaries.[29] This definition of the rule of law will be used as a starting point in order to develop the features that the rule of law acquires when limiting the power of the Union when acting externally.[30]

## B. … to the Challenges and Characteristics of the External

The rule of law in external relations maintains its core meaning as an organisational paradigm aimed at limiting the exercise of public power. The limits of the power are to be found in the law, as well as in more substantive legal principles, and judicial review makes sure that the power stays within the defined boundaries. If the development of the meaning of the rule of law internally has been driven by the CJEU borrowing from the Member States' legal traditions, the same cannot be fully said externally. The external relations of the Union are characterised by numerous and varied policies. The policies very much differ in terms of objectives and instruments used in order to develop and implement them. Therefore, if for certain external policies, such as anti-dumping, the Court has been active in establishing procedures aimed at giving effect to the rule of law and at limiting the power of the Union, for example, by extending the right to be heard,[31] the same cannot be said for other newer policies, such as the European Neighbourhood Policy, the EU External Energy Policy, etc. The reasons are manifold.

First, in recent years the external relations of the Union have faced an ever-increasing use of non-binding instruments (eg progress reports, impact assessments, etc) which despite the tendency of the Court to privilege substance over form in deciding which measures may be challenged, still frequently escape scrutiny.[32] They are adopted as internal documents (eg Commission Working Documents, Commission Communications to the Council, Commission Implementing Decisions, etc) or as unclassifiable documents (eg action plans, Memoranda of Understandings)[33] despite the fact that they are acts *de facto* addressed to individual third countries and have

---

[29] For a more extensive and elaborate definition of the meaning of the Rule of Law in EU law see the works listed in n 24.

[30] The author is aware that the definition of the rule of law as developed by the CJEU is not satisfactory; however, for the purpose of this chapter it will be used since it is the one enforced by the Court and recognised by the Union legal system. For a critical view on the definition of the rule of law in the EU, see G Palombella, *The EU Sense of the Rule of Law and the Issue of Its Oversight*, EUI Working Papers RSCAS 2014/125; and D Kochenov, 'EU Law Without the Rule of Law: Is the Veneration of Autonomy Worth It?' (2015) 34 *Yearbook of European Law* 74.

[31] Case C-49/88 *Al-Jubail Fertilizer v Council*, Judgment, EU:C:1991:276, para 15; see also HP Nehl, *Principles of Administrative Procedures in EC Law* (Oxford, Hart, 1999) 74–75.

[32] In relation to the difficulties posed by the CJEU in reviewing no binding acts in the internal domain, see J Scott, 'In Legal Limbo: Post-Legislative Guidance as a Challenge for European Administrative Law' (2011) 48 *CML Rev* 329.

[33] See, eg, EU Action Plan on Human Rights and Democracy 2015–2019, available at https://eeas.europa.eu/human_rights/docs/eu_action_plan_on_human_rights_and_democracy_en.pdf; Memorandum of Understanding on Strategic Partnership on Energy between the European Union and the Arab Republic of Egypt, available at http://eeas.europa.eu/archives/docs/egypt/docs/mou_energy_eu-egypt_en.pdf.

significant impact on them.[34] The documents clearly indicate what the individual third countries need to adopt unless they want to trigger negative sanctions.[35] The unclear legal nature of the documents seems to conceal the real function of the instruments. Moreover, it should not be neglected that in the EU legal discourse, the invasiveness of Union power in the activities of third countries is perceived as not harmful and, consequently, as not actionable. The Court, as of today, does not seem to have come to terms with this new legal reality; while the European Ombudsman is timidly trying to engage with this new form of external action.[36]

Secondly, if judicial review does not offer an effective answer in order to challenge the action of the Union externally, individuals and third countries will be reluctant to bring their claims to the Court. Therefore, if internally the Court has developed the principles giving effect to the rule of law on the real-life canvas of conflicts arising from EU law and the necessity to protect rights therein, externally this does not seem to be the most immediate solution. There are a few cases in which individuals have challenged before the Court activities of the type described above. However, in these cases the Court ignored (or maybe thwarted?) the opportunity of going beyond a purely formalistic approach in favour of one that would take into account the social reality and the implication of the Union's activities outside its borders. Arguably, the few cases that challenged the external activities of the type described in the previous paragraph that went all the way to the CJEU might have had a point in law (though not to say they would have won!) if the obligation to respect the rule of law externally would have been taken seriously.[37] For example, in one case,[38] a coalition of non-governmental organisations and Turkish citizens challenged the exclusion of some information from the Commission's progress report on Turkey.[39]

---

[34] See, eg, the Association Agenda between the EU and Georgia and the Georgia National Action Plan for its Implementation (Decree no 59 of the Government of Georgia, 26 January 2015) which indicates to transpose in national legislations the standards identified in the association agenda (the new name for action plans). Respectively, available at https://eeas.europa.eu/sites/eeas/files/associationagenda_2014_en.pdf and www.eu-nato.gov.ge/en/news/6015.

[35] For example, progress reports can inform the Council of lack of progress by a third state in certain essential areas of cooperation. Therefore, the Council might decide to suspend the entrance into force of the agreement or the agreement itself between the EU and the third country found to be lacking progress.

[36] In a recent case, the European Ombudsman derived from an internal action plan the obligation on the side of the Commission to conduct human rights impact assessments before concluding an agreement with third countries. Draft Recommendation on 26 March 2015 of the European Ombudsman on Complaint 1409/2014/JN against the European Commission.

[37] See Case T-367/03 *Yedaş Tarim ve Otomotiv Sanayi ve Ticaret AŞ v Council and Commission*, Judgment, EU:T:2006:96; Case T-346/03 *Krikorian v European Parliament, Council and Commission*, Order, EU:T:2003:348; Case T-2/04 *Korkmaz v Commission*, Order, EU:T:2006:97; Case T-292/09 *Mugraby v Council and Commission*, Order, EU:T:2011:418; Case C-581/11P *Mugraby v Council and Commission*, Order, EU:C:2012:466.

[38] *Korkmaz v Commission* (n 37).

[39] Progress reports are Commission Working Documents. The European Council invites the Commission to present the assessment of what each enlargement country has achieved over the last year in preparing for EU membership. The reports briefly describe the relations between the EU and the enlargement countries; they analyse the situation in each country in terms of the political and economic criteria for membership; and they review the country's capacity to implement European standards (ie gradually approximate its legislation and policies with the *acquis*).

The procedures indicating how progress reports should be drafted are numerous; however, since the procedures currently in place are simply internal self-imposed guidelines they could not be used by the applicant. This exclusion prevents the Court from being able to oversee procedural aspects in circumstances where substantive review would be difficult or even precluded.

Thirdly, certain principles giving effect to the rule of law internally would need to be moulded to the external reality before the Court could actually enforce them: the Court might be reluctant to grant procedural rights to third countries and third country citizens without a first step from the legislator.[40] For example, the protection of legitimate expectations might need to be revisited in light of the external relations context and its specific policy sector in order to pursue its function. The realm of external relations does not remain impenetrable from the creation of expectations. On the contrary, the wide net of activities listed above, together with the numerous European Parliament resolutions and political statements, have the effect of raising the expectations of individuals and third countries that the Union will act in a certain manner. Even if the expectations are not defined as legitimate under EU law,[41] the duty to state reasons and the importance of guaranteeing a certain level of legal clarity can help individuals and third countries to understand the purpose and role of the different instruments of the Union and understand what can be expected from them. Therefore, the protection of legitimate expectations in external relations can mandate the obligation to respect specific procedures. There is here a gap between the premises and values of the traditional conception of legal norms, and their application in external action.

In the absence of a powerful judiciary that could take the lead in guaranteeing the respect of the rule of law, its execution could be guaranteed thanks to inter-institutional conflicts or thanks to a strong motivation on the side of the Union to maintain its role as normative power in the international arena.[42] However, the legislator being composed by two institutions (ie the Council and the European Parliament) has different clashing interests. The Council has not yet showed any real intent to effectively limit the power of the Union in external relations; while the Parliament has only a relevant power in the area of financial assistance, where

---

[40] While, on the one hand, the Court in *Al-Jubail* was ready to extend the right to hear the other side also in case of acts of general application so as to protect external importers, on the other, this expansion was soon lowered in the *CEUC* case in order to limit the circle of beneficiaries of procedural protection to those parties which had a financial or economic interest at stake. Generally, the CJEU, in external relations has always been careful to recognise the political sensitiveness of certain situations: *Al-Jubail Fertilizer v Council* (n 31); Case C-170/89 *Bureau des Unions des Consommateurs (BEUC) v Commission*, Judgment, EU:C:1991:450.

[41] See *Mugraby v Council and Commission* (n 37) paras 57–71.

[42] See Preamble to the Lisbon Treaty: 'Confirming their attachment to the principles of liberty, democracy and respect for human rights and fundamental freedoms and of the rule of law'; and see M Cremona, 'Values in EU Foreign Policy' in P Koutrakos and M Shaw (eds), *Beyond the Established Orders: Policy Interconnections between the EU and the Rest of the World* (Oxford, Hart, 2011) 275; I Manners, 'Normative Power Europe: A Contradiction in Terms?' (2002) 40 *Journal of Common Market Studies* 235.

it has, nevertheless, started to show a real willingness to limit the power of the Commission.[43] It is the administration that has so far tried to impose on itself some guidelines on the procedures to be followed when drafting the policy instruments or when planning the disbursement of financial assistance.[44] The fact that administrative power has started to impose on itself some procedural guidelines as to how to exercise its powers shows a real need to find ways to constrain its action. Finally, it must not be forgotten that academia is also vested with the task of starting the debate.

The 'external rule of law', in the same way as the internal, is an organisational principle to the extent that it governs the exercise of the Union's power by subjecting it to the respect of principles and rules. The major difference lies in the change of interlocutors. Externally, the Union is required to respect the rule of law in its relations with those outside the EU legal system. This change demands to re-think the function of the rule of law and of its principles in light of the peculiarities of the external domain. In the absence of an active judiciary and of a powerful inter-institutional conflict that strives to guarantee the respect of the rule of law when the Union acts externally, the challenge is now to construct a methodological framework for moving the respect of the rule of law from mere utopian aim to enforceable organisational paradigm.

# IV. Rule of Law From Paper to Operationalisation: Structuring EU External Action

In order for the rule of law to acquire meaning when operating in the EU external domain, it is necessary to redefine and legally articulate the principles and rules giving effect to the rule of law internally with the aim of meeting the specificities of the external reality. EU law principles find their origins in national legal systems; they regulate the relation between the Member States' authorities and the Union; and between the national or Union authorities and the persons under their jurisdiction. Rethinking the internal principles, while keeping in mind the distinctive character

---

[43] In the most recent negotiations for the IPA II Regulation, the European Parliament pushed for the introduction of a 'Declaration by the European Commission on the strategic dialogue with the Parliament'. Under the declaration, the Commission is to conduct a strategic dialogue with the Parliament on the strategy and programming of financial assistance. The Commission according to the declaration 'will have to take into account the position expressed by the European Parliament on the matter'. Regulation (EU) 231/2014 of the European Parliament and of the Council of 11 March 2014 establishing an instrument for pre-accession assistance (IPA II) [2014] OJ L77/13.

[44] *Enlargement Package, Autumn 2012: Guidance Note*, Access to Document Team, Access to Documents Request (GESTDEM Reference 2013/3857); *ENP Package, 2014: Guidance Note*, EEAS Access to Documents, SG1 Corporate Board Secretariat (AD) Request (GESTDEM Reference 2013/5084); Commission Regulation (EC) 718/2007 of 12 June 2007 implementing Council Regulation 1085/2006 establishing an instrument for pre-accession assistance (IPA I) [2007] OJ L170/1.

of the decision-making process regulating the relationships with those 'outside' the Union's structure, is necessary for the sake of ensuring that the principles would also serve their function externally. The necessity of possibly tuning the principles derived from the rule of law in light of the domain should not be seen as a heresy. As Marise Cremona suggests in Chapter 1, 'principles operate in their particular context and the external context is simply a manifestation of that inherent contextual operation of principles'.[45] Principles giving effect to the rule of law can be understood as norms having a high degree of generality as to their content. They can be valid for a whole subject (eg contracts) or for a general branch of law (eg administrative law), but can also acquire sector specific connotations.[46] The content of the rule of law is malleable. The core idea of the rule of law, limiting the exercise of public power, entails the potential to adjust to changing realities.[47] The same CJEU in the *Al-Jubail* case recognised the distinctiveness of the anti-dumping policy so as to expand the right to hear the other side to acts of general application.[48]

The methodological framework for moving the respect of the rule of law from paper to operationalisation requires to first identify the most salient principles giving effect to the rule of law when the Union acts externally; secondly, to think about their content and scope; and finally to identify the rules translating the principles into concrete procedures. In order to identify the most salient principles giving effect to the rule of law when the Union acts externally, the following aspects need to be taken into consideration: the nature of the activities under analysis and the typology of the activities at stake. For example, the numerous instruments implementing the European Neighbourhood Policy are administrative in nature.[49] The administrative power within this space presents some tensions as to how it is exercised and controlled.[50] Thus, the first step in identifying the salient principles giving effect to the rule of law in this context is to pick those that are directly related to the administrative function.[51] Some of the principles deriving from the rule of

---

[45] Marise Cremona, Chapter 1.

[46] M D'Alberti, 'Diritto Amministrativo e Principi Generali' in M D'Alberti (ed), *Le nuove mete del diritto amministrativo* (Bologna, Il Mulino, 2010) 67.

[47] J Mendes, 'Rule of Law and Participation: A Normative Analysis of Internationalised Rulemaking as Composite Procedures' (2014) 12 *International Journal of Constitutional Law* 370; M Dawson, *Soft Law and the Rule of Law in the European Union: Revision or Redundancy?*, EUI Working Papers RSCAS 2009/24.

[48] 'It should be added that, with regard to the right to a fair hearing, any action taken by the Community institutions must be all the more scrupulous in view of the fact that, as they stand at present, the rules in question [Council Regulation (EEC) 3339/87 of 4 November 1987 imposing a definitive anti-dumping duty on imports of urea originating in Libya and Saudi Arabia] do not provide all the procedural guarantees for the protection of the individual which may exist in certain national legal systems.' *Al-Jubail Fertilizer v Council* (n 31) para 16.

[49] They are aimed at implementing the Union's primary political choice and they carry out administrative functions. They act as monitoring, agenda setting, standard setting and implementing acts.

[50] I Vianello, *EU External Action and the Administrative Rule of Law. A Long-Overdue Encounter*, (EUI PhD Thesis document on file).

[51] 'The rule of law tradition naturally fed into and informed development of EU Administrative law.' P Craig, 'EU Administrative Law and Tradition' in M Ruffert, *Administrative Law in Europe: Between Common Principles and National Traditions* (Groningen, Europa Law Publishing, 2013) 153, 161.

law have an impact primarily on legislative institutions, while others are aimed at the administrative duty.[52] Another example comes from the Union's sanction policy. The most important principles giving effect to the rule of law in the case of Union sanctions directed against third countries' citizens are fundamental rights. In *Kadi II*, the CJEU took largely the same view as in *Kadi I*, reiterating that the EU courts 'must, in accordance with the powers conferred on them by the Treaties, ensure the review, in principle the full review, of the lawfulness of all Union acts in the light of the fundamental rights forming an integral part of the European Union'.[53] Identifying the salient principles governing (or which should govern) the relations between the Union and its external partners requires to analyse the rule of law in its contextual reality. The identification of the most salient principles for each external policy does not imply that other principles might not be applicable. It just means that they are the first principles to be tackled in order to give effect to the rule of law in a specific policy domain. By protecting them first, the respect of other principles may follow. For example, from the obligation to protection the right of the defence in case of individual sanctions, proportionality considerations as to why a certain individual has been listed are to be followed. In *Kadi II*, the Court applied the full standard of review in light of the legal safeguards mandated by fundamental rights guarantees under EU law.[54]

Once the relevant principles giving effect to the rule of law in a given external policy are identified, their translation into rules requires first to think about their meaning and scope externally. Certain principles, especially those that operate both in the sphere of public and substantive law, acquire a different connotation externally. For example, Union internal law protects formal and substantive equality.[55] Formal equality requires that public authorities shall apply the law consistently and treat equally natural and legal persons in the same position; while substantive equality demands that the law must not discriminate between natural and legal persons on certain prohibited grounds (eg sex, race, religion, etc). If internally both formal and substantive equality must be upheld, externally this is not the case. Externally, substantive equality does not need to be respected unless the EU expressly commits itself to the respect of the principle of non-discrimination via international treaties or via autonomous measures. The EU can discriminate between third countries and third countries' citizens in terms of which substantive policy to offer (ie whether to grant preferential trade or visa liberalisation).[56] However, equality should be

---

[52] The changing requirements and conditions for implementing EU policies have pushed the CJEU to develop, in parallel to the constitutional law principles, also administrative law specific principles aimed at giving effect to the rule of law. HCH Hofmann, GC Rowe and AH Türk, *Administrative Law and Policy of the European Union* (Oxford, Oxford University Press, 2011) 143–45.

[53] Joined Cases C-584/10, C-593/10 and C-595/10 *Commission and others v Kadi* (*Kadi II* appeal), Judgment, EU:C:2013:518, para 97; Joined Cases C-402/05 and C-415/05P *Kadi and Al Barakaat International Foundation v Council and Commission* (*Kadi I* appeal), Judgment, EU:C:2008:461, para 326.

[54] See C Eckes, 'EU Restrictive Measures Against Natural and Legal Persons: From Counterterrorist to Third Country Sanctions' (2014) 51 *CML Rev* 869, 897.

[55] Tridimas, *The General Principles of EU Law* (n 24) 61.

[56] Marise Cremona, Chapter 1.

respected in the process of implementation of a specific external policy between natural and legal persons finding themselves in the same position. For example, in the case of the European enlargement policy, the Union does not have the obligation to include Moldova in the policy (despite the latter being a European country committed to the promotion of EU values); however, the Commission needs to use the same substantive and procedural standards when monitoring the candidate countries' ability to comply with the accession criteria.[57]

Another example of a principle which, for different reasons than equality, might need to be re-thought when applied externally is proportionality. At its most abstract level, the principle of proportionality requires that the action undertaken must be proportionate to its objectives.[58] However, if in external relations the objectives are general and abstract, the proportionality test is voided of its purpose. Therefore, the principle of proportionality, as well as the proportionality test, might need to be revisited when applied in relation to EU external action. Individual sanctions are a very good example. Is the freezing of assets of a suspected terrorist a proportional act in order to meet the objective of stopping terrorism? As Eckes suggests, most likely not. The evaluation must instead consider as far as possible the specificity of the case and must evaluate how the individual assets and actions of the targeted person contribute to terrorism.[59] Finally, the scope of the principles might need to be extended to embrace action of the Union that might have been thought impermeable from principles giving effect to the rule of law. The most obvious case is the one of individual sanctions, in respect of which the Court extended the application of fundamental rights to Council Decisions listing targeted individuals. A less obvious case might be to extend the scope of principles to non-binding acts in light of their impact on the third counties to which they are addressed.

The process of translating principles into rules requires taking into account the challenges posed by their application in the external realm. In some cases, the rules giving effect to the principles mandated by the rule of law as operationalised externally are to be found scattered in the different documents aimed at framing a specific policy;[60] while in other situations their 'construction' might be necessary. If such construction is necessary, the following approach is suggested. First, it is essential to understand what is the main function of the principles giving effect to the rule of law (eg in the case of participation, the function is defensive and collaborative).

---

[57] '[E]qual treatment and fairness of assessment across progress reports', European Commission Director General Enlargement, *Enlargement Package, 2012: Guidance Note*, Access to Documents Request (GESTDEM Reference 2013/3857).

[58] Tridimas, *The General Principles of EU Law* (n 24) 136.

[59] Eckes, 'EU Restrictive Measures Against Natural and Legal Persons' (n 54) 897.

[60] See, eg, EU Action Plan on Human Rights and Democracy 2015–2019 (n 33); Council Guidelines on implementation and evaluation of restrictive measures (sanctions) in the framework of the EU CFSP, Doc 11205/12 (15 June 2012); Regulation (EU) 236/2014 laying down common rules and procedures for the implementation of the Union's instruments for financing external action [2014] OJ L77/95; Joint declaration by the Council and the representatives of the governments of the Member States meeting within the Council, the European Parliament and the Commission on the development policy of the European Union entitled 'The European Consensus' [2006] OJ C46.

Once the function is clarified, existing case-law (if any) on the application of a specific principle in external action can help to clarify or to understand the problematics faced by 'the outsiders' or even the 'insiders' in holding the Union accountable in case of breach of that specific principle. Once the challenges have been singled out, the policy framework and the internal case-law on the principle are useful sources in order to identify specific rules that would ultimately give effect to the principle itself. Finally, in order to translate the principles into specific rules, the door might be opened to sources of legal obligation other than positive law. This should particularly be the case for policies that lack a clear legal framework indicating how the policies are to be developed and implemented;[61] or for policies in which non-binding measures (eg joint declarations) are privileged over positive law (eg Treaty Articles) as benchmark for determining the scope of Union action.[62] Opening to sources different from positive law should not be rejected on the basis of a strict formal reasoning. Self-imposed guidelines, rather than simply being envisaged as a tool to legitimise the Union's conduct, could instead be used to function as effective constraints on the Union's power.

The rule of law in external relations is a structural principle to the extent that it aims at constraining the actions of the Union intended to develop and implement EU political decisions. It is not concerned with the actual policy content. Symmetrically, the principles giving effect to the 'external rule of law' are only concerned with structuring the relations between the Union and the external partners; they do not challenge the political choices. Externally, the discretion of political decision-makers is accepted in assessing and determining which policy to offer or not to offer to third countries and to their citizens;[63] however, this same discretion is not approved as to the respect of procedural rules in the way the Union develops and implements its political decisions towards those outside its legal system.

# V. Conclusion

The rule of law as a structural principle in EU external relations law requires the Union to abide by certain principles in its relations with those outside the Union's legal structure. This obligation has nothing to do with the actual content of the Union policies; it is rather concerned with the action targeted at their development

---

[61] See the example of the European Neighbourhood Policy in Vianello, EU External Action and the Administrative Rule of Law (n 50).

[62] See the example of the European Consensus and the Development Cooperation instrument used by Marise Cremona, Chapter 1, citing M Broberg and R Holdgaard, *EU External Action in the Field of Development Cooperation Policy: The Impact of the Lisbon Treaty*, SIEPS Working Paper 2014/6, 46.

[63] As Cremona writes, 'the Courts appears to be reticent (non-interventionist) if not deferential as regards the policy choices of the political institutions in external relations'. M Cremona, 'A Reticent Court? Policy Objectives and the Court of Justice' in M Cremona and A Thies (eds), *The European Court of Justice and External Relations Law: Constitutional Challenges* (Oxford, Hart Publishing, 2014) 15.

and implementation. The obligation to respect the rule of law in the way the Union develops and implements its external action is mandated both by the Treaties as well as by the case-law of the CJEU and by the decisions of the European Ombudsman. If internally the construction of the rule of law has been driven by the Court borrowing from the legal traditions of the Member States, this was not (and in some cases cannot) be similarly done externally. Judicial review presents some practical and legal limitation in the context of EU external action; but also some inherent limitations rooted in the EU legal order. The obstacles on the way to judicial review, and the lack of institutional tension aimed at promoting the respect of the rule of law externally, should stimulate the academic community in thinking of ways of operationalising the respect of the rule of law externally. The methodology suggested by this chapter in order to achieve this goal is to identify the most salient principles giving effect to the rule of law in a given policy context, to think about their meaning and scope externally, and finally, once the principles are identified, the last step requires singling out the rules giving effect to the principles as operationalised externally.

The establishment of a framework of principles and rules giving effect to the rule of law in external relations has the potential, first, of critically evaluating the fundamental structures of the Union's action in external relations; and secondly, of offering to the Union's external partners the possibility of having a claim under EU law. Theoretically, external partners affected by the Union action would be empowered with the possibility of bringing a claim in case the EU would breach the principles and rules giving effect to the 'external rule of law'. Relations based on power alone are to be abandoned in favour of relations based on principles and rules. In this respect, it might be important to question whether the CJEU is on all occasions the correct institution to review the respect of the rule of law by the Union when acting externally.

The external relations of the European Union are numerous and varied. For some of them, the importance of respecting the rule of law is evident, for example in the case of individual sanctions. However, for others the impact of Union action is rather hidden and often diffuse. The importance of respecting the rule of law in Union external action must go hand in hand with the need to take an outward looking approach that would recognise the impact that Union action has on the third countries and individuals to whom the action is indirectly but inexorably addressed. A Union of law is undermined when its institutions knowingly and deliberately continue to adopt measures that are not in compliance with principles that are guaranteed by EU law.

# Part III

# Systemic Principles

# 10

# 'Building Coherent EU Responses': Coherence as a Structural Principle in EU External Relations

MIREIA ESTRADA CAÑAMARES

## I. Introduction

The quest for coherence, or consistency, in EU external relations has been a central topic in the academic and political debates in this field of Union action at least since the establishment of the European Political Cooperation (EPC, 1970).[1] Coherence, which found its way into EU external relations law with the adoption of the Single European Act (SEA, 1987),[2] has been referred to as a 'burning question', a 'recurrent theme' and a 'fervently discussed' issue, to mention but a few examples from the literature.[3] Likewise, references to coherence in the foreign policy of the Union are commonplace in official policy documents. For instance, *The EU's Comprehensive Approach to External Conflict and Crises* (2013) stresses that, following the creation of the position of the High Representative of the Union for Foreign Affairs and Security Policy–Vice President (HRVP) and the European External Action Service (EEAS), 'the EU has both the increased potential and the ambition—by drawing on the full range of its instruments and resources—to make its external action more consistent, more effective and

---

[1] Whereas the Treaties use the word 'consistency', the political and academic debates prefer 'coherence'. Regarding this confusion, see n 41 below. There are other notions in the Treaties that are linked to the idea of coherence presented in this chapter. This includes, for instance, the words 'cohesive' (Art 24(3), para 2 TEU), 'convergence' (Art 32, para 1 TEU) and 'complementarity' (eg Art 210(1) TFEU). See section III C below.

[2] The SEA referred to coherence in its Preamble and in Art 30(2)(d) and (5).

[3] HG Krenzler and HC Schneider, 'The Question of Consistency' in E Regelsberger *et al* (eds), *Foreign Policy of the European Union: From EPC to CFSP and Beyond* (Boulder, CO, Lynne Rienner, 1996) 133, 134; P Gauttier, 'Horizontal Coherence and the External Competences of the European Union' (2004) 10 *European Law Journal* 23, 25; C Gebhard, 'Coherence' in C Hill and M Smith (eds), *International Relations and the European Union*, 2nd edn (Oxford, Oxford University Press, 2011) 101.

more strategic'.[4] Remarkably, 16 provisions in the current version of the Treaties refer to the idea of coherence, many in the context of the Union's external action.[5]

Academic studies have generally assumed that coherence in EU external relations is desirable and have focused on how the institutional design and the legal framework can advance it. The debate has, however, been often vague in examining the nature and the notion of coherence in this field of EU action, probably driven by the same ambiguity that characterises references to coherence in the Treaties and case-law of the Court of Justice of the European Union (CJEU). The chapter focuses precisely on the questions that have been to some extent overlooked in the literature, and is aware that this means navigating difficult waters. It aims at understanding what can be considered 'an obsession' in the Union's foreign policy. This includes the examination of the reasons behind the quest for coherence in this area of EU action (section II). Likewise, the chapter analyses what the obsession is about, so it considers the notion of coherence in EU external relations (section III). Only after these questions have been addressed, is it possible to delve into the role of coherence as a principle of EU law that contributes to a broader political obsession (section IV). While not a technical principle pertaining exclusively to the legal domain, the chapter defends the interest of coherence as a principle that connects the *internal* character of individual structural principles, like conferral, to the *external* actorness of the Union in the world.

# II.  Making Sense of 'An Obsession'

The obsession with coherence in the external action of the Union, as reflected in the Treaties and in policy documents in this area, is based on the EU's perception of its *potential* as an international actor:

> But if we are to make a contribution that matches our potential, we need to be more active, more coherent and more capable.[6]

'Coherence' is a fixation with the policy and legal outcomes that the EU should produce in its external action in order to be effective as an international actor. There are two fundamental reasons behind the permanent quest for coherence in EU external relations. The first is the complex legal space in which the Union's external action is to be developed (we may call this 'the internal factor'). The

---

[4] Joint Communication to the European Parliament and the Council, *The EU's Comprehensive Approach to External Conflict and Crises*, JOIN(2013)30, 2.
[5] C Hillion, *Cohérence et action extérieure de l'Union Européenne*, EUI Working Papers LAW 2012/14, 1.
[6] European Council, *A Secure Europe in a Better World: European Security Strategy*, 15895/03 (12 December 2013) 13. Note that the policy document shared vision, common action: A strong Europe: A Global Strategy for the European Union's Foreign and Security Policy (June 2016) replaced the European Security Strategy.

second is the fact that the Union considers ensuring coherence a *conditio sine qua non* to its effectiveness on the international panorama ('the external factor').

The EU's system for external relations is one where multiple actors, policies and instruments operate simultaneously. The EU likes to refer to this as its wide *tool-box* to respond to international concerns. In doing so, the Union links its strength in the outside world not only to the existence of this wide range of tools, but also to the way in which it should use them—*coherently*. A great example is to be found in the 'Council Conclusions on the EU's Comprehensive Approach':[7]

> The European Union and its Member States can bring to the international stage the unique ability to combine, in a coherent and consistent manner, policies and tools rang-ing from diplomacy, security and defence to finance, trade, development and human rights, as well as justice and migration. This contributes greatly to the Union's ability to play a positive and transformative role in its external relations and as a global actor.

Organising the different tools of the Union is no easy task. Very often, the EU and its Member States operate in a truly parallel manner. This is, for instance, the case of the development cooperation field,[8] where the Union and its Member States program and implement their own aid programmes for each part-ner country.[9] The Common Foreign and Security Policy (CFSP), albeit generally requiring the unanimity of the Council, is not to affect the 'formulation and con-duct' of Member States' foreign policies.[10] Moreover, each EU policy area has its own instruments, like the Development Cooperation Policy, where, for example, the Instrument for Democracy and Human Rights Worldwide (EIDHR) and the Instrument contributing to Stability and Peace (IcSP)[11] can be used simultane-ously in cooperation with developing countries. Furthermore, the Union's institu-tions work towards objectives, such as poverty eradication and the strengthening of international security,[12] that are highly inter-linked on the ground. Yet these objectives are typically pursued in the context of policy areas that operate under decision-making processes that are not to affect each other:[13]

> CSDP [Common Security and Defence Policy] crisis management instruments and crisis response measures under the Instrument for Stability (IfS) pursue mostly short-term objectives, whereas development instruments by nature are oriented towards the long term. Although objectives and decision-making procedures are different, natural

---

[7] Council Conclusions on the EU's Comprehensive Approach, 9644/14 (12 May 2014) 2.

[8] Article 4(4) TFEU.

[9] As established in Art 210(1) TFEU, this should, however, happen with a high degree of coordi-nation, which is in practice mainly facilitated by Union delegations. See, eg, M Estrada Cañamares, 'A Legal Approach to Joint Programming in Development Cooperation Policy: Cooperation in Action Led by Union Delegations' in LN González Alonso (ed), *Between Autonomy and Cooperation: Shaping the Institutional Profile of the European External Action Service*, CLEER Working Paper 2014/6.

[10] See Art 24(1), para 2 TEU and Declaration No 13 annexed to the Lisbon Treaty.

[11] Regulation (EU) 235/2014 of the European Parliament and of the Council of 11 March 2014 establishing a financing instrument for democracy and human rights worldwide [2014] OJ L77/85, and Regulation (EU) 230/2014 of the European Parliament and of the Council of 11 March 2014 establish-ing an instrument contributing to stability and peace [2014] OJ L77/1.

[12] Articles 3(5) and 21 TEU.

[13] Article 40 TEU.

synergies and complementarities should be ensured ... The EU can use, in a coherent manner, different tools and instruments within their own mandates and decision-making processes to deliver on the shared objectives.[14]

This is a good example, showing that the challenging part of dealing with structural complexity lies in the need to respect the competences and the extent of the powers of actors, as well as the scope of policies. Noticeably, the political debate recognises that coherence is not only a matter of political will. There are 'objectives', 'instruments' and 'decision-making processes' to be respected. Furthermore, unlike in the case of the foreign policies of Member States, the different strands of EU external action (including the action of Member States) operate in a truly horizontal, *non-hierarchical* manner. There is no hierarchy between policies (eg CFSP/Common Commercial Policy (CCP)), no hierarchy between instruments (eg EIDHR/IcSP under the Development Cooperation Policy), and no hierarchy between actors (eg Commission/Council).[15] If the EU manages to be a coherent actor, we will consequently speak about a very *horizontal* coherence. The HRVP is a good example in this regard. Despite the important responsibilities over coherence that the Treaties entrust to her and her coordinating role, she cannot force Member States to follow concrete positions on the international scene.[16]

But coherence would not be an obsession in EU external relations if the Union did not consider it a *conditio sine qua non* to its effectiveness as an international actor ('the external factor'):

> The EU is stronger, more coherent, more visible and more effective in its external relations when all EU institutions and the Member States work together on the basis of a common strategic analysis and vision.[17]

The link between the idea of coherence and the effectiveness of the Union as an international actor can be found in the Treaties and the case-law of the Court of Justice.[18] This is especially clear in the context of the CFSP, as can be seen in Articles 24(3), second paragraph and 32, first paragraph of the Treaty on European Union (TEU):

> The Member States shall work together to enhance and develop their mutual political solidarity. They shall refrain from any action which is contrary to the interests of the Union or likely to impair its effectiveness as a cohesive force in international relations.

---

[14] *The EU's Comprehensive Approach to External Conflict and Crises* (n 4) 8. In a similar direction, in the Council Conclusions on Security and Development, 15097/07 (20 November 2007) 2), the Council claimed that the security-development nexus 'should inform EU strategies and policies in order to contribute to the coherence of EU external action, whilst recognising that the responsibilities and roles of development and security actors are complementary but remain specific'.

[15] 'A truly hierarchical foreign and security policy architecture—if it exists at all—is more typical of an individual State's constitutional set-up and bureaucratic machinery than of the condominium-type EU/CFSP structure and decision-making procedures.' A Missiroli, 'European Security Policy: The Challenge of Coherence' (2001) 6 *European Foreign Affairs Review* 177, 183.

[16] See, eg, Arts 18 and 27 TEU, and Declaration No 14 annexed to the Lisbon Treaty.

[17] *The EU's Comprehensive Approach to External Conflict and Crises* (n 4) 3.

[18] See, eg, Case C-246/07 *Commission v Sweden (PFOS)*, Judgment, EU:C:2010:203C, para 75.

Member States shall consult one another within the European Council and the Council on any matter of foreign and security policy of general interest in order to determine a common approach ... Member States shall ensure, through the convergence of their actions, that the Union is able to assert its interests and values on the international scene. Member States shall show mutual solidarity.

Likewise, we can find a similar link in Article 210(1) of the Treaty on the Functioning of the European Union (TFEU), in the context of the Development Cooperation Policy:

In order to promote the complementarity and efficiency of their action, the Union and the Member States shall coordinate their policies on development cooperation and shall consult each other on their aid programmes, including in international organisations and during international conferences.

Often the link between coherence and effectiveness finds its justification in the notion of EU actorness. Coherence serves the purpose of strengthening the actorness of the Union, which is indispensable for it to be ultimately effective as regards the objectives it pursues on the international scene. The EU acknowledges that the foreign policy domain is one where ascertaining one's power is crucial. The way in which actors perceive each other is fundamental in the struggle for power in world politics. By acting coherently, the EU understands that it can be a force for positive change. By being incoherent, it assumes that it can even *disappear* as an international player. The link between coherence and visibility shows that the Union is aware that it constantly needs to confirm its international identity.[19] The main challenge, in this respect, is obviously the fact that the EU shares the international space with each of its Member States and also that the Union is in relative terms still a very young actor. The EU needs to act coherently to be a credible international player, and be taken seriously by other actors. By way of example, Simon Nuttall mentions the Iraq War where, in his view: '[D]ifferences among the Member States ... deprived the Union of the credibility it needed to play an effective role'.[20] This idea of a lack of coherence that may lead to the EU not being recognisable on the international scene shows that the Union's assumption is not so much that coherence necessarily leads to effectiveness, as some authors seem to understand it, but rather that an incoherent Union cannot be an effective Union.[21]

On a more positive note, coherence allows the EU to show not only its existence but also its added value as an international player. This is why the 'European

---

[19] In fact, in the pre-Lisbon legal framework, ascertaining the EU's identity was one of the objectives of the CFSP. Currently, it is not an explicit external objective but it is mentioned in the Preamble to the TEU as one of the functions of the CFSP.

[20] S Nuttall, 'Coherence and Consistency' in C Hill and M Smith (eds), *International Relations and the European Union* (Oxford, Oxford University Press, 2005) 91, 94.

[21] For Antonio Missiroli the EU assumes that 'by acting unitarily and with a common purpose, the EU ... also becomes ipso facto more efficient and effective'. Missiroli, 'European Security Policy: The Challenge of Coherence' (n 15) 182.

Security Strategy' (2003) linked coherence to making 'a contribution that matches our potential'. We may also recall that the Council has recently stated that the coherent use of the EU's wide toolbox, 'contributes greatly to the Union's ability to play a positive and transformative role in its external relations and as a global actor'.[22] This statement implies an idea about what happens when the EU manages to work together with its 28 (soon to be 27) Member States, towards shared objectives. Is it not rare to see the Union trying to quantify the force of having the Union and its Member States working alongside one another?:

> The EU, both at its Member States and Community levels, is committed to meeting its responsibilities. Working together, the EU is an important force for positive change. The EU provides over half of the world's aid.[23]

In other instances, the rationale behind the coherence-effectiveness link responds to a more concrete idea of effectiveness. A clear example is the EU's long-standing agenda on 'Policy Coherence for Development', which follows an initiative led by the OECD and originally designed to accelerate progress towards the achievement of the Millennium Development Goals (MDGs).[24] Likewise, we can identify a recent trend to justify an increasing need for coherence on the basis of the existence of inter-linked realities on the ground:

> Preventing threats from becoming sources of conflict early on must be at the heart of our approach. Peace-building and long-term poverty reductions are essential to this. Each situation requires coherent use of our instruments, including political, diplomatic, development, humanitarian, crisis response, economic and trade co-operation, and civilian and military crisis management.[25]

In fact, one may wonder whether the EU is exploiting the existence of complex and inter-connected problems on the ground to legitimise itself as an actor that is particularly well placed to respond to today's global concerns,[26] because of the many tools it has at its disposal, and because of the way in which it can use them—in a

---

[22] See, respectively, *A Secure Europe in a Better World: European Security Strategy* (n 6) 13; and Council Conclusions on the EU's Comprehensive Approach (n 7) 2.

[23] Joint statement by the Council and the representatives of the governments of the Member States meeting within the Council, the European Parliament and the Commission on European Union Development Policy: The European Consensus [2006] OJ C46/1.

[24] See OECD and DG DEVCO's websites on 'Policy Coherence for Development': www.oecd.org/pcd/ and https://ec.europa.eu/europeaid/policies/policy-coherence-development_en.

[25] Council of the European Union, *Report on the Implementation of the European Security Strategy*, 17104/08 (10 December 2008) 14.

[26] This constitutes a critique of Niagalé Bagoyoko and Marie V Gibert to the EU incorporation of the security-development nexus, ie the idea that security and development challenges in the developing world can only be effectively tackled if addressed holistically and in an integrated manner. N Bagoyoko and MV Gibert, 'The Linkage between Security, Governance and Development: The European Union in Africa' (2009) 45 *Journal of Development Studies* 789. See the discussion regarding the recent proliferation of EU 'comprehensive approaches' in section III E below.

*strategically* coherent manner. For instance, Before the adoption of the "EU Global Strategy for Foreign and Security Policy" the EEAS' website claims:[27]

> Our world today is more connected, contested and complex … An EU Global Strategy on Foreign and Security Policy will enable the Union to identify a clear set of objectives and priorities for now and the future. On this basis the European Union can align its tools and instruments to ensure that they have the greatest possible impact.

The reasons that justify the obsession with producing coherent outcomes in EU foreign policy have a remarkable explanatory value as regards the function that coherence is supposed to fulfil in this area of EU action. Coherence in EU external relations should bring the EU as an external project forward ('the external factor'), while at the same time respecting the constituting elements of the Union's complex machinery for external relations ('the internal factor'). Far from being a vague political guideline, the emphasis on coherence in EU external relations says a lot about the nature of the EU as a complex international actor, and about the way in which the Union perceives that it can be most effective as regards its external objectives. It is a deliberate choice not to refer to structural complexity in EU external relations as a set of constitutional constraints, in spite of which the Union must ensure coherent outcomes. Dealing with the complexity characterising the Union's foreign policy machinery is inherent to the quest for coherence, to the extent that the latter would not exist without the former. To put it bluntly, if Member States decided that all policies in the Union's external action were to fall into the category of exclusive EU competences, would there be an obsession with coherence in this field?

Because of its place in the Treaties, coherence in EU external relations can be considered a *constitutional* obsession.[28] It is not only linked to how the Union organises its complexity *internally*, but it also has a clear *external* projection, as it is perceived as having a direct impact on the EU international actorness. It is, furthermore, a multi-faceted endeavour that depends on designing an adequate institutional set-up (eg is the EEAS fit for purpose?); managing to develop strategic coherence (eg from what substantive frameworks should coherent outcomes result?);[29] and acting with the right political will (eg do Member States take the coherence of the Union seriously?). Ensuring coherent outcomes depends, too, on the legal framework under which EU actors build external relations. Section IV of the chapter focuses on the role of the principle of coherence regarding this broad obsession.

---

[27] See n 6 above.
[28] Note that Loïc Azoulai goes as far as to claim that 'the external project is to affirm the presence and visibility of the EU on the international scene'. This corresponds to the 'external factor' of the quest presented in this section. See Loïc Azoulai, Chapter 2.
[29] Regarding the difference between strategic coherence and coherence at the level of individual measures, see section III E below.

# III. Coherence as the 'Dreamed' Outcome

The previous section has addressed the reasons behind the obsession with coherence in EU external relations in the treaties and in official policy documents. The analysis has already shed some light on what ensuring coherence in the Union's external action is about. It is an obsession with the outcomes produced as tangible and *external* results of having *internally* managed to organise a complex legal space.

This section claims that the complexity of the notion of coherence in the Union's foreign policy should not lead to the conclusion that we can say nothing substantial about it.[30] Although developing a one-sentence definition is not possible, this does not mean that we cannot elaborate on certain elements of the concept. The analysis refers to what coherence is, or at least clarifies what coherence in the Union's foreign policy is not. It focuses on what might be needed to be able to speak about coherent outcomes in EU external relations. It does not deny the fact that coherence presents specificities in each particular context where it is examined. In line with the views of Simon Nuttall, this chapter argues that coherence in EU external relations is 'a term of art', which has 'acquired overtones going well beyond its dictionary meaning'.[31]

## A. 'A Coherent EU Response' and 'Coherence between EU Responses'

This distinction results from the observation that coherence is a *relational* concept. Coherence can only be measured between different things, but which? There is a crucial difference between ensuring 'a coherent EU response' and preserving 'coherence between EU responses'. While the former refers to what might be needed to ensure coherence between different subjects (eg the EU/Member States, internal/external EU policies) in the same context (eg response to the 2015 refugee crisis), the latter, on the contrary, refers to coherence of the same subject (eg the Commission on human rights) in different, yet comparable, contexts (eg between 2012 and 2014 or in Kenya and South Sudan in 2014). Referring to these two notions without recognising this distinction leads to conceptual fuzziness regarding the quest for coherence in EU external relations. For instance, when Carmen Gebhard claims that 'practice has indeed shown that reaching coherence, eg in the form of a consistent common position or policy (ie in the vertical sense),

---

[30] 'It is then most challenging to define a single concept of coherence that would arch across all these issues, and provide an organizing function for Union external action in all its facets. One then finds oneself easily trapped between the need for abstraction and the need for a concrete definition of coherence.' B Van Vooren, *A Paradigm for Coherence in EU External Relations Law: The European Neighbourhood Policy* (Florence, European University Institute, 2010) 49–50.

[31] S Nuttall, *European Foreign Policy* (Oxford, Oxford University Press, 2000) 25.

often comes at the expense of functional depth'[32] she is not writing about the same idea of coherence that Marise Cremona reflects upon when she argues that there can be a tension between coherence and effectiveness as *real-politik*. Carmen Gebhard refers to the challenge of finding compromise solutions between the EU and its Member States to ensure 'a coherent EU response'. Marise Cremona, on the contrary, implies the need to recognise power differences in the Union's policy towards third states, which might require *incoherence* between EU responses in order to be effective.[33]

Understanding the quest for coherence as a direct response to structural complexity in EU external relations is not trivial. It means recognising that the obsession is primarily concerned with preventing the different policies, instruments and actors interacting simultaneously in the Union's foreign policy from developing in totally separate paths. Likewise, it means acknowledging that binding EU political actors with the decisions they took in similar situations is not the primary aim of the quest for coherence. In other words, it is much more an obsession with ensuring 'a coherent EU response' that with preserving 'coherence between EU responses'.

There are several arguments supporting this statement. First, references to coherence in the Treaties almost always appeal to coherence between different subjects operating simultaneously on the international scene. For instance, Article 7 TFEU and Article 21(3) TEU refer, respectively, to consistency 'between (the Union's) policies and activities, taking all of its objectives into account' and 'between the different areas of (the Union's) external action and between these and its other policies'.[34] Secondly, the link between the notion of coherence and the effectiveness of the Union as an international actor presented in this section shows a fear of not being able to provide concerted responses to specific international events (eg between the EU and the Member States). Thirdly, the quest for coherence in EU external relations dates back to the 1970s, when the germ of today's CFSP, the EPC, was established. The Union's foreign policy was then fragmented into the newly created EPC and the external dimension of the policies of the European Communities.[35] Fourthly, the HRVP and the EEAS, perhaps the most important institutional innovations regarding coherence after the entry into force of the Lisbon Treaty, are designed to bridge the persisting fragmentation between the CFSP/non-CFSP legal divide.[36]

---

[32] Gebhard, 'Coherence' (n 3) 110.

[33] See Marise Cremona, Chapter 1.

[34] Find other examples in the same direction in Art 13 TEU (coherence of the Union's 'policies and actions'); Art 16 TEU (coherence 'in the work of the different Council configurations'); and Art 214(1) TFEU (complementarity between 'the Union's measures and those of the Member States' in the field of humanitarian aid).

[35] In this direction see, eg, Gauttier, 'Horizontal Coherence and the External Competences of the European Union' (n 3) 25 and Nuttall, 'Coherence and Consistency' (n 20) 94–95.

[36] See Arts 18 and 27 TEU and Council Decision 2010/427/EU of 26 July 2010 establishing the organisation and functioning of the European External Action Service [2010] OJ L201/30. Along the same lines, see section III E below on the strategic powers of the European Council.

## B. Coherence and the Notions of Continuity and Equality

As explained in the foregoing, the primary focus of the obsession is on coherence between different subjects operating simultaneously, or on ensuring 'a coherent EU response', rather than preserving 'coherence between EU responses'. While it is true that the coherence of the Union as an international actor is often tested against previous EU responses in comparable situations, Article 13(1) TEU is the only provision in the Treaties that clearly mentions the notions of coherence and continuity listed together.[37] Linked to the idea of continuity, there is an idea of equality, suggesting that the EU should give similar solutions to similar problems.[38] Besides what has already been said about 'coherence between EU responses', we must recall that, as stated by Marise Cremona, 'equality does not imply that the EU in its external relations should not discriminate in terms of substantive policy ... between countries or individuals'.[39] Furthermore, we must be aware of the tension between forcing 'coherence between EU responses' at all costs and democratic considerations. From this perspective, Paul Gauttier has pointed at the need to tolerate a certain degree of incoherence as inevitable in 'an open decision-making process'.[40]

## C. Negative and Positive Coherence

In order to ensure 'a coherent EU response', the subjects we are comparing must not contradict each other (negative coherence or *consistency*) and they must, moreover, complement and reinforce each other (positive coherence). Negative coherence constitutes a necessary but insufficient condition for positive coherence.[41] Given the multiple policies, instruments and actors operating simultaneously in the field of external relations, to avoid unnecessarily contradictions and overlaps, it is essential that EU actors justify why they are entitled to act internationally and what exactly they are going to do when they act externally.[42]

The idea of positive coherence relates to the way in which the different subjects we are comparing (eg EU/Member States, Development Cooperation

---

[37] As will be seen in section IV below, there is, however, an important link between the principle of coherence and the idea of continuity.

[38] 'It would therefore be incoherent to treat in different ways two substantially similar situations.' S Bertea, 'Looking for Coherence within the European Community' (2005) 11 *European Law Journal* 154, 168.

[39] See Marise Cremona, Chapter 1.

[40] Gauttier, 'Horizontal Coherence and the External Competences of the European Union' (n 3) 24.

[41] Despite the fact that the English version of the Treaties uses the word 'consistency', it is widely accepted that it implies the idea of positive coherence described here. The fact that other language versions of the treaties refer to 'cohérence' (French), 'coerenza' (Italian) and 'coherencia' (Spanish), where in English we find 'consistency', is another argument in the same direction.

[42] As will be seen in section IV below, this is what the 'aim and content test' to decide on the adequate legal basis is about (see n 66 below).

Policy/Common Commercial Policy) can *complement* each other. The Treaties provide a more concrete idea of what this should look like in different contexts. For instance, in relation to the CFSP, we find references to the effectiveness of the Union as a 'cohesive force' and to the 'convergence' of Member States' actions.[43] As regards the development cooperation policy, very differently, the focus is on the need to ensure that EU and Member States' policies 'complement and reinforce each other'. From the perspective of coherence between different policies and activities of the Union, the TFEU recalls that the Union shall take 'all of its objectives into account'.[44] In the context of the CFSP, the idea is that of merging the different sentiments of the Council into one shared message, which Member States will then reproduce in the conduct of their own foreign policies. In relation to the Development Cooperation Policy, the focus is on making sure that the EU policy and those of the Member States ensure a greater impact together (because they reinforce each other) than if they did not coordinate at all. The requirement to take 'all of its objectives into account', which can be read as a requirement of *comprehensiveness*, has a normative character. It does not ask for coherence between whatever actors do; it asks for coherence with the objectives of the EU.[45]

## D. Coherence is Not Unity

As mentioned earlier in the chapter, coherence is intrinsic to structural complexity in EU external relations; the clearest expression of which is, of course, the CFSP/non-CFSP legal divide. This is why the challenge of ensuring 'a coherent EU response' encompasses doing so between CFSP and non-CFSP policy areas. In other words, reaching coherent outcomes does not require the total 'communitarisation' of the CFSP.[46]

A certain link between the notions of coherence and unity, however, can hardly be denied.[47] This association has to do with the 'external factor' behind the obsession with coherence. While the *internal* organisation of the EU's system for external relations must respect its constituting elements (its complexity), to confirm its identity on the international scene the Union needs to show *externally* a 'unified *modus operandi*'. The words of Advocate General Tizzano in *Hermès* are especially clear in this regard:[48]

---

[43] Articles 24(3), para 2 and 32, para 1 TEU.

[44] Articles 208(1) and 7 TFEU.

[45] This is why, for Anne Claire Marangoni and Kolja Raube: '[C]oherence makes the EU's commitment to comprehensive and global objectives credible'. AC Marangoni and K Raube, 'Virtue or Vice? The Coherence of the EU's External Policies' (2014) 36 *Journal of European Integration* 473, 478.

[46] Some authors have even claimed that a real communitarisation of the CFSP 'would finally make discussion of consistency irrelevant'. Krenzler and Schneider, 'The Question of Consistency' (n 3) 148.

[47] The fact that Art 26(2), para 2 TEU speaks about ensuring 'the unity, consistency and effectiveness of action by the Union' shows that these are linked but not interchangeable terms.

[48] Case C-53/96 *Hermès International v FHT Marketing*, Opinion of AG Tesauro, EU:C:1997:539, para 21.

The Community legal system is characterised by the simultaneous application of provisions of various origins, international, Community and national; but it nevertheless seeks to function and to represent itself to the outside world as a unified system. That is, one might say, the inherent nature of the system, which, while guaranteeing the maintenance of the realities of States and of individual interests of all kinds, also seeks to achieve a unified *modus operandi*.

The link between coherence and unity is also clear in the requirement of unity of international representation. In specific contexts, such as in the *PFOS* case, the coherence and effectiveness of the action of the Union can only be ensured with unity of EU international representation. The latter is, then, an expression of the principle of sincere cooperation as enshrined in Article 4(3) TEU, and it is directed or instrumental to the coherence and effectiveness of the action of the Union.[49] Furthermore, the connection between coherence and unity also explains the calls, especially in the context of the CFSP, for an EU single voice.[50] However, being realistic regarding the permanent character of structural complexity in EU external relations (at least in the near future) requires accepting that the Union will, at best, share a single message, reproduced by many different voices.[51]

## E. Coherent Outcomes and Strategic Coherence

The Union must ensure coherence in its external action in the midst of a set of non-prioritised and open-ended objectives. This is what Marise Cremona calls 'the absence of a *telos*' in EU external relations.[52] Coherence is only connected to advancing the Union's external objectives in a very indirect manner. It should strengthen the actorness of the EU, which is instrumental to its effectiveness as regards the objectives it pursues on the international scene. This is why a situation like the one in *Dermoestética*, where the Court used coherence as a criterion to test the adequateness of certain restrictions to the freedom of establishment and to provide services, is difficult to foresee in the area of EU external relations.[53]

---

[49] In a similar vein, see C Hillion, *Mixity and Coherence in EU External Relations: The Significance of the Duty of Cooperation*, CLEER Working Papers 2/2009, 4–7, and Case C-246/07 *Commission v Sweden (PFOS)*, Opinion of AG Poiares Maduro, EU:C:2009:589, paras 36–37.

[50] For example, the Preamble to the SEA referred to 'the need for Europe to aim at speaking ever increasingly with one voice and to act with consistency and solidarity in order more effectively to protect its common interests'.

[51] Christophe Hillion writes about 'the polyphonic nature of the Union's external action'. Hillion, *Mixity and Coherence in EU External Relations* (n 49) 3.

[52] See Marise Cremona, Chapter 1 and Arts 3(5) and 21 TEU.

[53] The Court concluded that restrictions introduced by the Italian government were not appropriate to guarantee the protection of public health since they were inconsistent. This was so because Italy 'introduced a prohibition on advertising medical and surgical treatments on national television networks while at the same time making it possible to broadcast such advertisements on local television networks'. Case C-500/06 *Corporación Dermoestética*, Judgment, EU:C:2008:421, para 39. In the same direction, see, eg, Case C-243/01 *Gambelli and others*, Judgment, EU:C:2003:597, paras 26 and 67. I thank Christophe Hillion for drawing my attention to these cases.

The Treaties leave ample space for political actors to define what substantive coherence should look like.[54] They foresee mechanisms to develop strategic documents, from which coherent outcomes or coherence at the level of individual measures should follow.[55] The idea of a certain degree of flexibility or political discretion in the design of strategic action is essential to the development of international politics. As long as strategic instruments are elaborated 'on the basis of the principles and objectives set out in Article 21 [TEU]',[56] EU actors keep a remarkable room for manoeuvre to decide on the Union's strategic partners and interests. This includes prioritising certain EU objectives over others and choosing policy mixes depending on the geographic and material scope of each strategic instrument.

Given the characteristics of the legal system for EU external relations, strategic documents are especially useful because, since they do not require a legal basis, they can bridge the CFSP/non-CFSP legal divide. For instance, Article 22(1) TEU establishes that the European Council shall identify the strategic interests and objectives of the Union that: 'shall relate to the common foreign and security policy and to other areas of the external action of the Union'.[57] Article 16(6), third paragraph TEU follows the former by stating that the Foreign Affairs Council (FAC): 'shall elaborate the Union's external action on the basis of strategic guidelines laid down by the European Council'.

In fact, we can identify a proliferation of strategic documents (often labelled 'comprehensive approaches') to certain material and geographical contexts after the entry into force of the Lisbon Treaty.[58] These documents are expressions of Member States' mutual solidarity (eg when adopted as FAC conclusions) and of inter-institutional sincere cooperation (eg when adopted as 'Joint Communications'),[59] and should contribute to enhancing coherence at the level of individual measures:

> The Council stresses that the comprehensive approach is both a general working method and a set of concrete measures and processes to improve how the EU, based on a common

---

[54] We may recall the extent to which the Court relied on the European Consensus on Development (2006), which defined a very broad scope for the EU's development policy. The Court did not question the content of the instrument; it emphasised, instead, the wide *consensus* reached around it. See European Consensus on Development (n 23) and, eg, Case C-377/12 *Commission v Council (Philippines II)*, Judgment, EU:C:2014:1903, para 19.

[55] 'A Union without a clear idea of what it is trying to do and where it is going will remain incoherent'. S Duke, 'Consistency, Coherence and European Union External Action: The Path to Lisbon and Beyond' in P Koutrakos (ed), *European Foreign Policy: Legal and Political Perspectives* (Cheltenham, Edward Elgar, 2011) 15, 29.

[56] Article 22(1) TEU.

[57] See *Strategic Agenda for the Union in Times of Change*, annexed to the European Council Conclusions of 26/27 June 2014 (EUCO 79/14). See also Art 26(1) TEU, on the strategic powers of the European Council in the CFSP context.

[58] For instance, the EU claims it has developed a comprehensive approach to Somalia and to the Sahel Region. Presentation of EU NAVFOR (Atalanta) and EUTM Mali, available at EEAS website, http://eeas.europa.eu/csdp/missions-and-operations/eu-navfor-somalia/mission-description/index_en.htm and www.eutmmali.eu/about-eutm-mali/the-eus-comprehensive-approach/.

[59] See, eg, Arts 13(2) and 32, para 1 TEU.

strategic vision and drawing on its wide array of existing tools and instruments, collectively can develop, embed and deliver more coherent and more effective policies, working practices, actions and results.[60]

The new prominence of comprehensive approaches in the EU external action is also directly linked to the fact that, after the entry into force of the Lisbon Treaty, the EU has an institutional structure (namely, the HRVP and the EEAS) that is fit to develop integrated strategies to external concerns. On a more critical note, one may draw attention to the self-interested use of comprehensive approaches by the EU. First, we may question whether the EU is exploiting the existence of interrelated problems on the ground to legitimise itself as a particularly or even uniquely well-placed actor. Secondly, allusions to the comprehensive approach allow the EU to present its strengths to address interrelated issues on the ground (its wide toolbox) without focusing on the problems created by the existence of so many different tools—the challenge behind the intention to use these tools *coherently*.

## IV. Coherence as a Principle

Analysing the principle of coherence in the context of EU external relations only after having addressed the obsession with coherence as an outcome in this field of Union action is a justifiable choice. It aims to stress that the principle of coherence can only be understood in the context of the broader objective that it contributes to. When reading of 'consistency' in the Union's external action in the Treaties, we may read the principle of coherence but also the obsession presented in the previous sections of this chapter.

Coherence is a *self-imposed* rule of conduct that should be respected throughout the development of EU external relations with a view to producing coherent outcomes. Member States have chosen, through successive treaty reforms, to reinforce the character of the Union as an international actor that acts in a coherent manner. Because of its location under Article 7 TFEU, coherence can be considered a 'Principle' of 'General Application' to the Union.[61] Since the entry into force of the Lisbon Treaty, the most important provisions regarding coherence, Article 7 TFEU and Article 21(3) TEU,[62] are within the jurisdiction of the Court of Justice. Despite the restricted role of the Court in the CFSP,[63] coherence is under its

---

[60] Council Conclusions on the EU's Comprehensive Approach (n 7) 1.

[61] Article 7 TFEU falls under Title II ('Provisions Having a General Application') of Part I ('Principles'). For an interpretation in the same direction, see Hillion, *Cohérence et action extérieure de l'Union Européenne* (n 5) 4.

[62] Article 21(3) TEU, in the specific context of the Union's external action, reads as follows: 'The Union shall ensure consistency between the different areas of its external action and between these and its other policies. The Council and the Commission, assisted by the High Representative of the Union for Foreign Affairs and Security Policy, shall ensure that consistency and shall cooperate to that effect'.

[63] Article 24(1) TEU.

control also in this context as a result of the single legal order brought about by the Lisbon Treaty reforms. Constitutional principles extend to all areas of EU action, including the CFSP.[64]

Besides the formal criteria to deem coherence as a principle of EU law, linked to its place in the Treaties and within the jurisdiction of the Court, there are two arguments regarding the function that coherence fulfils in EU external relations that support the same claim. First, the principle of coherence should guide the interpretation of a set of norms of a procedural and substantive nature in order to ensure 'a coherent EU response' to international events.[65] Article 7 TFEU is the clearest expression in the Treaties of what the principle of coherence is about. It reads as follows:

> The Union shall ensure consistency between its policies and activities, taking all of its objectives into account and in accordance with the principle of conferral of powers.

This provision shows the normative dimension of the principle ('taking all of its objectives into account'), as well as the procedural one ('in accordance with the principle of conferral of powers'). Likewise, it shows the negative and positive sides of coherence. The institutions of the Union and Member States must respect 'the principle of conferral of powers' (negative coherence) and take 'all of its objectives into account' (positive coherence). To ensure negative coherence, EU actors shall act only when they are competent to do so, within their powers and according to the procedures established in the law of the Union. The 'aim and content test' to decide on the adequate legal basis to be chosen to act internationally, according to which these choices must rest on objective factors amenable to judicial review, is essential in this regard.[66] It should allow all actors to understand why the EU is using a particular tool and what kind of activities are going to be carried out. This should avoid unnecessary overlaps (eg two EU actors doing the same).[67]

Furthermore, the different actors of the Union must ensure that their actions take all EU objectives into account and, thus, that these actions are not detached

---

[64] In the same direction see, eg, D Thym, 'The Intergovernmental Constitution of the EU's Foreign, Security and Defence Executive' (2011) 7 *European Constitutional Law Review* 453, and Hillion, *Cohérence et action extérieure de l'Union Européenne* (n 5) 5–7.

[65] For Christophe Hillion, coherence is a 'function of other EU legal principles'. C Hillion, 'Tous pour un, un pour tous! Coherence in the External Relations of the European Union' in M Cremona (ed), *Developments in EU External Relations Law* (Oxford, Oxford University Press, 2008) 10, 18. According to Marise Cremona, coherence 'finds its expression in a number of legal provisions and principles'; it 'operates to bring together—to structure—these fundamental legal principles'. M Cremona, 'Coherence in European Union Foreign Relations Law' in P Koutrakos (ed), *European Foreign Policy: Legal and Political Perspectives* (Cheltenham, Edward Elgar, 2011) 55, 59.

[66] See, eg, Case C-130/10 *Parliament v Council (Sanctions)*, Judgment, EU:C:2012:472, para 42.

[67] Notice, however, that the principle of conferral applies always, even when there is no need for a legal basis. This is clear, for example, in the *Council Note on EU Statements in Multilateral Organisations: General Arrangements*, 15901/11 (24 October 2011). The Note determines that statements by EU actors responsible for the external representation of the EU can only be prefaced by 'on behalf of the European Union' if they 'refer exclusively to actions undertaken by or responsibilities of the EU in the subject matter concerned including in the CFSP'. In every other instance, the expression 'on behalf of the EU and its Member States' has to be employed.

from the objectives pursued in other instruments or other policy areas. Despite
its normative dimension, coherence as a principle does not point at a specific
outcome. While it includes requirements of a substantive nature, it is not precise in
indicating what the response should look like. This is why the procedural dimension of the principle is much more important to build 'a coherent EU response'.[68]
When the attention is on the positive aspect of coherence, the principles of sincere
cooperation and mutual solidarity play a major role. When it is, instead, on the
need to respect the constituting elements of structural complexity, the principles
of conferral and institutional balance become central.[69]

Secondly, in the *Mauritius* case, the Court of Justice pointed to another dimension of coherence as a principle of EU action. By always acting in the same way,
the Union ensures procedural and normative *continuity* of its action. In *Mauritius*,
the Court held, on the 'requirements' of coherence and legal certainty, the need to
ground procedural legal bases for the negotiation and conclusion of international
agreements on substantive legal bases.[70] *Continuity* in the sense implied here does
not coincide with the notion of preserving 'coherence between EU responses'
presented earlier in this chapter. It is coherence over how we successively build
our responses, and not in the sense of adherence to the outcomes produced in
previous similar situations. Interestingly, this clearly distinguishes coherence as
a principle from coherence as a broad obsession. In the former, the main focus is
on the way in which the EU elaborates its responses, which is done with a view to
reaching coherent outcomes. In the latter, on the contrary, the centre of attention
is on the outcomes finally produced.

Understanding the principle of coherence as a commitment to a *continued* way
of acting internationally emphasises the character of coherence as an expression
of respect for the rule of law in the Union's external action. Along the same lines,
this perception stresses the *external* dimension of the principle. The principle of
coherence is not only an *internal* legal tool at the service of a broader EU obsession having an *external* dimension. Acting according to the principle of coherence
(eg respecting the principle of sincere cooperation)[71] has, in itself, an impact on
the EU's international actorness. By way of example, if the Union and its Member
States agree upon an arrangement to organise their action within an international

---

[68] Strategic instruments, which are expressions of the principles of sincere cooperation and mutual
solidarity, are crucial in this regard (see section III above).

[69] This is not to say that other rules and principles, such as exclusivity, pre-emption, subsidiarity
and proportionality, are not relevant to the overall coherence of the EU external action, but they are
much less important in this field than in other areas of Union law, which justifies why the principle of
coherence is especially relevant in the area of EU external relations.

[70] The Court states that anchoring the procedural legal basis to the substantive legal basis of a
measure 'ensures consistency, moreover, in the choice of legal bases for a measure'. Not doing so, on
the contrary 'would have the effect of introducing a degree of uncertainty and inconsistency into that
choice, insofar as it would be liable to result in the application of different procedures to acts of EU law
which have the same substantive legal basis'. Case C-658/11 *Parliament v Council (Mauritius)*, Judgment, EU:C:2014:2025, para 60.

[71] See, eg, Arts 4(3) and 13(2) TEU.

organisation, this is an expression of the principle of sincere cooperation, and ensures continuity over the way in which the Union acts within the organisation. This has, then, an impact on the image of the Union, since other members of the organisation perceive the EU as a coherent actor.[72] Interestingly, the principle of coherence confers a direct *external* dimension to other legal norms, like the principle of sincere cooperation.

The legal framework and the interventions of the Court of Justice are essential to facilitate that the institutions of the Union and Member States can respect the principle of coherence in the development of EU external relations. By clarifying and rationalising the complex legal system where these relations are to happen, it becomes easier to comply with the principle and, ultimately, to ensure coherent outcomes. This is why litigation before the Court of Justice in EU external relations can be a source of coherence in the long term, as it can lead to normative and procedural clarification in the legal framework.[73] This includes the role of the Court of Justice in finding pragmatic (and innovative) solutions to the limits posed by the principles of conferral and institutional balance, so that they allow for coherent outcomes. For instance, the judgment of the Court in the *PFOS* case on Sweden's duties flowing from the principle of sincere cooperation within a mixed agreement was criticised as placing a thin line between the principles of sincere cooperation and conferral. We can, however, defend the decision of the Court as a pragmatic one, guided by the need not to compromise the coherence of the Union's action. Noticeably, the Court based its interpretation of Sweden's loyalty obligations on the need 'to facilitate the achievement of the Community tasks and to ensure the coherence and consistency of the action and its international representation'.[74] From a very different perspective, the Court's unwillingness to accept the use of dual (CFSP/non-CFSP) legal bases does not seem to be a pragmatic interpretation of conferral, and certainly, it does not facilitate coherence between CFSP and non-CFSP measures.[75]

As regards the normative dimension of the principle of coherence, for instance the single set of EU external objectives, and the requirement to consider development cooperation objectives in all EU policies affecting developing countries, are meant to ensure normative coherence in EU external relations.[76] By way of

---

[72] See a similar example in Case C-25/94 *Commission v Council (FAO)*, Judgment, EU:C:1996:114.

[73] On a less positive note, attempts to over-codify and over-clarify the legal framework can diminish the flexibility of political actors in the Union's external action. This is what Bruno de Witte identifies as a problem of 'too much constitutional law' in EU external relations. B De Witte, 'Too Much Constitutional Law in the European Union's Foreign Relations?' in M Cremona and B de Witte (eds), *EU Foreign Relations Law: Constitutional Fundamentals* (Oxford, Bloomsbury Publishing, 2008) 3.

[74] *PFOS* (n 18) para 75; see also, for all, A Delgado-Casteleiro and J Larik, 'The Duty to Remain Silent: Limitless Loyalty in EU External Relations' (2011) 26 *EL Rev* 524.

[75] The Court has precluded the use of CFSP/non-CFSP legal bases in the context of restrictive measures since, to use a dual legal basis, it requires that the procedures for each legal basis are compatible. See, eg, *Sanctions* (n 66) paras 42–49.

[76] Articles 3(5) and 21 TEU and Art 208(1), para 2 TEU; see also Art 208(1), para 2 TFEU, specifying that the primary objective of the EU's Development Cooperation Policy is the reduction and, ultimately, the eradication of poverty.

example, regardless of whether the Union responds to an international security concern with a CSDP military operation, with CFSP restrictive measures, or with both, its action should show that it is an international actor that is strongly concerned with the protection of human rights.[77] These provisions, however, even if observed with the best intentions, are so open-ended that they are not able to prevent the EU from producing incoherent outcomes to international concerns.

The most crucial principles to ensure coherent outcomes are, certainly, the principles of mutual solidarity and sincere cooperation. We can find different provisions in the Treaties linking these principles to the coherence and effectiveness of the Union's action.[78] There is nothing new in establishing a link between loyalty principles and effectiveness.[79] Under public international law, this results from the principle of *pacta sunt servanda*. Broadly speaking, the idea is that we have created the Union and vested it with a set of objectives. We consequently need to be loyal to our partners and to the project (show good faith) and work towards those objectives. In a similar direction, Marise Cremona has stated that, by respecting the principles of sincere cooperation (and compliance), Member States 'defend the Community interest', which is a notion elaborated by the Court of Justice and clearly directed at the realisation of the Union's objectives.[80] In the context of EU external relations, coherence adds another layer to this argument: because of the complex system in which we are operating and our need to show a unified actorness, between loyalty and effectiveness we have added coherence. These links reinforce the quest for coherence as an *integrationist* one, aimed at bringing the EU as an external project forward.[81]

In the CFSP context, by exercising mutual solidarity, Member States can reach common approaches.[82] Solidarity, therefore, has a constitutive nature for the emergence of a CFSP common approach and at the same time fosters the coherence and effectiveness of the EU on the international scene. By way of example, the Conclusions of the FAC on the Ukrainian crisis are exercises of mutual solidarity between Member States and at the same time foster coherence. They create

[77] Articles 3(5) and 21(2)(b) TEU.

[78] See, eg, Arts 24(3), para 2 and 32, para 1 TEU, and Art 210(1) TFEU.

[79] Case C-105/03 *Pupino*, Judgment, EU:C:2005:386, para 42. This link is also obvious in Art 4(3) TEU, which establishes that: '[T]he Member States shall facilitate the achievement of the Union's tasks and refrain from any measure which could jeopardise the attainment of the Union's objectives'.

[80] 'If it is to be used as the basis for Member State obligations based on Article 10 EC it [the notion of Community interest] should be linked to the demands of the Community legal order ... These imperatives include the autonomy of the Community legal order, its primacy, and a reading of its scope and nature based on *effet utile*: an orientation towards completion of its objectives.' M Cremona, 'Defending the Community Interest: The Duties of Cooperation and Compliance' in M Cremona and B De Witte (eds), *EU Foreign Relations Law: Constitutional Fundamentals* (Oxford, Bloomsbury Publishing, 2008) 125, 169.

[81] 'The notion conveys the general aspiration of acting with even more unity, of becoming more cohesive, and thus of moving closer to an optimum level of integration. Hence, it is positively loaded in the sense that it directly appeals to the very core objectives of integration', C Gebhard, 'Coherence' (n 3) 110.

[82] See Art 32, para 1 TEU.

a common approach on the issue that Member States should adhere to in the conduct of their own foreign policies.[83]

Now that coherence is clearly within the jurisdiction of the Court of Justice, the question arises as to whether the Court may enforce it as such and, if so, how. In line with what has been argued throughout the chapter, it is reasonable to claim that the Court will not use the justiciability of the principle of coherence to bind institutions with specific political responses they produced in the past, since this is not what the principle is about. Nor does it seem realistic to foresee a situation where the Court would consider that an EU institution has failed to comply with the principle of coherence because it has adopted a measure without taking into account other EU objectives.[84] It is easier to imagine that the Court of Justice will use the strengthened position of the principle of coherence in the Treaties after the Lisbon Treaty reforms to reinforce its role in guiding other rules and principles of a procedural nature. This is, for example, what the Court has done in the *Mauritius* case, justifying rules to choose the right legal bases on the need to ensure coherence in the way in which the EU acts.[85]

Finally, coherence can be considered a *systemic structural* principle in EU external relations. Its main function is to direct other legal norms towards 'a coherent EU response', to some extent regardless of the substance of the outcome finally produced. This is why coherence is especially important in guiding other rules and principles of a procedural nature, and constitutes a structural principle in EU external relations. Furthermore, the fact that coherence attributes a shared function (ie to ensure 'a coherent EU response') to different structural principles justifies its characterisation as *systemic*.

## V. Concluding Remarks

The chapter has addressed the quest for coherence in EU external relations with a view to analysing how the principle of coherence contributes to this broader obsession. It has argued that the obsession directly relates to the outcomes that the Union should produce to show, *internally*, that is has managed to organise its complex legal machinery for EU foreign policy and, *externally*, that it is an actor than can respond coherently to international concerns. Respecting the constituting elements of structural complexity in EU external relations (eg acting in accordance with the principle of conferral) is part and parcel of the challenge of reaching coherent outcomes. Since the obsession focuses on the outcomes, we can think of it as an objective for political action. This should not, however, lead to

---

[83] See, for all, Council Conclusions on Ukraine, 12511/14 (15 August 2014).
[84] Article 7 TFEU.
[85] *Mauritius* (n 70) para 60.

the conclusion that coherence is an empty guideline (ie every actor aims at being coherent). It is a *constitutional* obsession that speaks about the nature of the Union as a complex international actor, and about how the EU understands that it can be most effective as regards the objectives it pursues in the world.

The chapter has claimed that there is an important distinction to be made between ensuring 'a coherent EU response' and preserving 'coherence between EU responses', and that the Union's obsession is primarily concerned with the former. Ensuring coherence between the EU and the Member States in the fight against ISIS is, thus, more important to the obsession than ensuring coherence between the electoral support offered by the Directorate-General for Development Cooperation to Burundi and Ethiopia for their 2015 general elections. Furthermore, section III has analysed that reaching coherence, as the 'dreamed' outcome, will depend, to a great extent, on whether the Union manages to develop *strategic* coherence. Given the open-ended and non-prioritised character of EU external objectives, strategic policy documents must identify strategic partners and interests, and prioritise certain EU objectives, depending on the geographical and material context. Coherence at the level of individual measures will then follow from these instruments.

Section IV of the chapter has, finally, addressed how the principle of coherence contributes to the broad political obsession. Coherence guides the application of a set of legal norms (eg principles of institutional balance and mutual solidarity) with a view to producing 'a coherent EU response' to international events. As the obsession with coherence has a clear external projection, this is the first way in which the principle of coherence attributes an *external* dimension to structural principles.

While the attention of the obsession is on the outcomes finally produced, the principle of coherence focuses on the way in which the Union builds its responses. It requires effort in the process of *building* 'a coherent EU response' to a given international concern, and a commitment to always *building* Union responses on the basis of the same rules and principles. This is the second way in which the principle of coherence confers an *external* dimension to structural principles. By repeatedly negotiating and concluding international agreements on the basis of the rules set out in Article 218 TFEU, which can be read as an expression of the principle of institutional balance, the Union shows an *identity* to its international partners. It shows, undoubtedly, a complex and inflexible *modus operandi*. But it also shows that the EU is an international organisation that *upholds* the rule of law, which can strengthen its credibility as a *promoter* of the rule of law on the international scene.

# 11

## The Search for Effectiveness and the Need for Loyalty in EU External Action

ANNE THIES

## I. Introduction

The European Treaties have never referred explicitly to a *principle* of effectiveness, but it has been argued that the Court of Justice of the European Union (CJEU) has recognised and developed it as one of the general principles of EU law.[1] In any case, it has been on the basis of effectiveness considerations that the CJEU recognised unwritten Member State obligations to strengthen the enforcement of EU law in the internal EU legal order. For instance, national courts, while enjoying procedural autonomy in principle,[2] have been requested to ensure the

---

[1] T Tridimas, *The General Principles of EU Law*, 2nd edn (Oxford, Oxford University Press, 2006) 418. According to Ross, the 'Court has elevated effectiveness into a constitutional principle', M Ross, 'Effectiveness in the European Legal Order(s): Beyond Supremacy to Constitutional Proportionality?' (2006) 31 *EL Rev* 476, 479, see also 495 *et seq*. Accetto and Zleptnig 'argue that effectiveness is one of the fundamental governing principles of Community law with overarching implications not just for individuals (and the protection of their Community rights) but above all for the coherence, integrity and the proper functioning of the Community legal order', 'governing the outcome of conflicts between the national and European legal orders'; see M Accetto and S Zleptnig, 'The Principle of Effectiveness: Rethinking Its Role in Community Law' (2005) 11 *European Public Law* 375, 376.

[2] For procedural autonomy considerations see Joined Cases 51/71–54/71 *International Fruit Co NV v Produktschap voor Groenten en Fruit*, Judgment, EU:C:1971:128, 1115, paras 3–4, where the Court referred to Member States' freedom to choose institutions in national systems when fulfilling obligations under (now) Art 4(3) TEU as 'solely a matter for the constitutional system of each State', and Case 33/76 *Rewe-Zentralfinanz eG and Rewe-Zentral AG v Landwirtschaftskammer für das Saarland*, Judgment, EU:C:1976:188, para 5, where the Court reiterated the Member States' freedom to designate courts and 'to determine procedural conditions' as well as the obligation to ensure equivalence and effectiveness. For a critique of the 'dual requirement of equivalence and effectiveness and the notion of "procedural autonomy"' in the context of the enforcement of EU law based rights before national courts, see M Bobek, 'Why There is No Principle of "Procedural Autonomy" of the Member States' in H-W Micklitz and B de Witte (eds), *The European Court of Justice and the Autonomy of the Member States* (Cambridge, Intersentia, 2012) 305.

effectiveness of EU law through the recognition of direct effect of EU law, the principle of state liability and the provision of effective judicial protection of natural and legal persons.[3] Whether or not one recognises a self-standing general principle of effectiveness, it is clear that the Court's focus, when referring to effectiveness in the internal EU legal order, has been on the enforcement of EU law and the functioning of the EU legal order.[4]

In Chapter 1, Marise Cremona categorised the principle of effectiveness, focusing in her analysis on the context of EU external action, as one of the systemic principles, which are concerned with 'the outcomes of those processes, or perhaps better, with building the EU's identity as a coherent, effective and autonomous actor in the world'.[5] She also observed that such systemic principles interact with what she categorised as relational principles, which 'govern the relationships between actors / legal subjects (not norms)',[6] such as the principles of conferral and sincere cooperation, in two ways: (a) the principle of effectiveness is being furthered by relational principles, as 'the Member States, for example, in an expression of the principles of loyalty and solidarity, are to refrain from any action "likely to impair [the Union's] *effectiveness* as a *cohesive* force in international relations" (Article 24(3) TEU)'; and (b) the principle of effectiveness (along with other systemic principles) 'serves to guide and shape [relational principles] and their implementation'.[7] It is through the lenses of such interaction that this chapter analyses recent case-law of the CJEU in the field of external action, in which the Court has relied explicitly or implicitly on effectiveness considerations to protect EU law, as well as the EU as a global actor. The chapter thereby focuses on cases in which the principle of effectiveness has either been employed as the immediate basis for the recognition of Member State obligations, or been applied when interpreting other (relational) principles, in particular the principles of conferral and sincere cooperation, to establish Member State obligations that correlate with the protection of EU law and the EU's own scope for manoeuvre as global actor.

The chapter recognises that the way in which the CJEU has employed effectiveness considerations regarding the impact of EU and international law in the

---

[3] Tridimas, *The General Principles of EU Law* (n 1) 418, with reference to Joined Cases C-46/93 and C-48/93 *Brasserie du Pêcheur v Germany* and *R v Secretary of State for Transport ex p Factortame Ltd*, Judgment, EU:C:1996:79, para 95; and Case C-5/94 *R v Ministry of Agriculture, Fisheries and Food ex p Hedley Lomas (Ireland) Ltd*, Opinion of AG Léger, EU:C:1995:193, paras 174–76.

[4] I categorised the principle of effectiveness as 'organisational principle' previously, by which I meant principles that constitute rules on 'how to exercise conferred EU, or retained Member State competence in the interest of shared objectives', whereas I classified certain rules related to/established on the basis of effectiveness considerations as 'interpretative principles' (direct effect and supremacy) and 'benchmark principles' (effective judicial protection); see A Thies, 'General Principles in the Development of EU External Relations Law' in M Cremona and A Thies, *The European Court of Justice and External Relations Law: Constitutional Challenges* (Oxford, Hart Publishing, 2014) 139, 140.

[5] Marise Cremona, Chapter 1.

[6] ibid.

[7] ibid.

context of EU external action is little different from its approach regarding EU internal law. National courts have been obliged to ensure the effectiveness of EU law and international treaties adopted by the EU, and to provide related remedies. This chapter argues that it is the protection of the EU's actorness on the global stage, and particularly so in areas of shared competence, that is different and novel. Confirming the interaction between EU systemic and relational principles as identified by Marise Cremona (see Chapter 1 and above), the chapter claims that the CJEU has taken effectiveness considerations into account when interpreting the reach of Member State obligations under the principle of sincere cooperation.[8] The chapter thereby highlights that because of effectiveness considerations, the CJEU has established that Member State obligations related to the EU's functionality as global actor can be triggered not only by legislative but also non-legislative measures adopted by the EU institutions. As a consequence of these developments, effectiveness considerations have imposed significant constraints on the Member States with regard to both their scope for international law-making in cooperation with non-EU actors (in substance) and their procedural capacity to take external action, even though in principle they have remained independent subjects of the international legal order. The chapter suggests that the wording of Article 4(3) of the Treaty on European Union (TEU) supports such approach, as it is EU law, other EU institutional acts, as well as EU objectives, which, once adopted or formulated in a lawful way by EU institutions, can trigger Member State constraints in any policy area.[9] At the same time, it is stressed that the EU principle of effectiveness can protect the EU's actorness only by clarifying the division between the EU and its Member States, while it cannot be relied on to increase the effectiveness and autonomy of EU as global actor outside the EU framework.

The remaining part of this chapter is divided into four sections. It starts with a short review of the principle of effectiveness as established in the internal legal order, highlighting that the Court has linked Member State obligations to the necessity to protect specific EU law and/or the (functioning of the) EU legal order (*effet utile*). In its subsequent section, the chapter turns to the reach of the principle of effectiveness and/or effectiveness considerations in the context of external action. It recognises, first, that EU law and the EU internal legal order continue to be very relevant when defining the institutional and constitutional

---

[8] The chapter thereby confirms Cremona's proposal that the principle of effectiveness (as one of the 'systemic principles' concerning the definition of actorness of the EU) serves to guide and shape the principle of sincere cooperation (as one of the 'relational principle' concerning the relationship between EU and its Member States) and its implementation; see Marise Cremona, Chapter 1.

[9] Article 4(3) TEU states that '[p]ursuant to the principle of sincere cooperation, the Union and the Member States shall, in full mutual respect, assist each other in carrying out tasks which flow from the Treaties. The Member States shall take any appropriate measure, general or particular, to ensure fulfilment of the obligations arising out of the Treaties or resulting from the acts of the institutions of the Union. The Member States shall facilitate the achievement of the Union's tasks and refrain from any measure which could jeopardise the attainment of the Union's objectives'.

space for EU external action, as they provide the basis for demarcating the EU's and its Member States' external scope for manoeuvre, most importantly in the making of international law. Yet, the chapter goes on to demonstrate that the CJEU has started to protect the functionality of the EU *as an external actor* by allowing effectiveness and related EU unity considerations to shape and further increase the reach of Member State obligations under the principle of sincere cooperation. In the absence of EU *legislation* that provides for particular EU external action and establishes correlating Member State obligations, the CJEU has recognised *non-legislative* measures adopted by the EU institutions (such as a strategy concerning the sequence of EU and international legislative steps)[10] as justifying Member State constraints in the interest of the EU's effectiveness as a global actor and has increasingly referred to the need for 'unity in international representation'.[11]

## II. Foundations and Role of the Principle of Effectiveness in the Internal EU Legal Order

The CJEU has established and applied the principle of effectiveness, which has resulted primarily in obligations imposed on the Member States and their domestic courts.[12] The CJEU relied on effectiveness considerations, together with Article 4(3) TEU,[13] to establish a whole range of other EU law principles in the interest of effectiveness of EU law and the functioning of the EU legal order as a whole: the principles of direct effect, supremacy, consistent interpretation and state liability. The Court has thereby emphasised the need 'to ensure fulfilment' of Treaty obligations.[14] Already in *Van Gend en Loos* (1963), the Court referred to the

---

[10] Case C-246/07 *Commission v Sweden (PFOS)*, Judgment, EU:C:2010:203. On the choice of law-making venues see B de Witte and A Thies, 'Why Choose Europe? The Place of the European Union in the Architecture of International Legal Cooperation' in S Blockmans, B Van Vooren and J Wouters (eds), *The Legal Dimension of Global Governance: What Role for the EU?* (Oxford, Oxford University Press, 2013) 23, on sequencing in particular, 34 *et seq.*

[11] See, eg, Ruling 1/78, EU:C:1978:202, paras 34–36 (by analogy with the European Atomic Energy Community (EAEC) Treaty); Opinion 2/91, EU:C:1993:106, para 36; Opinion 1/94, EU:C:1994:384, para 108; Case C-25/94 *Commission v Council (FAO)*, Judgment, EU:C:1996:114, para 48; *PFOS* (n 10) para 73.

[12] A Biondi, 'The European Court of Justice and Certain National Procedural Limitations: Not Such a Tough Relationship' (1999) 36 *CML Rev* 1271, 1277 *et seq*; Ross, 'Effectiveness in the European Legal Order(s)' (n 1) 477.

[13] See for wording n 9 above.

[14] Article 4(3), para 2 TEU. See also B de Witte, 'Institutional Principles in Judicial Development of the EU Legal Order' in F Snyder (ed), *The Europeanisation of Law: The Legal Effects of European Integration* (Oxford, Hart Publishing, 2000) 83, 88.

'effective supervision' [of EU law] by individuals (in addition to the Commission and the Member States) before acknowledging direct effect of Treaty provisions.[15] In *Grad* (1971), the Court recognised that '[i]t would be incompatible with the binding effect attributed to decisions ... to exclude in principle the possibility that persons affected may invoke the obligations imposed by a decision' and held that 'the effectiveness (*"l'effet utile"*) of ... a measure [imposing obligations on Member States] would be weakened if the nationals of that state could not invoke it in the courts and the national courts could not take it into consideration as part of Community law'.[16] The principle of supremacy was established in *Simmenthal* (1978) when the Court referred to the 'effectiveness of obligations undertaken unconditionally and irrevocably by Member States pursuant to the treaty' reflecting 'the very foundations of the Community' before establishing a national court's obligation to set aside national law conflicting with (what is now) EU law.[17]

Moreover, the Court established the principle of state liability, providing an independent remedy for natural and legal persons who suffered damage as a consequence of states' infringements of EU law that confers rights on individuals. The Court clarified that it 'would be contrary to the principle of the effectiveness of Community law' to 'make the reparation of loss or damage conditional upon the requirement that there must have been a prior finding by the Court of an infringement of Community law attributable to a Member State', 'since it would preclude any right to reparation so long as the presumed infringement had not been the subject of an action brought by the Commission ... and of a finding of an infringement by the Court'.[18] The Court continued its reasoning by stating that:

> [r]ights arising for individuals out of Community provisions having direct effect in the domestic legal systems of the Member States cannot depend on the Commission's assessment of the expediency of taking action against a Member State ... or on the delivery by the Court of any judgment finding an infringement.[19]

In *Köbler* (2003), the Court held that the 'full effectiveness of [EU] rules' protecting individuals also required that a decision of a national court, which infringed those rules, could trigger state liability.[20]

---

[15] Case 26/62 *Van Gend en Loos*, Judgment, EU:C:1963:1, 13. On the direct effect of Directives see Case 41/74 *Van Duyn v Home Office*, Judgment, EU:C:1974:133, para 15: 'Council Directive ... confers on individuals rights which are enforceable by them in courts of a Member State and which the national court must protect'.

[16] Case 9/70 *Franz Grad v Finanzamt Traunstein*, Judgment, EU:C:1970:78, para 5.

[17] Case 106/77 *Simmenthal*, Judgment, EU:C:1978:49, paras 18, 20, 22–23.

[18] *Brasserie de Pêcheur and Factortame Ltd* (n 3) para 95, with reference to Joined Cases 314/81, 315/81, 316/81 and 83/82 *Waterkeyn and others*, Judgment, EU:C:1982:430, para 16.

[19] ibid para 95.

[20] Case C-224/01 *Köbler v Austria*, Judgment, EU:C:2003:513, para 33.

Furthermore, the Court has recognised the principle of effective judicial protection as a general principle of EU law,[21] which could impose obligations on the Member States and their courts.[22] The Court has consistently held that:

> in the absence of Community rules governing the matter, it is for the domestic legal system of each Member State to designate the courts and tribunals having jurisdiction and to lay down the detailed procedural rules governing actions for safeguarding rights which individuals derive from Community law.[23]

Yet, the Court clarified, the Member States 'are responsible for ensuring that those rights are effectively protected in each case'.[24] The CJEU further specified that the effective enforcement of rights under EU law includes rights provided by EU secondary legislation.[25] The right to effective judicial protection has also been recognised as a fundamental right under EU law,[26] and Article 19(1), second paragraph TFEU endorsed Member States' commitment to 'provide remedies sufficient to ensure effective legal protection in the fields covered by Union law'.

Overall, the establishment and application of the principle of effectiveness for the protection of EU law and the EU legal order have played a significant role in the Court's case law on the exercise of power by the Member States in the light of their EU membership. Member State obligations related to the protection of natural and legal persons under EU law have been enforced before national courts,[27] and the European Commission and the CJEU have been primarily responsible for ensuring the overall effectiveness of EU law.[28] Effectiveness has been considered

---

[21] See, eg, Case C-432/05 *Unibet*, Judgment, EU:C:2007:163, para 37; Case C-268/06 *Impact*, Judgment, EU:C:2008:223, para 43.

[22] J Lonbay and A Biondi (eds), *Remedies for Breach of EC Law* (Chichester, Wiley & Sons, 1997); T Tridimas, 'Enforcing Community Rights in National Courts: Some Recent Developments' and J Temple Lang, 'The Principle of Effective Protection of Community Law Rights', both in D O'Keeffe and A Bavasso (eds), *Judicial Review in European Union Law, Liber Amicorum in Honour of Lord Slynn* (Alphen aan den Rijn, Kluwer, 2000), respectively 465 and 235; M Dougan, *National Remedies before the Court of Justice: Issues of Harmonisation and Differentiation* (Oxford, Hart Publishing, 2004).

[23] *Impact* (n 21) para 44, with reference to *Rewe-Zentralfinanz and Rewe-Zentral* (n 2) para 5; Case 45/76 *Comet*, Judgment, EU:C:1976:191, para 13; Case C-312/93 *Peterbroeck*, Judgment, EU:C:1995:437, para 12; *Unibet* (n 21) para 39; and Joined Cases C-222/05–C-225/05 *Van der Weerd and others* (2007), Judgment, EU:C:2007:318, para 28.

[24] *Impact* (n 21) para 45, with reference to Case 179/84 *Bozzetti*, Judgment, EU:C:1985:306, para 17; Case C-446/93 *SEIM*, Judgment, EU:C:1996:10, para 32; and Case C-54/96 *Dorsch Consult*, Judgment, EU:C:1997:413, para 40.

[25] See, eg, Case C-169/14 *Juan Carlos Sánchez Morcillo María del Carmen Abril García v Banco Bilbao Vizcaya Argentaria, SA*, Judgment, EU:C:2014:2099, para 27 *et seq*.

[26] See now also Charter of Fundamental Rights of the European Union, Art 47 See for scope of review required to be considered effective eg Case C-535/14P *Vadzim Ipatau, residing in Minsk (Belarus) v Council*, Judgment, EU:C:2015:407, para 42.

[27] See, eg, F Jacobs, 'Enforcing Community Rights and Obligations in National Courts: Striking the Balance' in J Lonbay and A Biondi (eds), *Remedies for Breach of EC Law* (Chichester, Wiley & Sons, 1997) 25–36.

[28] F Snyder, 'The Effectiveness of European Community Law: Institutions, Processes, Tools and Techniques' (1993) 56 *MLR* 19.

to be 'emerging as the driver of constitutional evolution',[29] and the principle of effectiveness has been conceptualised in its 'role as a guarantee for the functioning and coherence of the [internal EU] legal order'.[30]

# III. Effectiveness in the Context of External Action

As discussed elsewhere,[31] in addition to comprehensive studies on the EU as a global actor,[32] the *effectiveness* of the EU has been assessed with regard to its external policy-making and 'outputs';[33] the role and impact of newly introduced institutions, such as the European External Action Service (EEAS);[34] the upholding and promotion of EU values 'in its relations with the wider world';[35] the achieving of the EU Treaties' objectives;[36] and the EU's 'broader influence in the international system',[37] including through its involvement in international organisations.[38]

---

[29] Ross, 'Effectiveness in the European Legal Order(s)' (n 1) 477.

[30] Accetto and Zleptnig, 'The Principle of Effectiveness' (n 1).

[31] Thies, 'General Principles in the Development of EU External Relations Law' (n 4) 153 *et seq.*

[32] C Bretherton and J Vogler, *The European Union as Global Actor*, 2nd edn (Abingdon, Routledge, 2006); M Cremona, 'The Union as a Global Actor: Roles, Models and Identity' (2004) 41 *CML Rev* 553; C Hill and M Smith (eds), *International Relations and the European Union*, 2nd edn (Oxford, Oxford University Press, 2011); P Koutrakos, *EU International Relations Law* (Oxford, Hart Publishing, 2006); E Cannizzaro (ed), *The European Union as an Actor in International Relations* (Alphen aan den Rijn, Kluwer, 2002).

[33] L Aggestam, 'Introduction: Ethical Power Europe?' (2008) 84 *International Affairs* 1. See also KE Smith, *The EU in the World: Future Research Agendas*, LSE European Foreign Policy Unit Working Paper 2008/1, 23.

[34] R Balfour and H Ojanen, *Does the European External Action Service Represent a Model for the Challenges of Global Diplomacy?*, IAI Working Papers 2011/11; M Emerson et al, *Upgrading the EU's Role as Global Actor: Institutions, Law and the Restructuring of European Diplomacy* (Brussels, Centre for European Policy Studies, 2011); L Erkelens and S Blockmans, *Setting Up the European External Action Service: An Institutional Act of Balance*, CLEER Working Papers 2012/1; S Vanhoonacker and K Pomorska, 'The European External Action Service and Agenda-setting in European Foreign Policy' (2013) 20 *Journal of European Public Policy* 1316.

[35] Article 3(5) TEU; see with regard to, *inter alia*, the processes 'through which values are both imported and exported from the EU legal order', M Cremona, 'Values in EU Foreign Policy' in P Koutrakos and M Shaw (eds), *Beyond the Established Orders: Policy Interconnections Between the EU and the Rest of the World* (Oxford, Hart Publishing, 2011) 275, 313.

[36] KE Smith, *European Union Foreign Policy in a Changing World* (Cambridge, Polity, 2008) 237; M Cremona, 'Defining Competence in EU External Relations: Lessons from the Treaty Reform Process' in A Dashwood and M Maresceau (eds), *Law and Practice of EU External Relations* (Cambridge, Cambridge University Press, 2008) 34, 51 *et seq* (with reference to Opinion 1/03, EU:C:2006:81, and implied powers).

[37] Smith, *The EU in the World: Future Research Agendas* (n 33) 10, with reference to C Hill and M Smith, 'Acting for Europe: Reassessing the European Union's Place in International Relations' in C Hill and M Smith (eds), *International Relations and the European Union*, 2nd edn (Oxford, Oxford University Press, 2011) 404.

[38] With regard to negotiations in the context of the WTO, see, eg C-13/07 *Commission v Council (Vietnam)*, Opinion of AG Kokott, EU:C:2009:190, para 72; on the EU's influence at the United Nations on human rights issues, see, e.g. KE Smith 'Speaking with One Voice? European Union Co-ordination

The benchmarks for such assessments have been found predominantly in non-legal parameters and scholarship. This section neither intends to re-assess the actual global impact of EU positions or values, nor to measure the influence of the EU in international fora, which (at least partially) depend on external factors that remain largely unaffected by EU principles and EU judicial activity. Instead, it is interested in the *legal* implications of effectiveness considerations under EU law, as follows. As stated in the introduction, this chapter analyses whether and, if so, how the principle of effectiveness has been applied (and/or effectiveness considerations have been relied on) by the CJEU to constrain Member State external action in order to protect the effectiveness or effects of EU law or other EU institutional measures, on the one hand, and to protect the EU's own capacity to take external action, on the other. In the first scenario discussed below, it is an existing EU law or EU measure that is being protected from Member State interference or unilateral international law-making ('substantive dimension'). In the second scenario, it is the protection, or the carving out of the EU's scope for manoeuvre as an actor on the international stage, which usually correlates with Member State obligations ('institutional dimension'/'procedural dimension'). Both scenarios are discussed in the following paragraphs to provide a comprehensive basis for comparing the reach of the principle of effectiveness within the EU legal order with its reach in EU external action. Yet, it is the second scenario that deserves closer attention in the context of this book, as it is here that the CJEU has started to employ the principle of effectiveness in a way that is specific to the context of EU external action, going beyond the enforcement of EU law (which has been the focus of the principle's reach within the EU legal order) and strengthening the effectiveness of the EU as global actor in its own right.

## A. Effectiveness of EU Law and the EU Legal Order

Where EU Member States are involved unilaterally in the conclusion of international agreements, they have to exercise their retained powers in 'a manner consistent with [EU] law'.[39] In *Centro-Com*, the Court found that:

> the Member States cannot treat national measures whose effect is to prevent or restrict the export of certain products as falling outside the scope of the common commercial policy on the ground that they have foreign and security objectives.[40]

---

on Human Rights Issues at the United Nations' (2006) 44 *Journal of Common Market Studies* 113; see also D Mahnke and S Gstöhl (eds), *European Union Diplomacy: Coherence, Unity and Effectiveness* (Berne, Peter Lang, 2012).

[39] Case C-124/95 *R ex p Centro-Com v HM Treasury and Bank of England*, Judgment, EU:C:1997:8, para 25, with reference to Joined Cases 6/69 and 11/69 *Commission v France*, Judgment, EU:C:1969:68, para 17; Case 57/86 *Greece v Commission*, Judgment, EU:C:1988:284, para 9; Case 127/87 *Commission v Greece*, Judgment, EU:C:1988:331, para 7; and Case C-221/89 *Factortame and others*, Judgment, EU:C:1991:320, para 14. All of these cases concerned the Member States' obligation to comply with Treaty obligations.

[40] *R ex parte Centro-Com* (n 39) para 26.

In principle, EU Member States are obliged to give full effect to EU law when taking any action, both internally and externally, that falls within 'the scope of [EU] law'.[41] According to the CJEU, 'a specific issue which has not yet been subject to EU legislation may fall within the scope of EU law if it relates to a field covered in large measure by it'.[42] In the internal context, the effectiveness of the EU legal order is often directed at (or at the expense of) the Member States (eg enforcing EU law against them). Externally, Member States might also be prevented from pursuing their own law-making agenda, if there is conflicting EU law that they need to comply with. However, applying the principle of effectiveness to the external situation might have more far-reaching implications for Member States in that it means predominantly recognising the need to ensure that the EU and Member States are pulling in the same direction. As will be discussed in more detail below, the external context is therefore less about the enforceability and direct effect of EU law, and more about the need to allow for EU law and other EU institutional measures (eg those preparing legislative activities and other EU contributions in international fora) to have envisaged effects also outside the EU legal order—and that may mean that EU Member States are constrained in their capacity to take individual external action as separate subjects of the international legal order. What is important to remember here is that the wording of Article 4(3), second paragraph TEU, which has been relied on for the development of the principles of effectiveness and other principles related to it, such as direct effect and supremacy, provides the basis for recognising Member State obligations triggered by EU Treaties, secondary EU law and other institutional acts.[43]

EU institutional acts (as referred to by Article 4(3) TEU)[44] that have the capacity to define the scope for Member State external action include legally binding instruments adopted by the EU institutions (see Article 288 of the Treaty on the Functioning of the European Union (TFEU)) as well as international agreements adopted by the EU (see Article 216(2) TFEU). The Court has held since *Haegeman* (1974) that an international agreement concluded by (what is now) the EU constitutes an 'integral part of the EU legal order'.[45] The EU concludes an international agreement through Council Decision (Article 218(6) TFEU); as a result, it

---

[41] Case C-260/89 *Elliniki Radiophonia Tiléorassi AE and Panellinia Omospondia Syllogon Prossopikou v Dimotiki Etairia Pliroforissis, Sotirios Kouvela, Nicolaos Avdellas and others (ERT v DEP)*, Judgment, EU:C:1991:254, para 42.

[42] See, eg, Case C-240/09 *Lesoochranárske zoskupenie VLK v Ministerstvo životného prostredia Slovenskej republiky*, Judgment, EU:C:2011:125, para 40 (regarding the CJEU's capacity to interpret provisions of a mixed agreement).

[43] Article 4(3), para 2 TEU: 'The Member States shall take any appropriate measure, general or particular, to ensure fulfilment of the obligations arising out of the Treaties or resulting from the acts of the institutions of the Union'.

[44] See n 9 above.

[45] Case 181/73 *Haegeman v Belgium*, Judgment, EU:C:1974:41, para 5. See, for a detailed study of the effects of international agreements within the EU legal order, M Mendez, 'The Enforcement of EU Agreements: Bolstering the Effectiveness of Treaty Law?' (2010) 47 *CML Rev* 1719; M Mendez, *The Legal Effects of EU Agreements: Maximalist Treaty Enforcement and Judicial Avoidance Techniques* (Oxford, Oxford University Press, 2013).

is of a legal nature that is equivalent to EU law adopted in the internal legal order with regard to resulting Member State obligations, while taking precedence over such internal law obligations for the Member States.[46] Moreover, the CJEU has held that agreements concluded by both the EU and some or all of its Member States ('mixed agreements') 'have the same status in the [EU] legal order as purely [EU] agreements, as these are provisions coming within the scope of [EU] competence'.[47] As a consequence, 'in ensuring respect for commitments arising from an agreement concluded [also] by the [EU] institutions, the Member States fulfil, within the [EU] system, an obligation in relation to the [EU], which has assumed responsibility for the due performance of that agreement'.[48] Member States are bound to comply with their obligations under the Charter of Fundamental Rights of the EU when implementing 'Union law',[49] which includes the implementation of international agreements concluded exclusively by the EU and mixed agreements, at least to the extent they fall within the scope of EU law.

The principles of direct effect, supremacy and consistent interpretation, which have been developed in the interest of the effectiveness of EU law, have also found their way into the law of EU external relations in that they remain applicable with regard to EU law that originates in the EU's international law obligations. The CJEU has considered international treaty provisions to be directly effective— and thus enforceable against Member States—if the 'wording [,] purpose and nature of the agreement' do not preclude direct effect, and 'the provision contains a clear and precise obligation which is not subject, in its implementation or effects, to the adoption of any subsequent measure'.[50] In the absence of direct

---

[46] See, eg, C-228/06 *Mehmet Soysal and Ibrahim Savatli v Bundesrepublik Deutschland*, Judgment, EU:C:2009:101, para 58 *et seq.*

[47] C-459/03 *Commission v Ireland (Mox Plant)*, Judgment, EU:C:2006:345, para 84, with reference to Case C-13/00 *Commission v Ireland*, Judgment, EU:C:2002:184, para 14.

[48] *Mox Plant* (n 47) para 85, with reference to Case C-13/00 *Commission v Ireland* (n 47) para 15. See already Ruling 1/78 (n 11) para 36. See also Commission Communication, *European Disability Strategy 2010–2020: A Renewed Commitment to a Barrier-Free Europe*, COM(2010)636 (15 November 2010) note 4 ('The UN Convention will be binding on the EU and will form part of the EU legal order'), and at 4 where the Commission acknowledges the role of both the EU and its Member States to ensure 'effective implementation' across the EU of the UN Convention.

[49] Charter of Fundamental Rights of the European Union, Art 51(1). See for recent interpretation of Art 51(1), Case C-617/10 *Åkerberg Fransson*, Judgment, EU:C:2013:105. Accordingly, it is settled case-law 'that the fundamental rights guaranteed in the legal order of the European Union are applicable in all situations governed by European Union law, but not outside such situations. In this respect the Court has already observed that it has no power to examine the compatibility with the Charter of national legislation lying outside the scope of European Union law. On the other hand, if such legislation falls within the scope of European Union law, the Court, when requested to give a preliminary ruling, must provide all the guidance as to interpretation needed in order for the national court to determine whether that legislation is compatible with the fundamental rights the observance of which the Court ensures' (para 19). See for detailed analysis of the reach of general principles and fundamental rights under the Charter, M Dougan, 'Judicial Review of Member State Action under the General Principles and the Charter: Defining the "Scope of Union Law"' (2015) 52 *CML Rev* 1201.

[50] *Lesoochranárske zoskupenie VLK* (n 42) para 44; see also Case C-265/03 *Simutenkov*, Judgment, EU:C:2005:213, para 21 (Communities/Russia Partnership Agreement); and Case C-372/06 *Asda Stores*, Judgment, EU:C:2007:787, para 82 (EEC/Turkey Association Agreement).

effect of international treaty provisions, the CJEU has confirmed Member States' obligation to interpret domestic law consistently with the EU's international obligations, also in the context of a mixed agreement. While the Court recognised that it remained the responsibility of the Member States 'to lay down detailed procedural rules governing actions for safeguarding rights which individuals derive from EU law', the principle of effectiveness required that this 'must not make it in practice impossible or excessively difficult to exercise rights conferred by EU law'.[51] The CJEU held that in order 'to ensure effective judicial protection in the fields covered by [EU] law' Member State courts were under the obligation 'to interpret ... national law in a way which, to the fullest extent possible, is consistent with the objectives laid down in [the invoked international agreement]'.[52] As a consequence, the Member State had to grant an environmental organisation access to a domestic court to challenge a decision taken following administrative proceedings liable to be contrary to EU environmental law, which had been foreseen by the international treaty provision at stake but not by domestic law.

At the same time, Article 351(2) TFEU obliges Member States to 'take all appropriate steps to eliminate the incompatibilities [with the Treaties]' where those result from Member State agreements concluded prior to their EU membership. In cases brought by the Commission, the CJEU held that Austria and Sweden had infringed their obligation to eliminate Treaty incompatibilities,[53] because they had kept in force international investment agreements that contained 'provisions which guarantee the free transfer, without undue delay and in freely convertible currency, of payments connected with an investment'.[54] The CJEU recognised that certain Treaty provisions[55] 'confer on the Council the power to restrict, in certain specific circumstances, movements of capital and payments between Member States and third countries',[56] and that it was the 'effectiveness' of those provisions that required their '[immediate application] with regard to the State to which they relate', possibly including some of the states signatories to the claimants' investment treaties.[57] While it could be argued that the Court identified a merely hypothetical incompatibility that might arise between the restrictive Council measures

---

[51] *Lesoochranárske zoskupenie VLK* (n 42) para 47 *et seq*. See also n 2 above.
[52] ibid para 50.
[53] Case C-205/06 *Commission v Austria*, Judgment, EU:C:2009:118, para 45; Case C-249/06 *Commission v Sweden*, Judgment, EU:C:2009:119, para 46.
[54] *Commission v Austria* (n 53) para 24 (investment agreements entered into with the Republic of Korea, the Republic of Cape Verde, the People's Republic of China, Malaysia, the Russian Federation and the Republic of Turkey); *Commission v Sweden* (n 53) para 25 (Argentine Republic, the Republic of Bolivia, the Republic of Côte d'Ivoire, the Arab Republic of Egypt, Hong Kong, the Republic of Indonesia, the People's Republic of China, the Republic of Madagascar, Malaysia, the Islamic Republic of Pakistan, the Republic of Peru, the Republic of Senegal, the Democratic Socialist Republic of Sri Lanka, the Republic of Tunisia, the Socialist Republic of Vietnam, the Republic of Yemen and the former Socialist Federal Republic of Yugoslavia).
[55] (Then) Arts 57(2), 59 and 60(1) EC.
[56] *Commission v Austria* (n 53) para 35; *Commission v Sweden* (n 53) para 36.
[57] *Commission v Austria* (n 53) para 36; *Commission v Sweden* (n 53) para 37.

and the Member States' investment agreement obligations vis-à-vis third states, it is suggested here that the Court aimed to protect 'effectively' the Treaty provisions that confer such power on the Council. It is not an abstract/general power of the Council in a particular policy area that might be exercised in one way or another, but specific instruments the exercise of which would foreseeably clash with Member States' guarantee to third states to allow for free transfer of capital. It is in the light of the effectiveness of Treaty provisions that the Court refers to the 'practical effectiveness of those [Council] measures', which would be incompatible with lengthy international treaty negotiations following the adoption of the Council's unilateral restrictive measures, or uncertain effects of the use of other international law mechanisms, such as suspension, or (partial) denunciation.[58] The Member States' expressed intention to introduce a clause reserving certain powers to regional organisations to ensure compatibility with their Treaty obligations was not considered sufficient, as no steps had yet been taken.[59] The Court concluded by stating that the effect of its ruling concerning the incompatibilities of investment agreements with third countries with the Treaty was not limited to the defendants in the present cases, and that the Member States had to assist each other and take a common attitude, facilitated by the Commission.[60] It was therefore the Court's effectiveness considerations concerning the application and implementation of Treaty provisions that led to the recognition of a positive duty on the Member States concerning their external action and interaction with non-EU states.

## B. Effectiveness of EU *Action*?

As shown in the previous paragraphs, the principle of effectiveness operates in the context of external relations in the same way as in the internal EU legal order in that it protects the full effect of EU *law*. In that respect, the principle of effectiveness has certainly had legal implications for the Member States' capacity to act as subjects of the international legal order, even though recognising a *principle* for that purpose might not add much to the more general question of the reach and binding nature of EU law vis-à-vis the Member States. What is less certain, however, is whether the principle of effectiveness triggers legal obligations for Member States also in the absence of EU law that either shapes a particular kind of external action[61] or confers expressly the capacity to act on the EU, which Member States should respect.[62] In other words, are there legal obligations of the Member States

---

[58] *Commission v Austria* (n 53) paras 39–40; *Commission v Sweden* (n 53) paras 40–41.
[59] *Commission v Austria* (n 53) paras 41–42; *Commission v Sweden* (n 53) paras 42–43.
[60] *Commission v Austria* (n 53) paras 43–44; *Commission v Sweden* (n 53) paras 44–45.
[61] See, eg, cases cited at n 39 above.
[62] See, eg, cases cited at n 53 above.

in the interest of protecting other aspects of (politically) desired effectiveness of the EU as a global actor, independently of specific (substantive) legal obligations or constraints under EU law that the principle of effectiveness can enforce? What have been the tools of the CJEU to ensure the functionality of the EU as actor on the international stage on the basis of effectiveness considerations?

In the *Mox Plant* case, the Commission had claimed, *inter alia*, that Ireland, by instituting arbitral proceedings within the framework of UNCLOS (a mixed agreement ratified by both the (now) EU and its Member States) had exercised competence that belonged to (what was then) the Community, and that this act was:

> liable to create confusion in non-member countries which are parties to the Convention with regard to the external representation and internal cohesion of the Community as a contracting party, and is highly damaging to the *effectiveness* and coherence of the Community's external action. (emphasis added)[63]

The CJEU held that Ireland had infringed both its obligation of having recourse to the CJEU for the settlement of intra-EU Member State disputes (now Article 344 TFEU), and its 'duty of prior information and consultation' of the competent Community institutions on the basis of the duty of cooperation (under (now) Article 4 TFEU and Article 192 of the European Atomic Energy Community Treaty).[64] Despite the reasoning submitted by the Commission, the Court did not address the implications of Ireland's conduct for the effectiveness of the Community's external *action*. Instead, the Court focused again on protecting the effectiveness of Community *law* and its uniform interpretation when considering that the Member State's submission of 'a dispute … to a judicial forum such as the Arbitral Tribunal involve[d] the risk that a judicial forum other than the Court will rule on the scope of obligations imposed on the Member States pursuant to Community law'.[65]

Yet, there have been other cases in which the CJEU has acknowledged Member State obligations, where the Court's reasoning has focused more on the EU's capacity to speak with one voice and act effectively as global actor than merely on the effective enforcement of EU law. In those cases, the Court has identified negative and positive Member State obligations that correlate with joined representation and/or an increased scope for manoeuvre of the EU institutions in the interest of the EU's effectiveness on the international stage. As a consequence, the capacity of the EU to act (effectively) on the international stage in itself gained significance. It is argued here that the Court has started to protect

[63] *Mox Plant* (n 47) para 159 *et seq.*
[64] ibid para 182.
[65] ibid para 177. In Opinion 2/13, EU:C:2014:2454, para 201 *et seq*, the CJEU confirmed its exclusive jurisdiction for disputes between Member States and between the EU and Member States, which required an 'express exclusion of the ECtHR's jurisdiction' in the accession agreement in order to be compatible with Art 344 TFEU.

the EU's external functionality as global actor through a combined application of the principles of effectiveness and sincere cooperation as laid down in Article 4(3) TEU. In that context, the Court has referred to concepts of coherence, consistency and unity to fill the gap of substantive EU law that could determine Member State external action. It has been on the basis of those concepts that the Court has provided the basis and rationale for Member State obligations that go beyond the mere enforcement of EU law in the interest of the EU's effectiveness as global actor in international fora. More specifically, as will be demonstrated through an analysis of relevant judgments in the following paragraphs, the Court has started to include effectiveness considerations to help its interpretation of the scope of the principle of sincere cooperation, and to give it substance in specific contexts.[66] It should be emphasised from the start, however, that the EU's capacity to act internationally itself or through the Member States, which has been protected by the Court in that context, continues to be firmly rooted in the internal EU legal order in that it had been legitimised by lawfully adopted EU law or other institutional acts. In that respect the reach of the principles of effectiveness and sincere cooperation is (again) comparable to the way they interact within the EU internal legal order.

In the light of the complexities of the EU legal order and division of (external) competences according to a variety of different policy areas, it comes as no surprise that different circumstances of external action should be distinguished and will provide the structure for the following discussion regarding the protection by the CJEU of the EU's functionality and effectiveness as global actor: first, the need to protect exclusivity of EU competence (where it exists) by requiring Member States to act as 'trustees' of the EU in international fora; and secondly, in areas of shared competence the recognition of Member State obligations in order to accommodate the EU as global actor next to its Member States.

## (i) Protecting Exclusivity: Member States as Trustees and the EU's Effective Say

The Court has protected the effectiveness of the EU as a global actor by obliging Member States to act as trustees of the EU in areas of exclusive competence where the EU is excluded from negotiating an international treaty or from taking measures within the framework of an international organisation.[67] Effectiveness considerations have been employed (beyond the establishment of exclusive

---

[66] For analysis of the discussed cases in the light of (predominantly) the principle of sincere cooperation, see P Eeckhout, *EU External Relations Law*, 2nd edn (Oxford, Oxford University Press, 2011) 241 *et seq*.

[67] See for a detailed analysis of relevant case-law until 2011, M Cremona, 'Member States as Trustees of the Union Interest: Participating in International Agreements on Behalf of the European Union' in A Arnull, C Barnard, M Dougan and E Spaventa (eds), *A Constitutional Order of States? Essays in EU law in Honour of Alan Dashwood* (Oxford, Hart, 2011) 435.

competence) when recognising Member State constraints regarding their operating at the international level. Such constraints have been recognised in order to allow for the full exercise of EU exclusive competence, as well as to avoid the adoption of rules without the input of the EU (either in the form of unilateral measures, international treaty law or measures adopted within an international organisation) that might affect EU rules. It is suggested that the principle of effectiveness has thereby interacted with the principle of conferral as well as the principle of sincere cooperation.

## (a) Unilateral Measures and Conclusion of Treaties

In a case brought by the Commission against the United Kingdom, the Commission had criticised the United Kingdom for adopting unilateral fishery conservation measures, *inter alia*, by claiming that 'measures of this type could not be effectively adopted except for the whole of the Community'.[68] Without referring to the principle of effectiveness, the Court held that:

> Member States are subject to special duties of action and abstention in a situation in which the Commission ... has submitted to the Council proposals which, although they have not been adopted by the Council, represent the point of departure for concerted Community action.[69]

In the absence of specific legal obligations under EU law to act in one way or the other, which could have been protected/enforced by the principle of effectiveness, Member States were reminded of their EU membership, which required them to make room for joint action once the EU had prepared the exercise of its competence. Such 'special duties' have been analysed against the principle of sincere cooperation and loyalty obligations of the Member States.[70] It is suggested here that effectiveness considerations underpinned the Court's reasoning. Making reference to the exclusive nature of the EU's competence, the Court reminded the Member States of their role as 'trustees of the common interest'.[71] The Court referred not only to other legislative measures that framed the matter, but also to 'requirements inherent in the safeguard by the [EU] of the common interest and the integrity of its own powers' when recognising:

> not only an obligation to undertake detailed consultations with the Commission and to seek its approval in good faith, but also a duty not to lay down national conservation measures in spite of objection, reservations or conditions which might be formulated by the Commission.[72]

---

[68] Case 804/79 *Commission v United Kingdom*, Judgment, EU:C:1981:93, para 9.
[69] ibid para 28; confirmed in Case C-266/03 *Commission v Luxembourg*, Judgment, EU:C:2005:341, para 59; and Case C-433/03 *Commission v Germany* [2005] ECR I-6985, para 65.
[70] See n 69 above.
[71] *Commission v United Kingdom* (n 68) para 30.
[72] ibid para 31.

It was therefore at least partially the capacity of the EU to exercise its exclusive competence effectively that justified Member State constraints.

The exercise of EU competence was also at stake in the context of Opinion 2/91 that concerned the adoption of a Convention on chemicals at work, which was negotiated within the International Labour Organization (ILO). The ILO does not allow for EU membership but deals with issues that fall within areas of exclusive and shared EU competence. As a consequence, the EU Council and Commission agreed on procedures regarding the negotiation of Conventions adopted by Member States in the context of the ILO. In Opinion 2/91, the Court held that external (what is now) EU competence had to be 'exercised through the medium of the Member States acting jointly in the [EU's] interest',[73] having held that the ILO Convention to be adopted fell within exclusive EU competence and aspects within shared competence.[74]

At the beginning of its observations on 'the substance' in Opinion 2/91, the Court stated, *inter alia*, that:

> the Community's tasks and the objectives of the Treaty would ... be compromised if Member States were able to enter into international commitments containing rules capable of affecting rules already adopted in areas falling outside common policies or of altering their scope.[75]

Even though the Court did not refer explicitly to (what is now) Article 4(3) TEU, this statement confirms the necessity for Member States to refrain from external action that would interfere with their legal obligations under the existing body of what was then Community law (see section III A above). Yet, the Court went beyond simply affirming such a negative Member State obligation. In order to (effectively) protect the existing body of Community law, Member States had to *cooperate* with the Community institutions when concluding and implementing a Convention of the ILO falling in part within EU and in part within Member State competence. The Court reiterated the importance 'to ensure that there is a close association between the institutions of the Community and the Member States both in the process of negotiation and conclusion and in the fulfilment of the obligations entered into'.[76] Because the Community was not entitled under international law to conclude an ILO Convention itself, the Member States had to do so as its 'medium'.[77] While the Court did not address any matters of 'effectiveness' of the Community on the international stage, the Court linked the duty of cooperation to the 'requirement of unity in the international representation of the Community'.[78] The Court thereby started to protect the united involvement

---

[73] Opinion 2/91 (n 11) para 5.
[74] Cremona, 'Member States as Trustees' (n 67) 437.
[75] Opinion 2/91 (n 11) para 11.
[76] ibid para 36.
[77] ibid para 37.
[78] ibid para 36. See also Opinion 2/94, EU:C:1996:140, para 108.

of the EU on the basis of the principle of loyalty, providing the basis and rationale for Member State obligations that go beyond the mere enforcement of EU law towards protecting the EU's effectiveness as global actor. The Court referred to the Community's unity as a global actor to support the recognition of Member States' positive obligations to involve the Community in their international law-making.

## (b) Other Measures within Treaty Regimes

In *Commission v Council*, the CJEU considered the arrangement between the Council and the Commission regarding their participation and voting rights in the UN Food and Agriculture Organization (FAO) to represent 'fulfilment of [the] duty of cooperation between the Community and the Member States in the FAO', and 'that the two institutions intended to enter into a binding commitment towards each other'.[79] The contested Council Decision, which indicated to the FAO that the draft agreement fell within shared competence and that the Member States had the right to vote, was considered by the CJEU to be in breach of the arrangement. In its reasoning, the Court stated, *inter alia*, that the Council had 'prevented the Commission from presenting the common position' and:

> since the content of the Agreement could still be changed until the time when the text was adopted, the fact that the right to vote was given to the Member States prevented the Community from having any *effective say* in the deliberations which would precede the final decision on the text of the Agreement. (emphasis added)[80]

Moreover, 'the fact that the Member States voted in accordance with the common position gave other States and the FAO the impression that the thrust of the Agreement did not fall within the exclusive competence of the Community'.[81] The inter-institutional agreement concretised the duty of cooperation, had legal effects for the institutions and the Member States (as represented by the Council) and could then be (effectively) protected, not least in the interest of an effective EU participation on the international stage. The Court protected the effectiveness of the Community as global actor by employing the principle of sincere cooperation (as further defined by the inter-institutional arrangement) in order to make space for the Community's position to be voiced at the international level without potentially conflicting Member State action.

As in the ILO (see previous section), the membership of the International Maritime Organization (IMO) is open only to states, and does not allow for participation of the EU.[82] All EU Member States are members of the IMO, but the IMO deals with many issues that fall within areas of EU competence, including

---

[79] *FAO* (n 11) para 49.
[80] ibid para 34.
[81] ibid para 35.
[82] Convention on the International Maritime Organization (adopted 6 March 1948, entered into force 17 March 1958) 289 UNTS 3, Art 4. The IMO has concluded a cooperation agreement with the EU, available at www.imo.org/en/About/Membership/Pages/IGOsWithObserverStatus.aspx.

environmental protection and maritime safety. In the *IMO* case, the Court had to decide on the capacity of Greece to submit a national position within the IMO for monitoring compliance with international rules.[83] Even though the parties agreed on the existence of EU exclusive competence in the area of transport at stake, it was controversial whether exclusive EU competence would only affect the conclusion of an international agreement,[84] or whether Member States were also prevented from taking unilateral measures within an international organisation because those measures (and its consequences) could be considered to be affecting EU rules.[85] In the view of the Commission, since the adoption of the Regulation implementing the relevant international agreement, the EU had 'enjoyed exclusive competence to assume international obligations in the area covered by that regulation'.[86] As a consequence, it was only the EU that could ensure proper application at EU level and discuss with other IMO contracting parties 'the correct implementation of or other subsequent developments in those standards'.[87]

The Court observed 'that, under Article 3(1)(f) EC, the setting of a common policy in the sphere of transport is specifically mentioned as one of the objectives of the [EU]', and that under (what was then) Article 10 EC 'the Member States must both take all appropriate measures to ensure fulfilment of the obligations arising out of the ... Treaty or resulting from action taken by the institutions and also abstain from any measure which might jeopardise the attainment of the objectives of the Treaty'.[88] According to the Court, as a consequence of reading those Treaty provisions together:

> to the extent to which [EU] rules are promulgated for the attainment of the objectives of the Treaty, the Member States cannot, outside the framework of the [EU] institutions, assume obligations which might affect those rules or alter their scope.[89]

On the one hand, the Court protected the effectiveness of existing EU rules against effects of international rules that might be adopted as a consequence of Member States' unilateral measures within the international organisation. On the other hand, the Court again seems to have relied on effectiveness considerations when interpreting the reach of the principle of sincere cooperation in the interest of a functional EU external action system: Member States had to refrain from unilateral action in order to protect the EU's actorness in an area of EU competence and respect EU objectives defined by the EU institutions (and their ability to define them) by acting jointly as trustees of the EU.

---

[83] Case C-45/07 *Commission v Greece (IMO)*, Judgment, EU:C:2009:81.

[84] See, eg, n 69 above.

[85] See M Cremona, 'Extending the Reach of the AETR Principle: Comment on *Commission v Greece* (C-45/07)' (2009) 34 *EL Rev* 754, 762.

[86] *IMO* (n 83) para 14.

[87] ibid para 14.

[88] ibid paras 15–16, with reference to Case 22/70 *Commission v Council*, Judgment, EU:C:1971:32, paras 20–21.

[89] ibid para 17, with reference to *Commission v Council* (n 88) para 22.

In the *OIV* case brought by Germany against the Council, the CJEU recently acknowledged the Council's capacity to adopt decisions under Article 218(9) TFEU[90] on EU positions to be adopted in an international organisation, even if the EU is itself not a party to the organisation's agreement.[91] Germany had requested the annulment of a Council Decision that established the position to be adopted on behalf of the EU with regard to certain resolutions to be adopted in the framework of the International Organisation of Vine and Wine (OIV). The EU only holds 'guest' status in the OIV, while 21 EU Member States are members of the organisation.[92] The challenged Council Decision had been adopted on the basis of Article 218(9) TFEU, which entitles the Council to '[establish] the positions to be adopted on the Union's behalf in a body set up by an agreement, when that body is called upon to adopt acts having legal effects'.[93] According to the Council and the Commission, this legal basis had been appropriate, as OIV recommendations relating to oenological practices and methods of analysis, to be adopted internationally following the Member States' involvement, were capable of causing changes of EU law,[94] as EU legislation referred to OIV standards, and thereby incorporated them into EU law.[95] According to Germany and other Member States supporting its claim, Article 218(9) TFEU was 'not applicable in the context of an international agreement which, like the OIV Agreement, has been concluded by the Member States and not by the European Union'.[96] The rules and practices covered by OIV recommendations did not fall within the area of exclusive EU competence but within the area of agriculture, for which the Member States retained (shared) competence.[97] Moreover, the recommendations could not be considered 'acts having legal effects', as OIV recommendations were not acts that were binding on the EU under international law; instead the legislation incorporating those recommendations were unilateral acts of the EU legislature, 'which [are] not capable of transforming those recommendations into binding acts of international law, particularly with regard to third countries'.[98] The Council contended that the EU

---

[90] Article 218(9) TFEU states that '[t]he Council, on a proposal from the Commission or the High Representative of the Union for Foreign Affairs and Security Policy, shall adopt a decision suspending application of an agreement and establishing the positions to be adopted on the Union's behalf in a body set up by an agreement, when that body is called upon to adopt acts having legal effects, with the exception of acts supplementing or amending the institutional framework of the agreement'.

[91] Case C-399/12 *Germany v Council*, Judgment, EU:C:2014:2258.

[92] ibid para 5.

[93] '9. The Council, on a proposal from the Commission or the High Representative of the Union for Foreign Affairs and Security Policy, shall adopt a decision suspending application of an agreement and establishing the positions to be adopted on the Union's behalf in a body set up by an agreement, when that body is called upon to adopt acts having legal effects, with the exception of acts supplementing or amending the institutional framework of the agreement.'

[94] Case C-399/12 *Germany v Council*, Opinion of AG Cruz Villalón, EU:C:2014:289, para 25.

[95] *Germany v Council* (n 91) para 46 *et seq.*

[96] ibid para 29.

[97] ibid para 34.

[98] ibid para 36.

had exclusive competence in the field and that what was decisive for the applications of Article 219(9) TFEU was that OIV recommendations have legal effects within the EU because of the EU legislature's decision to incorporate them into EU legislation.[99]

Following the Commission's argument, the Court held that the applied legal basis did not require the EU to be a party to the pertinent agreement, so the wording of Article 218(9) TFEU '[did not prevent] the EU from adopting a decision establishing a position to be adopted on its behalf'.[100] Moreover, the EU had competence for the common organisation of the wine markets, and the Member States were to '[act] jointly' in the interest of the EU by presenting an adopted EU position.[101] As a consequence, the lack of EU membership in the OIV did not prevent the EU from applying Article 218(9) TFEU.[102] The Court also held that the OIV recommendations contributed to the international harmonisation of practices and standards that were capable of 'decisively influencing' the content of EU legislation by incorporation.[103] It concluded that the Council had rightly used Article 218(9) TFEU as the basis for adopting the contested Decision.[104]

Similar to the *IMO* case, the Court had to address the interplay between the EU's capacity to exercise its competence through the Member States on the international stage, this time following the adoption of a Council Decision, and the Member States' retained capacity to act on the global stage as members of an international organisation. It is noteworthy that the Court did not refer to 'effectiveness' of EU law or action, even though, as observed by Cremona, the Court gave 'an interpretation to Article 218(9) TFEU that—while textual—was fundamentally influenced by the principle of effectiveness' and led the Court to conclude that the principle of conferral was not contravened.[105] While focusing on the EU's capacity to establish positions to be adopted in the international forum that had to be 'effectively' protected, the Court only implicitly recognised constraints on the EU Member States in that they had to refrain from exercising competence through international law-making in the context of agriculture, which the Court seemed to consider an exclusive EU competence in this case.[106] In addition to protecting the EU's own scope for manoeuvre, the reason for recognising such Member State constraint seemed again to be the fact that Member States' international involvement can have legal effects within the EU legal order and, as submitted by the Commission,[107] would therefore affect also those EU Member States that are

---

[99] ibid para 46.
[100] ibid paras 49–50.
[101] ibid paras 51–52.
[102] ibid para 55.
[103] ibid para 59 *et seq.*
[104] ibid para 66.
[105] See Marise Cremona, Chapter 1.
[106] According to Art 3(2) TFEU, '[t]he Union shall also have exclusive competence for the conclusion of an international agreement when its conclusion is provided for in a legislative act of the Union or is necessary to enable the Union to exercise its internal competence, or insofar as its conclusion may affect common rules or alter their scope'.
[107] *Germany v Council*, Opinion of AG Cruz Villalón (n 94) para 25.

not members of the OIV. In other words, the Court recognised legal constraints on Member States' international law-making activity: (a) to protect the effectiveness of a Treaty provision that enables the EU to pursue its objectives through its own law-making on the international stage; and (b) to protect the effectiveness of existing secondary EU law that would possibly be modified as a consequence of Member States' unilateral involvement in international law-making.

As shown in the previous paragraphs, the Court has been keen to protect the single voice of the EU in areas of exclusive competence, even where the EU has not been present in international fora. More specifically, the Court has recognised Member State obligations to act as trustees of the EU in order for the EU to exercise its powers in full. While the Court might have been in favour of protecting or increasing the capacity of the EU to act in international fora through its Member States, it was careful to link related Member State constraints to EU law and the EU legal order. On the one hand, the Court has protected the scope and means for the EU to exercise its *exclusive competence* effectively. On the other hand, the Court has protected *EU law* by constraining Member States' capacity to take measures on the international stage, such as their involvement in international treaty negotiation, or the adoption of unilateral measures outside or within an international organisation, that might change or clash with the relevant EU law. The Member States have been obliged to make room for the EU institutions to exercise EU competence once it has been conferred on the EU, and Member States have been prevented from triggering changes of, or challenges to, the existing body of EU law. We can therefore conclude that the protection of 'actorness' has been anchored in the principle of conferral and the binding nature of EU law for the Member States. At the same time, the Court relied on effectiveness considerations to interpret the reach of the principle of sincere cooperation under Article 4(3) TEU, which in turn provided the basis for establishing Member State duties.

## (ii) Accommodating the EU as Global Actor Next to its Member States

The previous section focused on the way in which the CJEU has protected the EU's actorness in areas of *exclusive* competence by imposing obligations on Member States regarding their international activities. The following section of the chapter focuses on cases in areas of *shared* competence in which the Court has protected the EU's actorness both in international treaty negotiations and within the ambit of existing international treaty regimes. What makes this area of case-law even more controversial than the one addressed in the previous section is that in areas of shared competence, both the EU and (some of) its Member States are recognised as relevant actors at the international level in principle. It is suggested that the Court has applied the reasoning established in the context of exclusivity in order to strengthen the effectiveness of the EU as global actor with the capacity to speak with one voice in international fora also where Member States continue to be present as separate subjects of the international legal order because of their (in theory) shared competence in the area. The Court has been willing to protect the effectiveness/functionality of the EU external action system, the EU's actorness, and objectives as defined by the institutions (and their ability to define them)—rather than the integration objective—when recognising Member State duties on the basis of Article 4(3) TEU. The Court's reasoning has been based on notions of uniformity and unity in the EU's international representation, filling the gap of EU law obligations regarding a particular Member State's 'behaviour'/conduct (such as substantive law (see section III A above) or the need to allow for the exercise of EU exclusive competence (see section III B (i) above). More specifically, the Court has interpreted the principle of sincere cooperation as imposing far-reaching Member State obligations to refrain from unilateral exercise of retained competence once such obligations were, according to the Court, triggered by EU institutional measures that preceded the actual exercise of EU shared competence and/or on the basis of expected effects of international measures on EU law. Again, it is suggested that it has been the effectiveness of the EU as global actor, as well as potential implications of unilateral Member State measures for the EU legal order, that underlie the Court's reasoning.

Already in Ruling 1/78, the Court held that the [then] Community's participation in an international convention in addition to its Member States was crucial to ensure that the convention would 'function [within the ambit of Community law] in an effective manner'.[108] Given that the Convention had not yet been ratified at this point, the situation was different from other cases, in which the effectiveness of international treaty provisions, which had become an integral part of the EU legal order, was at stake.[109] It is noteworthy that the Court linked effectiveness considerations regarding (what is now) the EU as global actor again to the principle of conferral in that it protected the exercise of EU competence within its limits.[110] Given that Member States had conferred competence on the EU, the EU's capacity to exercise such conferred competence also in international fora had to be protected, and (related to the outcome of such exercise in addition to Member States' involvement) it was necessary to conclude the international agreement in the form of a mixed agreement in order to ensure its effective implementation in the EU legal order once ratified.[111] The Court protected the 'actorness' of the Community by holding that:

> unilateral action by the Member States in this regard, even if it were collective and concerted action, would have the effect of calling in question certain of the essential functions of the Community and in addition of affecting detrimentally its independent action in external relations.[112]

In order for the Convention to be implemented, there needed to be a 'close association between the institutions of the Community and the Member States both in

---

[108] Ruling 1/78 (n 11) para 32. Even though the case concerned the EAEC Treaty and not the EEC Treaty, the Court placed this ruling into its case-law on the principle of loyalty under the EEC Treaty; see Eeckhout, *EU External Relations Law* (n 66) 242.

[109] See n 45 above.

[110] See for the principle of conferral Arts 4(1) and 5(1), (2) TEU.

[111] See n 47 above.

[112] Ruling 1/78 (n 11) para 33.

the process of negotiation and conclusion and in the fulfilment of the obligations entered into'.[113] The Court clarified that the Convention, once concluded by the Community, would become an integral part of Community law, its application would require close cooperation between the institutions and the Member States, and that implementing measures would need to be taken by the Community and the Member States in accordance with the division of competences provided by the Treaty.[114]

In sum, effectiveness considerations provided the basis for: (a) protecting the Community's capacity to exercise its competence conferred upon it by the Member States (even if at the expense of Member States' international treaty-making capacity); and (b) the future reach of the international convention once concluded and binding within the internal Member State/Community legal order. Rather than requiring the Member States to act as trustees of the Community during treaty negotiations (see previous section), the functionality and effectiveness of the Community as global actor in its own right was protected by imposing an obligation on its Member States to accommodate the Community in the relevant international forum. For this purpose, Member States had to ensure close association with the institutions during the negotiation and conclusion of the international convention, and to refrain from unilateral action that could undermine the EU's voice presented by the Commission on the international stage in areas of Community competence.

In cases brought by the Commission against Germany and Luxembourg in areas of shared competence, the CJEU held that:

> [t]he adoption of a decision authorising the Commission to negotiate a multilateral agreement on behalf of the Community marks the start of a concerted Community action at international level and requires for that purpose, if not a duty of abstention on the part of the Member States, at the very least a duty of close cooperation between the latter and the Community institutions in order to facilitate the achievement of the Community tasks and to ensure the coherence and consistency of the action and its international representation.[115]

The Court (again) did not refer to effectiveness considerations, and these cases also have been analysed as part of the case-law on the principle of sincere cooperation.[116] Yet, the Court's conclusions protected the Commission's capacity to negotiate (effectively) the multilateral agreement as it had been envisaged by the Council Decision. Member State obligations were the corollary to the Commission's scope for manoeuvre, and, in absence of a specific EU law provision on the content of what was to be negotiated at the international level, it was

---

[113] ibid para 34.
[114] ibid para 36.
[115] *Commission v Germany* (n 69) para 66, with reference to *Commission v Luxembourg* (n 69) para 60. As observed by Cremona in 'Extending the Reach of the AETR Principle' (n 85) 763, this situation differed from the situation in the case brought against Greece (*IMO*, see n 83 above), where the Community was considered to hold exclusive competence, so that there was no need for the 'start of concerted action' as had been identified in the cases against Luxembourg and Germany.
[116] See n 66 above.

the interest in the 'achievement of the Community tasks' and 'the coherence and consistence of the action in its international representation' that the Court aimed to protect. According to the Court, the Member States' measures to ratify and implement the agreement without consulting the Commission 'jeopardised the implementation of the Council Decision' and 'consequently the accomplishment of the Community's task and the attainment of the objectives of the Treaty'.[117] Even though the legally binding nature of the Council Decision could trigger the applicability of the principle of effectiveness as employed in the internal EU legal order in principle, the lack of content regarding the outcome of the international treaty negotiations made it difficult to link relevant Member State obligations to particular obligations resulting from the Council Decision (*effet utile*). It can be argued here that the Court started to refer to concepts of coherence, consistency and unity to fill the gap of substantive EU law that could have determined Member State external action by limiting the scope for international law-making (due to its conflicting content), or by imposing particular procedures. The capacity of the Community to act (effectively) on the international stage in itself gained significance. It has to be emphasised, however, that the Community's capacity to act internationally was firmly rooted in the internal legal order in that it had been legitimised by lawfully adopted Community law (here the Council Decision) that preceded the EU's exercise of shared competence.

The *PFOS* case added a further dimension to the Court's case-law when recognising, in the absence of a legal instrument adopted by the EU, Sweden's obligation to refrain from unilateral action in the context of a mixed agreement. While in previous cases the Court had identified Member State obligations to refrain from unilateral external action that would (a) infringe binding (substantive) EU law (*Centro-Com*);[118] or (b) undermine the EU's position as an international negotiator that had been conferred by a legally binding EU measure (*Commission v Germany*; *Commission v Luxembourg*),[119] the Court (c) recognised in *PFOS* that also an EU 'strategy, which although not a formally adopted decision may, as in this case, nonetheless carry implications for the Member States'.[120] The Court acknowledged that the identified EU 'strategy' imposed on Member States the obligation to refrain from unilateral action to protect the EU and its Member States' capacity to exercise 'their negotiating power with regard to other parties to [an international] Convention'.[121] The Court thereby further merged the principles of effectiveness and loyal cooperation by providing two different lines of reasoning.

---

[117] See, eg, *Commission v Germany* (n 69) paras 69, 73, and *Commission v Luxembourg* (n 69) paras 63, 67.

[118] *R ex p Centro-Com v HM Treasury and Bank of England* (n 39).

[119] See, eg, *Commission v Germany* (n 69); *Commission v Luxembourg* (n 69); see text at n 115 above.

[120] M Cremona, 'Case C-246/07, *Commission v Sweden (PFOS)*, Judgment of the Court of Justice (Grand Chamber) of 20 April 2010' (2011) 48 *CML Rev* 1639, 1640. See *PFOS* (n 10) paras 77 *et seq*, 89 *et seq*.

[121] See, eg, *PFOS* (n 10) para 104.

On the one hand, the Court referred to the consequences that Sweden's action could have for the EU through the 'adoption of international legal rules', which are binding on all parties to the Convention[122]—a reasoning again related to the effectiveness of EU law (see also *OIV*). In that respect, the CJEU seemed to consider it crucial that the EU law-making activities envisaged under the EU strategy (including the envisaged sequence of domestic and external law-making activities in the field)[123] would be 'effective', and that this would not be guaranteed if a Member State's unilateral action creates legally binding obligations also for the EU that conflict with the EU's own law-making activities. Because of the implications of Sweden's unilateral external action on the legal order of the EU, Sweden needed to refrain from such unilateral external action. On the other hand, the Court referred in *PFOS* to what it then called for the first time 'the *principle* of unity in the international representation of the Union and its Member States' (emphasis added) to constrain Member States' action related to their implementation of the Stockholm Convention, which had been concluded by the EU and its Member States as a mixed agreement.[124] It was thus not only the content of the strategy that Member States were asked to advocate on the international stage, but also the EU's ambition—arguably formulated in that strategy—to act jointly, and with one voice only, within the framework of the Stockholm Convention. In that respect, the Court built on its case-law on the principle of loyalty (eg Opinion 2/91).[125]

It is therefore argued here that the Member States' respect for such EU strategy and envisaged joint external action was required in the *PFOS* case to ensure

---

[122] ibid para 100 *et seq*.

[123] See n 10 above.

[124] *PFOS* (n 10) para 104; see also para 73 (with reference to prior decisions, in which the Court referred not to the 'principle' but to the 'requirement' of unity in the international representation of the Community. Also in the context of mixed agreements, the Court had stressed already in *FAO* (n 11) para 48, that it was essential to ensure close cooperation between the institutions and the Member States, both in the process of negotiation and conclusion and in the fulfilment of the commitments entered into; according to the Court 'that obligation to cooperate flows from the requirement of unity in the international representation of the Community' (with reference to Ruling 1/78 (n 11) paras 34–36; Opinion 2/91 (n 11) para 36; and Opinion 1/94 (n 11) para 108.

[125] As argued before, the requirement/principle of unity can hardly be considered as imposing an absolute obligation on Member States to adapt their external action to what the EU institutions do, or intend to do, merely on the basis of unity, without providing further justification for the existence of such principle of unity and its interrelationship with the allocation of competence; see Thies, 'Development of EU External Relations Law' (n 4) 157, with reference to the Opinion of AG Poiares Maduro in *PFOS*, who considered the unity of international representation of the (then) EC and its Member States not to have 'an independent value' but 'merely an expression of the duty of loyal cooperation under [then] Article 10 EC'; he stated that '[t]he question whether such unity is required by the duty of loyal cooperation can be resolved only by analysing the obligations laid down in a specific agreement'; see Case C-246/07 *Commission v Sweden*, Opinion of AG Poiares Maduro [2010] ECR I-3317, para 37. See, however, E Neframi, 'The Duty of Loyalty: Rethinking Its Scope through Its Application in the Field of EU External Relations' (2010) 47 *CML Rev* 323, 353, who considered the (then called) *requirement* of unity to be an autonomous external action objective, which is 'not an explicitly provided objective, but one deriving from the objective of the assertion of the EU identity on the international scene', which could be jeopardised by unilateral and diverging international action of the EU and the Member States.

the effectiveness of the EU legal order *and* the capacity of the EU institutions to exercise the EU's shared competence in a particular and united way.[126] The principle of sincere cooperation was interpreted as imposing constraints on Member States to make space for EU external action as envisaged by an EU institutional act (the strategy), which was of a non-legislative nature. While it has been highlighted elsewhere that the Court would need to clarify what formal criteria will need to be met to recognise an EU institutional act, which is not a legislative one, as legitimate trigger for further Member State constraints in areas of shared competence under Article 4(3) TEU,[127] it can be concluded here that it is the impact of effectiveness considerations on the interpretation of the principle of sincere cooperation that has provided the legal basis for Member State EU law obligations in the interest of the effectiveness of EU external action, going beyond the mere enforcement of Member States EU law obligations.

# IV. Conclusion

This chapter has added two observations to Marise Cremona's categorisation of the EU law principle of effectiveness as one of the systemic principles of EU law that is concerned with building the 'EU's identity … in the world'.[128]

First, the chapter suggested that the principle of effectiveness can indeed be considered systemic in that it protects EU law also in the context of EU and its Member States' external action, thus protecting the EU as an entity with its own law that Member States cannot derogate from when exercising their sovereignty in foreign affairs. In that respect, the CJEU has relied on effectiveness considerations in the same way as in the EU internal legal order where relevant EU *law* shaped external action of the EU and/or its Member States. Once EU law (a) has been adopted in the EU Treaties, in the form of secondary legislation (that defines or constrains future external action), or by ratification and adoption of an international agreement, and (b) is binding on the EU and/or its Member States, all relevant actors, namely the EU institutions and Member States, need to comply with it in their external action falling within the scope of EU law. The Court has

---

[126] Interestingly, according to AG Maduro in *PFOS*, Sweden's unilateral action was not affecting the capacity of the EU to exercise its competence by submitting proposals within the international organisation, nor would the EU be bound by the rules; Opinion of AG Poiares Maduro (n 125) para 38 *et seq.* Yet, he concluded that 'Sweden's actions may jeopardise the exercise of the Community's competence not because of their subject-matter, but because they undermine the Community's decision-making process' (para 47).

[127] A Thies, 'Shared Competence and the EU Member States' Obligation to Refrain from Unilateral Action: *PFOS* and Beyond' in J Díez-Hochleitner, C Martínez Capdevila, I Blázquez Navarro and J Frutos Miranda (eds), *Últimas tendencias en la jurisprudencia del Tribunal de Justicia de la Unión Europea [Recent Trends in the Case-law of the Court of Justice of the European Union] (2008–2011)* (Madrid, La Ley, 2012) 703–28, 714, 726–28.

[128] See n 5 above.

recognised Member State obligations to ensure the effective implementation of EU law when ruling on the reach of EU law obligations in Member State external action (*Centro-Com*);[129] the scope of obligations resulting from the EU's agreements with third states within the Member States' domestic legal orders (*Simutenkov*);[130] the obligations to renegotiate or withdraw from Member State agreements with third states to comply with EU Treaty obligations (*BITs* cases);[131] and, finally, the obligation to make room for the EU's decision formulating an EU position (based on the TFEU) to be adopted by those Member States party to an international agreement to which the EU is not itself a member and to refrain from unilateral action that could affect existing EU law (*OIV*).[132]

The second claim of this chapter is that the CJEU has started to protect the effectiveness or functionality[133] of the EU in its external action and, related to this, the EU's scope for manoeuvre as a global actor also in the absence of EU law that defines or constrains future external action. For this purpose, the CJEU has recognised Member State obligations on the basis of the principle of sincere cooperation in the light of effectiveness considerations regarding the EU's capacity to act in international fora. In such cases, one can identify, on the one hand, a correlation between the EU law constraints imposed on Member States in their capacity as subjects of the international legal order that are separate from the EU as a whole and, on the other, the Court's commitment to respect and protect the EU's own scope for manoeuvre and potential impact on the international stage. While EU law might continue to provide the core reasoning when recognising Member State obligations (eg the *acquis communautaire* argument in *PFOS*[134] and *OIV*),[135] there seems to be judicial commitment to allow for a (single) voice of the EU to be heard, with unified action and involvement at the international level, which requires the Member States' loyalty and commitment to the successful operation of the EU on the global stage. This is so even if it necessitates Member States refraining from unilateral action altogether (*PFOS*).[136] Yet, while this might further shape the constitutional space for EU external action, it has been pointed out throughout this chapter that Member State obligations have to be triggered by lawfully adopted EU acts, but not necessarily legislative measures of the EU institutions within the ambit of their capacity to further define EU objectives or take related initiatives.

---

[129] See n 39 above.

[130] See n 50 above.

[131] See n 53 above.

[132] See n 91 above.

[133] Arguing in favour of focusing on the importance of 'internal functionality' rather than effectiveness, see CJ Bickerton, *European Union Foreign Policy: From Effectiveness to Functionality* (Basingstoke, Palgrave Macmillan, 2011); according to Bickerton (118), 'foreign policy cooperation is oriented as much towards the balancing of the positions of different actors within the Union as it is to securing specific outcomes in theatres across the world',.

[134] See n 10 above.

[135] See n 91 above.

[136] See n 10 above.

To conclude, within the internal EU legal order, effectiveness considerations have been made by the CJEU with the ambition to protect EU law and the functioning of the EU legal order as a whole. The context of EU external action poses particular challenges to the application of the principle of effectiveness. More specifically, the interest in the effectiveness of the EU as a global actor goes beyond the shared goal of implementing EU law within all the Member States' legal orders, and of ensuring the functioning of the EU's internal legal order. EU external action involves political decision-making and participation in international fora. EU law principles cannot have any significant impact on the actual outcome of international negotiations or law-making in international organisations. Yet the degree of unity of EU positions to be presented in international fora and the implementation of international law binding on the EU are subject to rules stemming from the EU constitutional legal order. The Court has started to protect the EU's actorness by focusing on the unity of the EU's external voice. As stated above, the Court has relied on effectiveness considerations to interpret the reach of Member State obligations on the basis of the principle of effectiveness. It has thereby developed tools to strengthen the functionality of the EU external action system, in the absence of a substantive legal framework, relying on the recognition of the ability of the EU institutions to define objectives and take action, which imposes constraints on the Member States' capacity to take unilateral action as subjects of the international legal order.

However, the Court has so far been careful to link such tools and constraints back to EU law and the EU legal order, rather than recognising the autonomy of the EU as global actor per se, in order to justify the constraining effects the Court's decisions have had on Member States' own international scope for manoeuvre. This observation sheds new light on the recognition of effectiveness as a 'driver of constitutional evolution',[137] which has arguably become a self-perpetuating characteristic of European integration within the EU internal legal order. The CJEU faces challenges in the external sphere of EU action that exclude such development in that context: most importantly, the external dimension of EU action is neither embedded in the EU's core set of objectives regarding the internal market,[138] nor subject to a continuous judicial dialogue between the CJEU and national Member State courts that could ensure the acceptance and sustainability of EU law principles.[139] As a result, it remains crucial for the Court to link its decisions on what needs protection on the basis of effectiveness considerations and related Member State obligations back to EU law and the EU legal order in order to legitimise any further development of the constitutional and institutional framework in which EU external action takes place.

---

[137] See n 29 above.

[138] For the lack of final *telos* in EU external action, see Marise Cremona, Chapter 1.

[139] For a discussion of this and other constitutional challenges regarding the judicial development of general principles in the context of external relations, see Thies, 'General Principles in the Development of EU External Relations Law' (n 4) 159, 163.

# 12

## The Principle of Autonomy: An Adolescent Disease of EU External Relations Law?

JED ODERMATT

## I. Introduction

Autonomy means self-rule. An entity that possesses autonomy has the ability to choose a path for itself, without the influence, direction and control of others. Autonomy, however, is not absolute. It does not so much describe an absolute quality of an entity, but the relationship of that entity with others, and in particular the ability of that entity to define this relationship.[1] A legal body, such as the European Union, is 'autonomous' in relation to other actors or another legal order. In the context of the EU, the concept of autonomy is closely tied to the notion of the EU as a 'new legal order',[2] one of the foundational myths that were used to develop the building blocks of the Union legal order, such as direct effect and primacy. From its early days, this concept of internal autonomy—the idea that the EU is not only a new legal order, but also one that is distinct from its Member States—was instrumental in developing this EU legal order. As the EU developed greater external competences, and increased its interaction with external actors, questions arose regarding the EU's relationship with third states and other organisations and the effects that this might have on EU law. It was

---

[1] B de Witte, 'European Union Law: How Autonomous is Its Legal Order?' (2010) 65 *Zeitschrift für öffentliches Recht* 141, 142: '[T]he autonomy of EU law is not absolute but relative; it does not mean that EU law has ceased to depend, for its validity and effective application, on the national law of its member states, nor that it has ceased to belong to international law'. In this discussion on autonomy, 'self-rule' does not refer to the issue of *kompetenz-kompetenz* whereby a court has the competence to decide upon the extent of its jurisdiction.

[2] Case C-26/62 *Van Gend en Loos v Administratie der Belastingen*, Judgment, EU:C:1963:1: '[T]he Community constitutes a new legal order of international law'; Case 6/64 *Costa v ENEL*, Judgment, EU:C:1964:66: 'By contrast with ordinary international treaties, the EEC Treaty has created its own legal system'. See JHH Weiler, 'The Transformation of Europe' (1991) 100 *Yale Law Journal* 2403; JHH Weiler and UR Haltern, 'The Autonomy of the Community Legal Order: Through the Looking Glass' (1996) 37 *Harvard International Law Journal* 411.

in this context that the Court of Justice of the European Union (CJEU) turned towards external autonomy, that is, the idea that the integrity of EU law and the EU legal order should not be undermined by the international action of the Union or the Member States. While the internal and external elements of autonomy are closely entwined, this chapter focuses on the external element, an issue that is now an important one in the law of EU external relations.

The EU Treaties do not refer explicitly to the principle of autonomy, and it has mostly been developed through the jurisprudence of the CJEU. Although the term has only been employed in more recent case-law, the principle has a longer history. Early discussions about the principle of autonomy focused on this internal threat, that is, the EU's autonomy vis-à-vis its Member States. One can see how it would be difficult to develop an EU legal order if the Member States were able to dismiss EU law because it conflicts with their own legal systems or national legislation. The concept of autonomy was therefore important in developing the principles of direct effect and primacy, which are based on the idea that the EU represents a new legal order, one that differs from the system of public international law. Barents argues, for instance, that '[a]lthough the EC is based on a document which bears the name "treaty", this has but a formal meaning. In a material sense the EC Treaty has the character of an autonomous constitution and, as a result, it constitutes the exclusive source of Community law'.[3] In *Costa*, the Court referred to EU law as 'an independent source of law'[4] and makes a strong link between this idea of the EU as a 'new legal order' and the concept of autonomy. The fact that the Union had legal personality and powers, exercised independently of the EU Member States, was not always self-evident, and had to be developed over time. The idea of the EU legal order as autonomous and independent played a significant role in this development.

The focus on internal autonomy gave way to a protection of the external dimension of autonomy. The EU further developed its relations with external actors and has participated in its own right at the international level; it seeks to influence, and is influenced by, its complex interactions with other entities. As these interactions have become more common and more complex, a new 'threat'[5] emerged: the idea that EU law could be undermined, not only by conflicting national legislation, but by international law. This not only means that international law and EU law may come into direct conflict. It also means that international law may not always recognise the separate actorness of the EU, in the sense that it may view the Union, not as a distinct legal entity on the international plane, but as merely a reflection of the collective will of the EU Member States, or may treat EU law as simply an international law regime, with all that means in terms of hierarchy of norms and rules of treaty conflict. The concept of autonomy, first developed with regard to

---

[3] R Barents, *The Autonomy of Community Law* (The Hague, Kluwer Law International, 2004) 112.
[4] *Costa v ENEL* (n 2).
[5] M Parish, 'International Courts and the European Legal Order' (2012) 23 *European Journal of International Law* 141, 142: 'A new threat has recently emerged to the consistent application of EU law, namely interpretation of EU law by the ever growing range of international tribunals that sit outside the domestic legal order of any particular state'.

the relationship between the Union and the Member States, became a concept that would help navigate the EU's relationship with the wider international legal order.

This chapter discusses how the concept of autonomy has developed into a principle in EU external relations law and how it relates to other systemic principles such as effectiveness and coherence. It discusses how the CJEU has developed a relatively narrow principle into a more broad and overarching concept, one that determines how the EU should interact with other entities and the wider international legal order. Section II discusses the concept of autonomy in international law and international organisations. The principle of autonomy is not unique to the EU legal order, but is touched upon in discussions about international organisations generally. The chapter then turns to the question of how autonomy has developed as a self-standing principle in EU law. It focuses on how the principle of autonomy has been given effect in two key fields of EU external relations. Section III discusses the principle of autonomy in relation to the EU's participation in forms of dispute settlement outside those established by the Treaties. Section IV then turns to the question of how the Court deals with norms that originate outside the EU legal order, in particular its relationship with international law. These are only two manifestations of the principle of autonomy, which has developed into a more all-encompassing constitutional principle. This was revealed in Opinion 2/13, in which the Court ruled that the agreement designed to allow the EU to become a contracting party to the European Convention on Human Rights was rejected because it 'is liable adversely to affect the specific characteristics of EU law and its autonomy'.[6] While the Court's reasoning is open to criticism, its conclusions are perhaps less surprising when viewed as the latest judgment in a line of case-law in which the principle of autonomy has developed into a broad and far-reaching principle. In contrast to some of the other principles discussed in this volume, the precise meaning of autonomy, and the limits of the concept, are still being developed. The final section discusses how the Court's application of autonomy can have negative effects. It discusses how, by seeking to protect the EU legal order, the application of this principle may also impede the effectiveness of the EU's external action and compromises its ability to act on the international plane. The Court's focus is almost entirely on what might be called the negative dimension of autonomy; it is about ensuring that the EU legal order is protected from external threats. It is less concerned, however, with the positive dimension of autonomy, which entails providing the EU with the ability to act effectively as a distinct actor on the international stage.

'Autonomy' has been described as a 'concept'[7] or as an 'idea'[8] but should it be regarded as a legal principle in the same way as other principles discussed in this

---

[6] Opinion 2/13, EU:C:2014:2454.

[7] N Tsagourias, 'Conceptualizing the Autonomy of the European Union' in R Collins and ND White (eds), *International Organizations and the Idea of Autonomy* (London, Routledge, 2011) 339: 'The concept of autonomy has been embedded in the legal and political culture of the European Union and has been the harbinger of important legal and political developments'.

[8] R Collins and ND White (eds), *International Organizations and the Idea of Autonomy* (London, Routledge, 2011).

volume? As Marise Cremona explains, principles, unlike rules, are norms of a fundamental character, and rules must conform to these underlying principles. 'Autonomy' may appear quite different from other structural principles, such as the duty of sincere cooperation, or the principle of transparency. Indeed, autonomy is often presented as a more foundational concept, one that differs from other principles, such as direct effect and primacy.[9]

The concept of autonomy was instrumental in developing these foundations of the EU legal order, but it was not until later that the concept of autonomy developed into a more concrete principle in EU external relations law. Principles are of a general character, but may be translated into more specific rules. In the cases discussed in this chapter, we see how the Court translates the principle of autonomy into more specific rules. These are *manifestations* of the autonomy principle, not elements of the principle itself. For instance, the obligation under Article 344 of the Treaty on the Functioning of the European Union (TFEU), whereby EU Member States may not submit disputes on EU law to any method of dispute settlement other than those provided in the EU Treaties, is one such manifestation of the principle. The rule is designed to protect and preserve the integrity and unity of EU law. Yet one should not equate these particular manifestations, such as the protection of the Court's judicial monopoly, with the principle itself. Further, even in instances where the Court does not explicitly invoke autonomy, the underlying principle may still be the motivating force behind the Court's reasoning. As shown in section IV, the principle of autonomy can help explain the Court's approach to the reception of international law in the EU legal order, even if the term 'autonomy' is seldom invoked explicitly.

## II. Autonomy in International Law

The debate about autonomy arises not only in relation to the European Union; it is also a phenomenon that is discussed more widely in public international law. In particular, 'autonomy' is debated in international law and international relations literature, when it concerns the degree to which international organisations exercise independent powers. This stems from a foundational issue at the heart of all international organisations. On the one hand, international organisations are composed of states, and their founding instruments are normally international legal instruments, often a treaty, entered into by those states. The organisation remains dependent upon its members, both in terms of its legal existence, but also

---

[9] J-W van Rossem, 'The Autonomy of EU Law: More is Less?' in RA Wessel and S Blockmans, *Between Autonomy and Dependence: The EU Legal Order under the Influence of International Organisations* (The Hague, TMC Asser Press, 2013) 13, 18: 'In any event, the bottom line of this argument is that autonomy is not exactly in the same league as, say, primacy, fundamental rights protection or judicial review, but forms the premise upon which such fundamental principles of EU law are built'.

in terms of its day-to-day functioning. Decision-making, funding, and the actions of an international organisation, often require the input of the member states. On the other hand, when an international organisation with legal personality is created, a new legal subject is established, one that may possess a certain level of autonomy from its membership. This reflects the underlying paradox of international organisations: they are at the same time made up of states and constrained by their founding instruments, but have also been tasked with the powers and institutional structures to act with a certain level of independence *from* those states. As the International Court of Justice stated in the *Legality of Nuclear Weapons* case, one of the intentions of treaties establishing international organisations 'is to create new subjects of law endowed with a certain autonomy'.[10] The level of autonomy enjoyed by a given organisation differs from organisation to organisation.

The autonomy of international organisations is often presented as a positive development in international law.[11] The international legal order is still one dominated by states. When an international organisation is capable of developing a certain degree of autonomy from its members, this can be seen as strengthening international law, since an international organisation may be more likely to achieve its foundational objectives without being hindered by the political interests of states. In this way, the development of greater institutional autonomy addresses a certain flaw in the international legal order, that is, the fact that state interests and geopolitics can prevent an international organisation from fully exercising its functions and realising its objectives.[12] This development of an autonomous legal order is thus often viewed as a form of institutional maturity. In an international legal order which is characterised as decentralised, state-centric and lacking enforcement mechanisms, the development of international institutions possessing a greater degree of autonomy can be viewed as a positive development, one that strengthens the effectiveness of international law.[13]

This is the 'internal' dimension of autonomy. It refers to the relationship between an international organisation and its members and the degree to which an organisation exercises independent powers. While the autonomy of

---

[10] *Legality of the Use by a State of Nuclear Weapons in Armed Conflict* (Advisory Opinion) [1996] ICJ Rep 66, 75.

[11] 'For some time, in fact, the assumption amongst many international lawyers seems to have been that whatever independence and influence an organization gained at the expense of its member states was necessarily good for the functioning of the organization and, in turn, whatever was good for the functioning of the organizations was necessarily beneficial for the advancement of international law.' R Collins and ND White, 'Introduction and Overview' in R Collins and ND White (eds), *International Organizations and the Idea of Autonomy* (London, Routledge, 2011) 2.

[12] '[T]he lack of institutional autonomy in international law is seen as the fundamental stumbling block in the way of realizing an international rule of law': ibid 23.

[13] '[I]t cannot be excluded that autonomy has been seized upon by international legal scholars as a political banner under which one could demonstrate support for the role of international institutions—seen as a necessarily positive development—as opposed to the sovereign prerogatives of states, seen as harmful to the general interest.' J D'Aspremont, 'The Multifaceted Concept of Autonomy of International Organizations: A Challenge to International Relations Theory?' in R Collins and ND White (eds), *International Organizations and the Idea of Autonomy* (London, Routledge, 2011) 63, 77.

international organisations can have certain positive elements, states are wary of allowing an organisation to develop too much, lest it become a Frankenstein's monster, a body that is able to act without the necessary level of control by its members.[14]

Autonomy can also describe the relationship from the other angle, that is, the relationship between the organisation and public international law more generally.[15] In this case, autonomy refers, first, to the extent to which the organisation has become an independent actor in its own right on the international plane. It also describes the extent to which the legal order has developed to become somewhat 'impermeable' to external influences.[16] This argument can be found, for example, in the discussion of self-contained regimes in international law. A self-contained regime is a 'sub-system' of international law; not only does it regulate a certain sphere of activity, it also contains its own secondary rules, largely (or completely) replacing general international law.[17] The International Law Commission's study on the fragmentation of international law recognises that a system may develop into a self-contained regime over time.[18] The EU legal order has for a long time been described as a self-contained regime in international law,[19] although whether the EU should be considered as a fully self-contained regime remains disputed.[20] International lawyers are beginning to recognise that international organisations can also possess this type of 'external' autonomy.

The two elements of autonomy are closely entwined. Internal autonomy can be seen as beneficial to the international legal order, as it allows the organisation to contribute to the international community by taking decisions independently of states. At the same time, as the organisation develops greater internal autonomy, it may seek to act in a 'state-like' manner by seeking to protect and preserve its institutional autonomy from *external* influences. In this way, the organisation, like a state, begins to give normative priority to its internal legal order over obligations

---

[14] See A Guzman, 'International Organizations and the Frankenstein Problem' (2013) 24 *European Journal of International Law* 999.

[15] F Dopagne, 'Sanctions and Countermeasures by International Organizations: Diverging Lessons for the Idea of Autonomy' in R Collins and ND White (eds), *International Organizations and the Idea of Autonomy* (London, Routledge, 2011) 178, 187: 'The autonomy of the international organization can indeed refer either to the relationship between the latter and its member states or to the link between the legal system of the organization and general international law'.

[16] 'Autonomy as institutional independence is also what gives the organization the possibility of acting as an independent member of the international community', D'Aspremont, 'The Multifacted Concept of Autonomy of International Organizations' (n 13) 70.

[17] E Klein, 'Self-Contained Regime', *Max Planck Encyclopedia of Public International Law*, available at opil.ouplaw.com/home/EPIL.

[18] International Law Commission, *Fragmentation of International Law: Difficulties Arising from the Diversification and Expansion of International Law*, UN Doc A/CN.4/L.682 (13 April 2006) 1–256, and UN Doc A/CN.4/L.702 (18 July 2006) para 157.

[19] Weiler, 'The Transformation of Europe' (n 2) 2422: 'The Community legal order ... is a truly self-contained legal regime with no recourse to the mechanism of state responsibility, at least as traditionally understood'.

[20] See B Simma and D Pulkowski, 'Of Planets and the Universe: Self-contained Regimes in International Law' (2006) 17 *European Journal of International Law* 483, 518.

stemming from international law. The principle of autonomy, therefore, is not only relevant in relation to the EU legal order, but is a concept discussed regarding international organisations generally.

While autonomy exists as a concept in public international law, it has developed into a self-standing principle with a more precise legal meaning in EU law. In the context of the EU's external relations, autonomy may be termed a structural principle in that it plays an important role in establishing the EU as an international actor with the ability to determine its interaction with other international legal regimes. The way in which this principle has been developed and applied in practice is discussed in the next sections.

## III. Autonomy and Judicial Competition

One of the main ways in which the principle of autonomy manifests itself in the external relations case-law is when the Court seeks to preserve its exclusive jurisdiction to interpret and apply EU law. These cases all relate to the EU's and the Member States' participation in forms of judicial dispute settlement outside the context of those set out in the Treaties. The Court has held that in principle, the EU and its Member States are open to use other such modes of settlement, and may join a treaty that employs binding methods of dispute settlement. However, the Court has set out certain conditions, the most important of which is that such participation must not violate the autonomy of the EU legal order.[21] The Court's aim is to ensure that no body other than the CJEU is capable of interpreting and applying EU law, even indirectly. It has been argued that this stems from the 'selfishness' of the Court.[22] De Witte, for instance, argues that the autonomy of the EU legal order 'is put forward as a rhetorical shield to help to protect the Court's own exclusive jurisdiction' in a way that is 'rather unfriendly towards the "rest" of international law'.[23] The principle of autonomy is not designed only for the benefit of the Court, however; it is also for the benefit of the EU legal order. The Court's desire to ensure uniform and consistent interpretation of EU law stands as a valid reason for asserting autonomy. Seen in this way, the Court's protection of its judicial monopoly is a means by which to preserve this autonomy, and is not only motivated by a need to preserve its own prerogatives and powers.

---

[21] See Opinion 1/91, EU:C:1991:490, para 40: 'An international agreement providing for such a system of courts is in principle compatible with Community law. The Community's competence in the field of international relations and its capacity to conclude international agreements necessarily entails the power to submit to the decisions of a court which is created or designated by such an agreement as regards the interpretation and application of its provisions'.

[22] B de Witte, 'A Selfish Court? The Court of Justice and the Design of International Dispute Settlement Beyond the European Union' in M Cremona and A Thies (eds), *The European Court of Justice and External Relations Law: Constitutional Challenges* (Oxford, Hart Publishing, 2014) 33.

[23] De Witte, 'European Union Law' (n 1) 150.

One can understand how rival courts and tribunals interpreting EU law in a way that diverges from that of the CJEU may have the effect of undermining the unity and consistent application of EU law. The problem, however, is that the preservation of this goal can often come at the expense of another important goal, namely the EU's effective participation in the international legal order.

The Court's judicial monopoly is safeguarded by Article 344 TFEU:

> Member States undertake not to submit a dispute concerning the interpretation or application of the Treaties to any method of settlement other than those provided for therein.

It is not self-evident that this provision is intended to apply to the participation of the EU Member States in international dispute settlement mechanisms. Since *MOX Plant*,[24] this provision has been applied to the participation of the EU and the Member States within international dispute settlement mechanisms. Article 344 TFEU raises a number of questions. What should be considered another 'method of settlement', especially when there is a vast array of dispute settlement mechanisms? Does this apply only to judicial bodies, or also to non-judicial dispute resolution procedures? When does a dispute concern the 'interpretation or application of the Treaties'? Is this the case, for example, when the rival court or tribunal is called upon to interpret EU law only indirectly, such as provisions of an agreement that closely resemble EU law? Moreover, does it apply to interpretations of EU law that are merely incidental or procedural, such as in identifying the appropriate party in a case? Or, more radically, does it mean that the EU is prevented from joining a dispute settlement body simply because there is a *possibility* that Member States *might* bring claims against one another concerning EU law? Is it concerned only with inter-Member State disputes or is it an expression of a more general principle of exclusivity of jurisdiction? In answering these questions, the Court has had to strike a balance between preserving its judicial monopoly, on the one hand, and allowing the EU to participate in international dispute settlement, on the other.

The Court addressed many of these questions in *MOX Plant*,[25] a case that arose from a dispute between the United Kingdom and Ireland regarding a nuclear facility situated on a site at Sellafield in the United Kingdom, on the coast of the Irish Sea. Ireland instituted arbitral proceedings against the United Kingdom at the international level, pursuant to the dispute settlement provisions in UNCLOS.[26] The European Commission regarded Ireland's use of arbitral proceedings as a violation of EU law and brought proceedings against Ireland, *inter alia*, for failing to fulfil its obligations under Article 292 of the EC Treaty (TEC) (now Article 344 TFEU). While the arbitral tribunal considered that it had prima facie jurisdiction, it noted that the dispute between Ireland and the United Kingdom before

---

[24] Case C-459/03 *Commission v Ireland (MOX Plant)*, Judgment, EU:C:2006:345.
[25] ibid.
[26] United Nations Convention on the Law of the Sea (UNCLOS), Art 287 (adopted 10 December 1982, entered into force 16 November 1994) 1833 UNTS 3, and UNCLOS, Art 1, Annex VII.

the CJEU would be binding under EU law, and might therefore lead to conflicting decisions. The tribunal decided to suspend the proceedings.[27]

The Commission argued that the dispute between Ireland and the United Kingdom was essentially a dispute concerning the interpretation of EU law, and that the CJEU therefore had exclusive jurisdiction to hear the dispute. The Court found that Ireland, by submitting the dispute to an arbitral tribunal, had breached its obligation under Article 292 TEC. The judgment drew a certain amount of criticism from academics in both EU law and international law.[28] Klabbers, for instance, argued that 'the Court's attitude is worrisome: it does aspire to build a fence around EU law, thus running the risk of placing the EU outside international law'.[29] Prost argued that the judgment 'artificially "Communitarises" whole portions of the law of the sea and asserts, in absolute terms, the autonomy and superiority of the Community system over the universal regime of the UN'.[30] Much of the criticism stemmed from the fact that the Court examined the issues solely through the lens of EU law, without acknowledging that the wider dispute concerned issues of international law and dispute settlement.[31] The judgment is also important in that the Court invoked the principle of autonomy in order to determine the relationship between EU law and the international legal order more generally. It held that an international agreement could not 'affect the allocation of responsibilities defined in the Treaties and, consequently, the autonomy of the Community legal system'.[32] Autonomy is not used here just to preserve the role of the Court, but as a way to protect the allocation of responsibilities in the EU legal order.

In *Mox Plant*, Article 292 TEC was used as a means to prevent Member States from bringing disputes against one another involving EU law. It allowed the Commission to initiate proceedings on the basis of Article 344 in cases where a Member State has made use of international dispute settlement processes against another EU Member State. But could the very *possibility* of the Member States bringing these proceedings in the first place violate Article 344 TFEU? This question was addressed in Opinion 2/13. Article 33 of

---

[27] See President's Statement of 13 June 2003, *Ireland v United Kingdom (MOX Plant)*, available at http://pcacases.com/web/sendAttach/877, para 11: 'The Tribunal considers that a situation in which there might be two conflicting decisions on the same issues would not be helpful to the resolution of this international dispute. Nor would such a situation be in accord with the dictates of mutual respect and comity that should exist between judicial institutions deciding on rights and obligations as between States, and entrusted with the function of assisting States in the peaceful settlement of disputes that arise between them'.

[28] 'For an international lawyer, this is a stunning case.' M Koskenniemi, 'International Law: Constitutionalism, Managerialism and the Ethos of Legal Education' (2007) 1 *European Journal of Legal Studies* 8, 9.

[29] J Klabbers, *Treaty Conflict and the European Union* (Cambridge, Cambridge University Press, 2009) 148.

[30] M Prost, *The Concept of Unity in Public International Law* (Oxford, Hart Publishing, 2012) 42–43.

[31] '[T]he Court analysed matters primarily, if not solely, through the prism of Community law.' S Boelaert-Suominen, 'The European Community, the European Court of Justice and the Law of the Sea' (2008) 23 *International Journal of Marine and Coastal Law* 643, 676.

[32] *MOX Plant* (n 24) para 123.

the European Convention on Human Rights (ECHR) allows contracting parties to bring inter-state disputes. The Court found that the 'very existence of such a possibility' of the EU or Member States utilising Article 33 ECHR with respect to a dispute involving EU law would violate Article 344 TFEU.[33] The Court stresses that the ability to bring such a dispute to the European Court of Human Rights (ECtHR) 'goes against the very nature of EU law'.[34] It does not seek to prevent, as in *Mox Plant*, Member States from initiating proceedings against one another, it prevents them from entering into an agreement that allows for such a possibility.

The issue of inter-state disputes does raise concerns about autonomy. This is because the ECHR Accession Agreement would have allowed EU Member States to bring proceedings before the ECtHR that deal with issues of EU law, without the CJEU having been able to address those issues. The issue of inter-state proceedings was also addressed in the View[35] of Advocate General Kokott. However, as she rightly points out, such an issue can be fully addressed using the EU's own institutional framework, such as the Commission initiating proceedings against the Member State, as was the case in *Mox Plant*. Kokott also stresses that numerous international agreements to which the EU and the Member States are party already allow for inter-state proceedings. If it were the case that a proposed agreement must *expressly* forbid inter-state cases in order to be valid under EU law, then 'this would implicitly mean that numerous international agreements which the EU has signed in the past are vitiated by a defect, because no such clauses are included in them'.[36]

The Court is requiring a principle of EU law, one that is already adequately safeguarded using the EU's own constitutional controls, to be addressed through a clause in an international agreement. By requiring 'the express exclusion of the ECtHR's jurisdiction'[37] over these inter-state disputes, the Court significantly expands the requirements under Article 344. It does not merely require Member States to refrain from a certain action; it obliges them to include in an international agreement a provision that excludes the dispute settlement body's jurisdiction over certain cases. No such clause can be found in the World Trade Organization (WTO) Agreement or UNCLOS, and the Court does not explain clearly why the ECHR situation differs from these other forms of dispute settlement. The Court's rationale, that 'if the EU or Member States did in fact have to bring a dispute between them before the ECtHR, the latter would, pursuant to Article 33 of the ECHR, find itself seized of such a dispute'[38] applies equally to

---

[33] Opinion 2/13 (n 6) para 208.
[34] ibid para 212.
[35] Opinion 2/13, View of AG Kokott, EU:C:2014:2475, para 118: 'In my view, the possibility of conducting infringement proceedings (Articles 258 TFEU to 260 TFEU) against Member States that bring their disputes concerning EU law before international courts other than the Court of Justice of the EU, with the added possibility that interim measures may be prescribed within those proceedings if necessary (Article 279 TFEU), is sufficient to safeguard the practical effectiveness of Article 344 TFEU'.
[36] ibid para 117.
[37] Opinion 2/13 (n 6) para 213.
[38] ibid para 209.

these other forms of settlement. This is an example of how the Court's approach to the principle of autonomy emphasises the negative dimension, that is, the desire to protect the EU legal order *from* international law. Yet this requirement, by stipulating that the Union can only take part in dispute settlement procedures when such a clause exists, undermines the EU's positive autonomy. Such an interpretation of Article 344 jeopardises the EU's ability to participate effectively in the wider international legal order. By requiring that internal issues be taken into account at the international level, the Court has made it more difficult in practice for the Union to take part in these agreements.[39]

The Court also employed the principle of autonomy in its reasoning in Opinion 1/91, in which it was asked to decide on the compatibility of the European Economic Area (EEA) Agreement with the Treaties. In contrast with *Mox Plant*, this and similar cases relate to proposed agreements that include forms of dispute settlement. The Court has held consistently that such a dispute settlement body should only have jurisdiction to interpret and apply the international agreement at issue, and should not be capable of interpreting EU law. While this may seem a rather straightforward requirement, this can be quite complex in practice, particularly in the cases of a mixed agreement, where the EU and Member States are both parties. One of the questions that arose in relation to the EEA Agreement was whether the Court of the European Economic Area, established by the agreement, would be interpreting and applying EU law. In particular, since the EU and the Member States were parties alongside one another, the EEA Court would have had the power to determine who would be the correct party in a given case, either the Member State(s) or the Community. According to the Court, this conferral of jurisdiction would allow the EEA Court to rule upon the allocation of competences of the Community and the Member States, and therefore, would 'likely adversely affect the allocation of responsibilities defined in the Treaties and the autonomy of the Community legal order'.[40] As in *Mox Plant*, the Court is essentially safeguarding its judicial prerogative, but it is doing so in order to protect the allocation of responsibilities in the EU legal order.

We see similar issues being played out, for instance, when the EU seeks to participate in agreements covering investor-state dispute settlement, especially now that the Union has competence in the field of foreign direct investment.[41] The text of the Canada–EU Comprehensive Economic and Trade Agreement (CETA),

---

[39] T Locke, 'The Future of the European Union's Accession to the European Convention on Human Rights after Opinion 2/13: Is It Still Possible and is It Still Desirable?' (2015) 11 *European Constitutional Law Review* 239, 255: 'This stance again reveals the Court of Justice's lack of trust in the EU's own legal order. The consequence of this is that the EU is becoming an even more awkward partner on the international plane. Requiring the protection of the autonomy of EU law in a watertight manner requires an externalisation of internally resolvable issues, which is new and worrying because it makes the EU a difficult partner to deal with'.

[40] Opinion 1/91 (n 21) 6.

[41] See H Lenk, *Investor-State Arbitration Under TTIP: Resolving Investment Disputes in an (Autonomous) EU Legal Order*, Swedish Institute for European Policy Studies (SIEPS) 2015:2. Articles 206 and 207 TFEU explicitly mention 'foreign direct investment' as part of the EU Common Commercial Policy.

for instance, includes a 'domestic law clause' (Article 8.31(2) 'Applicable Law and Interpretation') under which the tribunal 'shall not have jurisdiction to determine the legality of a measure, alleged to constitute a breach of this Agreement, under the domestic law of the disputing Party'. The inclusion of such a clause was intended to preserve the judicial monopoly of the CJEU to interpret EU law. Whether this would be enough to satisfy the Court, especially in light of Opinion 2/13, remains debatable, since it may still allow an incidental review of EU law.[42]

In Opinion 2/13, the Court discussed a different institutional innovation designed to protect EU autonomy: the co-respondent mechanism. This procedure was designed to allow both the EU and a Member State to become parties to ECtHR proceedings and was introduced primarily in order to prevent the ECtHR from making rulings on who is the correct party to a case involving the EU and/or its Member States, and thereby indirectly ruling on issues of competence.[43] The CJEU found that the design of the co-respondent procedure still violated the autonomy of the EU legal order. In certain circumstances, the ECtHR would have been asked to determine whether it was plausible that the conditions of co-respondency were fulfilled, thereby asking the ECtHR to make an indirect assessment of competence. According to the CJEU, interpreting EU law in such an indirect and incidental way still gives rise to concerns over autonomy.

The Court summarised its position on what the principle of autonomy requires in Opinion 1/00[44] on the establishment of a European Common Aviation Area. In a passage that has been referred to a number of times since, the Court stated that the preservation of autonomy of the Union legal order requires two main features:

> [F]irst, that the essential character of the powers of the Community and its institutions as conceived in the Treaty remain unaltered ... Second, it requires that the procedures for ensuring uniform interpretation of the rules of the ECAA Agreement and for resolving disputes will not have the effect of binding the Community and its institutions, in the exercise of their internal powers, to a particular interpretation of the rules of Community law referred to in that agreement.[45]

The Court sets out two key conditions. The first relates to the preservation of the 'essential character' of the powers of the Union and its institutions. The second seeks to ensure that an outside dispute settlement body would not have the power to interpret EU law if it is to have binding effect on the Union. This presents what was understood as a narrow understanding of autonomy. This narrow conception is focused primarily on preserving the exclusive powers of the Court

---

[42] CETA, Art 8.31(2) states that 'the Tribunal may consider, as appropriate, the domestic law of the disputing Party as a matter of fact. In doing so, the Tribunal shall follow the prevailing interpretation given to the domestic law by the courts or authorities of that Party and any meaning given to domestic law by the Tribunal shall not be binding upon the courts or the authorities of that Party'.
[43] Opinion 2/13 (n 6) paras 215–35.
[44] Opinion 1/00, EU:C:2002:231.
[45] ibid para 12.

to interpret the Treaties and EU law.[46] De Witte, for instance, summarising the Court's position in these cases, states that 'the theme of the autonomy of the Community legal order is mentioned recurrently, and relates essentially to the preservation of the Court's own exclusive power to interpret Community law'.[47] However, what we see in these cases is not the preservation of the Court's powers for its own sake; in each instance a more fundamental issue is at stake.

This broader conception of the principle of autonomy began to emerge in Opinion 1/09. Here, the Court was called upon to decide whether a proposed European and Community Patents Court (ECPC), which would have jurisdiction to hear actions related to European and Community patents, was compatible with the EU Treaties. One of the controversial aspects of the agreement establishing the ECPC was that it allowed the Patent Court to refer a question to the CJEU relating to questions concerning EU law. This was designed to be a way of safeguarding autonomy, by ensuring that the CJEU still has the final say on the interpretation of EU law. The Court stressed that an:

> international agreement concluded with third countries may confer new judicial powers on the Court provided that in so doing it does not change the *essential character of the function of the Court* as conceived in the EU and FEU Treaties.[48]

What is an 'essential' character or function of the Court? The CJEU found that one of these essential elements is the ability of the courts of the EU Member States to refer questions to the CJEU. The preliminary ruling mechanism in the draft agreement would essentially deprive the national courts of this function in this field of law.[49] This role of the national courts, the Court asserts, is 'indispensable to the preservation of the very nature of the law established by the Treaties'.[50] The judgment holds that the Member State courts have an essential role in the interpretation and application of EU law, and that this function cannot be delegated to the international level.[51] Here, we see that the principle of autonomy is not simply concerned with the judicial monopoly of the Court; rather, the Court links the concept of autonomy to the broader notion of safeguarding the 'essential characteristics of the European Union legal order'.[52] The Court is nevertheless still safeguarding its own authority, since the national courts are under the authority

---

[46] Locke, 'The Future of the European Union's Accession to the European Convention on Human Rights after Opinion 2/13' (n 39) 243: 'A narrow conception of autonomy, such as this, is appropriate as it serves the legitimate purpose of protecting the integrity of the EU law while retaining the EU's capacity as an external actor'.

[47] De Witte, 'European Union Law' (n 1) 150.

[48] Opinion 1/09, EU:C:2011:123, para 75 (emphasis added).

[49] ibid para 81: 'The draft agreement provides for a preliminary ruling mechanism which reserves, within the scope of that agreement, the power to refer questions for a preliminary ruling to the PC while removing that power from the national courts'.

[50] ibid para 85.

[51] See R Barratta, 'National Courts as "Guardians" and "Ordinary Courts" of EU Law: Opinion 1/09 of the ECJ' (2011) 38 *Legal Issues of Economic Integration* 297.

[52] Opinion 1/09 (n 48) para 65.

of the CJEU in a way that an international court is not.[53] What constitutes the 'essential characteristics' remains an open and debated question. Opinion 1/09 illustrates the broadening of the principle of autonomy, and can be seen as laying the groundwork for the rationale used in Opinion 2/13, discussed below.[54]

## A. Autonomy and International Courts

The EU seeks to play a more active role in shaping, developing and strengthening international law. The support of international dispute settlement mechanisms should be a large part of this. International dispute settlement can help to bolster international law and the rule of law by establishing some of the features often missing in the international legal order, such as judicial review and enforcement. Participation in international dispute settlement by the EU is also a way to ensure that the Union observes its own international obligations. This would be especially important in the ECHR context, since there is currently no external mechanism to monitor the EU's compliance with human rights norms. The Court has been reluctant to accept the role of other courts, however. Parish argues that:

> The Court of Justice should learn to be more relaxed about other international tribunals adjudicating on EU law. International courts are a growth industry, and it is inevitable that investment treaty law, international trade law, and a host of other areas of international law that international courts have mandates to apply overlap with the ever-expanding ambit of EU law.[55]

The increasing number and density of international courts and tribunals, of course, gives rise to a number of challenges to supranational courts such as the CJEU. How, then, should the principle of autonomy be interpreted? The Court has interpreted it in a way that establishes a high threshold for the Union to participate in international dispute settlement procedures. Yet, as discussed in the next section, the principle of autonomy has also been used in order to determine the conditions under which international law, including the decision of international courts, can be given effect in the EU legal order. Since the Court is capable of playing this gatekeeper role, it should not be so reluctant to allow EU participation in international dispute settlement. The CJEU can and does give priority to its own rules and constitutional legal order. Yet in doing so, the Court should be mindful of the fact that there are many benefits associated with the EU and its Member States participating in this wider legal order. The Union's ability to act independently on the international stage is an expression of the Union's autonomy.

---

[53]  ibid paras 86–88.

[54]  On Opinion 1/09 as a 'warning sign', see D Halberstam, '"It's the Autonomy, Stupid!" A Modest Defense of Opinion 2/13 on EU Accession to the ECHR, and the Way Forward' (2015) 16 *German Law Journal* 105, 111. 'The Patent Court Opinion, in turn, held that the application of EU law must remain in the hands of the EU judiciary, which includes national courts but excludes courts in which Member States and non-Member States participate together. Both were strong assertions of the autonomy of EU law and the necessity of maintaining the integrity of the EU's constitutional architecture.'

[55]  Parish, 'International Courts and the European Legal Order' (n 5).

# IV. Autonomy and Norms Originating Outside the EU

The previous section discussed briefly how the principle of autonomy has been used in the context of dispute settlement procedures, which is the main context in which the principle has been applied in practice. Yet the principle is employed in other aspects of EU external relations law, even if the language of autonomy is not used explicitly. The best example of this is instances where the Court is called upon to deal with the effects of international law within the EU legal order. As the EU enters into a greater number of international agreements and takes part in international organisations and other international bodies, international norms are increasingly invoked before the Court. This can range from provisions of treaty law, both binding and non-binding on the Union, customary international law, general principles of law, as well as a growing number of rules that might be categorised as 'soft law', which are not strictly binding but may nevertheless be influential. In recent years, the Court has had to determine how to give effect to these norms, and under what conditions. In developing these rules, the principle of autonomy has played an important role.

Some have argued that the principle of autonomy, as applied in the external dimension, means that the Court has become rather 'unfriendly' towards international law.[56] What this really means is that the relationship between the EU and international legal orders is to be determined solely by the rules in the EU legal order itself. It is not saying that the EU is no longer a part of the international legal order, nor that international law cannot have an effect within the EU legal order, but that this relationship can only be determined by reference to internal rules, and, more concretely, that the essential characteristics of EU law, especially the primary role of the Court in interpreting EU law, cannot be prejudiced by international law.

The complex issue of the Court's approach to international law has been discussed extensively in academic literature.[57] In recent years, the Court's approach to international law has been described as being more 'closed' or 'unfriendly' towards

---

[56] '[T]he EU has a much less friendly disposition towards international law than is commonly assumed', J Klabbers, 'The Validity of EU Norms Conflicting with International Obligations' in E Cannizzaro, P Palchetti and RA Wessel (eds), *International Law as Law of the European Union* (Leiden, Martinus Nijhoff, 2012) 111, 112.

[57] F Martines, 'Direct Effect of International Agreements of the European Union' (2014) 25 *European Journal of International Law* 129; C Kaddous, 'Effects of International Agreements in the EU Legal Order' in M Cremona and B de Witte (eds), *EU Foreign Relations Law: Constitutional Fundamentals* (Oxford, Hart Publishing, 2008) 291; J Klabbers, *The European Union in International Law* (Paris, Pedone, 2012); J Wouters, A Nollkaemper and E de Wet (eds), *The Europeanisation of International Law: The Status of International Law in the EU and its Member States* (The Hague, TMC Asser Press, 2008); M Mendez, *The Legal Effects of EU Agreements: Maximalist Treaty Enforcement and Judicial Avoidance Techniques* (Oxford, Oxford University Press, 2013); K Lenaerts, 'Direct Applicability and Direct Effect of International Law in the EU Legal Order' in I Govaere, E Lannon, P van Elsuwege and S Adam (eds), *The European Union in the World, Essays in Honour of Marc Maresceau* (Leiden, Martinus Nijhoff Publishers, 2014) 45.

public international law, often in contrast with its more open earlier case-law, which was seen as being more receptive to international norms. The literature tends to contrast the CJEU's recent emphasis on the autonomy of the EU legal order with its earlier 'friendliness' towards public international law. Asserting the EU's autonomy is therefore viewed as the CJEU further isolating itself from public international law.[58] Respect for international law and the preservation of the autonomy of the EU legal order are sometimes presented as mutually irreconcilable goals; the Court being presented as 'oscillating between what may be called deference to international law and insistence on the autonomy of the EU legal order'.[59]

The Court of Justice famously applied the principle of autonomy to explain the relationship between the EU legal order and public international law in *Kadi I*.[60] The Court explicitly invoked the autonomy of the Union legal order in its reasoning, stating that 'an international agreement cannot affect the allocation of powers fixed by the Treaties or, consequently, the autonomy of the Community legal system'.[61] *Kadi I* is also important since it further underlines the fact that the principle of autonomy is not simply about preserving the role of the Court, but is a much broader constitutional principle.[62] Autonomy is concerned with preserving the 'fundamental characteristics' of the EU legal order. These include, according to the Court, the protection of fundamental rights, respect for the rule of law, and the judicial review of EU acts, all of which cannot be prejudiced by an international agreement. What constitutes the essential characteristics of the EU legal order is open to debate. In Opinion 2/13, the Court found that the principle of mutual trust was one of these essential characteristics.[63]

The principle of autonomy also plays a role in cases where the Court is asked to determine what legal effect, if any, is to be given to agreements to which the EU

---

[58] F Hoffmeister, 'The Contribution of EU Practice under International Law' in M Cremona (ed), *Developments in EU External Relations Law* (Oxford, Oxford University Press, 2008) 37, 56: 'In other words, as the EC Treaty was not subject to ordinary international treaty rules, but rather interpreted from a constitutional perspective, the Community isolated itself from public international law to a certain degree in its "early strive for autonomy"'.

[59] HG Krenzler and O Landwehr, 'A New Legal Order of International Law: On the Relationship Between Public International Law and European Law After *Kadi*' in U Fastenrath, R Geiger, D Khan, A Paulus, S von Schorlemer and C Vedder (eds), *From Bilateralism to Community Interest, Essays in Honour of Judge Bruno Simma* (Oxford, Oxford University Press, 2011) 1004.

[60] 'The Court's judgment in *Kadi I* is a further landmark in the process of defining the autonomy of EU law from international law', P Eeckhout, 'Human Rights and the Autonomy of EU Law: Pluralism or Integration?' (2013) *Current Legal Problems* 1, 27. Joined Cases C-402/05P and C-415/05P *Kadi and Al Barakaat International Foundation v Council and Commission* (*Kadi I*), Judgment, EU:C:2008:461.

[61] *Kadi I* (n 60) para 282.

[62] Van Rossem, 'The Autonomy of EU Law' (n 9) 17: '[W]hat spurred the ECJ's appeal to the autonomy of the EU legal order was not so much a somewhat narrow concern for its exclusive jurisdiction, as a more general and more profound concern for the constitutional integrity of this legal order'.

[63] Opinion 2/13 (n 6) para 168: 'This legal structure is based on the fundamental premiss that each Member State shares with all the other Member States, and recognises that they share with it, a set of common values on which the EU is founded, as stated in Article 2 TEU. That premise implies and justifies the existence of mutual trust between the Member States that those values will be recognised and, therefore, that the law of the EU that implements them will be respected'.

is not a party, but all its Member States are. This question arose, for instance, in *Intertanko*, with respect to Marpol 73/78,[64] and *Air Transport Association of America*, with respect to the Chicago Convention on International Civil Aviation.[65] The Court held that the obligations under these agreements would only be binding upon the Union in cases where there had been a full transfer of the powers under the agreement to the Union.[66] The Court has set a very high threshold for the theory of functional succession to apply, and this has only occurred in rare instances.[67] From the viewpoint of preserving the autonomy of the EU legal order, one can see why the Court would pursue this approach. Allowing international agreements into which only the Member States have entered, but which the Union has not, to bind the Union would go against the idea of the Union as a separate and distinct entity. To do otherwise might threaten the unity of the EU legal order.[68]

The principle of autonomy also plays a role in cases where the Court has been called upon to determine the legal effect of agreements entered into by the EU Member States before their entry into the Union. This issue is governed by Article 351 TFEU, which states that while international agreements entered into by the Member States before they joined the Union will continue to apply, the Member States are also under an obligation to eliminate incompatibilities between EU law and those earlier international agreements. This Article has two elements; the first is about preserving the Member States' prior agreements, while the obligation to eliminate incompatibilities is motivated by the need to preserve the integrity of EU law. In case-law applying Article 351 TFEU, the Court has emphasised the latter goal.[69] This again can be seen as being motivated by the

---

[64] Case C-308/06 *Intertanko and others*, Judgment, EU:C:2008:312. See J-W van Rossem, 'Interaction Between EU Law and International Law in the Light of *Intertanko* and *Kadi*: The Dilemma of Norms Binding the Member States but Not the Community' (2009) 40 *Netherlands Yearbook of International Law* 183.

[65] Case C-366/10 *Air Transport Association of America and others v Secretary of State for Energy and Climate Change*, Judgment, EU:C:2011:864. See G De Baere and C Ryngaert, 'The ECJ's Judgment in *Air Transport Association of America* and the International Legal Context of the EU's Climate Change Policy' (2013) 18 *European Foreign Affairs Review* 389.

[66] For a discussion on the Court's use of the theory of 'functional succession' see J Wouters, J Odermatt and T Ramopoulos, 'Worlds Apart? Comparing the Approaches of the European Court of Justice and the EU Legislature to International Law' in M Cremona and A Thies (eds), *The European Court of Justice and External Relations Law: Constitutional Challenges* (Oxford, Oxford University Press, 2014) 249.

[67] The most notable being Joined Cases 21/72–25/72 *International Fruit Company and others v Produktschap voor Groenten en Fruit*, Judgment, EU:C:1972:115, para 18. See also Case 38/75 *NV Nederlandse Spoorwegen*, Judgment, EU:C:1975:154, para 21.

[68] Van Rossem, 'The Autonomy of EU Law' (n 9) 36: 'In *Intertanko* and *Air Transport Association of America*, the Court's decision not to incorporate an international agreement to which the Union is not formally bound, primarily seems to have stemmed from a desire to defend the unity of the Union legal order'.

[69] See Case C-205/06 *Commission v Austria*, Judgment, EU:C:2009:118; Case C-249/06 *Commission v Sweden*, Judgment, EU:C:2009:119; Case C-118/07 *Commission v Finland*, Judgment, EU:C:2009:715; *Kadi I* (n 60) para 304. *Air Transport Association of America and others* (n 65) para 61: 'Although the first paragraph of Article 351 TFEU implies a duty on the part of the institutions of the European Union not to impede the performance of the obligations of Member States which stem from an agreement prior to 1 January 1958 ... that duty of the institutions is designed to permit the Member States concerned to perform their obligations under a prior agreement and does not bind the European Union as regards the third States party to that agreement'.

broader principle of autonomy.[70] The prior agreements of the Member States must be respected, according to the Court, but this cannot undermine the unity and integrity of the EU legal order. Autonomy is put forward as a shield to protect this integrity and unity of the legal order.[71]

In these instances, the Court is applying the principle of autonomy, a concept originally developed to assert the primacy of EU law over national law, to the EU's wider relationship with international law. In both instances, the underlying rationale is the same: since the EU is a distinct and autonomous legal order, it cannot be undermined by the invocation of norms that originate outside that legal order, whether they derive from the Member States' legal systems or from international law.[72] At its heart, this means that the relationship between EU law and international law is to be determined by the CJEU itself, according to its own constitutional principles. As Advocate General Maduro boldly stated in his Opinion in *Kadi I*, 'in the final analysis, the Community Courts determine the effect of international obligations within the Community legal order by reference to conditions set by Community law'.[73] *Kadi I* and other cases stressing the autonomous nature of the EU legal order have been criticised for essentially isolating the Union from international law. De Búrca, for instance, criticises the Court for following an 'internally-oriented approach and a form of legal reasoning which emphasized the particular requirements of the EU's general principles of law and the importance of the autonomous authority of the EC legal order'.[74] Autonomy is presented as a rather blunt instrument to detach the EU from international law. However, the reality is more nuanced, and is more concerned with the Court's ability to determine the ways in which international law is given effect in the EU legal order. The next section discusses how the EU's application of this principle can lead to some negative consequences; while there is a need for the Court to preserve the autonomy of the EU legal order, this can and should be balanced against other goals and principles, including the EU's goal of respecting international law.[75]

---

[70] Klabbers, for instance, argues that 'while ostensibly safeguarding anterior member state agreements, [Art. 351] has always been more about achieving a balance between the protection of those earlier treaties and the protection of the autonomy of the EC's legal order—and that is a charitable reading'. J Klabbers, 'Beyond the Vienna Convention: Conflicting Treaty Provision' in E Cannizzaro (ed), *The Law of Treaties Beyond the Geneva Convention* (Oxford, Oxford University Press, 2011) 192, 203.

[71] See N Lavranos, 'Protecting European Law from International Law' (2010) 15 *European Foreign Affairs Review* 265.

[72] 'The reference to the autonomy of the Community system in its relation to *international law* echoes much older references in the European Court's case law to the autonomous nature of Community law in relation to the *law of its member states*' (original emphasis). De Witte, 'European Union Law' (n 1) 142.

[73] Joined Cases C-402/05P and C-415/05P *Kadi and Al Barakaat International Foundation v Council and Commission*, Opinion of AG Poiares Maduro, EU:C:2008:11, para 23.

[74] G de Búrca, 'The European Court of Justice and the International Legal Order After Kadi' (2010) 51 *Harvard International Law Journal* 1, 44.

[75] This duty stems from Art 3(5) TEU, which sets out that the EU 'shall contribute ... to the strict observance and the development of international law' and Art 21(1) TEU providing that the EU's 'action on the international scene' should be guided by 'respect for the principles of the United Nations and international law'. See Wouters, Odermatt and Ramopoulos, 'Worlds Apart? Comparing the Approaches of the European Court of Justice and the EU Legislature to International Law' (n 66).

## A. Autonomy as a Structural Principle in Opinion 2/13

The EU Member States included an obligation in the Lisbon Treaty, that '[t]he Union shall accede to the European Convention for the Protection of Human Rights and Fundamental Freedoms'.[76] It should be borne in mind that accession was one of a number of approaches the EU could have taken to address the fact that the Union was not a contracting party to the European Convention on Human Rights. The Union could have sought simply to strengthen its own internal human rights mechanisms. In fact, this is what it sought to do through the EU Charter of Fundamental Rights and Freedoms. Alternatively, the Court could also have found the EU to be subject to the obligations under the Convention via the theory of 'functional succession' discussed above.[77] This would have meant that the EU would be subject to the obligations in the ECHR under EU law through implied succession, rather than the EU being formally bound as a matter of international law. It would also have meant that the EU would not have been able to participate in the institutional mechanisms related to the ECHR, most importantly the ECtHR. Both of these approaches were perceived as inadequate and would have failed to address the gap in human rights protection stemming from the EU not being a party to the ECHR.

It was decided that this gap in human rights protection should be addressed by the EU joining the ECHR as a full party. The legal significance of such as step should not be underestimated, both from an EU law and public international law perspective.[78] From the perspective of EU law, it would be the first time the EU had opened up its legal order for external scrutiny in the field of human rights, with judicial supervision backed up by binding commitments under international law. From an international law perspective, this would be the first time that an international organisation had submitted itself to a form of binding judicial review in the human rights sphere. It would also mean that the ECHR system would have to be modified to allow participation by a contracting party that is not a state. Accession, therefore, was not merely a cosmetic procedure; it would have had important consequences for both the international and EU legal orders.

EU accession was to be a long process. An important step in the journey were the negotiations for a draft Accession Agreement, setting out the conditions under which the EU would accede, and outlining the changes that would be made to the ECHR to allow EU participation. In negotiating the Agreement, the drafters, composed of the EU and the 47 Council of Europe members, had to balance two competing objectives. On the one hand, they sought to ensure that the EU would

---

[76] Article 6(2) TEU.

[77] T Ahmed and I de Jesús Butler, 'The European Union and Human Rights: An International Law Perspective' (2006) 17 *European Journal of International Law* 771, 788: '[I]t is possible to argue that, although the EU has not become party to a human rights treaty itself, the obligations incurred by its Member States by virtue of their membership of such treaties might impose obligations on the EU per se'.

[78] J Odermatt, 'The EU's Accession to the European Convention on Human Rights: An International Law Perspective' (2014) 47 *New York University Journal of International Law and Politics* 59.

accede, as far as possible, on the same footing as other contracting parties. Not only would this ensure that the EU was not given special treatment, it would also help guarantee that the rights in the Convention would be protected in a similar manner, irrespective of whether the violation stemmed from a Member State or from the EU. On the other hand, since the EU is not a state, and therefore differs in many respects from other state contracting parties, certain arrangements needed to be made to take into account this difference. The drafters had to strike a balance between treating the EU as a normal contracting party, while at the same time acknowledging the unique nature of the EU and its legal order. Importantly, the drafters had ensured that any agreement respected the principle of autonomy.

In addition to the principle of autonomy found in EU law, the drafters of the Lisbon Treaty also included further constitutional safeguards, set out in Article 6(2) TEU and Protocol No 8.[79] Article 6(2) highlights that 'accession shall not affect the Union's competences as defined in the Treaties' whereas Protocol No 8 states that any draft agreement must also 'ensure that accession of the Union shall not affect the competences of the Union or the powers of its institutions'. The text of the draft Accession Agreement and its negotiating history has been discussed in detail elsewhere.[80] The Accession Agreement introduced a number of institutional innovations to the ECtHR system, such as the co-respondent mechanism and prior involvement procedure. These were designed particularly to ensure that the autonomy of the EU would be preserved.

In accordance with the procedure in Article 218(11) TFEU, the CJEU was asked to deliver its opinion on whether the draft Accession Agreement was compatible with the EU Treaties and EU law. In Opinion 2/13, the Court found that it was not. The Court based its opinion mostly on the argument that the modalities of accession enshrined in the Accession Agreement would violate the autonomy of the EU legal order. Opinion 2/13 is the most important judicial pronouncement on the principle of autonomy to date. Most importantly, it established the principle of autonomy as a broader and more all-encompassing doctrine than previously thought, and will have important ramifications for the EU's future external relations.

This chapter does not seek to explore further the Court's reasoning in full.[81] Rather, it seeks to understand a puzzling question. Why did Opinion 2/13 come as such a surprise? The Court did not have minor qualms over the Accession Agreement, issues that might have been remedied by amendments to the

---

[79] Protocol (No 8) relating to Article 6(2) of the Treaty on European Union on the Accession of the Union to the European Convention on the Protection of Human Rights and Fundamental Freedoms.

[80] See X Groussot, T Lock and L Pech, *EU Accession to the European Convention on Human Rights: A Legal Assessment of the Draft Accession Agreement of 14 October 2011*, Fondation Robert Schuman European Issues 2011/218, 3; P Gragl, 'A Giant Leap for European Human Rights? The Final Agreement on the European Union's Accession to the European Convention on Human Rights' (2014) 51 *CML Rev* 13; J-P Jacqué, 'The Accession of the European Union to the European Convention on Human Rights and Fundamental Freedoms' (2011) 48 *CML Rev* 995, 1006.

[81] B de Witte and Š Imamović, 'Opinion 2/13 on Accession to the ECHR: Defending the EU Legal Order Against a Foreign Human Rights Court' (2015) 40 *EL Rev* 683.

agreement or declarations made at the time of accession. This was essentially the approach taken by the Advocate General, who, although finding similar faults in the Accession Agreement as the Court, still gave her approval. Rather, the Court came at the Accession Agreement with a sledgehammer.

The reaction to Opinion 2/13 was generally one of surprise and shock.[82] Academic discussion prior to the Opinion did not see serious concerns with the Agreement. All EU Member States which submitted observations to the Court agreed that the draft Accession Agreement was compatible with EU law and the agreement had the support of the European Commission, the Parliament, the Council as well as the Advocate General. Perhaps what made the Opinion all the more surprising was the fact that the Court itself played an indirect role in the drafting process. In particular, the drafters sought to address the concerns included in a Joint Communication of the Presidents of the CJEU and ECHR, which set out some of the essential conditions of any accession agreement.[83] Some of the institutional innovations found in the Accession Agreement, such as the procedure to allow prior involvement of the CJEU, can be traced back to this document, which clearly states that such prior involvement would be a necessary condition. Given all of these factors, in addition to the clear legal requirement for the EU to accede to the Convention established by Article 6(2) TEU, one can see why Opinion 2/13 caused such surprise. In fact, it is not so much the outcome of the Opinion that is shocking as much as the language and legal reasoning used to support it. In contrast with the more conciliatory approach of the Advocate General, Opinion 2/13 adopts a more abrasive and assertive tone.

What can explain this puzzle, and what does it tell us about the principle of autonomy? One possible explanation is that the Court was acting out of self-interest. According to this argument, the Court was simply against EU accession to the ECHR and sought to do all it could to kill off or delay this process. The idea is that the Luxembourg Court could not accept any judicial rival that would potentially rule on the legality of EU law. While this concern may have played some role in the

---

[82] Some of the early reactions include: W Michl, 'Thou Shalt Have No Other Courts Before Me', *Verfassungblog*, 23 December 2014, www.verfassungsblog.de/en/thou-shalt-no-courts/; A Buyse, 'CJEU Rules: Draft Agreement on EU Accession to ECHR Incompatible with EU Law', *ECHR Blog*, 20 December 2014, http://echrblog.blogspot.co.uk/2014/12/cjeu-rules-draft-agreement-on-eu.html; A Duff, 'The European Union is in Deep Trouble with Its Top Court', 7 January 2015, http://andrewduff. blogactiv.eu/2015/01/07/the-european-union-is-in-deep-trouble-with-its-top-court/; S Peers, 'The CJEU and the EU's Accession to the ECHR: A Clear and Present Danger to Human Rights Protection', *EU Law Analysis*, 18 December 2014, http://eulawanalysis.blogspot.co.uk/2014/12/the-cjeu-and-eus-accession-to-echr.html; J Odermatt, *A Giant Step Backwards? Opinion 2/13 on the EU's Accession to the European Convention on Human Rights*, FRAME Working Papers (20 February 2015), available at www.fp7-frame.eu/working-paper-a-giant-step-backwards-opinion-213-on-the-eus-accession-to-the-european-convention-on-human-rights/; A O'Neill, 'Opinion 2/13 on EU Accession to the ECHR: The CJEU as Humpty Dumpty', *EUtopia Law*, 18 December 2014, http://eutopialaw.com/2014/12/18/opinion-213-on-eu-accession-to-the-echr-the-cjeu-as-humpty-dumpty/.

[83] Joint Communication from Presidents Costa and Skouris (CCBE, 24 January 2011), available at www.ccbe.eu/fileadmin/user_upload/document/Roundtable_2011_Luxembourg/Joint_communication_from_Presidents_Costa_and_Skouris_EN.pdf.

Opinion, it is unhelpful to think of Opinion 2/13 as purely political. It is unhelpful because it obfuscates the fact that the Opinion *was* based on existing case-law and legal reasoning. Until this point, however, this reasoning had not led to such a drastic outcome as in Opinion 2/13.

The Court's Opinion may seem less surprising when one examines the line of case-law on the autonomy of the EU. In particular, the Court's emphasis on autonomy is foreshadowed in Opinion 2/94, the first time it was asked to decide on the EU's accession to the ECHR. Referring to possible accession, the Court held that:

> Such a modification of the system for the protection of human rights in the Community, with equally fundamental institutional implications for the Community and for the Member States, *would be of constitutional significance* and would therefore be such as to go beyond the scope of Article 235. It could be brought about only by way of Treaty amendment.[84]

Opinion 2/94 is often presented as being based on the lack of competence for the EU to accede. The drafters of the Lisbon Treaty addressed this lack of competence by providing a duty to accede in Article 6(2) TEU. Although this addressed the competence issue, it did nothing to address the more fundamental questions raised by EU accession, the conclusion that such a step 'would be of constitutional significance'. This underscores the paramount importance given to the principle of autonomy. Article 1(a) of Protocol No 8 requires that the 'specific characteristics of the Union and Union law' be taken into account in the accession agreement and so this was included as an essential condition for accession. Yet the Court refers to the 'specific characteristics *and the autonomy* of EU law' treating the two as separate but related elements.[85] Despite there being a clear legal obligation for the EU to accede enshrined in the TEU, the Court emphasises that this still must be done in a way that does not prejudice the autonomy of the EU legal order.

As discussed above, one can think of narrow and broad conceptions of autonomy. The narrow version tends to link autonomy to the powers and role of the Court. One of the recurrent criticisms of Opinion 2/13 is that the Court appears to have applied a much broader version of autonomy than it had in its previous case-law. Locke argues, for instance, that in Opinion 2/13 'the Court of Justice moved the goalposts and, without expressly admitting it, extended the meaning of the autonomy of EU law'.[86] The argument is that the drafters sought to safeguard autonomy according to its narrow conception whereas the benchmark used by the Court employs a much broader understanding of the principle.

The drafters of the Accession Agreement seem to have approached the question based on the narrow conception of autonomy, that is, that respect for the principle of autonomy essentially required safeguarding mechanisms designed to preserve the role of the CJEU. The Court is extremely critical of this approach:

---

[84] Opinion 2/94, EU:C:1996:140, para 35 (emphasis added).
[85] Opinion 2/13 (n 6) para 258 (emphasis added).
[86] Locke, 'The Future of the European Union's Accession to the European Convention on Human Rights after Opinion 2/13' (n 39) 243.

The approach adopted in the agreement envisaged, which is *to treat the EU as a State and to give it a role identical in every respect to that of any other Contracting Party*, specifically disregards the intrinsic nature of the EU and, in particular, fails to take into consideration the fact that the Member States have, by reason of their membership of the EU, accepted that relations between them as regards the matters covered by the transfer of powers from the Member States to the EU are governed by EU law to the exclusion, if EU law so requires, of any other law.[87]

At first, this reasoning seems difficult to support. The Accession Agreement makes very clear that the EU is not a state; the Preamble even emphasises this:

[H]aving regard to the specific legal order of the European Union, which is not a State, its accession requires certain adjustments to the Convention system to be made by common agreement.[88]

The fact that a complex accession agreement was needed at all is based on the idea that the EU requires certain treatment for it to accede to the ECHR.

The Court's criticism, however, was of the approach taken by the drafters. That is, they sought to treat the EU as a state in all respects, but would include 'certain adjustments' where necessary. The drafters started from the principle that each contracting party should be treated in the same manner, unless special circumstances required different treatment. For the Court, it was the other way around; the unique nature of the EU legal order should have been the starting point. These two starting points were so different that the Accession Agreement was possibly doomed to fail. The Court did not have problems with the technical design of the building, but with the very foundations on which it was built. This can only be rectified, not with modifications, but by re-building from the ground up. One could argue that such an approach goes against the clear will of the Member States, who included ECHR accession as a constitutional obligation. Unlike other international agreements to which the EU seeks to accede, the EU Treaties *require* the Union to join the ECHR. Yet the fact that the Court would adopt such an approach, in the face of such strong support, serves to emphasise just how important a constitutional principle autonomy has become.

The passage quoted above also shows that the external dimension of autonomy is concerned not only with the action of the EU, but also with the Member States, who have accepted that their mutual relations 'as regards the matters covered by the transfer of powers from the Member States to the EU are governed by EU law to the exclusion, if EU law so requires, *of any other law*' (emphasis added). The role and status of the EU Member States as parties to the ECHR, which would be transformed into a mixed agreement upon EU accession, would also be affected by the EU's accession to the ECHR. This is quite different from the internal dimension of autonomy, where the Court emphasises the distinct nature of the EU legal order vis-à-vis the EU Member States. The external dimension of autonomy as a

---

[87] Opinion 2/13 (n 6) para 193 (emphasis added).
[88] *Draft Accession Agreement, Final Report to the CDDH*, Council of Europe Doc 47+1(2013)008rev2 (10 June 2013).

structural principle requires one to imagine the Member States as an important element of this structure. The effect of EU accession on the role and status of the EU Member States as parties to the ECHR is something that was arguably overlooked by the drafters and perhaps another reason why the Court's Opinion came as a surprise.

# V. Conclusion: Evolution of Autonomy

Autonomy is a somewhat paradoxical concept. In the context of international organisations, it relates to the idea that as a legal person, the organisation is both independent from, but at the same time dependent upon, its Member States. Similarly, the EU is the international organisation that exercises the most independence from its Member States, and the Court has long emphasised the separate legal nature of the EU. Yet at the same time the Union is highly dependent upon the Member States in order to carry out its functions[89] and they remain an essential element in the EU constitutional structure.

This paradox also applies to the external dimension of autonomy. The EU has become a global actor in its own right and, especially since the Lisbon Treaty, it has espoused the principles of multilateralism and international cooperation. At the same time, its case recent case-law has stressed the autonomy of the EU legal order, in a way that emphasises the Court as the gatekeeper able to decide the conditions under which international law can take effect within the EU. The way in which the Court has sought to preserve this autonomy has meant that it has appeared rather hostile to international law and towards international dispute settlement mechanisms. This approach to autonomy can in turn undermine another goal, the EU's ability to become a strong and effective global actor. The EU is a part of, and seeks to participate in, the international legal order, but at the same time seeks to preserve its autonomy vis-à-vis that legal order: 'On the one hand, the EU's autonomy is a product of international law; on the other, it must distance itself from the international legal order to cement and strengthen its autonomy'.[90] Cannizzaro, Palchetti and Wessel point out this apparent contradiction: 'The ambiguity lies in its claim to be an open society, which aims to play an increasingly active role in the global legal order, while simultaneously presenting itself as

---

[89] P-J Kuijper and E Paasivirta, 'EU International Responsibility and Its Attribution: From the Inside Looking Out' in M Evans and P Koutrakos (eds), *The International Responsibility of the European Union: European and International Perspectives* (Oxford, Hart Publishing, 2013) 35, 41–42: 'The EU ... is the victim of a paradox in international relations. It seeks to act as a strong and unified actor towards the outside world in international relations and that is what it is supposed to do according to its latest charter, the Treaty of Lisbon. However, because of its basic structure, it is highly dependent on its Member States for carrying out its policies and implementing its laws, including in the field of international relations'.

[90] Collins and White, 'Introduction and Overview' (n 11) 14.

an isolated monad, safeguarding the autonomy of its domestic system of values'.[91] Others have pointed out that, if the EU seeks to portray itself as a body committed to respecting international law, we should expect its Court to show a more open or integrationist attitude towards international law.[92] It seems, however, that the opposite is the case in practice.[93] The more the EU seeks to present itself as an actor in its own right at the international level, to participate in the development of international law, the more the Court seeks to stress the autonomy of the EU legal order.

This may not be as contradictory as it first appears. Perhaps we should expect that an entity so tightly woven into the fabric both of the international legal order and that of its Member States would need to assert its autonomy even more strongly. Eckes argues, for instance, that because of the nature of the EU legal order, it needs more protection than that of a well-established state.[94] According to this argument, we should expect the CJEU, as the guardian of the EU legal order, to be more assertive in protecting what might be viewed as threats to autonomy, both external and internal. The assertion of autonomy can be seen as a necessary reaction to greater interaction with other actors and legal orders.[95] Autonomy in this respect is viewed as being closely interlinked with the EU's constitutional maturity.[96] However, the need to assert its autonomy in this way, especially the need to include specific clauses in agreements to protect EU autonomy, can also mean that the EU is not yet mature.

[91] E Cannizzaro, P Palchetti and RA Wessel, 'Introduction: International Law as Law of the European Union' in E Cannizzaro, P Palchetti and RA Wessel (eds), *International Law as Law of the European Union* (Leiden, Martinus Nijhoff, 2012) 1.

[92] G de Búrca, 'After the EU Charter of Fundamental Rights: The Court of Justice as a Human Rights Adjudicator?' (2013) 20 *Maastricht Journal of European and Comparative Law* 168, 183. 'If the EU perceives of itself as a uniquely internationally engaged entity, and as a political system founded on the idea of transnational legal and political cooperation, we would be inclined to expect that its Court of Justice would reflect something of this internationalist orientation too'.

[93] Locke, 'The Future of the European Union's Accession to the European Convention on Human Rights after Opinion 2/13' (n 39) 244: 'While this would suggest that in contrast to some states, which robustly defend the idea of their own sovereignty, the Union would be more open to integration into an international human rights mechanism, the Court has used this argument to achieve the exact opposite'.

[94] 'Also, the Court of Justice did not have an alternative. It took the perspective of European law. This is the only possible option. After all, the European legal order, despite its ongoing constitutionalisation, remains an international organization that needs to defend its autonomy more firmly than a well-established state, both towards the inside and towards the outside.' C Eckes, 'Protecting Supremacy from External Influences: A Precondition for a European Constitutional Legal Order?' (2012) 18 *European Law Journal* 230, 250.

[95] '[A]utonomy is relational. Autonomous orders interact with other orders and this inevitably leads to the normative and legal interpenetration. The question then is how a particular order can preserve its autonomy under conditions of intense interaction with other orders. It is submitted that the autonomy of otherwise juxtaposed orders is preserved only if such normative or legal penetration occurs according to the rules of the receiving order.' Tsagourias, 'Conceptualizing the Autonomy of the European Union' (n 7) 345.

[96] Van Rossem, 'The Autonomy of EU Law' (n 9) 28: '[O]ne could argue, the more constitutionally mature the EU becomes, the more protective the shield of the concept of autonomy in the face of the international legal order'.

There comes a point, moreover, when the assertion of the EU's autonomy by the Court undermines the EU's ability to participate effectively at the international level. This chapter has argued that the concept of autonomy is a broad one, and as Opinion 2/13 demonstrates, can sometimes lead to rather unexpected outcomes. It is not simply about safeguarding the role of the Court, but ensuring that the 'essential characteristics' of the EU legal order are preserved. Such an abstract concept can have problems, particularly when the EU seeks to enter into international agreements and take part in dispute resolution mechanisms. Without clear guidance on the limits of the principle of autonomy, negotiators on behalf of the EU cannot be confident that certain clauses will not give rise to concerns. The Court in Opinion 2/13 required that every possible legal issue, even if slight or hypothetical, be resolved in the Accession Agreement. Rather than showing faith in the robustness, flexibility and maturity of the EU legal order, the Court requires that safeguards be put in place at the international level to preserve EU autonomy.

The principle of autonomy has also been used by the Court to develop the EU's relationship with international law more generally. Without clearly defined boundaries, it can be used to justify a more restrictive attitude towards international law.[97] There are good reasons for seeking to preserve the integrity of Union law from being undermined by international law, yet autonomy should not be the only guiding principle in developing the EU's relationship with international law. Autonomy should also take into account other principles, including the Union's respect for international law. The EU exists in a larger world of other states and international organisations and benefits from participation and interaction in the international legal order; international law is in turn also strengthened by the participation of the Union in international agreements and dispute settlement mechanisms. Autonomy is currently defined primarily in terms of exclusion, even isolation, and not in terms of engagement and integration. Such an approach to the principle of autonomy can diminish the EU's ability to participate in this system, and undermines many of the principles it seeks to protect.

---

[97] K Ziegler, *Autonomy: From Myth to Reality—or Hubris on a Tightrope? EU Law, Human Rights and International Law*, University of Leicester School of Law Research Paper 15–25 (2015) 43: 'The shift to an abstract "principle" of autonomy is a dangerous precedent likely to be used to justify whatever restrictive approach to international law is considered appropriate'.

# INDEX